Mr. Novak

Mr. Novak

An Acclaimed Television Series

By

Chuck Harter

BearManorMedia.com

Published in the USA by:
BearManor Media
PO Box 71426
Albany, Georgia 31708-1426
www.bearmanormedia.com

ISBN (trade) 978-1-62933-164-5
ISBN (trade paper) 978-1-62933-163-8

Printed in the United States of America
Typeset/design by Ranjit Sandhu.
Cover/book design by Chuck Harter.

Table of Contents

Introduction by
Richard Donner

Making *Mr. Novak* was a wonderful period in my life. Our inspired and ingenious producers, E. Jack Neuman and William Froug, created families on screen and on set. To be a part of the *Novak* family was a great honor and learning experience. I'm so pleased that Chuck Harter is bringing the *Mr. Novak* experience to a wider audience. After you've read his detailed, behind-the-scenes account, I hope you'll consider yourself part of the *Novak* family.

Richard Donner.

Foreword

"Mr. Novak": A TV Gem from the 1960's

by Martin Landau

Several months ago I received a text asking me to call Chuck Harter. Curiosity got the better of me and I made the call.

A well-spoken male voice answered the phone, and after the polite hellos I asked, "Why are you contacting me?"

He replied, "In the early 1960's you did a couple of guest-starring roles on a black-and-white television series that ran on NBC for a couple of seasons, entitled *Mr. Novak*."

As he spoke, my memory kicked into gear and I thought back to a weekly TV series about a young teacher and his daily problems at an average American high school.

It starred James Franciscus as the title character with Dean Jagger and Burgess Meredith as School Principals Albert Vane and Martin Woodridge.

The driving force and reason for the show being on the air was its hands-on showrunner, Executive Producer and Creator, E. Jack Neuman.

I remembered being cast and playing two completely diverse characters on *Mr. Novak* episodes way back in 1963 and 1965 and how intelligently written they were, which certainly wasn't always the case when dealing with episodic television in the 60's.

Harter asked if I would agree to an interview if he sent me DVD copies of the two shows I appeared in. I agreed to participate and hadn't, in fact, seen the shows since the 60's, more than half a century ago.

He then said, "Neither has anyone else seen them! That's why I'm writing the book, to right a wrong that's been perpetrated all of these 55 years since the series went off the air. Nothing has ever been done with *Mr. Novak* since the original run although it had been honored with dozens of awards from various scholastic and educational organizations, at the time, for its excellence, intelligence and adult handling of pertinent subject matter. The powers that be somehow allowed the entire series to fall through the cracks, after its summer re-runs. It completely disappeared. It is as if it never existed. It's doubtful if any person who is under 35 years of age today has ever heard of *Mr. Novak*. It is safe to say that no teen-aged high school student living in this country today, has ever seen a *Mr. Novak* episode."

The work that Chuck Harter has been doing over the last several years in researching his book deserves to be rewarded. He is completely focused on bringing *Mr. Novak* back and to the forefront of our consciousness, because of its excellence, important perspectives and entertainment value. Harter believes if there is anything that deserves to be resurrected and preserved it's the entire two years of *Mr. Novak*. The fact that the series is very difficult to find and view is why he is so ferociously trying to correct what he considers one of television history's major oversights. His knowledge and his devotion to both seasons of *Mr. Novak*, and all the episodes, always strikes me as selfless and impressive, and increases my amazement whenever we speak. That kind of devotion to something worthwhile deserves accolades and as many allies as possible.

Harter has reminded me of the lasting value of the two episodes I appeared in during *Mr. Novak*'s brief stay on the air. "Pay the Two Dollars" and "Enter a Strange Animal" each contained issues that are still timely and topical in today's world, half a century later. After I viewed the DVDs that Harter sent, many memories came vividly back to me. "Pay the Two Dollars" was an episode in which Mr. Novak is accused of getting physical with a dishonest male student during an attempt to break up a fight among several boys. The student's father threatens to sue Novak with the intention of getting him fired. My character, a lawyer, is brought in to handle Novak's case and recommends a settlement out of his laziness. Novak refuses to admit to anything untrue and won't settle, forcing a court case. It was a moving show about personal integrity and courage. "Enter a Strange Animal" dealt with the new-fangled individual desk-top teaching machines (computers) first introduced in the 1960's. My character represents the company that manufactures the machines and being opposed by a humanistic teacher (Nehemiah Persoff) who is against the idea of electronics in the class room. As a fast-talking salesman of the computer company, who has lots to say, I chose to talk and behave like a non-feeling impersonal machine. The importance of human interaction with students was realistically presented. It was very prophetic as all classrooms now use computers as part of the teaching methods.

James Franciscus, the star of the series, was a consummate and professional actor who was always very present for our scenes together. His dedication to his character was a large part of the success of the show. The scripts were well written and the directors were first-class. I found the time spent working on the series to be very rewarding for me as an actor and creative artist.

Meeting with Chuck Harter has allowed me to appreciate the *Mr. Novak* series anew, and realize the value of his efforts. *Mr. Novak* allowed its viewers to examine subjects like racism, bullying, cheating and other problems of high school life with clarity, insight and superior scripting, in an engaging format way ahead of its time and through a 1960's lens. None of the content of this fifty-year-old series seems dated or old-fashioned, not the topics or the presentation. Granted, the clothing styles, black-and-white images, and less than hi-def resolution tells us this is a series from another time, but the story telling holds up in other wonderful ways. *Mr. Novak* was a production of outstanding qualities that honestly endure. This show deserves to be rediscovered with official DVD releases or rebroadcasts on cable TV.

Chuck Harter has produced a superlative book that is both fascinating and informative.

Long Life to *Mr. Novak*! and Three Cheers to Chuck Harter!

Acknowledgments

Ranjit Sandhu for his immense assistance in technically bringing this book to fruition.

Ben Ohmart of Bear Manor Media for this opportunity to tell the story of *Mr. Novak*.

Sandy Grabman of Bear Manor Media for advice, encouragement, and friendship.

Marian Collier (Neuman) for generosity, encouragement, and friendship.

Laure Georges (Gonzalez) for enthusiasm, encouragement, and friendship.

John T. Taylor at www.fccj.us/MrNovak/mrnovak.html for inspiration, assistance, and **episode discs**.

Bruce Remy of www.rockandrollondvd.com for initial inspiration, encouragement, and **episode discs**.

Barbara Kramig of the John Marshall High School newsletter.

Eddie Blick for research advice.

Pat Dawson for the Marian Collier contact.

Sam Gasch for his graphics skills.

The late Bob Birchard for advice and encouragement.

Ol Sach = goodolsach@yahoo.com for **episode discs**.

William Wellman, Jr., for Kitty Wellman contact.

Bradley Meinke of Columbia College for Christian College photo. (Columbia College Archives.)

Vakil Smallen of N.E.A. archives.

Ned Comstock of U.S.C. for his usual great archival assistance.

Stu Shostack for Sherry Jackson contact.

Amy Roy (Donner's assistant) for processing Richard Donner Introduction.

Ronald V. Borst of Hollywood Movie Posters 6727½ Hollywood Blvd., Los Angeles, CA 90028, for **episode discs**, conducting Johnny Crawford interview, and encouragement.

Steve McCracken for graphics expertise and program installation.

Diane Albert for copies of *The TV Collector*, of which all back issues are available at dianealbert@happyretrogirl.com, and encouragement.

Ebay.

The Staff at the Margaret Herrick Library in Beverly Hills.

The Los Angeles Public Library on 5th Street.

Richard Donner for his Introduction.

Martin Landau for his Foreword.

Walter Koenig for his Afterword.

Ani Berberian for taking the author photo (Ani Berberian Photography).

For granting interviews…

Lane Bradbury, Marian Collier, Richard Donner, John D. F. Black, Bob Schultz, Ed Asner, Frankie Avalon, Diane Baker, Barbara Barrie, Beau Bridges, Brooke Bundy,

Johnny Crawford, Pat Crowley, Davey Davison (Silverman), Tony Dow, Richard Evans, Richard Eyer, June Harding, Jimmy Hawkins, Peter Helm, Allen Hunt, Sherry Jackson, Randy Kirby, Tommy Kirk, Walter Koenig, Martin Landau, Louise Latham, June Lockhart, Tom Lowell, David Macklin, Alison Mills (Newman), Brenda Scott, David Shiner, Julie Sommars, Tisha Sterling, Buck Taylor, Beverly Washburn, Marc Wanamaker, Kitty Wellman, John Franciscus, Laure Georges (Gonzalez), Wes Wheadon, Dr. G. Keith Dolan, Diane Albert, John T. Taylor.

If I have omitted anyone to thank for contributions, help or assistance, I regret my lapse of memory. Please note that I do appreciate all the efforts that *everyone* has done over the past two years regarding this book project.

All photos/images contained in this book came from the Author's Own Collection, The Martin Grams, Jr., Collection, Marian Collier's E. Jack Neuman Archive, or where otherwise noted. In some cases, images are presented in less-than-pristine condition due to their historical importance.

A note about interview sourcing. I always found it a bit awkward when reading a chapter of a book to find interviews either sourced in a list at the end of the chapter or in the back of the book. This required moving back and forth and was both time-consuming and would break the flow of the reading. In this book, the first time a person is quoted the date (where remembered) is noted directly after the quote. Additional quotes from this same interview are ended with Int. for interview. This approach will allow the reader not to have to disrupt the narrative by flipping the pages.

Dedications

James Franciscus (Teacher John Novak) &
Dean Jagger (Principal Albert Vane)

E. Jack Neuman (Creator/Producer) &
Marian Collier (Teacher Marilyn Scott)

Laure Georges (Gonzalez) —
Forever Mr. Novak's Biggest Fan and Favorite Student.

Prologue

The origin of this book began with an unsolicited package in the mail that I received in early 2015. Bruce Remy is a friend of mine who lives in upstate New York. He runs a company called rockandrollondvd.com and has over 20,000 rare music, Broadway shows, and television rarities. Every now and then he would send me a package of rare music discs. In this particular parcel was a stack of DVDs marked "*Mr. Novak.*" I called him and inquired about this unexpected gift. Bruce told me it was 24 episodes of an old series about a high school teacher. Apparently, the shows had been taped when *Novak* aired on the TNT Network in the late eighties. After thanking him I thought about the show and vaguely remembered it being on TV when I was very young. In those days, our family had one set and my dad, being in the Air Force, wanted to watch *Combat*. As this was broadcast opposite the teacher series, I never saw any episodes. The young girls in my classes brought in teen magazines with articles on James Franciscus. I became aware of the handsome star of the show. As the series never aired in reruns, by the late sixties I had forgotten about it. In the ensuing decades I would occasionally see a brief reference to the show in books or articles on the history of television. There were always positive views on the program. I set the discs aside and although I appreciated Bruce's generosity, I wondered if the show would hold up or appear dated and redundant.

A few weeks later, I decided to watch an episode. I viewed the pilot, "First Year, First Day," and by the end of it was pleasantly surprised. The acting of Dean Jagger as the principal and James Franciscus as the title character was excellent. It had a realistic script and the production values were outstanding. There was a second episode on that first disc, "The Risk," and I viewed that as well. It too was very good and my curiosity about the show was piqued. I found myself wanting to buy a book on the *Mr. Novak* series to learn more about it. After checking Amazon.com I discovered that there wasn't a book. I was disappointed but figured that the show would be covered in depth in a biography on James Franciscus. This too did not exist and I surfed the internet until I found a *Mr. Novak* site by veteran teacher John T. Taylor. It is located at www.fccj.us/MrNovak/mrnovak.html. He titled it "My Favorite Teacher TV Series." The content was informative and clearly a labor of love. I called John and he told me how much he loved the show when a fledgling teacher and that it had helped him to become a better educator. He would even use episodes of the series in his classes. I was puzzled that such a program of apparent quality and influence had been largely forgotten. After doing a little preliminary research it became apparent that Mr. Novak had won many awards and that it was a ground-breaking series in the history of dramatic television.

I decided that I would write a book not only to have a creative project but also to discover more about this unique program. After drafting a proposal, I contacted Ben Ohmart, the head of BearManor Media publishing, and he soon issued a contract. Many months later the results are in your hands. This has been an incredibly fulfilling journey for me and I have encountered dozens of great people who either granted interviews, provided materials and assistance or just offered encouragement. Two people in particular really made this trek a great experience. Marian Collier portrayed teacher Marilyn Scott on the show and eventually married series creator E. Jack Neuman. She was incredibly helpful and encouraging and really went the extra mile. Her generosity in allowing me full access to her Neuman archives has really embellished the quality of this book. Laure Georges Gonzalez was an extra on the show and is a devout fan even to the current day. The memories of her teenage love of the show were beautiful and heartfelt. She too offered much enthusiasm and positive energy. This television production achieved a great deal and is worth discovering and remembering. So hurry along because it's just about time for first period to begin in the classroom of Mr. Novak.

Chapter One

Headmaster —
E. Jack Neuman

The man who created and produced the classic *Mr. Novak* series had no high school experience beyond having attended one in his youth. Professionally he held a degree in law, just like his father, but never practiced, deciding instead on a career as a radio, film, and television writer. In fact, when the idea of a TV series set in a high school was suggested to him, he didn't think there'd be enough stories to sustain it beyond three weeks.

Ernest Jack Neuman was born in Toledo, Ohio, on February 27, 1921. He was the only child of E. Jack Sr. and Agnes Neuman. E.J.'s father was a lawyer and his mother a housewife. As a small child, he showed an aptitude for reading and writing. The family moved to Denver, Colorado, when E.J. was a boy and he attended Cathedral Grade School. The young Neuman was an avid reader of magazines and pulp fiction. He was a big fan of radio and listened to programs of the day with a particular fondness for detective shows.

Neuman senior high school photo

Neuman graduated from Regis Jesuit High School in 1938 and then attended Colorado State College in Greeley. While a student at the school, he originated a college radio program emanating from the campus called *Campus Broadcast*. He also took over the station break on CBS at 6:55 A.M. and reported news of the world for a five-minute period. Neuman enjoyed working in the medium and was determined to explore his options in both writing and broadcasting after his school years ended.

E.J. then switched to the University of Missouri where he enrolled in the School of Journalism. He maintained a straight-A average and would often do extra-credit assignments to further his knowledge of journalistic criteria. Before he could complete the course, he entered the Marines and was assigned to the radio division of Special Services. While there he wrote and adapted dramatic scripts for the War Department. These were well received and E.J. enjoyed creating these shows for the military. He was convinced that his decision to become a writer in the field of entertainment was the correct path to take.

In 1943 he wrote his first radio script for the *Suspense* program. It was titled "The Strange Death of Charles Umberstein" and was the story of an Allied Spy who feels the noose of discovery slowly tightening. It was well received at the time and remains a favorite among fans of old-time radio. Neuman returned to writing in 1945 while recovering in the Naval Hospital at San Diego from tuberculosis, which he had contracted in the South Pacific. He sold his second radio script to the *Romance* program. Titled "Love Is News," the story concerns a meek little man from Cleveland who discovers romance on a South Pacific island. It starred Irene Tedrow and Fred MacKaye and aired on June 19, 1945. Shortly thereafter he sold his first screenplay, *The Silver Bandit*, to King Brothers Productions. The film was not produced. Neuman was honorably discharged from the Marines in 1946 with the rank of Sergeant.

Pondering his next move, and remembering his father's occupation as a lawyer, E.J. enrolled at UCLA's law school. Based on his literary experience while in the service, he was soon hired by CBS radio as a staff writer. Neuman placed a script with the *Meet Miss Sherlock* program called "Wilbur and the Widow." The scenario concerned amateur detective Jane Sherlock and featured Sondra Gair in the title role. During this period E.J. was associated with KFI radio for thirteen weeks and worked with J. Walter Thompson and the May and Bennett Advertising Agency. As a CBS staff writer, he was assistant producer for the *Bullocks* radio show, "The World We Are Fighting For," This successful first experience with production gave him a new career goal along with his desire to keep improving his writing skills.

The following year Neuman placed three radio scripts. They were for popular series *The Whistler*, *Garden of Art*, and *Hawk Larabee*. His reputation as a writer of quality stories was being noticed by executives of the radio networks. E.J. was an author for the CBS series *Free for All*. This was a weekly game show in which listeners wrote in asking for different items. While on the air, emcee Wes Battersea would read the requests substituting the word "blank" for the article

Maury Cohen MC (center) and Neuman go through the daily mail for *Free for All*. The program receives close to 10,000 letters weekly.

sought. A studio audience member would be allowed three guesses to identify the item. If they were right, they'd win a "prize box" that would contain anything from a John Fredericks hat to an electric typewriter. In late 1948 E.J. asked to be released from his CBS contract and became a freelance writer. He had gained a great deal of experience from his time at CBS but wanted to be more in control of his career.

Neuman's first major assignment as a freelancer was the new radio series *Joe Canto, Private Eye*. It starred Barton Yarborough as professional investigator Jeff Regan. His superior, Anthony Lyon, was voiced by Wilms Herbert. The premise was that Regan would receive assignments from his boss whom he was not on friendly terms. The second episode, "The Prodigal Daughter," was written by E. Jack Neuman. He went on to write 14 more shows before the end of the year. The series' name was later changed to *Jeff Regan, Investigator* and Jack Webb took over the lead. The series was popular and Neuman's reputation as a writer increased. E.J. would pen a few more stories for the Regan series in 1949 and began to write for other dramatic shows such as *The Whistler* and *The Adventures of Rocky Jordan*.

In September of 1949 Neuman wrote his first script for the popular *Suspense* series. He had been hired by radio producer William Spier. E.J. wrote several stories for *Suspense* as well as other series such as *Escape*, *Johnny Dollar*, and *Sam Spade*. Around this time, he was again hired by Spier to write scripts for the *Sam Spade* series and continued to do so for the next two years. In the fall of 1950 he made a return visit to Denver and was profiled in a local paper:

> Eight years ago a Denver youth barely out of his teens packed a suitcase full of his belongings and, with $10 in his pocket, set out for Hollywood via the "thumb" route. He told his mother not to expect him back until he became a successful radio writer. E. Jack Neuman, a writer of the CBS *Suspense* and the NBC *Sam Spade* radio dramas, returned to Denver Thursday for a short holiday visit with his mother, Mrs. A. C. Jennings. For several years one of radio's half-dozen top writers, Jack, his mother agreed, had made the grade in Hollywood. A unique feature of Neuman's stories, many Denver friends and acquaintances have been startled to find, is that his characters invariably bear their names. An awed producer once asked Neuman how he managed to conceive such a colorful array of fictitious names. "I dream them up at night," was the reply.

In October of 1950 Neuman wrote a script for the *Dr. Kildare* radio series called "Joe Finley's Ulcer." The regulars were Lew Ayres as Dr. Kildare and Lionel Barrymore as Dr. Gillespie. The *Dr. Kildare* characters and program were to return a decade later in a most prominent way for the young writer. He would play a large role in the television adaptation of the popular radio series. E.J. continued to create scenarios for *Suspense* and *Sam Spade* and also penned a script for *Richard Diamond, Private Detective*. Motion picture star Fred MacMurray purchased a story from Neuman:

> Ever since *Double Indemnity*, Fred MacMurray has been looking for another thriller. Now he thinks he has found it in "Windy City Six," a radio script he'll play this week. So sold is Fred on the yarn that he bought it from E. Jack Neuman before it even goes on the air.

The episode aired on the *Suspense* series on February 8, 1951, to positive reception. During the summer of 1951, Neuman wrote six more scripts for *Dr. Kildare* and continued creating stories for *Suspense*. A wire-service blurb described his dedication to authenticity through research.

> E. Jack Neuman, who frequently writes about crime for "Suspense," will enter UCLA in June to take a special course in criminal law." — 6/23/51.

As a freelancer, Neuman was always seeking new avenues for his literary efforts. He had been working regularly in the radio field for half a decade, and had made many contacts in the industry. In the fall he began writing for the popular CBS *Lineup* series. It was a realistic police drama that gave radio audiences a look behind the scenes at police headquarters. Neuman became head writer and produced a total of eleven scripts that that aired through the fall of 1952. The show was based in San Francisco. Neuman and the director would often ride with the police while they were investigating crimes. Fresh ideas for scripts would often arise from the actual police cases. E.J. would also read dozens of daily newspapers to get potential stories. This attention to research and realism would become a trademark of E. Jack Neuman's approach to script writing and production.

Neuman was prolific during the year of 1953 with a total of 22 radio scripts that were produced for various series such as *Yours Truly, Johnny Dollar, Escape, Suspense, On Stage* and *Rogers of the Gazette*. He also married Irene Booth with whom he would have four children. E.J. wrote a script for the prestigious *Hallmark Hall of Fame* series which showcased his "Alfred Noble" story on December 13, 1953. The production starred Hallmark veteran Lionel Barrymore with John Hoyt and Charlotte Lawrence in supporting roles. The producer and director was William Froug. He and Neuman worked well together and became friends. They would collaborate ten years later on the pilot of the *Mr. Novak* television series.

During the early years of the fifties, E.J. was increasingly aware of the expanding television industry and its need for superior script writers. Neuman wrote his first story for the CBS video series *You Are There*. The program blended history with modern technology and presented great events of the past. Dramatic recreations were utilized along with modern-day reporters who would interview the historical protagonists. The host was Walter Cronkite, who would anchor the show from New York. At the end of each episode Cronkite would summarize the events depicted in the teleplay. The series had aired on radio for several years to great success.

Neuman's episode was "The Surrender of Corwallis at Yorktown" and aired on December 27, 1953. It was directed by Bernard Girard and featured actors Paul Birch, Paul Burke, John Larch, and DeForest Kelley. The episode was well received by both the critics and the public.

In the new year of 1954 Neuman continued to write radio scripts for various series as *Suspense, On Stage*, and the prestigious *Hallmark Hall of Fame*. E.J.'s episode "Nurse Edith Cavell," aired on March 7, 1954, and starred "first lady of the American theatre" Helen Hayes. The producer was once again William Froug. Lionel Barrymore narrated the drama about a British nurse who was shot by the enemy in World War I for

Helen Hayes, "first lady of the American theatre," confers with writer E. Jack Neuman (left) and producer Bill Froug on her starring role as "Nurse Edith Cavell," tonight at 9 on WTAG-CBS' Radio Hall of Fame.

aiding Allied prisoners. The program garnered positive reviews and Neuman's reputation as a writer of quality scripts was solidified within the television industry.

E.J. wrote his second TV script for the *You Are There* series with "The Surrender of Corregidor," which aired in April. He continued to write in the radio medium with scripts for several different series, but would soon be focusing his literary efforts almost exclusively for television.

Neuman's next foray into TV came with his story for the debut of the *Climax* series, "The Long Goodbye." It received positive reviews in the trades:

> If this new teleseries lives up to its opener in future plays, it should be the number one hour-long dramatic show. Using Raymond Chandler's novel, with an excellent adaption by E. Jack Neuman, the first vehicle resulted in a gripping murder mystery, beautifully acted and directed, and loaded with suspense.

E.J. wrote a few more scripts for *Suspense* and *Escape* during the remainder of the year and then turned his attention to scenarios for television. While he would continue to write radio scripts through the end of the decade, his career in that field had essentially come to an end.

October 1954 brought a small-screen adaptation of *The Lineup* radio show which was broadcast on the CBS network. The show was based on actual cases from the San Francisco Police Department and was filmed on location. It starred Warner Anderson as Lt. Detective Ben Guthrie, Tom Tully as Inspector Matt Greb with Marshall Reed in the role of Inspector Fred Asher. The first episode, "The Paisley Gang," was reviewed in a trade publication:

> Adult treatment and good acting characterize *The Lineup*.... Producer Jaime del Valle uses new Eastman Tri-X for outdoor night shots, filming almost entirely on location, and thereby generates a remarkable sense of authenticity. E. Jack Neuman's script throbbed with tingling excitement.

Neuman wrote two more segments of this popular detective series. In the following year of 1955, with E.J. now focusing on television, scripts were provided for *Gunsmoke* and *Matinee Theatre*. He also managed to squeeze in a pair of stories for the radio series *Yours Truly, Johnny Dollar*.

The new year of 1956 found Neuman writing some of his final scripts for the radio medium. He also penned "The Big Dry" for the television series *Frontier*. E.J. spent a great deal of the year developing concepts while attending UCLA where he took several creative-writing classes. He received straight A's in his courses and gained further knowledge and insight into his chosen profession. Neuman's constant desire to improve his skills in the craft of writing would reap big dividends in the busy year of 1957. Around this time, he achieved a degree in law from UCLA. Although he would never practice, the information gained would be beneficial for many future projects.

Panic! was an anthology series that was hosted by actor/producer Westbrook Van Voorhis. It was produced by Al Simon Productions, Inc., and aired on NBC. Neuman wrote a total of five scripts for the series during the year. His final *Panic!* story was for an episode broadcast in early 1958.

He also wrote three scripts for the detective program *Meet McGraw*. The series was produced at the Desilu studios. It starred Frank Lovejoy in the title role. Neuman also managed, in this very productive time, to pen two episodes for the anthology program *West Point*. This was his first effort in writing for a series that concerned education and student life.

In 1958 E.J. continued his literary efforts with a story for the western series *Cimarron City* and three scripts for *Jefferson Drum*. This was also a western series but primarily concerned the crusading efforts of a newspaper editor. It aired on NBC and was produced by future game-show tycoons Mark Goodson and Bill Todman. One of the writers on the series was future *Star Trek* creator Gene Roddenberry.

As the 1950's came to a close, Neuman wrote three scripts for the popular *Wagon Train* series. They were all well received. Neuman had expressed to several friends and colleagues his desire to move beyond writing and become a producer. His experience of over a decade in both the radio and television fields had given him a full knowledge of all creative aspects of programming. Although it would take a few years for this desire to become a reality, Neuman was determined to advance his career in this new direction.

The first year of the new decade saw Neuman's final script for radio, which was accepted by the *Suspense* series. It was titled "The Mystery of Marie Roget" and aired on February 7, 1960. He had written well over a hundred scenarios that were produced in his radio career and his reputation was exemplary.

The remainder of the year brought forth a plethora of new television scripts that were placed with *Bonanza*, *The Untouchables*, *Dante*, and *The Westerner*. E.J. was now in demand as a writer of quality stories that could be tailored to individual series. In an undated interview at the time, his increasing frustration at changes to several of his scripts was reported:

> I wrote scripts that were accepted, but many times when I saw them on the screen they barely resembled what I intended.

In the fall of 1960 a script by E.J. was submitted to Rod Serling's *Twilight Zone* series. It was titled "The Trouble with Templeton" and was accepted and used with little if any changes. The episode was directed by veteran Buzz Kulik and starred Brian Aherne as Booth Templeton and Pippa Scott as his first wife Laura.

It followed a familiar theme that Serling favored which was a desire to go back in time to better days. The script's plot concerned an aging theatre actor who is unhappy in both his personal and professional life. Templeton grieves for his late first wife and sees his current young spouse flirting with a gigolo. He attends a rehearsal of a play and is met by an arrogant young director who chides the actor for being late. Embarrassed by this condescending treatment, Templeton leaves and finds himself in a speakeasy. He encounters his first wife Laura and is astonished to see everyone exactly as they were thirty years earlier. She assumes him to be in aging makeup and won't listen to any questioning of the odd

Brian Aherne and Pippa Scott

circumstances. His former wife ends up slapping Booth and tells him he doesn't belong with her in the past. Laura tells the actor to go back to where he came from. Booth returns to the theatre, asserts himself and the play's rehearsal continues.

The episode received positive reviews and both the lead performance by Brian Aherne and Neuman's script were singled out for praise:

> Although plot smacks of the familiar, unique treatment of story and a fine performance by Aherne make it a spell-binder. — Decatur Illinois *Herald*, 12/9/60.

Neuman remembered writing the script years later while speaking author Mark Scott Zicree of *The Twilight Zone Companion*:

> I had often toyed with the notion of "You can't go home again," and it should have been, "you shouldn't go home again, ever," which is what I was trying to say here. I wrote it in about a day.

Neuman's years of experience meant he could write such an excellent script in a short period of time. The episode remains a high point in the *Twilight Zone* series and is a favorite among its fan base.

In the year of 1961 Neuman contributed two scripts for ABC's police drama *The Asphalt Jungle*, which starred Jack Warden and Arch Johnson. He also wrote two scenarios for NBC's crime drama *Cain's Hundred*. This program starred Peter Mark

Raymond Massey and Richard Chamberlain

Richman as a former mob lawyer who teamed up with the FBI to bring gangsters to justice.

On September 28, 1961, a new drama series debuted on the NBC network. *Dr. Kildare* starred Richard Chamberlain as a young physician and veteran actor Raymond Massey as Dr. Gillespie who was the young doctor's superior. It was filmed on the MGM lot in Culver City and was based on the characters and situations that had been depicted in the motion picture series. The show was an immediate hit and made Chamberlain a TV superstar.

While the series was in development, the lead was offered to James Franciscus who had previously been a regular on the *Naked City* show:

> E. Jack Neuman, who developed the show for TV, had decided Franciscus was perfect for the role. Sagal, slated to direct the pilot, agreed. Studio brass concurred. There was one hitch. The pilot had to roll immediately in order to be ready for the next selling season — and Franciscus was riding out the final period of an option that committed him to another series, *Band of Gold*, which found a sponsor but no network time slot. "I loved the Kildare story, and the script was one of the finest written. My *Band of Gold* option had just seventeen days to go." — *TV Guide*, 11/16–22/63.

Kitty, his wife at the time, recalled the loss of the Kildare role:

> Jim was naturally disappointed not to get the lead. He found it funny that the producers chose Richard Chamberlain, who resembled my husband. Jim thought that Dick was great in the lead and the *Dr. Kildare* show was an excellent dramatic series. — Interview.

Neuman wrote three episodes for the program. They were "Twenty-Four Hours" and "Admitting Service" in 1961 and "Gravida One" in 1962. As was his custom, he extensively prepared before he wrote the scripts:

> Prior to formulating his pilot script for the TV series, Neuman spent two months at Los Angeles County Hospital doing clinical work with a young intern, fresh out of medical school. He covered every area of a young intern's life from emergency duty to assisting in the delivery of babies. But his primary objective was observing his young intern friend — the stresses, strains, mistakes, joys, sorrows — and his dedication to medicine and his patients. — E. Jack Neuman Press Biography.

The premiere episode, "Twenty-Four Hours," was well received with Neuman's script mentioned as a contributing factor to the show's success:

> Ahhhhh — here's a winner — the new Dr. Kildare show. So far it's the best new show of the season. The NBC series fairly reeks of authenticity, of the smells and flavor and realism of life in a hospital. Writer Jack Neuman is tossing liberal doses of medical jargon into the script without apology, assuming his audience has intelligence. I particularly enjoyed the way Neuman brought out, with only the barest of explanations, the rigid caste system that exists in the medical profession. — Terry Turner, *Chicago Daily News*, 9/29/61.

Neuman was highly regarded at the MGM studios for his integrity and dedication to quality. These attributes would be beneficial when he created the *Mr. Novak* series. His working relationship with Boris Sagal would continue for Neuman's next project, the first he would both write and produce:

> I was going to write and direct as well. Then it struck me that there's always someone who is telling the director what to do. That was the fellow, I decided, I'd like to be, the executive producer. — Undated blurb.

E.J.'s initial foray into the role of producer came with his concept and development of a series based on the famous San Francisco trial lawyer, Jake Ehrlich:

> "My San Francisco connection gave me the idea for *Sam Benedict*," Neuman said. "I talked about it with Jake Ehrlich, who liked the idea.
> "Jake has been with us on every phase of the series," Neuman said. "He's consulted about every story. He either comes down to MGM in Hollywood or I hustle up to San Francisco."

Neuman's law degree from UCLA and his usual preparation gave the new series a great advantage. He spent many hours in courtrooms, absorbing the legal atmosphere. The director of the pilot was Boris Sagal, who went on to helm several episodes of the series. Veteran actor Edmond O'Brien portrayed the title role of Sam Benedict. He had won an Academy Award for *The Barefoot Contessa* and had appeared in many motion pictures

Edmund O'Brien as Sam Benedict

and television shows. The story concept was in sharp contrast to previous legal series and would focus on the character of the trial lawyer as revealed by his cases, rather than on the individual cases themselves.

The show premiered on September 15, 1962, with a Neuman script, "Hannigan." It was directed by Boris Sagal and aired on NBC. The series' producer would be William Froug with Neuman producing the pilot. The initial reviews were for the most part positive:

Sam Benedict, MGM-TV's new hour-long entry in its courtroom sweepstakes, is an excellent, high powered drama which packs several stories into the fast-moving show. "Benedict" is a man of strong convictions, and his denunciation of capital punishment, in the opening seg which was the pilot, is a case in point. Yet E. Jack Neuman deftly avoids the trap of preachment, this is all woven in as an integral part of the story itself. — Daku, *Variety*, 9/17/62.

A new lawyer series, but with a change of pace. Overall the production spells class, quite reminiscent of the "Dr. Kildare" production and that's not bad. The interesting E. Jack Neuman script was above par. — Hank Grant, *The Hollywood Reporter*, 9/17/62.

The series continued into the fall of 1962 as a respected production. Ehrlich's national fame as a trial lawyer contributed to interest in the show. Unfortunately, it was scheduled opposite the extremely popular *Jackie Gleason Show* and never achieved ratings of any consequence. It soon became evident that the series would probably not be renewed in the spring after the contracted episodes were broadcast.

In contemplating his next project, Neuman recalled a conversation with his associate Boris Sagal. An undated article portrayed this exchange:

Sagal: "Hey, how about doing a series about a high school teacher?"

Neuman: "Well, it doesn't sound so good to me. What do we do when we're finished with smoking in the school basement, the star half back who is a lousy English student and the kids who run off to get married?"

A short time later however, Neuman dropped into a high school during school hours. "It was an entirely different picture than I'd thought," he said. "Then I started talking to administrators and getting an idea of their problems and what school life is like. Young people today are begging for discipline and understanding," he said. "They aren't the way they were shown in *Dobie Gillis* or *Our Miss Brooks*."

Finally he had an idea for a central character — "a practical idealist, a man who wants nothing more than a chance to take a crack at ignorance eight or ten hours a day, a great hero for the public."

E. Jack Neuman and Boris Sagal at their office on the MGM lot

Chapter Two

New School — Filming
the Pilot for *Mr. Novak*

Producer E. Jack Neuman began to contemplate and prepare the concepts for his television series based on a high school. He didn't want to make the humorous type of programs that had previously appeared. Both *Mr. Peepers,* with Wally Cox, and *Our Miss Brooks,* with Eve Arden, had been successful sitcoms. Neuman wanted to use a more serious approach. This had never been done on network television. It would be a concept that would bring much popularity, respect, and admiration to the forthcoming series. Neuman later recalled his own educational background and views on his school years:

> I had a Jesuit education myself, and I was a reluctant learner, but later on I certainly appreciated the way they kept hammering away at me all the time, and got an enormous respect for education. And it was just the right time. Up until that time, any attempts to depict teaching or teachers or school were done with high comedy. — *The TV Collector*, Vol. 2, No. 44, 9–10/89.)

In the fall of 1962, E.J. visited a few schools in the Los Angeles area and spoke with various teachers and students. He quickly gained insight into aspects of the educational system and began to approach the executives at MGM-TV about his new show's concepts:

> When I first had the idea that there might be a television series dealing with a schoolteacher there was quite a bit of excitement — not from schoolteachers — but from people in the broadcasting business. They thought it was a dandy idea. Several of them mentioned the success of the *Peepers* and *Brooks* programs and assumed I would be delivering a series in a similar comedic tone. I told them I would get back to them after some additional scholastic research. — Washington Education Association Speech, 4/17/64.

Neuman returned to the schools he had previously visited and spoke further with the educators:

> The schoolteachers I spoke to were very suspicious — if not downright hostile. I couldn't blame them. They complained that motion pictures and television had treated education as a farce comedy too many times. As I continued my research it seemed to me that in the serious, crucial business of education there was a quiet giant of a drama happening every day in every type of school in the country. I assured the teachers and principals that I had every intention of using a dramatic and realistic approach to the new show. They were pleased to hear this and promised their full cooperation. — Ibid.

Neuman soon decided that he wanted to portray the high school experience in his pilot script and series:

> I eliminated the elementary level of schooling simply because it presented impossibly expensive production problems using children en masse. The college level seemed less attractive to me than the secondary because the students in a high

school have not quite set their minds and are more malleable and unpredictable. Once I decided on a secondary school background I said I was going to try to make a high school teacher the most popular hero ever seen on film. In short, I wanted to see if a man without a gun or badge or a horse or a stethoscope could capture a few million hearts. I also wanted to put the distorted image of the teenager back into a proper, authentic perspective. — Ibid.

Sagal and Neuman during the pilot filming
at John Marshall High School

E.J. had kept in contact with his former collaborator Boris Sagal while he was conducting research and having initial discussions with the television executives. Sagal agreed to direct a pilot episode and became involved in the development of the show. He would share a "Created by" credit with Neuman when the series eventually aired. E.J. wrote a treatment and approached MGM-TV about financing the pilot. His sterling reputation and previous quality work at the studio on *Dr. Kildare* and *Sam Benedict* prompted a favorable response by the studio.

Neuman then contacted Joseph Stefano and asked him to write a pilot script for the new series. The dramatist was a veteran of the motion picture and television industry. He had written scripts for popular anthology series *Playhouse 90* and *General Electric Theatre*. Stefano had penned the scenario for Alfred Hitchcock's *Psycho* and was well respected in the business. He acquired Neuman's research notes and began to develop the pilot script.

While Stefano was writing the pilot, Neuman began thinking of a location for filming. He knew that it would be economical to use a High School in the Los Angeles area. If the pilot could be filmed over the Christmas vacation of December 1962, actual students could be used as extras. After some consideration, he settled on what would be his series' "Jefferson High School."

John Marshall High School was located in the Los Feliz district of Los Angeles at 3939 Tracy Street. It served grades nine through twelve and was part of the Los Angeles Unified School District. It was named after jurist John Marshall, who served as the fourth Chief Justice of the United States for three decades. An appealing aspect of the school to Neuman was that it was racially integrated. Students of various ethnic backgrounds came from Los Feliz, Atwater Village, East Hollywood, Northeastern Koreatown, Elysian Valley, and Silver Lake. Designed by architect George M. Lindsey in the Collegiate Gothic style, and constructed in 1930, John Marshall High School first opened its doors on January 26, 1931, with approximately 1,200 students and 48 teachers. The principal in 1962 was W. Bruce Kirkpatrick. Neuman negotiated with the school and it was agreed that the filming of the pilot would begin on December 26, 1962, during Christmas vacation.

E.J. worked closely with Stefano in fashioning the pilot script. He envisioned two leads for the new series. The first would be teacher John Novak, who was just beginning his career in education. Novak would be naïve but with a sense of integrity and dedicated to providing the best possible learning experience for his students. The other lead would be Principal Albert Vane, a veteran with many years of participation in the educational field. He would be a mentor to young Novak and would also benefit from the teacher's determination and drive. This approach of an older associate and his young novice had been successfully used in the *Dr. Kildare* series. Veteran actor Raymond Massey portrayed Dr. Gillespie and Richard Chamberlain starred as the young Dr. Kildare. The interplay between the two had been a major contribution to that programs' success.

As December began, Neuman and Sagal began the casting process for the actors in the pilot. The producer's initial choice for the lead role could have started the series with some potentially unwelcome publicity:

> The first guy that was gonna do it was Richard Crenna. He was perfect, because he had starred in the [high school] comedy thing with Eve Arden [*Our Miss Brooks*]. Crenna was doing *The Real McCoys* and couldn't get out of it. — *The TV Collector*, 9-10/89.

Neuman's concept for the new show was *not* to do the humorous approach. In retrospect, it is probably good that Crenna wasn't available. His familiarity from the comedy series would have worked against his acceptance in a serious role. The title role ended up going to a young performer who was a veteran of the acting profession:

> They brought James Franciscus up, and, he's a very personable guy, and, you know, it was like a couple of years before — I couldn't cast *Dr. Kildare* and they brought up some guy named Richard Chamberlain, and I said, "Oh well, what the hell, I guess I'll try him. — *The TV Collector*, 9–10/89.

Franciscus had been the first choice for the lead when *Dr. Kildare* went into production. His contractual option with a pilot had prevented him from taking the part. It is more than probable that Neuman remembered this and it may have contributed to Franciscus getting the role of teacher John Novak.

James Franciscus was born in Clayton, Missouri, on January 31, 1934. In the summer of 1953, Jim enrolled as an apprentice in a summer stock theatre in Massachusetts. He entered Yale University that September with the intention of becoming an English major. Franciscus soon became involved with theatre training. He wrote and produced three of his own works and acted in many others. Each summer — five in all — he performed in summer stock. The big break came during his third year at Yale:

> In his junior year, a Walt Disney scout spotted him in a production of *The Great Gatsby* and he was asked to read for a role in *A Light in the Forest*. "Talk about butterflies," said Jim. "It was my first experience before a camera and I clammed up. I didn't get the part." But the director was so impressed with the novice that he signed him for the lead role in the movie, *Four Boys and a Gun*. After filming was completed, Franciscus interrupted his acting career, returned to Yale and completed his Senior Year. — Christopher Gardner, "In a Class by Himself," *New York Sunday News*, 10/25/63.

In 1957, he received a Bachelor of Arts degree in English and Theatre Arts from Yale University, from which he graduated magma cum laude. After commencement, he spent the summer in Europe, still undecided as to whether he wanted to spend full time in front of cameras or a typewriter. Opting to pursue an acting career, Franciscus appeared on several series such as *Have Gun, Will Travel; Studio One in Hollywood*; and *The Silent Service*.

His first major role was that of Detective Jim Halloran in the half-hour version of ABC's *The Naked City*, which debuted in the fall of 1958. During the year of production, Jim began to be featured in both fan magazines and soon built up a following among teenage girls. His handsome countenance and nice-guy image propelled him into being a minor celebrity among youthful television viewers. During this time, an alarming incident caused the young actor considerable distress:

> I was skating one day in Central Park in New York. Some girls recognized me from the series and crowded around for my autograph. It was going all right until the management told the girls to get off the rink. Then they were worried they wouldn't get their turn, and they started grabbing at my collar, my tie, etc. When the mob scene was over, I was left standing with only my pants and my skates on. — Bob Thomas, "Mr. Novak Doesn't Want to Be a Teen-Age Sensation," AP, 3/3/64.

He was shaken by this potentially dangerous situation and began to question the validity of fame. This early example of fan hysteria was to be amplified to a great degree during the *Mr. Novak* years. James Franciscus would eventually acquire firm convictions about the type of publicity and availability he would allow to the press and public.

The young thespian acted in the *Naked City* series for its first season of 1958–1959. In the spring Jim left the show because he didn't wish to remain in New York City for the location filming. Franciscus then appeared in a few features such as *I Passed for White* in 1960 and *The Outsider*, with Tony Curtis, in 1961. He also acted in several TV series such as *The Twilight Zone*, *The Rifleman*, *Rawhide*, and *Alfred Hitchcock Presents*. James Franciscus had built a reputation in the industry as a professional and competent actor. The coverage in the various fan publications continued to increase.

His next series was CBS' *The Investigators* in which he played insurance fact-finder Russ Andrews. It debuted on October 5, 1961, and was canceled at the end of December. Franciscus was not very upset by the end of his second series:

> It was very bad, really and only lasted 13 weeks. But it put me enough in the clear financially so I could afford to wait out a good role. And wait I did, nearly a year and a half for *Mr. Novak*. — Ruth E. Thompson, "Mr. Novak Starts Sophomore Year on TV," Greenfield, Massachusetts, *Recorder-Gazette*, 9/19/64.

Franciscus was very happy to receive the lead role of teacher John Novak:

> I was hooked by the series before a scene was ever shot. From the outset, I thought it was dramatically sound. I liked the conception, the purpose. — "Mr. Novak No Fan of Magazines," Columbus, Indiana, *Republic*, 10/10/64.

His wife Kitty remembered his happiness at receiving the lead role:

> When Jim was cast as Mr. Novak he was pleased. He had originally wanted to be a teacher and achieve a degree in that profession. Jim went into his acting career so this part "killed two birds with one stone" as he told me. He thought the series would help people. — Int.

E. Jack Neuman's choice of the actor to portray Principal Albert Vane was a clear-cut decision:

"I found out right away that a high school is only as good as its principal. The school itself was always a reflection of who was at the top. If he was a weak toady [person], the school was generally ill-run; if he was a strong man, whatever personality he had, the whole school had the same personality."

"How many men did they test for the part?"

"One... Dean Jagger," says Neuman. "Dean Jagger was the epitome of a thoughtful, firm guy who knew he had to do the job with humor or he'd get killed." — *The TV Collector*, 9–10/89.

Dean Jeffries Jagger was born in Lima, Ohio, on November 7, 1903. He attended Wabash College but dropped out in his sophomore year. For a few semesters, he taught all eight grades in an elementary school before heading for Chicago. He studied acting at the Lyceum Arts Conservatory and acquired considerable skills and experience. Jagger later performed in vaudeville, on radio, and the stage. Through the 30's and 40's he acted in many Broadway plays, including the original production of *Tobacco Road*.

Jagger made his film debut in *The Woman from Hell* (1929) with Mary Astor. He went on to become a successful character actor and appeared in dozens of films during the 1930's. The breakthrough part came in 1940 with the title role in *Brigham Young*. He continued to appear in many films during that decade and acquired a reputation as a skilled and professional thespian. Jagger won the 1949 Academy Award for Best Supporting Actor for his role of Lt. Col. Harvey Stovall in *Twelve O'Clock High*.

During the 1950's he appeared in such popular films as *The Robe*, *White Christmas*, *Bad Day at Black Rock*, and Elvis Presley's *King Creole*. Although he preferred to work in motion pictures, he did act in a few television series such as *Lux Video Theatre*, *Schlitz Playhouse*, *Zane Grey Theatre*, and *Playhouse 90*.

At the beginning of the following decade, Jagger performed on some popular television shows such as *The Twilight Zone*, *General Electric Theatre*, and *Dr. Kildare*.

A creative artist of integrity and conviction, Jagger was always very choosy about the parts he accepted. His agreement to portray the Principal was carefully considered:

> I feel an actor should not accept any role willy-nilly. It is much better to bide one's time until the thing that appeals, that you can believe in, presents itself. I stayed out of much television because so much of what I saw and so much of what I read seemed strictly matter-of-fact surface emotion. Then along came *Mr. Novak* — a sincere, honest effort to entertain and inform. A chance to do immeasurably good to a segment of our population that is sadly taken for granted — the teacher and the nation's teenagers. — "Key to Youth is found by Mr. Novak Star," *Chicago Tribune*, 11/15/63.

E. Jack Neuman had very definite ideas about the characters of his two leads and discussed them at length with Franciscus and Jagger:

> When I told Jim about the role I pointed out that Mr. Novak was going to be a maker of mistakes. I told the same thing to Dean Jagger. They were delighted at the prospect of creating heroes where heroes have always existed but have rarely been seen. Mr. Novak is often a misuser of English — even if he is an English teacher. And Mr. Vane very often is an indecisive stutterer — even though he is a decision maker. Mr. Novak feels that he has the right to accept or reject a drink, to fall in or out of love, to hate or admire a student, a fellow faculty member, or anyone else. He feels that being a schoolteacher does not exempt him from being a human being. — W.E.A. Speech, 4/17/64.

Franciscus and Jagger with Sagal at John Marshall

The plotline of the pilot script concerned the first day of the new semester at Jefferson High School. Shortly after arriving at the educational institution, fledgling teacher John Novak notices that his car has been damaged. He discovers that a brilliant student of his caused the dent. The boy agrees to pay for the damage and announces that he's quitting school to work full time at his father's auto body shop. Mr. Novak uses unconventional methods to convince the boy to remain at Jefferson High.

A part of the episode concerned an orientation presentation at the school's auditorium. Many John Marshal students would be used in this scene as well as other segments of the production. Just before the Christmas break recruitment began to obtain extras for the pilot. Student Laure Georges recalled the excitement of an opportunity to be part of a television production:

> There was a sign-up list for any students who wanted to be extras in the pilot. It was to start the day after Christmas and we would be needed for three days. A lot of us signed up and were soon notified that we would be used. We were to be paid $10 a day and a box lunch. The main reactions to our being chosen were joy, excitement and disbelief. I remember jumping up and down and hugging my friends when we realized this was truly going to happen. — Interview.

L-R: Jagger, Asner, Collier, Franciscus, and Franken

Rounding out the cast and portraying teachers at Jefferson High were Steve Franken as Jerry Allen, Donald Barry as Coach Mr. Gallo, Paul Genge as Mr. Christopher, and Shirley O'Hara as Mrs. Clyde. Attractive actress Gloria Talbott had been hired as the third lead in the role of Assistant Principal Miss Harvey. Noted character actor Ed Asner received featured billing and was cast as educator Mr. Stern. Just prior to the filming date of December 26th, a young actress, who was to become very popular on the forthcoming series, was added to the ensemble:

> I got a call from a casting agent at MGM. The call came in around noon and said to report to the studio for an interview at 6:00 p.m. It was for the part of a school teacher. I remembered teachers from my school days as being frumpy and thought they wouldn't hire me because I was too good looking. I picked out a conservative black suit and reported to the MGM casting department. I didn't wear much makeup and was prim. Boris Sagal met with me and explained the role. I did a few lines such as "Good morning, Mr. Novak" and so on. I asked Boris if he had someone else in mind and he said Sandra Giles. I told him her boobs were bigger than mine but I was the better actress. He said I had the part of Home Ec. teacher Marilyn Scott and we went to a Christmas party. — Marian Collier Interview, 9/21/16.

Marion Collier's arrival on the set included an incident that was very ironic considering her marital future:

I was supposed to report to MGM on December 26 at 5:30 A.M. I knew that I shouldn't wear black and couldn't find anything to wear. I called a friend and told her I needed a conservative dress that wasn't too sexy looking. She lent me a powder blue dress with a high neck.

I drove over to John Marshall High School and went into the gym and met with makeup and hair. I knew most of the crew from MGM and was happy to see them. After make-up I was taken outside and introduced to E. Jack Neuman and was told to stand next to him for a photo. I wondered who he was and asked him who was the damned fool who said to shoot the day after Christmas. He replied that he was and I asked him what he did. He replied that he was the Producer. I said that he must be the one to count the money and he laughed. After a few photos were taken, the photographer asked for a shot of him kissing me. He did and it was quite a prophetic shot since we ended up getting married seven years later. Jim Franciscus came out and posed with me for a few photos. He was very handsome and was quite proper and nice. After the photos were taken, I was told that I would have to change the dress as it was too sexy and was sent to wardrobe where I was assigned a less revealing outfit. — Ibid.

The John Marshall student extras were finding the filming to be a most enjoyable experience:

Miss Scott and Mr. Novak

I had a friend whose father was the assistant director of the pilot. I was selected and remember that we were told to walk around the hallways or sit in a classroom. James Franciscus was very nice and easy to talk to. He was very handsome and available to chat between scenes. Dean Jagger was perfect as the Principal. He was a gentle and friendly guy but not as available as Jim. They sat the actors outside the school between takes. It was a big deal for the students because they hadn't been on a movie set and they could see how things were filmed. The girls drooled over Jim Franciscus because he was so handsome. — Wes Wheadon Interview.

There was a lot of anticipatory waiting between setups but it wasn't boring. Jim and Mr. Jagger were friendly to the students. I remember constantly going up and down staircases while the classes were changing. I also spent time sitting in

Mr. Novak's classroom and there were some outdoor scenes where I'd sit with the other students in clusters. Jim Franciscus was the consummate DREAM BOAT!!! My girlfriends and I were totally crushing on him during the filming. — Laure Georges (Gonzalez), Int.

Character actor Ed Asner had positive impressions of the pilot's filming.

Jim and Marian during lunch break at John Marshall

E. Jack Neuman had hired me for the role of teacher Mr. Berg. He was very good to me and a good writer and producer. Jim Franciscus had a great smile that he used a lot. I thought he was more interesting when he wasn't smiling. I worshipped Dean Jagger as an actor. He never made a false move. You came away from a scene with him a smarter individual. His scene in the pilot where he tells the new teachers about our forthcoming jobs was a magnificent one. Marian Collier was very winsome and I flirted constantly with her. She was delightful. Steve Franken was hopping all over the place and was funny between takes. I liked the script and thought it could be a dignified and interesting show. An intelligent show. — Ed Asner, Interview, 9/30/15.

The filming at John Marshall ended on December 28. It had been a harmonious and productive shoot. Creator E. Jack Neuman felt that he had gained insight from the actual students of the high school:

Filming completed at John Marshall High School with approximately 1,000 regular students playing themselves, already has been in itself a rewarding, enlightening adventure. It didn't take long for us to discover that here was no group of trained extras, willing to take direction blindly. They had to know the story, what roles they played in it, what they were supposed to do and why they were supposed to do it. They were forever asking questions — but each question revealed their inquisitiveness, their curiosity, their intelligence, their emotions and their wonderful vitality. By the time the first day was over, all of us had an instant and severe lesson in today's teen-agers, their thinking and their sincerity — a lesson we will utilize throughout the series. — "Back-to-School Visit Opens Producer's Eyes," Youngstown, Ohio, *Vindicator*, 7/11/63.

Marian Collier also had a sense of optimism about the future of *Mr. Novak*:

When the shoot was finished we all had a real good feeling about the show being picked up by the network. It felt like we had done something that was both classy and groundbreaking. — Int.

The students who had appeared in the pilot also had a sense of hope and anticipation of the show being selected for broadcast in the fall of 1963. Wes Wheadon received optimistic news:

> All of us who were in the pilot hoped the show would be sold so they would continue to film at John Marshall. Some of the crew and the actors told us that they were pretty sure the show would make it to the air. We were informed that it would probably be a few months before they would know. — Int.

Laure Georges and her classmates were very excited at the possibility of further participation if the pilot sold:

> It had been an amazing three days and my girlfriends and I were so happy and thrilled to be in an actual TV show. We were told that if and when the show was sold to the network, that they would probably come back to John Marshall to do some more filming. Some of the students would be used as background extras in the actual episodes. We all were really hoping that would happen. — Int.

James Franciscus had performed well in the shoot. He told his wife Kitty that he too was optimistic:

> Jim said the pilot filming went very well. He liked and respected Dean Jagger and felt that all of the principals did a fine job. He had a good feeling about the show being picked up and hoped it would become his third series. — Int.

Editing and post-production concluded on January 8, 1963. E. Jack Neuman had successfully put his vision of a new type of television series on film. Now it was time to sell it to the studios and begin the real creation of Jefferson High School.

Mr. Novak

NBC Television • Fall 1963

Chapter Three

Prep School —
Sale of Series, Early Publicity
and Initial Production

The final editing of "First Year, First Day" wrapped on January 8, 1963.

Everyone involved was very pleased with the finished pilot and E. Jack Neuman began negotiations with MGM-TV to add *Mr. Novak* to the 1963 season's programming. One month later the anticipated outcome was revealed in the trades:

METRO FIRMS NBC-TV HR. SERIES — Firmed for next season was *Mr. Novak*, costarring James Franciscus as a young high school teacher and Dean Jagger as the principal. "*Novak*" will deal with the problems besetting a young teacher in a metropolitan school. Producer will be E. Jack Neuman, who with director Boris Sagal created the property. Pilot script was written by Joseph Stefano. NBC and MGM-TV will be partners in "*Novak*." — *Daily Variety*, 2/8/63.

In early March there was an exciting event for the faculty and students of John Marshall High School. The pilot film was scheduled to be shown in the school auditorium. In attendance were E. Jack Neuman, Boris Sagal, Dean Jagger, James Franciscus, and wife Kitty and a capacity audience of happy students, many of whom were extras during December's filming. Laure Georges was really looking forward to the screening:

Excitement, joy, and bliss belonged to my school friends and me as we filed into the auditorium. We had felt so lucky to be extras and it had been three days of feeling like stars on our own turf. The word had gone out that *Mr. Novak* had been picked up for the fall line-up on NBC and it felt like a miracle. As we settled in our seats we kept shrieking until the principal asked us to settle down. As the film rolled, we became hysterical each time one of us showed up on screen. It was our finest hour — literally. After the filming many of the students, including myself crowded around James Franciscus in the hallway. It was an awesome day. — Int.

Laure Georges beams happily, two to our right of James Franciscus

Kitty Franciscus and her husband were pleased with the favorable reception:

> Jim was so happy with the students' and faculty's encouraging response to the showing of the pilot film. On the way home he told me that he felt very positive about this third series and couldn't wait for the new season's filming to begin in May. It was so cute to see all the girls gathering around my husband. — Int.

Franciscus, wife Kitty, and executives after the screening at Marshall

Robert Sarnoff, Board Chairman of the National Broadcasting Company, received a congratulatory telegram. It was from Hazel A. Blanchard, President of the National Education Association, praising the pilot film. It read in part:

> If subsequent episodes of "*Mr. Novak*" live up to the high promise of the pilot film, we will be pleased to alert our entire National Education Association membership — which now includes more than 834,000 classroom teachers and school administrators — to the new series. "*Mr. Novak*" should be a credit to your fall schedule."

The National Education Association would subsequently become involved in many areas of *Novak's* publicity and production.

Daily Variety announced on March 15 that the *Mr. Novak* series would be slotted into NBC's Tuesday line up from 7:30 to 8:30 P.M.

During March, E. Jack Neuman visited five cities gathering material and promoting the forthcoming show:

> "This is strictly a dramatic series, although there will be liberal doses of humor. It's an honest attempt to portray the high school student for what he is — a practical, hard-working idealist swinging a good hard blow at the problems of ignorance."
>
> Neuman is going across the country, showing the film, and doing research into the problems faced by high school teachers. Along with press interviews, he is promoting the new show with displays at schools and State Education Associations. "One of the biggest problems is to convince the faculties that *Mr. Novak* will not ridicule them or make them out to be a bunch of pawns in the hands of silly students.
>
> "Nor do we make out the students to be juvenile delinquents. By and large, today's high school students are pretty sharp kids. Not all teachers are old maids or schoolmarms, but many of them are young, beautiful, and intelligent. And in this

series we have several good-looking women instructors." In Jim Franciscus, Neuman has made an excellent choice to play the title role. He exudes warmth, sincerity, and a certain amount of charm. In the initial episode, Mr. Novak makes a few mistakes on opening day of school, including going against the express wish of the principal. Not all the problems are solved at program's end. And in solving some of them, Neuman has not resorted to the usual clichés, but rather he has found realistic, believable answers. — Del Carnes, "Promoting the Teachers," *Denver Post*, 3/20/63.

Dr. G. Keith Dolan was the Principal of San Bernardino High School. He attended a conference that included a presentation by Neuman. The administrator would soon become a small part of the fledgling series:

At the conference, a 16mm print of "First Year, First Day" was shown to a great reception by the educators in attendance. Afterward, there was a request for anyone to become a script advisor. I wrote them and agreed to participate. I would receive scripts and made comments on them and a studio representative would take me to dinner and take notes. There would be a $50 payment for each script I reviewed. It was impressive to me that the Producers wanted the shows to be as authentic as possible. I ended up reviewing about three scripts each for the two seasons. There was one script that was so flawed that I recommended that it not be made and as far as I know it wasn't. — Dr. G. Keith Dolan, Interview, 11/8/16.

The beginning of April brought an announcement that William Froug would be the producer of the forthcoming series. He was a veteran of the television industry and had won an Emmy for an *Alcoa-Goodyear* segment and a Screen Producers Guild award for a *Playhouse 90* film that he had produced at Screen Gems.

Froug discussed the forthcoming series in a *Daily Variety* article:

> TV invades the classroom next season. MGM-TV is readying *Mr. Novak*, which has as its background a high school. *Novak* is an hour-long series to be on NBC-TV, is described as a "teenage *Defenders*" by Bill Froug, producer of the series. Froug is not one to underestimate the intelligence of the teenager. "Teenagers," he declares, "have the most adult minds today. You can't hook them with pap. We're taking the position that high school is a cross-section of America." With this approach, Froug is planning offbeat stories, some of a controversial nature. NBC-TV has okayed this approach, and the result is some very interesting stories are currently in preparation. There is one yarn about a conscientious objector. Still another deals with a Negro high school boy who cynically wonders why he should be concerned about graduating, his attitude being "I'll wind up being a Pullman porter anyway." Another story deals with a high school girl who wins a contest for her essay on patriotism, but because she criticizes the town in which she lives, townspeople don't want to give her the reward. What she has said is the truth, but they resent her for it. There's a provocative story about a high school youth involved in cheating. He's one of those ambitious characters who runs for class prez and wins, but he does this by the worst kind of cheating and conniving. His view-point being the goal justifies the tactics. Sixteen writers are already busy at their typewriters, knocking out this non-pap type of merchandise for Froug. On paper, as the saying goes, this has all the earmarks of being one of the next season's more interesting new ventures. — Dave Kaufman, "On All Channels: TV's Campus Capers," 4/23/64.

Along with the two leads from the pilot, returning actors to the new series included Marian Collier as Home Economics teacher Marilyn Scott and Steve Franken as instructor Jerry Allen. New regulars cast as educators were Kathaleen Ellis as Ann Floyd and Stephen Roberts as Math teacher Stan Peeples. Additions to the new cast were Vince Howard and André Phillipe. E. Jack Neuman recalled their casting:

> Vince Howard, who played the black teacher — I was at a club one night which featured a lot of comic talent and singers. He was standing there with a big bass baritone voice, singing like hell, and I cast him right there. He had never acted a day in his life. André Phillipe played the French teacher. He was so damned agile, he could play the piano and dance and fence and all that and use that French accent. He came knocking on the door one day, and I was always on the lookout for the right people. — *The TV Collector*, 9–10/89.

Marian Collier was impressed by her costars:

> Jim was a good-looking guy and was a good actor. An excellent actor. I found out later that he had gone to Yale. Dean Jagger was the one. Truthfully I think the show would have been good but not as good if Dean wasn't there. He was the major one

and a natural. Vince Howard was my buddy. He had never acted before and turned out to be a great actor. Stephen Roberts was funny and perfect for the role of the fussy type teacher. André Phillipe was a character and very talented. He was more of an entertainer. The whole company was like a family. It was a very happy shoot and we all became close. There was never any trouble in the first season. — Int.

Vince Howard as Pete Butler, Stephen Roberts as Stan Peeples.

Gloria Talbott, who portrayed Assistant principal Miss Harvey, had been scheduled to return to the role in the new series. However, a broken leg rendered her unavailable. For the initial filming of new episodes, the part was left open. By early June the part would be recast with an actress who would prove to be a favorite with the audience and the production.

An important factor in the future excellence of the new series was the first-class technicians and crew. These seasoned professionals gave the show a genuine quality of lighting, sound, sets, and photography. Property Master Bob Schultz recalled his joining the *Mr. Novak* team:

> I had worked on features and was on a guarantee at MGM and had just finished working on *How the West Was Won*. At the time the studio was very quiet and there were only two TV series going and they put me on *Mr. Novak* when it started. There were a number of highly skilled and experienced technicians on salary that were not being utilized by the studio. They ended up working on *Novak* and brought the new show up to a technical level of motion picture features. Everyone was very professional on the set and they were the best crew. The cinematographer was Dick Kline. He was a first-class technician and would go on to film all sixty episodes of the series. Dick knew how to achieve great results on the hurried production schedules of a weekly television series. The show's visual quality really helps it to hold up after so many years. — Interview.

Although some exteriors would be filmed at John Marshall during the forthcoming season, most scenes of Jefferson High School would be confined to the MGM lot in Culver City.

The corridors and classrooms and Principal's office was built on the lot. The sets were pre-lit so it was easy to film as there wasn't a lot of set up time needed. If a school auditorium was needed for a scene, the real one at John Marshall would be utilized during weekend filming. — Interview.

The actor playing the Principal of Jefferson High School was a man who stood by his convictions. He told a syndicated writer that his belief in the new series was absolute:

Dean Jagger says his *Mr. Novak* series, coming on NBC next fall, will concern itself with provocative themes — even segregation. When he was asked if he didn't feel that sponsors might object, because of a danger of a Southern boycott, Jagger answered: "If there's any problem, I'll talk to the sponsor myself. This is something I feel strongly about and I'm going to do it." — "Jagger Series to Be Provocative," *The Pittsburgh Press*, 6/1/63.

Miss Phipps counsels pregnant student (Pat McNulty) at Jefferson High

The first episode filmed was "Hello, Miss Phipps" which began production on May 29. The working title had been "Age Cannot Wither or Custom State." It starred veteran actress Lillian Gish as a social hygiene teacher who receives complaints from parents about her outspoken ways. A young actor named Allan Hunt was featured in this installment:

When *Mr. Novak* was first in production the word was out among all of us young actors that the new series was a treasure trove of possibilities for our age group. It was an especially rewarding experience for me because of Lillian Gish. There was quite a buzz about her coming to the set. She came in stone hard on her lines... her movements... her close-ups. She did everything in one take and never flubbed any lines. She was a real inspiration. James Franciscus was very personable... very quick to shake your hand... always pleasant... but he always had his nose buried in the script. — Interview.

E. Jack Neuman was determined that there would be no interference by any executives from NBC:

I forbade them on the set. I would not allow them to look at dailies, or anything like that. I just said, "You want it done, this is the way it's gonna be done." I didn't want their input, 'cause it was usually inept. And they went along with it. They always wanted a thorough treatment of the script before it was written, so they could examine it. And the way I usually did that was, I'd write the script, ask the secretary to draw up a treatment for it, and it was [filmed] by the time they got the treatment, and they went along with that." — *The TV Collector*, 9–10/89.

In this early stage of production, the suits were not interfering with the producer's concepts. Bob Schultz noticed MGM's lack of interest in the TV shows that were being produced on the lot:

MGM had its head in the sand because they would not recognize television. Features were the main part of the studio. The TV shows that were successful were the outside shows that came in and were owned by other people and just used MGM facilities. They didn't really want to have anything to do with TV. It was like, "Just let them shoot... and do their own thing." Our production staff, which was very small, did all the work. — Int.

Neuman would frequently rewrite scripts submitted by other writers. The series was a result of his vision and he wanted the best possible scripts for each episode. Schultz would observe this dedication:

Jack had so much energy and he'd bounce around the set in and out of his office after he'd done some rewrites. That was his expertise... rewriting someone else's script. He had a bungalow on the lot and some nights he'd be in there typing like crazy until 9 or 10 at night to try and fix a script. — Ibid.

Marian Collier also observed Neuman's dedication to the show:

In the first season Jack was very present. He would come on the set every morning and every afternoon. He would check on how things were going. He was a writer and then became a producer to save his lines because he didn't want anyone to change his words. He would sometimes have pages of script revisions. — Int.

The next episode filmed was "My Name Is Not Legion," which had begun as "One for the Girard Money, Two for the Show." It was the story of a brilliant but erratic student who has trouble adjusting to academic life at Jefferson High.

During this time an additional member of the regular cast was hired. Jeanne Bal was cast as Jean Pagano, the Assistant Principal of Jefferson High. She had originally planned on attending college to major in journalism To pass the summer months before the fall term started, she auditioned as a lark for a Los Angeles Light Opera musical and spent the next four years traveling in road companies of *Guys and Dolls* and *South Pacific* among other hits. Tiring of the road, she relocated

to Los Angeles. In the early 1960's she guest starred in many series including *Thriller*, *Route 66*, *Bonanza*, and *Wagon Train*. She reflected on accepting her role in the new *Novak* series:

> It is no secret that Jeanne turned down other series before accepting *Mr. Novak*. What made her say yes to this one? "The part," she answered. "Jeanne Pagano, the assistant principal, is a woman who has had experience and lived. She's not a door opener, as I call the roles so many of my actress friends end up playing. You know, the ones in little aprons. What really sold me on playing Jean Pagano was that when Mr. Neuman offered me the role he was able to give me a complete picture of Jean Pagano — her origin, family background, early life and other significant facts. To me that was of the greatest importance. For when you really know the character you're playing, just who and what you are supposed to be, you can add meaning to everything you do. I took this role knowing full well that James Franciscus and Dean Jagger are the stars. But my role has so many factors... it can go in many directions." — J.D. Sipiro, "TV's Fair Ladies," *Milawaukee Journal-Sentinel*, 11/10/63; and Aleena MacMinn, "Having a Bal with "Mr. Novak," *Detroit Free Press*, 2/9/64.

Marian Collier was impressed with the new vice principal:

> I thought Jeanne was perfect for the part. She was beautiful, personable, and a very good actress. She became a real favorite with the cast and crew. Jeanne was always letter perfect in her dialogue and worked very hard. — Int.

"The Private Life of Douglas Morgan, Jr." was directed by television veteran Richard Donner. It was the story of a class clown who becomes a conscientious objector in order to be excused from compulsory ROTC training. It starred young Peter Helm:

Peter Helm and Franciscus during filming of "Douglas Morgan"

Richard Donner was a great director. He gave good suggestions. He allowed me to do what I wanted to do and didn't correct very much. James Franciscus really looked the part and I could play off him well. He was a good actor and a good guy. Dean Jagger would improvise a lot. He'd change lines around and do new stuff but it was always natural and good for the character. Jeanne Bal was a sweet lady and worked well in our one scene together. It was an easy crew to work with and a great atmosphere on the set. — Interview.

Richard Donner had worked in the industry since 1960 and helmed many episodes of series' television including six episodes of the *Sam Benedict* program. He found the experience of directing of the *Novak* series to be a positive one:

When I was hired I fell in love with the whole group. At the end of the day we'd go into E. Jack's office and I'd have a glass of something with him. Not only would you discuss the next day's filming which was great, but he'd get into the characters' lives. I loved those sessions. E. Jack was a special man and he'd back you to the hilt. An hour show's shooting time was six days. There were no rehearsals. If you were lucky you'd bring in your cast the night before... as a favor... otherwise it was a union problem... and you'd block that night. Jim was wonderful as Mr. Novak. He knew his lines but most importantly he knew the character and was good in the role. He had the utmost respect for Dean Jagger. Dean was as professional as the day is long. I never butted heads with him and respected him. Jeanne Bal was very happy go lucky... a sweet lady... well trained and professional. With my background as an actor... I always loved working with actors that had a freedom for improvisation. — Interview.

Marian Collier appreciated Donner's style of direction:

Richard Donner was the best. He was an excellent director. He made it fun and he really worked well with the actors. He was not a dictator and would allow the actors to bring their own interpretations to the scenes. If it wasn't good he would say so. — Int.

James Franciscus's media coverage was increasing with publicity about the forthcoming series. He was featured in both TV magazines as well as publications geared toward a teenage audience. A prominent monthly was *'TEEN*, which catered to young girls with articles on grooming, lifestyles, fashion, and career choices. This was not the typical film and music-star fan magazine. Franciscus discussed the new show in the July 1963 issue:

> "The way I look at it," Jim enthuses, "*Mr. Novak* is a show all teens, teachers and parents can identify with. It won't cook up any phony yarns about JD's and teenage misfits. It won't portray teens as a group with no individuality. It'll treat them as individual human beings, just as they really are... and this is important. Novak as a character is about 28 or 29, single, and dedicated to his profession. He loves teaching and admires most of his students. He gets emotionally involved with many of them and this is where the stories come from." — '*TEEN*, 7/63.

E. Jack Neuman continued to give interviews publicizing the upcoming new series:

> We're trying to be scrupulously honest. And we've had no resistance. They say make the shows as true as you can. So we're going into educational problems, discuss them on our level. We'll deal with teacher's problems, with salaries, problems between an individual teacher and the faculty. We've put our school in a mythical city because we will attack school boards and criticize education. Student problems will be as real as we can make them. Our school is integrated of course. What we're really trying for is to foster the real image of the modern high school teacher, to foster the respect a man deserves who whets the appetite for learning. And we want to get as many of those young and eager faces as we can on the screen. — Cecil Smith, "The TV Scene: Realistic View of High School Days," *Los Angeles Times*, 7/2/63.

Herschel Bernardi and Franciscus during production of "I Don't Even Live Here"

"I Don't Even Live Here" lensed next and starred Herschel Bernardi as a teacher who is so desperate to be liked that he gives all his students A's.

"To Lodge and Dislodge" followed and featured Kim Darby in her first prominent role. She later recalled her pride in achieving this initial role of importance:

> When she was 16, she landed a little theatre role in "The Miracle Worker." Producer E. Jack Neuman was in the audience one night and asked her to audition for his "Mr. Novak" TV series. Her professional debut was on the show playing a blind girl named Julie who falls in love with her teacher. "After that one week of work was over. I went home and cried and cried. It was the first time I had ever been part of something that was my own, with people wanting me because I was me." That was in 1963 and people continue to compliment her on that performance, no slight accomplishment when viewers generally forget what they watched last night. — "True Grit Heroine Becomes an Activist," Wilson, North Carolina, *Daily Times*, 10/31/70.

The episode featured several teenaged members of the Foundation for the Junior Blind. E. Jack Neuman admired the attitudes of the handicapped students:

> Boris (Sagal) called me from the high school; he said, "Can you get down here?" And he said, "I photographed them coming off the bus, and they got in class a little early and one of 'em had a guitar — you wanna hear what I photographed?!?" And he had 'em singing. Well, it was so marvelous, all these blind kids singing away and never whimpering for sympathy or anything, and all of 'em with plans to go to college and be in professions and what not. — *The TV Collector*, 11–12/89.

The group was shown in episode singing Woody Guthrie's "This Land Is Your Land."

Marian Collier was uplifted by the blind students' optimism:

Marian offers encouragement
to an aspiring actress

> I had lunch with one of the blind students who appeared in the episode. She was telling me that she wanted to be an actress. I told her that there was no reason that she couldn't be. All of the blind students were so positive and happy. They were a real inspiration to the cast and crew. They were wonderful. Kim Darby was excellent in the lead and it really helped her career. — Int.

Tony Dow was known for his role of Wally in the *Leave It to Beaver* series. "To Lodge and Dislodge" was the first of his three appearances as student newspaper Editor George Scheros:

> Episode director Boris Sagal always seemed to me to be very serious. He was the co-creator of the show so he really knew what he was doing. Kim Darby was very good as the blind student... very convincing. She was very quiet and perfect for the role. James Franciscus was a good guy. He wouldn't hang out with us but was always really pleasant. He was just like he was on the show. In those days, if you did a scene with another actor they'd look right at you. He did a lot of looking away with quick motions. I'd never seen anybody else use that technique. It was very natural. Dean Jagger had great charisma and power in his acting. He was the most powerful person on the set and everybody knew it. I'd never seen another actor while playing an authoritarian role toss off some of his lines in a throwaway fashion. It made him seem somewhat absent minded. He would walk off screen into his office and still be talking. — Interview.

Tony Dow as George Scheros,
editor of Jefferson High
student newspaper

"Love in the Wrong Season" featured a storyline about a potential love affair between a shy student and his teacher. It was directed by Ida Lupino who had become a respected director in the television industry. The guest stars included Disney star Tommy Kirk as the pupil and television veteran Pat Crowley as the instructress. Tommy Kirk was distressed with his experience on the show:

> My agent got me an interview with Ida Lupino. I read a few lines and was informed that I had been cast as the shy boy. On the set Lupino was very intense... serious... all business. I had a terrible time communicating with her and we argued a lot. I was very uncomfortable with the experience. At this stage in my life I was in a great deal of turmoil in both my personal and professional life. At one point when I was arguing with Lupino, Franciscus injected himself into the conversation and told me to shut up and do what she wanted. His presence was severe and rather formal. It was one of the nastiest experiences of my career. The only good thing was Pat Crowley who was very professional. We worked well together but I was glad when the episode's filming wrapped. — Interview.

Pat Crowley had an entirely different experience:

> I was blown away by the story. An untold one at that time. Ida Lupino was beautiful, kind, helpful, brilliant, and so talented. She was the first of the female directors and as fine as any men I worked with. I don't remember any problems working with Tommy Kirk. He was very good in our scenes together and played the awkward student with sensitivity and grace. There are no memories of any clashes on the set. James Franciscus was a gentleman and a dream to work with. He was a very handsome man and a serious actor who was welcoming and generous to me. I was

> totally intimated by Dean Jagger, which worked well for the story as he was my boss. I couldn't wait to work with him and he lived up to my expectations. Overall, it was a very good experience for me. — Interview.

"He Who Can Does" went into production and starred Edward Mulhare as a novelist with unorthodox views who is scheduled to speak at Jefferson High.

Marian Collier had been cast as a Home Economics teacher. She was finding the role to be a bit difficult:

> I hadn't had much experience in Home Ec. One time I had to carve a roast that was on a board. Every time I tried to cut it... it would fall

on the floor. Finally, they put a nail in it so I could finish the scene. I was raised in a very ethnic family. A Romanian family of seven. At the dinner table we had a knife and fork and that was it. So when I had to teach the kids how to set a table, they had to show me how to do it. When I did the pilot, they didn't say what kind of teacher I'd be. Then I became the Home Ec. teacher. — Int.

The National Education Association was becoming more involved with the upcoming series:

> Noerdlinger Heads Up NEA Info Bureau Here — Motion Picture, television and radio Information Center of National Educational Assn. has been established in L.A. with quarters in Kirkeby Center, Westwood. Heading up the new branch of NEA with its 860,000 members is Henry S. Noerdlinger, formerly associated with C. B. DeMille Productions and MGM research department. Center will serve the mass communications media as they interpret education to the public. Noerdlinger's first contact will be with MGM-TV's "Mr. Novak," drama series about a high school teacher. — *Daily Variety*, 7/30/63.

The NEA also provided *Mr. Novak* with a technical advisor who would play a large role in the accuracy of the program. John Ryan had been a teacher for fifteen years. He would appear in various episodes and would write the last show of the first season.

Neuman appreciated his knowledge and input:

> He was the guy that showed you how to walk in the door... there are certain things you have to watch very carefully — like... the class is over; everybody gets up and leaves except one girl... make sure the door stays open. Things you would never think of. All the tiny little details that any teacher, would, right away, say, "Hey, come on!" Well, we didn't break any of those rules; we were very rigid about that. Another one was you'd never touch a kid. And the certain basic rules in handling children: don't back 'em against a wall and give 'em no way out, 'cause then you're gonna have an animal at bay and both of you are gonna make a big mistake. — *The TV Collector*, 9–10/89.

"X Is the Unknown Factor" featured David Macklin as a brilliant student who is ultimately caught cheating. Brooke Bundy played his girlfriend. The boy is scheduled to receive a scholarship and pressure is put on Novak to pass him even though he has produced inferior work. There was a guest appearance by noted educator Dr. Frank Baxter. His similar appearance to Dean Jagger provided an amusing scene. The show was directed by Richard Donner. Macklin, like many other youthful actors, found working on the show to be a good experience:

> I liked the script and the character. Richard Donner was my favorite director. He was good humored, open, and cooperative. He was willing to talk to and communicate with the actor. Brooke Bundy was great. She was fun to be around and work with. James Franciscus was the best. He was friendly, cooperative, and

generous. He even let "us kids" hang out in his trailer while on location at John Marshall High School. I was glad to work with TV's *Mr. Science* Dr. Frank Baxter. A memorable shoot. — Interview.

Brooke Bundy also found her first stint on *Novak* to be enjoyable:

> David Macklin was always very professional... very dedicated to the role. He was a serious actor. I was intimated by James Franciscus because he was a highly trained actor and I wasn't. He was very gracious and professional and it was great to work with him. I learned a lot from him. Richard Donner was a wonderful director. He was very intense and would take you aside and discuss the role and ask what you might do with it. He allowed an actor to contribute to the characterization. Donner was very cinematic. — Interview.

The episode's director was impressed by the realistic storyline:

> If the student had been excused his cheating then the school would have acknowledged his achievements. Instead, after confessing his transgression, the student is denied his scholarship. E. Jack Neuman was very successful because 99% of TV shows lived in a world of accepted fantasy. Jack lived in a world of reality. — Int.

The beginning of August brought a major change to the series as it was preparing for initial transmission in late September:

> MGM-TV Releases Froug So He Can Do "Zone" — MGM-TV has granted producer William Froug his release from its *Mr. Novak* series, so that he can become producer of Cayuga Productions *Twilight Zone* series. E. Jack Neuman, exec producer and creator of *Novak*, will produce the Metro series pending appointment of a successor to Froug. — *Daily Variety*, 8/2/63.

The star of the new series had been an English major with an interest in journalism at Yale and would soon find an outlet for his writing skills:

> Jim Franciscus' new TV series, "*Mr. Novak*," has put Jim in line to write an advice column for *'TEEN Magazine* starting in September for high schoolers — Jim plays a high school teacher in "*Mr. Novak*." — *Pasadena Star-News*, 8/18/63.

The advance publicity for the forthcoming season had prompted this widely read magazine to request Franciscus to communicate with his anticipated youthful audience.

The first episode filmed in August was "The Risk," which concerned a teacher who was a reformed alcoholic. He had been a mentor to young Mr. Novak and was now seeking a position at Jefferson High. Complications ensue when his young wife shows up drunk at the school. Sherry Jackson played the alcoholic spouse and was enthusiastic about participating in the new series:

Franciscus, Jagger, Alexander Scourby, and Sherry Jackson during filming of "The Risk"

I was excited about the part as I had been known as a teenage actress. The role of the wife looked to be a challenge and I was up for it. There was a lot of buzz about the new series and I knew it would be a good move to be on it. Michael O'Herlihy was a great director and guided me in my scenes and made me feel wonderful about what I was doing. Alexander Scourby, who played my husband, was beautifully spoken and a very nice man. He was so good in the part. His scene where he reads "The Raven" was riveting. He alluded to his first wife who had died. James Franciscus was very attractive and very pleasant. I was excited to work with him and later attended a party at his house which was fun. I was really looking forward to working with Dean Jagger. I had seen him in *Twelve O'Clock High* and other movies. He was an impressive kind of person in the way that he handled himself and was personable. He was also funny and nice.

My big scene was when I showed up drunk at the high school and embarrassed my husband. In preparing myself I wanted to be realistic and not overdo the drunkenness. Michael O'Herlihy was crazy about my performance and really complimented me after it was done. It was almost embarrassing. I was always proud of doing the *Mr. Novak* series. Being on the show really elevated my status in the industry. I now had been regarded as an adult woman who could do dramatic parts. It really opened some doors and was a good experience. — Sherry Jackson, Interview, 9/25/16.

Racial prejudice was dealt with in "A Single Isolated Incident," in which an African American student is pelted with garbage and threats are made to other black undergraduates.

Principal Vane counsels Gloria Caloméé as a student
traumatized by racial prejudice

A beautiful rebellious pupil, played by Joey Heatherton, was the subject of "To Break a Camel's Back."

Mr. Novak is frustrated by antagonistic
student, Joey Heatherton

As September began a new member was added to the creative team on *Mr. Novak*:

Robert Stambler, assistant producer of last season's *Sam Benedict* TV series, signed by MGM-TV as associate producer of *Mr. Novak* series, to begin September 24, 7:30 to 8:30 P.M., on NBC-TV network. Mr. Stambler replaces Robert Thompson, who is leaving program to concentrate on writing a screenplay. — *Broadcasting*, 9/16/63.

Stambler had previously served in the capacity of associate producer on *The Beachcomber* TV series.

Two days before the season premiere E. Jack Neuman gave a final interview promoting his upcoming show:

"Ours is a story about teachers... it's a dramatic show not a comedy series... it deals with the problems of teachers as well as students. When I started studying for this series I began in New York. We are trying to get a perspective of a cross section... and 90 per cent of what we do is based on what's been related to us. This is as fresh a show as we'll get on TV this year. There'll not always be a happy ending or a successful conclusion but what we do will be dramatic and revealing. Yes, we'll deal with sex problems.... Sex is the most predominant things in the mind of teen-agers... we can't avoid it, so we use it. One of the episodes that we filmed was how a teacher gets involved with one of her pupils.... So we see what it's like when a teacher finds a boy has a terrible crush on her... or a girl student with a man teacher. We're doing this through the National Education Association which has thousands of teachers as their members.... Through them I got to students, teachers and principals and learned about their problems.

"We lay the camera right on the high schoolers' faces to show the public they're not 'kooks,' not 'ding dongs'.... It's an exciting project for us to work on.... We learn something new each day.... When the kids come out to the studio the set changes.... It fills us with youth and makes it immensely attractive." So the school bell rings, Mom and Pop and all you kids.... Perhaps some of the problems you faced or are confronted with now will be presented. So come 7:30 Tuesday it'll be time for class with *Mr. Novak*. — Turner Jordan, "Novak Bows Soon," *Birmingham News*, 9/22/63.

E. Jack Neuman had pursued his creative vision for the new series and it was now time for Jefferson High School's Freshman semester to begin.

Chapter Four

Freshman Year — Mr. Novak's First Season (First Half)

The *Mr. Novak* television series debuted on September 24, 1963. It aired on Tuesday night during the 7:30-to-8:30 time slot and was broadcast on NBC. "First Year, First Day" received primarily positive reviews and the show appeared to be a hit. Typical of these critiques was the coverage in the trade publication *Daily Variety*:

"*Mr. Novak*," Metro's new series about a high school teacher, is an excellent dramatic effort, a worthy stablemate to the Culver City lot's "*Dr. Kildare*." Joseph Stefano's well-written script skillfully captures the aura of a high school, he endows his characters with life-like realism, and absorbing characters and situations emerge. Unquestionably, "Novak" is one of the standouts of the new season which heretofore has been generally drab. It's a slick, class production benefitting not only from the fine story, but from overall better-than-average performances, and the perceptive direction of Boris Sagal, who created the series with producer E. Jack Neuman. Overall production is excellent.

As the teacher, Franciscus performs with conviction and restraint. He's ideally cast as the young tutor who defies "the system" to meet what he considers his responsibilities on his own. The spirit of dedication and zeal comes over solidly, yet humanly, so that the teacher isn't a stuffed shirt. Dean Jagger is excellent as the principal, a man of firmness, who also has humor, compassion and consideration. Lee Kinsolving's portrayal of the would-be dropout was well-shaded and realistic. Gloria Talbott, Stephen Franken, Ann Shoemaker, Edward Asner and Marian Collier provided good support. Lyn Murray's score adds much to the overall. "Mr. Novak" should be around for a number of semesters. — Daku, *Daily Variety*, 9/26/63.

Reviews of all of the first season's telecasts can be found in the episode guide.

Mr.Novak

Novak's a new kind of hero: a hip, handsome high-school teacher with a more than passing-or-failing interest in his students. James Franciscus, Dean Jagger co-star.

PREMIERE TONIGHT 6:30
NBC CHANNEL 5

The September issue of *'TEEN* magazine contained the first of many monthly columns written by James Franciscus. Although he was wary of the TV and movie fan magazines, he had agreed to write the columns for this quality teen publication. The columns would include such varying topics as cheating, classroom romances, scholastics versus athletics, volunteer work, teenage support groups, and more. Franciscus's wife Kitty recalled his commitment to writing for *'TEEN* magazine:

Jim really took his writing of the columns seriously. Even though he had a heavy schedule with the series, he enjoyed writing them. As he originally wanted to be a journalism major at Yale, he was in his element. *'TEEN* had a large circulation and Jim told me he was glad to make a constructive impact on his many young fans of the show. According to the publisher, the reaction to his columns was very positive and Jim was pleased with the response. — Int.

Diane Baker and Franciscus in "A Feeling for Friday"

Subjects of all of the columns can be found in the appendix.

The production of new episodes continued with "A Feeling for Friday" which featured Diane Baker as a former flame of Novak:

It was a satisfying experience working on the series. *Mr. Novak* was a quality production in the acting, direction, and scripts. A series of class and distinction. I especially loved the writing which was honest and thought provoking. James Franciscus was a first-rate actor to work with. — Interview.

The next episode to be filmed was "Pay the Two Dollars" in which Mr. Novak is accused of injuring a student. The teacher feels he is innocent but is asked to settle by a lawyer played by Martin Landau:

I thought my character of attorney Victor Rand was of a guy who preferred to take the simple route. As a lawyer, he chose what he did so he didn't have to work so hard. He wasn't a trial lawyer but in this case he had to be one. Part of resistance was self-doubt. I liked to see confusion in a character. — Interview.

In several scenes the lawyer is absent mindedly playing with a small puzzle. Landau conceived this seemingly incongruous action to add shade and depth to his characterization:

The use of puzzles that the attorney played with was my idea. A character who amuses himself takes the easy road. He

Martin Landau, left, Jeanne Bal and James Franciscus in a scene from the "Mr. Novak" series drama on KSD-TV Tuesday at 6:30 p.m.

wanted to settle but came across Mr. Novak who states he's innocent and is a guy who refuses compromise. I was impressed with him even though he scared me. In a later scene with Jim in a bar my character was playing with two intertwined nails. Jim liked that so much he tagged the scene by taking the nails from me and playing with them. That was spontaneous and came out of the moment. Jim Franciscus was very professional and always letter perfect. E. Jack Neuman ran the show. He was a very good writer and producer and excellent at what he did. He would sometimes come to the set to observe filming. — Interview.

Tom Lowell played the injured student and was pleased to be cast in the episode:

> When I received the script, I thought it was an interesting character, and much different from the characters I usually got cast in, the very pleasant typical teen. This guy was a real jerk. James Franciscus was a very sincere actor, giving you the same performance in your close up as he did in the master shot. I did not meet with Dean Jagger. I think they lifted the scene in which he is laughing at some school assembly from another show. He was not around when I was there. — Interview.

Dean Jagger had been absent during filming as he was sidelined by an illness which would reappear during the series' run:

> Early "casualty" of the new season is Dean Jagger of "Mr. Novak" — ulcers. Hospitalized in La Jolla, Jagger will be out of the Metro series a fortnight, Jim Franciscus takes over the full load for the next couple of segs. — Army Archerd, "Just for Variety," *Daily Variety*, 9/30/63.

The September issue of the NEA Journal carried an article entitled "Meet Mr. Novak." This monthly publication of the National Education Association praised the new show and described the superior level of research toward authenticity that would characterize the series:

> As Executive Producer E. Jack Neuman told 9,000 teachers who previewed the pilot of Mr. Novak at the NEA convention this summer in Detroit, "We're gathering stories which we hope will cover the whole range of problems teachers face always with our eyes on the importance of the teacher's job on the American scene." A stickler for accurate detail, Neuman ordered the show's writers to spend hours in their neighborhood high schools. To further ensure that *Mr. Novak* accurately reflects real problems and real schools, the first draft of each script is submitted to the NEA, which in turn reviews it with panels of working educators — high school teachers and administrators for the most part. Hardworking and enthusiastic *"Novak"* panels now include teachers from many Southern California school districts. They are backstopped by panels of educators recruited from a number of Eastern and Midwestern cities.

In early October, a brief piece in a syndicated show business gossip column mentioned a possible feud between the two leads of the show:

MR. NOVAK' TURNED IN A STRAIGHT-A REPORT CARD....EMERGED AS
ONE OF THE BEST OF THE NEW SERIES."--Los Angeles Times

THE BEST THING THUS FAR IN THE CURRENT T.V. SEASON."--Denver Post

'MR. NOVAK', A BELIEVABLE SCHOOL TEACHER IS SUPERBLY PLAYED
BY JAMES FRANCISCUS."--Chicago Tribune

MR. JAGGER AS THE HIGH SCHOOL PRINCIPAL, SO EXTRAORDINARILY
NATURAL HE SEEMS ALMOST TO BE IMPROVISING ON THE SPOT."
--Chicago's American

COMPLETELY HONEST AND SCORED ONE OF THE FIRST BULL'S-EYES
OF THE NEW SEASON."--San Francisco Chronicle

SHOULD BE AROUND FOR A NUMBER OF SEMESTERS."--Daily Variety

'MR. NOVAK' IS THE MOST ADEPT, DRAMATICALLY SURE NEW SERIES
I'VE SEEN SO FAR THIS YEAR."--Tulsa World

"...IT IS MOST HEARTENING TO SEE THE TEACHING PROFESSION PORTRAYED WITH SUCH WARMTH, THE
ADMINISTRATION DEPICTED WITH THE UNDERSTANDING, THE YOUTH OF AMERICA SHOWN IN ALL ITS
WONDERFUL COMPLEXITY AND SCHOOL FEATURED AS A DYNAMIC PLACE...'MR. NOVAK' SHOULD BE A
CREDIT TO YOUR FALL SCHEDULE."   -Hazel A. Blachard, President National Education Association, in wire to Robert Sarnoff, Board Chairman National Broadcasting Co., Inc.

MR. NOVAK

METRO-GOLDWYN-MAYER TELEVISION PRESENTS "MR. NOVAK"...STARRING JAMES FRANCISCUS AND DEAN JAGGER
WITH JEANNE BAL · EXECUTIVE PRODUCER E. JACK NEUMAN · CREATED BY E. JACK NEUMAN AND BORIS SAGAI

POUTY PAIR — Dean Jagger and Jim Franciscus, stars of "*Mr. Novak*," retire to opposite sides of the set when not emoting. They just don't like each other and apparently make no bones about it.

This perceived conflict was without factual basis. Both actors had a great deal of dialogue to learn and prided themselves on being letter perfect. After a scene was completed they would retire to their dressing rooms to run lines.

Franciscus' wife Kitty never saw evidence of any dislike between the two actors:

> I remember Dean and Jim liking each other. They had total respect. There was never a feud between them. I was on the set once and after a take Dean and Jim laughed at some kind of private joke. Jim liked him a lot. — Int.

Property master Bob Schultz also saw no antagonism between the series' leads:

> I was on the set every day for both seasons and never saw *any* feuding between Jim and Dean. They were always cordial and respected each other as professional actors. Dean was like, "Just show me the words." Sometimes Jim would make a suggestion for a line reading but there was never any animosity between them. Jim and Dean always worked well together. — Int.

Marian Collier didn't observe any discontent between the main actors:

> I never saw any feuding per se between Jim and Dean. If anything, I think if anything Jim may have slightly resented everyone going to Dean. When Dean was on the set, he was *it* — but there was no feud. Jim and Dean were cordial professionals who respected each other. — Int.

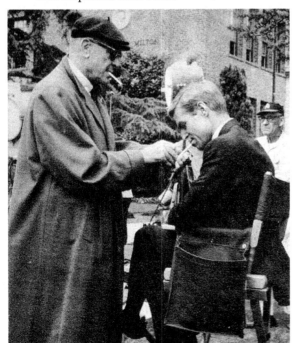

Dean and Jim take a smoke break during filming

In the forthcoming year, the press would attempt to create a conflict similar to that which had occurred between Richard Chamberlain and Raymond Massey on the *Dr. Kildare* set.

October brought the broadcasts of "To Lodge and Dislodge," "I Don't Even Live Here" and "X Is the Unknown Factor."

During this time, after a slight delay due to Dean Jagger's illness, "A Thousand Voices" went into production. It was the story of a rebellious youth. The lead was played by popular singer Frankie Avalon who had been known for frothy teen musicals:

Peter Ford and Frankie Avalon in
"A Thousand Voices"

I was really looking forward to working on the show. It was my first dramatic role and I liked the part of the alienated teenager. It was a real stretch from my previous acting and Richard Donner's directing skills helped me to achieve a very good performance. Franciscus and Jagger were great actors and I learned a lot by working with them. The episode had an unhappy finish as my character ended up a lost soul. It was realistic and cutting edge. — Interview.

An especially well-done episode about racial discrimination, "A Single Isolated Incident," aired later in October. It concerned abuse against an African American coed and was generally praised by the critics. There was a harrowing performance by semi-regular Gloria Calomeé in the lead.

As the month of October was ending, production began on "The Boy Without a Country," which told the tale of a Russian exchange student who had trouble adapting to life in an American school. The part was played by neophyte actor Walter Koenig:

A month earlier I had tested for the lead. I had never done any dialects. My father was from Russia and I remembered how he spoke. Joe Augusta was the casting director. I had worked with him on a low budget film called "*Strange Love.*" He called me to read for the role of Aleksei. I read for a previous director who liked my stoic interpretation of the character who I felt was uncomfortable in his new home in America. I didn't hear for a day or so and called Joe. He told me they weren't happy with the script and were reworking some aspects of the production. In the down time the director decided to test other actors. Another read wildly different from my subdued interpretation and the director loved the new kid. I was told to come in again and read. I was quiet and read the way I did the first time. The director wanted me to read like the other kid and I refused. He gave the other boy the part. Shortly thereafter Dean Jagger became ill and they postponed the episode.

Mr. Novak is puzzled by Russian
exchange student Aleksei's aloofness
(photo courtesy of Walter Koenig)

Four weeks later the first director had left. I came in and read for episode director Michael O'Herlihy. I did one line in the Russian accent and got the part. Michael was a very quiet director who let me go on my way. James Franciscus was a nice guy but not too personal. All the girls were swooning over him but he took it with a grain of salt. Dean Jagger was a good pro. He was a pleasant man and a great actor who was very considerate to me when we went over our scenes together. It was a nice experience and my first guest-starring role on television. — Interview.

Koenig's portrayal of the Russian student on *Mr. Novak* would help him at a later date to acquire his game changing role of Ensign Chekov on *Star Trek*.

In some of the earliest episodes there was a hint of a romance between Mr. Novak and Miss Scott. This potentially intriguing concept was lessened as the series progressed. Marian Collier was disappointed at this revision:

I always thought it was because Jim didn't want a romance with another teacher. He always wanted somebody new each week. That was my guess as to why the romance didn't develop. The scripts didn't advance our relationship, so I had to accept it even though I would have liked a romance with Mr. Novak. Jim and I were both opposites and it would have been good. Who knows, maybe it was a network decision or a result of Jim's increasing popularity with teenage girls. — Int.

The last episode to be broadcast in October was "The Risk."

James Franciscus continued to give interviews publicizing the series:

We think ours is the first regular show to present teachers in a realistic and attractive manner. They are not shown as clowns or eccentrics as they have been on past programs. Mr. Novak is a high school teacher who is bright, intelligent, served in Korea and made up his mind that teaching was important. He also has a sense of humor. It is the type of character anyone would be proud to play. Our teenage students are not juvenile delinquents or crackpots either, as they've often been portrayed. This is not a running *"Rebel without a Cause"* series. We're trying to show all sides of school life and to portray our students as young adults. Some of them can run afoul, as anybody does, but on the whole they are depicted as fine citizens. — Anthony LaCamera, "Mr. Novak Doing Right by Teachers," *Boston Record American*, 10/20/63.

Cathy Ferguson (Sherry Jackson) makes a drunken appearance at Jefferson High in "The Risk"

The month of November brought production of "The Song of Songs." This storyline concerned a coed's father who accuses Novak of teaching lewd and pornographic material. Character actor Edward Arnold portrayed the father and the daughter was played by young Brooke Bundy:

Jeanne Bal and Brooke Bundy in "The Song of Songs"

Edward Arnold was so funny in real life and he was so intense in his part. I loved working with him. James Franciscus had an effect on me as an actress to dig deep and be good. He was so committed and engaged and it was contagious to work with him. He remained to read lines and act off camera when a lot of series' regulars wouldn't or would use a stand in. I was very impressed by that. He was very polite when he excused himself to work on his lines. Jeanne Bal was very funny between takes and was light. She was real professional and a cool lady. The character she played was very much like she was. I was glad to appear on the show as it was a respected series which provided work for a lot of young actors like myself. A great experience. — Int.

A positive review of the series by Cleveland Amory was presented in the prestigious *TV Guide*:

The show as a whole, produced by E. Jack Neuman, deserves special mention. In a relatively undramatic everyday area of life, with no violence, little crime and a merciful absence of neurotic sex, it somehow manages not only to be continuously interesting, but to face up to the country's No. 1 problem, the place where all other problems begin, the blackboard jungle. And if it doesn't wipe the slate clean — it is too honest a show for that — it at least chalks up some grounds for hope. — 11/2–8/63.

The other teachers at Jefferson High as portrayed by the series' regulars would usually be seen in short segments. It was rare that any of them would play a prominent role in an episode. Marian Collier regretted this decision:

I never understood why the other teachers were restricted to brief scenes in the show. I guess the emphasis would have been on the guest stars and the rest of us were just fellow teachers. It couldn't have been an economic factor because we were paid so little anyway. I would have liked to have had larger parts. I don't recall any discussion about this among the regulars. We just accepted it and were glad to be working. — Int.

In a few later episodes, Vince Howard had some lengthy scenes and Marian would be featured in an episode of the second season.

A predicament that would plague the series throughout the run would be its ratings figures. In a time of no VCRs and homes with one TV set, night and time placement were very important. The first indication of this problematic situation was revealed in a Nielsen ratings report. *Mr. Novak* aired opposite ABC's popular *Combat* war series, which earned a placement of 41 with 18.8 share. CBS broadcast *Marshall Dillon*, which was a *Gunsmoke* rerun in their 7:30 to 8:00 P.M. slot. This was followed by the first half of the powerhouse *Red Skelton Show* which placed 8. with a 24.6 share. *Mr. Novak* placed 52 with a share of 17.9. (*Broadcasting*, 11/4/63.)

Combat and the first half of the *Red Skelton Show* would continually beat *Mr. Novak* during the rest of the season. These were established programs that had built up a considerable viewing audience. Among the 32 new shows of the 1963 season *Mr. Novak* placed 9th according to *New York Times* critic Jack Gould.

Student Laure Georges was a devout fan of the series and Jim Franciscus. There was no way she was going to miss her favorite program:

> Once the *Mr. Novak* series began airing on Tuesday evenings, that time slot became sacred to my friends and me. Back in the day very few families had more than one TV set. Several of my girlfriends experienced *Novak* withdrawal symptoms if they were unable to see the show, due to their dads watching *Combat*. Laure to the rescue! We also owned one TV set but my dad worked nights and my mom had no objection to allowing my friends to join me for this extremely special event. Of course, all of us had to have our chores and homework done before *Mr. Novak* aired. Talk about motivation! Tuesday became "Novak Night" for us, followed by discussions in hushed tones at school. We analyzed every minute of what had occurred. Jim Franciscus was SO dreamy and we all had crushes on him. — Int.

"Hello, Miss Phipps," which featured Lillian Gish as a controversial hygiene teacher, was broadcast.

The star of *Mr. Novak* was becoming increasingly popular with his fans. Columnist Hedda Hopper revealed a night of glory for the television star:

> James Franciscus leads 3500 high school students, made up of bands from all over the area, during the UCLA-Washington game half time. Three guesses what they'll play. "The Mr. Novak March." — 11/8/63.

"To Break a Camel's Back," starring sex symbol Joey Heatherton as a problematic student, aired to good reviews for the sexy star.

"The Exile" was the story of a dropout who wanted to return to daytime classes at Jefferson High. Regulations prevent this and it was an abject lesson to remain in school. The role of the unhappy student was played by Richard Evans:

> I had to audition at MGM. Director Michael O'Herlihy was in his office. I was ready to read from the script but instead he asked if I read poetry. When I said that I did, he gave me the part. The entire script surprised me as I'd seen nothing on series

TV to match the impact of the story by E. Jack Neuman. The final scene with Dean Jagger, from an actor's point of view, was remarkable. I felt an immediate connection with him. His off-center, somewhat eccentric delivery seemed fresh... unexpected... a bit different each take. James Franciscus was a very serious guy, quiet, reserved, much like the character of Novak. Virginia Christine, who played my mother was very sweet and a real pro. The filming went very well and this story of a desperate young man in a depressing situation was very dramatic and real. I walked onto the sound stage on Friday, November 22, and was stunned to see that nothing and no one was moving. I had not heard the news of JFK's assassination. Everyone was stunned and immobilized. Eventually a few attempts were made to get something on film. One actor was simply unable to handle his lines and the shoot wrapped early. The bar around the corner from MGM was packed that night and well into the morning. — Interview.

Mid-November brought a ray of hope to the producers of *Mr. Novak* with the announcement that the series had received a positive TvQ rating and ranked number

Franciscus, Evans, and Collier in "The Exile"

4 among the new shows. When Nielsen ratings were low but the quality of the production was first-rate, programmers would frequently look to the TvQ ratings for encouragement. A high score meant that those who had seen the series liked it, but that too few had seen it.

Television Magazine recognized the critical acceptance of *Mr. Novak* and other new series that had not achieved high ratings:

Although critics and Nielsen ratings rarely agree, Television Magazine has polled 15 of the nation's leading critics on the new shows, asking which they think are the critical hits of the new season. The leaders, on which 10 or more agreed are fine additions to the TV spectrum, include, "*The Richard Boone Show,*" "*Danny Kaye Show,*" "*East Side, West Side,*" "*Mr. Novak,*" "*My Favorite Martian,*" "*Hollywood and the Stars.*" Only "*Martian*" drew a high Nielsen rating. — Cecil Smith, "The TV Scene," *Los Angeles Times,* 11/13/63.

Two new episodes aired in the later part of November. These included "A Feeling for Friday" and "Pay the Two Dollars" with Martin Landau.

Franciscus and Jagger appeared on the November 16–22 cover of *TV Guide* magazine. The title of the featured article was "It's Back to School for a Yale Grad," and, along with a career history of Franciscus, it reported his disdain for fan-magazine-type publicity:

> Franciscus has put his foot down. He'll sit still for no fan-magazine quotes or pictures. In the selected press interviews he does grant, he demurs at discussion of his friendships or social life. "Not that the guy has anything to conceal. He just has that kind of exaggerated idea of the importance of his conservative image, what with this new schoolteacher series and all," says one reasonably close friend. "Actually he's a very nice guy — and what else is there to say about him? He's completely devoted to his wife, family and work in about that order." — 11/16–22/63.

Franciscus would relax his views on certain types of fan magazines such as the teen-orientated publications and would cooperate with photo sessions and interviews.

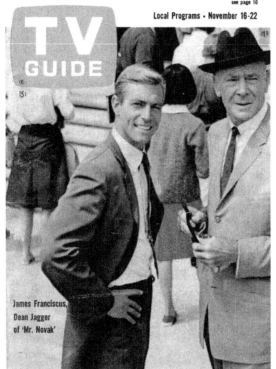

FAR EAST TELEVISION – IT'S FAR OUT
see page 10
Local Programs · November 16-22

James Franciscus, Dean Jagger of 'Mr. Novak'

Mr. Novak appeared on the front cover of three issues of *TV Guide*, now considered collectable items today, sold on internet auction houses and web sites including Ebay

He would, however, grow increasingly disturbed by the TV and movie magazines prying into his private life and would remain reluctant to allow them access. The *TV Guide* article contained praise for the young actor by both his co-star and producer:

> "A very nice boy," echoes Dean Jagger, the skilled veteran who shares top billing in *Mr. Novak*. "Very hard worker, too." "He's the most conscientious and at the same time the most talented actor to come along since Richard Chamberlain," says executive Neuman. "He was really born to play this English teacher, Mr. Novak."

Mr. Novak was in many ways a dialogue show. Jim Franciscus had a lot of lines in each episode and was determined to give his best during the filming. Marian Collier often saw this dedication:

> Jim never hung out with us. He was very private. We did our scenes and that was it. He was very conscientious. He was always running his lines in his dressing room and was always letter perfect. He was not a nasty guy or anything like that. Jim was a real professional and a nice guy. In fact, I sometimes would ask him how to do a line or a bit of business. He told me to just think about it and say the words. — Int.

"I'm on the Outside" starred Teno Pollick as a Hispanic student who mistakenly accuses Novak of prejudice was produced. This episode gave regular Vince Howard a lengthy dramatic scene as the boy's guidance counselor.

A program concerning anti-Semitism was filmed next with a brilliant student on Novak's debating team who taunts a Jewish member of the team. Titled "Sparrow on the Wire," it starred a young Beau Bridges:

> *Mr. Novak* was one of the first jobs I landed on my own. Jim Franciscus was a total professional but approached his work with a great sense of joy. This spirit spilled over to the whole cast and crew. He was very kind to me and inspired me to give my very best. Dean Jagger was a performer I had admired growing up and he did not disappoint. *Mr. Novak* was a groundbreaking series and I was so fortunate to be a small part of it. The show took on some really tough subjects, such as religious persecution, bullying, and teacher's rights. These were subjects that up to this time were not seen on network television. Appearing on such a prestigious program really boosted my early career onto a higher level. — Interview.

As the show had been on the air for three months, James Franciscus was realizing its impact on the youthful viewing audience:

> As in past generations, young people are generally sold short by their elders, who are unwisely too short of patience to realize that teens may appear smart-alecky but actually are putting on a defensive front in a search of answers to problems that may frighten them. You should read my fan mail. It's not the gushy, illiterate stuff you may suspect from so-called swooning teen girls, but serious, thoughtful and thoroughly mature attitudes.
>
> This series, I'm happy to say, relates the problems of high school students as a majority, not the delinquent few. It also targets teachers in various episodes for plot exposition of their innermost feelings. I believe this is equally important. Many teens regard their teachers as stuffy, if completely knowledgeable squares, with little capacity for emotional feeling beyond anger or disapproval. If we can make youngsters realize that their teachers are as capable of defensive armor — thus, the controlled emotions — as they are, I think that alone would make this series worthwhile. — Hank Grant, "Teen Agers Discover New Hero in Teacher Series," Bell-McClure Syndicate, 12/3/63.

Dean Jagger's ulcers had sufficiently healed to allow his restricted return to the series. He would acquire a driver to transport him to and from the studio and wouldn't have to work past 4 P.M.

December brought airings of "Love in the Wrong Season," "The Boy Without a Country," and "A Thousand Voices". The series continued to be very popular with the youthful viewing audience and Jim Franciscus's stardom was increasing. A newspaper article revealed his heavy work schedule and contained a bit of charming honesty from co-star Marian Collier:

"With 'Mr. Novak,' I work six days a week and don't get to do much but barbecue in the backyard or watch a football game on TV." There is of course, a great deal of interest in teaching on the "Mr. Novak" set, and, as Mr. Franciscus said, everyone involved is glad to be improving the American conception of that worthy personage, the high school instructor.

But no one said anything more telling than pretty Marian Collier, the actress who plays Thomas Jefferson High's domestic science teacher and Mr. Novak's romantic interest. Asked if she'd like to marry a teacher in real life, Miss Collier quickly shook her head. "I must be honest," she said. "They don't make enough money. Maybe if this program helps improve that condition, I'd marry one." — James Devane, "TV Stars Franciscus and Chamberlain Visited," *Cincinnati Enquirer*, 12/11/63.

E. Jack Neuman received the John Swett Award from the California Teachers Association. It was presented to him during a luncheon at the Ambassador Hotel in Los Angeles. The award was in the form of a citation which read in part:

> This award recognizes the care taken by Mr. Neuman to produce the first dramatic television show seriously attempting to portray realistically the contributions and problems of schools and teachers and the vibrant youth they serve. This effort has resulted in a unique and invaluable service to public education throughout the nation.

Marian Collier and the rest of the cast and crew were delighted by all of the recognition for excellence:

> When the show kept getting so many awards we were all just so proud. They made us feel we were really contributing something positive

MATTER OF PRINCIPAL

Fan mail drawn by NBC-TV's "Mr. Novak" series suggests that veteran Dean Jaggers is pushing youthful James Fran-ciscus in viewer popularity. They co-star as high school principal Albert Vane and English teacher John Novak respectively.

to the audience other than just an hour of entertainment. Evidently the academic institutions felt we were playing school teachers in a positive, realistic way. Jack was particularly thrilled since the show was his baby. — Int.

Many awards would be forthcoming over the next few years to the producer, cast, and series. The majority of these would be given by educational institutions. A complete list of all the awards presented to *Mr. Novak* can be found in the appendix.

FRANK ALBERTSON (left) and James Franciscus co-star in "The Death of a Teacher" on Mr. Novak at 7:30 p.m., Tuesday, on NBC-TV. Franciscus plays the title role in the weekly series.

In mid-December, one of the best episodes of *Mr. Novak's* first season was produced. "The Death of a Teacher" and was written by E. Jack Neuman and directed by Richard Donner. The story concerned a popular teacher dropping dead of a heart attack on campus. This tragedy impacts both the students and a veteran teacher who becomes fearful of his own health. Tony Dow again appeared as George Scheros:

Richard Donner was one of the top television directors of the time. He used a lot of extreme close-ups which was a very progressive style at the time. The way he handled the teacher's death scene was fabulous. It was understated and natural. It was very realistic. This was a cutting-edge show and dealt with serious subjects. The teacher who wanted to quit out of fear of overwork. I hung around to watch a lot of the filming because I continually learned from both Donner and the principals. — Int.

The pressure and hectic pace of filming had taken a toll on the veteran actor who played Principal Vane. Jagger discussed his difficulties in an article from the *Milwaukee Journal-Sentinel*:

The tall and amiable Jagger talked of the strange parallel in his life's activities — starting off at 16 as an honest to goodness teacher in the backlands around Fort Wayne, Ind., and today, at 60, the head man of a thriving, if mythical, institution known as Jefferson High School. Jagger said he never liked teaching. When he gave up the profession after two terms he certainly hadn't the faintest idea he'd wind up acting a principal's role for a living. And from the zooming popularity ratings of the show, it is reasonable to think he could wind up his career in that role. "That is, if these ulcers don't get me first," he adds. Three times this season, the show's first, Jagger has been hospitalized for short periods — and he's constantly in pain. The

"Mr. Novak" schedule — often from dawn to midnight — is a torturous one even for the younger members of the cast. — 12/8/63.

In an interview with syndicated newspaper writer, Bill Thomas, Franciscus discussed the series' critical approval and growing popularity:

Of the show's success to date, Franciscus told us, "Our ratings are now running ahead of *Dr. Kildare*'s at this time in its first year. But we're not exactly a mass audience appeal series. It's a more selective group we attract. However, our audience is gaining steadily and we expect this trend to continue. Before three-fourths of the season is past, we anticipate a very respectable rating." While the show's growth in popularity has been a more gradual thing, "the critical response has been excellent from the first," he said. Among the new shows, we and *East Side, West Side* and *The Richard Boone Show* have received the best critic's notices. We heard from many teachers, and, overall, they say we are giving valid portrayals. They are our stiffest critics, you know, and we are pleasing them. Students also, by and large, like the show.

"The series has included Negro roles from the start of the season because they are present in public schools and are very much a part of the school scene. An interesting thing happened when we did one episode on the specific problem of school integration. We learned later that a number of southern cities had 'cable failure' that night, and, as a result, were unable to receive it." — "James 'Mr. Novak' Franciscus: Teaching and Acting are Alike," *TV Times*, 12/14–20/63.

Dean Jagger was again working regularly on the show. As a veteran of the longer shooting times of motion pictures, he was finding the relatively brief schedules of television production to be a challenge:

"Television is a new part of the acting business. It hasn't all the craftsmanship that I knew on the stage and in films. But it is important, and that's why I wanted to be a part of it." For Jagger, the adjustment to an hour-long weekly series has not been easy. Recently he suffered a collapse that absented him from filming. "I was trying to do too much. I had an illness that kept me out, and I tried to go back to work too soon. Then I really got hit. It was the first time in my life I didn't have complete control. It scared me. I didn't like it. And I began to wonder if I should undertake something like a series. But I came back and the people in charge at MGM have been wonderful. They told me they didn't want me doing too much. They want me to spare myself, and I've been trying to do just that. It seems to be working out well now. I'm a word polisher. That was training in the theatre and the movies, and it's hard for me to reconcile myself to the television schedule. We could do so much better if we simply had a day's rehearsal before each show. It's impossible for an actor to come in cold and do his best work before the camera. We finish a script one night and begin the next morning on another. It's pretty tough to get top quality that way." — "Dean Jagger Finds TV a Big Switch from Films, Stage," AP, 12/21/63.

Director Richard Donner observed Jagger's discomfort and frustration:

Dean Jagger was a tough old bird.... Somewhere at that moment in his life he felt that it had all gone downhill and he was doing television. He had been a great film actor. He gave his all to the role of the principal but somehow felt it was beneath him. He needed to make a living. He never let you know of his frustrations. It must have been hard on him. There was tension between Dean and Jim but Jim respected Dean and probably realized the veteran actor's frustration. In my relationship with the two of them I never saw anything except you could see in Jim's eyes that he was holding back. I think he did it out of respect. The tension was on screen and did affect the show in a good way. — Int.

Franciscus's popularity was on the increase and the wire services carried this charming blurb as Christmas approached:

James Franciscus, star of NBC-TV's Tuesday night series, has received an average of 1,300 letters a week since the program's debut. Most of the mail is from high school coeds who say they would want to transfer to Jefferson High next season. — 12/22/63.

Up to this time there had not been any memorabilia released in connection with the series. This was odd as many shows of the time had paperback novels, lunch boxes or other items available for purchase. Laure Georges had been frustrated by this lack of *Mr. Novak* merchandise but received a surprise on December 25:

As I got more and more enamored with the show, I tried to find some memorabilia to keep in my room on display. I had pictures of Jim from the teen

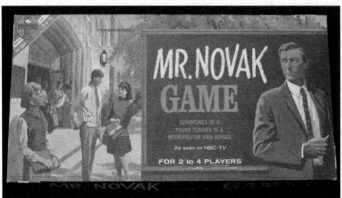

mags but my searches in the department stores yielded no results. By December I had given up on the idea and was concentrating on holiday plans, my boyfriend and other activities. On Christmas morning I noticed a rectangular package under the tree, marked "open last" in my Mom's handwriting. I finally opened it and OMG. It was a *Mr. Novak* board game! What a spectacular gift-an item I didn't even know existed. It had a great painting of Jim on the cover. The premise of the game was the winner would become Senior Class President. Very cool. Playing my new game gave an added dimension to our Tuesday evenings (Novak night). That gift from my Mom was such a treasure. — Int.

Details and illustrations of the game appear in the appendix.

The next episode to air was "My Name Is Not Legion." This was followed by the production of "Chin Up, Mr. Novak" which would prove to be the final episode filmed during 1963. It would prove to be a departure for the series with a comedic storyline. Veteran actress Hermione Baddeley guest starred as a 75-year-old British exchange teacher who brings her own unique and successful way of teaching to Jefferson High.

Jim Franciscus, having sent out letters to high school papers asking them to interview him, told how happy he was about topping Tony Curtis in the Sour Apple tourney. — Mike Connolly, "Rambling Reporter," *The Hollywood Reporter*, 12/30/63.

Hermione Baddeley in "Chin Up, Mr. Novak"

The Sour Apple Awards were presented each year by the Hollywood Women's Press Club. This year's winners had been announced at a swank industry event:

Sour Apple awards for the most unco-operative actress and actor went to Ann-Margret and James Franciscus, who plays the co-operative school teacher in the TV show, "Mr. Novak." The awards were announced at a luncheon at the Beverly Hills Hotel. — 12/18/63.

Neither star had attended the ceremony. Jim Franciscus had been developing an increasing annoyance with the fan-magazine coverage of his career. He would grant interviews with newspaper reporters, high school writers and, in an intriguing twist, would oblige teen magazines. In the forthcoming year, he would continue to develop a hatred for the fan magazines and would again receive the Sour Apple Award.

At some point in late 1963 there had been a change in location filming. All previous location scenes had been filmed at John Marshall High School. Bob Schultz recalled the use of a new substitute for Jefferson High:

> Hamilton High School, near Culver City, began to be used for some of the location filming because the parking was better for the crew. They had a more expansive outer campus. It was a long walk up to the entrance to the school which would be easier to film because John Marshall was closer to the street. Hamilton was much closer to the MGM studios in Culver City. There would still be some location filming at John Marshall during both seasons as well as Hamilton. It depended on what was required. — Int.

Alexander Hamilton High School was located at 2955 S. Robertson Boulevard in Los Angeles. It opened in the fall of 1931 and carried grades nine through twelve. Like John Marshall, it had a culturally diverse student body.

The last day of 1963 featured the airing of a new episode, "He Who Can Does." This was an intriguing show in which Edward Mulhare starred as a controversial novelist who addresses the student body with his unorthodox views. The writer had been a former flame of Miss Pagano and she protests his appearance. This program showcased the increasing visibility of Jeanne Bal, who had become a favorite with audiences.

Mr. Novak had firmly established itself as a television series of class and quality with an increasing popularity with viewers. The new year of 1964 promised even greater triumphs.

A tough-minded but idealistic high school teacher is spoken of respectfully by his students....

mr. novak

STARRING JAMES FRANCISCUS & DEAN JAGGER

TUESDAY 7:30 PM

WGAL-TV CHANNEL 8

Chapter Five

Midterm — Mr. Novak's First Season (Second Half)

The year of 1964 began with some great news for fans of the television series. It appeared that the faculty and students at Jefferson High would be returning for a sophomore year:

> MGM-TV and the "*Mr. Novak*" cast should soon be getting a belated Christmas gift soon from NBC — what else, but the word to continue for another year. — Hank Grant, "On the Air," *The Hollywood Reporter*, 1/2/64.

The ratings, though still on the lower side, had continued to improve. James Franciscus' popularity with his teenage audience was also on the rise. For the most part, critical reviews of the series had been positive and it was a prestige program for NBC. The various awards from academic institutions had also garnered favorable publicity for the show.

Several fan magazines mentioned the physical similarity between the stars of *Dr. Kildare* and *Mr. Novak*. The television doctor commented on this perceived likeness in a syndicated blurb:

> Richard (Dr. Kildare) Chamberlain and James (Mr. Novak) Franciscus look somewhat alike. At least, some of their fans think they do, but the two actors don't see it. Recently Chamberlain visited Franciscus' set to congratulate Jim on the success of the series. And Dick reported another person who sees the resemblance. "My mother likes you very much," Dick said. "Now she can see me twice a week." — "TV Scout," *Abilene Reporter-News*, 1/2/64.

"Mr. Novak" and "Dr. Kildare" at an industry function in Hollywood

The first episode to be filmed in the New Year was "Fear Is a Handful of Dust." It concerned an introverted but extremely bright girl who Novak encourages to develop her talent for caricatures. The guest star was young Brenda Scott:

> I was very shy in my personal life at that stage. I liked Abner Biberman's direction. He would discuss my character with me. James Franciscus was very much like he appeared. He was very courteous... nice... good looking. He was not a chatty person but he was very professional on the set. Mr. Novak was a great role for him. There was a scene in the girl's locker room. My character looks in a mirror and tries to look pretty. She then bursts into tears of frustration and draws on the mirror. I had done that type of scene before in other productions. I had played many disturbed children. I never played a pretty girl. Tony Dow, who was in the episode, was professional to work with and a good guy. — Interview.

Brenda Scott as Sue Johnson in
"Fear Is a Handful of Dust"

Tony Dow found working on this episode to be an interesting experience:

> Brenda Scott was really good as the shy student and I thought at the time she was really cute. The narrative was a fascinating psychological study told in an adult manner. It was a story that had a moral to it which was presented in a low-key manner. — Int.

The first episodes to air in 1964 were "The Song of Songs" and "The Exile."

In mid-January, "How Does Your Garden Grow?" went into production. It starred Barbara Barrie as an inexperienced and frightened substitute teacher who had difficulty instructing her class. She enjoyed working on the episode:

> I had seen a few episodes of *Mr. Novak* and thought it was good... intelligent. I loved the script and I also loved my character of the frightened teacher. It was very well written and gave me a lot to work with. Director Michael O'Herlihy was very, very good. He allowed me to do my work and was extremely sensitive but well organized. Jim Franciscus was a lovely guy and great to act with. Cinematographer Richard Kline was so nice to me. I remember his reaching down to take my hand as I left the set. I think we had a little crush on each other. — Interview.

"Sparrow on the Wire," which starred Beau Bridges, aired next.

The ratings were on the increase as was reported in the *NEA Reporter*:

NBC-TV series *Mr. Novak* heads the list in the latest Nielsen compilation of this season's new dramatic shows with a rating of 19.2. This means that nearly one-fifth of all home TV sets are tuned to the show every Tuesday night. — 1/17/64.

Although *Combat* and *The Red Skelton Show* were still far ahead in the overall ratings, this encouraging report meant that *Mr. Novak* was acquiring more viewers with each new episode that aired.

"One Way to Say Goodbye" went before the cameras and starred Kathryn Hays as a former Jefferson High student who returns to visit her alma mater. Mr. Novak falls in love with her at first sight and they find they have a lot in common. This romantic episode was directed by Richard Donner:

> It was E. Jack Neuman's vision to have *Mr. Novak* episodes on such groundbreaking subjects as racial discrimination, unwed mothers, drugs, and cheating. He was quite liberal in his belief in storytelling, although he didn't use it as a platform. With that said, he was always steeped in entertainment. There would be an occasional comic episode and brief elements of humor would be found in many of the dramatic stories. This romantic installment was a nice change of pace. I enjoyed using a lighter touch for a change. — Int.

Tom Nardini had a small role as a student who gets in an off-campus fight with Mr. Novak. He was a newcomer to the acting profession and later discussed working with Franciscus in an interview with *Movie Life* magazine:

Franciscus with Kathryn Hays in
"One Way to Say Goodbye"

I was real nervous. I had heard that Jim was a cold fish and I was afraid. I'd only done two other TV shows in my life. I got pretty friendly with him. Although at my first impression of Jim he came off, oh not conceited, but it irritated me to be around him. I don't know why; it was weird and he acted tough really, as though "This is what I'm going to do and that is what you are going to do." The first day I thought Jim was a pretty cold egg. The second day I had some difficult scenes with him and he offered suggestions to me which he didn't have to. We had a fight scene and the help he gave me was really invaluable. He also showed me how to place myself so that the lights would show me to an advantage. Not many stars do that. I got to know him as a person. I know now that he isn't cold or conceited, it's just something you have to overcome when you first meet him. When we were through filming Jim came over and congratulated me. Dick Donner, the director, also gave me a big handshake and thanked me. *Me.* They were the ones who took a chance on me. — 10/64.

In the 15th annual nationwide poll of television critics and editors conducted by "Television Today," *Mr. Novak* and James Franciscus were voted tops in their category. *The Alfred Hitchcock Hour, What's My Line?, Garry Moore, Twilight Zone,* and *Patty Duke* were also judged as being the best in their categories. None of these performers or series was in the Nielsen top fifteen.

The end of the first month of 1964 brought the airing of "The Private Life of Douglas Morgan, Jr." The NEA continued to praise the *Novak* series and devoted an entire page in the current issue of their publication, *Education U.S.A.*:

> Teachers seem to have found in Mr. Novak, and his principal Mr. Vane, the sort of colleagues with whom they would like to identify, and in the problems with which Novak and Vane cope each week the sort of challenges which confront them from day to day in the classroom. Producer E. Jack Neuman, who created the series, spent months touring high schools throughout the nation to learn about the real situations that would make believable, honest dramas. Neuman also expects writers who aspire to write for Mr. Novak to visit schools also in order to learn about the situations that face faculty and student body in the American high school today. — 1/28/64.

Neuman had prepared a 12-page guide to potential writers of the series. It is reproduced in the appendix.

James Franciscus was receiving much coverage in the teenage fan magazines and his popularity was elevating him to becoming a teen idol. During the 1960's television studios often encouraged its stars to make vocal pop records if they had achieved a teenaged fan base. Syndicated columnist Hedda Hopper had the scoop as January came to a close:

When Metro learned that Jim Franciscus has a lovely singing voice, a song was written in for him in a Novak sequence on TV, and now the company's trying to persuade him to make records. — 1/29/64.

The star of *Mr. Novak* was wary of becoming a recording artist. He wanted to be taken seriously as an actor and had aspirations for a feature film career in the future.

James Franciscus appeared on a March of Dimes telecast that was aired from Pittsburgh on February 1. He would lend his celebrity presence to several charity events during the run of the series.

New episodes, "The Death of a Teacher" and "I'm on the Outside," aired in early February.

James Franciscus had agreed to address several high school journalism majors. He was unprepared for the volatile exchange that occurred:

The world's best known English teacher, James Franciscus, star of TV's popular "Mr. Novak" series, bravely exposed himself to a mass examination by 48 Los Angeles high school journalism majors the other afternoon. The idea was that the kids could throw a lot of interesting questions at him about conducting his make-believe classroom. Some good still pictures, a few blurbs in the papers might result, the NBC publicists figured. But the conference immediately got out of hand. Franciscus was rocked back on his heels by the very first query and from that point on the session boiled into a controversy about whether a Hollywood star had any right to a private life of his own. "Why," demanded a pretty, aspiring writer, as the bell rang, "were you singled out by the Hollywood Women's Press Club to be awarded the sour apple of 1963?" Franciscus was taken aback, but only momentarily. He suddenly sprang into such a heated defense that it appeared he relished getting his feelings before the youngsters — as an object lesson to them, perhaps.

"Truthfully, I have never turned down an interview with any legitimate publication," he began. "That includes a lot of teen magazines. But I want to point out to you that a good 60% of the membership in that women's club write for the so-called fan magazines. I refuse to talk to them. They produce cheap trash. I hope none of you reads that stuff. It's the most disgusting sensational journalism I've ever come across. And it's aimed at teens. I read Playboy — an adult magazine — but Playboy wouldn't be caught dead printing the suggestive junk the mags run. I hope I win the sour apple award next year, and for many years to come. It's the nicest thing that has happened to me since I came to Hollywood."

On his daily routine as an actor: "I'm up at 6 in the morning and on the set before 8. Between scenes I'm studying my lines. I grab a sandwich in my dressing room while learning more lines. We're generally through for the day at 7 or 8 — but often we go to midnight. Then I go home and say goodnight to my children, who don't answer because they're asleep in bed." At this point one student inquired; "Then when do you find time for your family?" To which Mr. Novak replied candidly: "That's exactly what they're been asking me." — undated article from Neuman archives, circa 2/64.

This vehement condemnation of the fan magazines was not appreciated by the writers and editors. A backlash was developing in which some publications would print lies intending to portray Franciscus in a bad light. An example would be the story in the February issue of *TV Radio Mirror* which showcased the "feud" between Richard Chamberlain and Jim Franciscus. The article stated that a director walked off the show because of the star's attitude. It also mentioned the "antagonism" between Dean Jagger and Franciscus. There was no truth to these accusations, but the lies would continue for the rest of the series' run. James Franciscus's handsome face would sell a lot of issues, but the slanderous attacks would persist.

Franciscus' wife Kitty never saw any feud between her husband and the star of *Dr. Kildare*:

Jim and Dick Chamberlain never had a feud. They were cordial professionals and might occasionally encounter each other on the MGM lot. Both of their series required long hours of hard work so there was little if any time to socialize. We moved in different social circles than Dick but we would sometimes run into him at an industry event. He and Jim would exchange pleasantries. This so-called feud by the fan magazines was another reason my husband wanted to stop giving them interviews. — Int.

Dick Chamberlain and Jim Franciscus
at the TV Guide Awards

"Day in the Year" went into production. It concerned the death of a Jefferson High student who dies of a drug overdose. Character actor David Sheiner made his first appearance in this episode as a doctor. He was very impressed by the actors on the series:

James Franciscus was the most professional actor that I ever worked with. He hit his marks brilliantly and was a terrific technician. There was a stiffness about him which worked very well for his part. Dean Jagger was a very good actor but on a personal level was not forbidding but came very close to it. Marian Collier was fine as Miss Scott the Home Ec. teacher. She was very bubbly and very attractive. The *Mr. Novak* series was beautifully done. It was well cast and the scripts were good. It was a positive experience for me. —Interview.

Sheiner would appear in two episodes of the second season as a music teacher Paul Webb.

The principal of Jefferson High received an honor that was most satisfying to the actor who portrayed him:

Jagger and Neuman very pleased with their Secondary School Principals Awards

Chicago — Honorary life membership in National Assn. of Secondary School Principals was presented Saturday, at the organization's annual convention, in Conrad Hilton Hotel, to Dean Jagger who plays the principal in MGM-TV's "*Mr. Novak*" series on NBC, Also honored were E. Jack Neuman, executive producer of the series, and Robert F. Kinter, NBC president. — *The Hollywood Reporter*, 2/10/64.

A wire service story later recounted a humorous incident regarding the new honorary member:

"Dean Jagger attended a convention of the National Association of Secondary School Principals. He was in the hotel lobby when another convention delegate approached him, and said he recognized him but just couldn't remember what school and city he was from. 'Jefferson High, TV,' said Jagger, casually." — 4/12/64.

The humorous "Chin Up, Mr. Novak" episode aired next and was followed by the production of "Moment Without Armor." This episode featured Jeanne Bal in the lead. In the story she is attacked by an unknown assailant. An incorrigible student, with a politically powerful father, taunts her. She loses control, slaps him, and faces disciplinary action. "Fear Is a Handful of Dust" followed and received good notices.

E. Jack Neuman celebrated his birthday on February 27 with a cake that read "Happy Birthday to the Father of Mr. Novak." The cast was in attendance and it was a festive occasion.

An episode about a pregnant senior who won't be allowed to graduate began filming as the month of February was ending. It starred Noreen Corcoran as the distraught student.

Proving that imitation is the sincerest form of flattery, the success of the *Mr. Novak* show had inspired several television producers:

> *Mr. Novak* (it is the highest rated new series of the season) has already spawned three new pilot films which are being submitted to networks for approval. One is an elementary school series, and the other two are set in high school. — Hal Humphrey, "Mr. Novak Improves Image of Teacher," *Richmond Times-Dispatch*, 2/29/64.

Further evidence of *Mr. Novak*'s influence was noted in *Daily Variety*:

> "Sparrow on the Wire" segment of MGM-TV's "Mr. Novak" will be shown at the March 18 meeting of the Encino chapter of B'Nai B'rith. Episode deals with anti-Semitism. — 3/3/64.

"The Tower," with Heather Angel as elderly geometry teacher whom Principal Vane is forced to retire, aired next to good reviews. The three primary actors associated with the series would soon receive honors which included a prestigious award that was particularly gratifying to leading man of the series:

> James "*Mr. Novak*" Franciscus is the holder today of a Golden Apple Award presented by the Los Angeles Association of Secondary School Administrators. Three other TV personalities were honored by the organization last night at the annual dinner for city school administrators at the New Continental Hotel in Hollywood. They were Art Linkletter, Miss Jeanne Bal, who also appears in the "*Novak*" series; and Dean Jagger, who portrays the principal in the show. In accepting his award Franciscus said it made up for the Sour Apple he received from the Hollywood Women's

Heather Angel, aged by makeup magic, plays a retired school teacher who provokes police and Dean Jagger

Press Club. — "'Novak' Series TV Stars Win Golden Apples," *Los Angeles Herald-Examiner*, 3/12/64.

A trade announcement brought good news for fans of the series:

> The "faculty" of MGM-TV's "*Mr. Novak*" series, starring James Franciscus and Dean Jagger, will remain virtually intact for next season, according to executive producer E. Jack Neuman. Presiding over the group as administrators will be Jagger as the principal and Jeanne Bal as his assistant. Faculty is headed by Franciscus and, and other returning faculty members include Marian Collier, Kathleen Ellis, André Phillipe, Stephen Roberts, Vince Howard, Larry Thor, John Ryan, Jim Dawson, Marjorie Corley. Only member of this year's faculty not available is Steve Franken who will be starring in his own series. — *The Hollywood Reporter*, 3/13/64.

This would prove to be true with one regrettable exception.

A syndicated blurb gave Franciscus's answer to the studio's request of him to make records:

> Jim Franciscus nixed an MGM plan to have him become Mr. Novak, the singing school teacher, via the studio recording company. Guess he figures a singing medic (Dr. Kildare) is enough for one studio. — 3/14/64.

Richard Chamberlain had been recording for the MGM record label for some time and had achieved three hit singles.

The last show of the season, which starred Marta Kristen as a zealous student who alienates her classmates, went into production:

Franciscus, Marian Collier, and Marta Kristen in "Senior Prom"

"Senior Prom," final episode of MGM-TV's "*Mr. Novak*" for current season, rolls today with Michael O'Herlihy directing. Immediately after completion of this episode, the series begins work on the first two episodes for the next season, winding production April 10 and resuming June 4. — *The Hollywood Reporter*, 3/16/64.

This announced first shooting date did not occur. The first episode of the second season, "The People Doll: You Wind It Up and It Makes Mistakes," would not begin filming until June 1. This delay gave the cast and crew a summer vacation of a few months.

The romantic "One Way to Say Goodbye" aired next and was another fine episode directed by Richard Donner.

The attractive assistant principal of the series would soon win her own award:

> Jeanne Bal was given Barstow High School's "Paddle Award" which producer
> E. Jack Neuman will permanently install in office set of "*Mr. Novak.*" — *Daily
> Variety*, 3/19/64.

This would prove to be ironic in lieu of events that would occur in the summer.

The California Teachers Association Southern Section held their Eleventh Annual Communications Awards ceremony Los Angeles. The *Mr. Novak* series' positive and sympathetic depiction of teachers was lauded. Awards were given to the executive producer and the leading players of the program which read:

> E. Jack Neuman for creating the first valid "image" of a courageous, imaginative,
> dedicated teacher and presenting it to millions of viewers each week; and especially
> for his complete and continuous cooperation with CTA-SS, NEA, and local teacher's
> associations in seeking advice, counsel, and promotional assistance.
>
> James Franciscus, who has interpreted the character of "Mr. Novak" in a skillful
> and sympathetic manner, and has achieved the extremely difficult goal of becoming
> a new idol for youthful viewers, while also becoming one of whom the teaching
> profession is proud and for whom the general public has developed affection, interest
> and respect.
>
> Dean Jagger, whose skill in portraying the character of Mr. Vane, principal of
> Jefferson High School, has enhanced respect for school administrators, increased
> understanding of the difficult problems which they must handle, and underscored
> the need for outstanding human qualities in this difficult but vital function. —
> 3/20/64.

AWARD-WINNING TRIO. Three of the people who have supplied the main reason NBC TV's *Mr. Novak* show will be coming back next fall, hold the award they were presented recently by the California Teachers' Association, SOUTHERN SECTION. They are JAMES FRANCISCUS (left), who has the title role in the series; JEANNE BAL who plays Miss Pagano, the assistant principal at Jefferson High; and E. JACK NEUMAN, creator and executive producer of the series. Missing when the picture was made was a key member of the team, Principal Albert Vane, portrayed by Dean Jagger. Miss Bal is holding his award from the CTA/SS. (Original caption.)

That same day an announcement was featured in *Daily Variety* that a major change was in store for the awarded series:

> MGM-TV has assigned Leonard Freeman to produce its "*Mr. Novak*" series next season. "*Novak*" is produced this season by E. Jack Neuman, co-creator with Boris Sagal of the series. Neuman will continue as exec producer and Freeman will also write several episodes for the series. — 3/20/64.

Leonard Freeman was a veteran of the television industry. He had written many teleplays since 1952. Such well-liked series as *Schlitz Playhouse*, *Lassie*, *Lux Playhouse*, and *Alcoa Theatre* had all accepted scripts from the writer. He had produced 28 episodes of the popular *Route 66* series during the 1961–62 schedule. Freeman also served as executive producer of 12 episodes of *The Untouchables* during its 1962–63 season.

Marian Collier had observed E. Jack Neuman's exhaustive schedule on the first season and understood the installation of the new producer:

> Jack would already be at the studio when I arrived for hair and makeup. When I would leave in the evenings he would still be there. He would put in over twelve hours every day as well as weekends. I don't think he could handle the hours anymore and Leonard Freeman came in. — Int.

Bob Schultz had a different opinion on the arrival of the new producer:

> Leonard Freeman was assigned by MGM. The suits wanted it to be the way they envisioned it. This was the studio's decision. Jack had no say in it. Freeman was basically a stooge for MGM. His job was to be sure the shows were produced and on budget. He was like a production manager. — Int.

TWO OF THE MEN BEHIND MR. NOVAK: E. Jack Neuman (left), who will continue as executive producer for the second season of *Mr. Novak*, talks with **Leonard Freeman,** who will handle production reins for the series. Creator of *Mr. Novak* with Boris Sagal, Neuman wrote and produced seven of the series' 30 original teleplays and produced 12 others. Freeman, whose film credits include production of 30 *Route 66* episodes and 13 episodes of *The Untouchables*, also has written more than 100 original teleplays.

Neuman's exhaustive dedication the series had resulted in a string of excellent episodes. He was now developing two new projects for MGM and NBC. E.J. would not be as hands on in the second season and many of the major decisions in content would be made by Freeman. The program would morph into his vision and the changes would not all be positive.

Representatives of the NBC network had generally allowed Neuman freedom to make the show as he wanted. But with increasing viewers and publicity there had been some opposition to his scenarios. The prestigious *Saturday Review* reported this friction between business and creativity:

> Neuman, like a few other television producers who are attempting to deal with current social issues in their programs, has conflicts with network officials. NBC shares ownership of the series with MGM and has the last word in story approval. The producer admits that he has "generally carte blanche," but there have been occasions when he and network representatives have clashed over happy endings. He did one story on Mr. Novak in which a boy who cheated in class was given a second chance, cheated again, and was tossed out of school. The network wanted the boy redeemed, but it ultimately gave Neuman's hard ending the green light. In another show, when the producer wanted a student to persist to the bitter end with downbeat behavior, the network overruled him and compelled a happy ending. It's a matter of give and take. The network has to hold the line for upbeat endings that harmonize with the sponsor's message (and perhaps with the wishes of the audience), yet network officials also see the wisdom of not over frustrating their creative talent. The dilemma is a normal condition of our sponsored, mass-circulation broadcasting system. — Robert Lewis Shayon, "The Businessman as Critic," 3/21/64.

Bob Schultz had witnessed some of the conflicts between Neuman and the studios executives:

> E. Jack had some disagreements with MGM executives late in the first season about storylines. There had been some publicity about their clashes. Jack was a forceful guy and the suits might have considered him to be trouble. You didn't tell E. Jack Neuman how to go somewhere when he's the creator and writer of the series. Jack had to have had a major disagreement to have them put another producer on the second season. — Int.

"Day in the Year," with the narcotics storyline was the next show to air.

While the behind the scenes changes and conflicts were happening, James Franciscus's popularity with his fans was ever increasing. Hedda Hopper reported this growth in her column:

> Jim (Mr. Novak) writes for a teen-age magazine and gets thousands of letters. It seems that high school kids have adopted him as their father confessor and adviser. — 3/26/64.

One high school kid who adopted Franciscus as her adviser was Laure Georges:

> I read every one of Jim's columns in *'TEEN* magazine and loved them. They were well written and my mom encouraged me to devour his words of wisdom. I was taking an English Lit course at John Marshall and chose to read and deliver an oral report on *To Kill a Mockingbird*. I had seen the movie with Gregory Peck the year before and was fired up to read the book after seeing the movie. Jim had written a column which said that's its very enriching to read the book and not totally rely on the movie

to grasp the meaning of a story. I asked my English Lit teacher if I could read the column along with my book report for extra credit. She said yes and after I read both I received an A. It was as if Mr. Novak himself helped me to get the top grade. It was really cool. — Int.

A newspaper article summed up the first season's successes for the program and its executive producer:

Mr. Novak ranks by the important standards as the most successful new program of the season. It hasn't been among the top ten or twenty programs according to total audience, but it has consistently placed high in dozens of polls around the nation that reflect preference and loyalty. Producer Jack Neuman has undoubtedly received more plaques and citations — mostly from professional educational organizations — than any producer in Hollywood. Every teacher and high school student to whom I've talked thoroughly enjoys and approves of the program. And probably no program on the air has approached the unanimity of praise from TV columnists and critics. — Ernie Kreiling, "Mr. Novak Video's Top New Progam," Alhambra, California, *Post-Advocate*, 3/28/64.

"Moment Without Armor" aired on the last day of March. The series and its leading men had been nominated for several awards. There would be both losses and wins.

The show had been nominated for "Favorite New Series" in the *TV Guide* Awards but lost to *The Fugitive*. James Franciscus had won "Most Promising New Star, Male" in the *Motion Picture Daily-Fame Magazine* Poll of 1963. The series won the National School Bell Award for Dramatic Interpretation of Education Series.

The new producer of the forthcoming second season was already seeking stories that would be both truthful and provocative:

Leonard Freeman has Herman Groves scripting a yarn dealing with the death of a high school football player during scrimmage, of how the death affects teachers and students. Yarn asks if competitive sports programs are worth the 18–20 high schoolers killed every year playing football. — *Daily Variety*, 4/1/64.

A distressed Cathy Williams
(Noreen Corcoran) confides in
Principal Vane in
"Fare Thee Well"

Another new episode, "Fare Thee Well," featuring Noreen Corcoran as a pregnant student, was broadcast on April 7. The final new installment of *Mr. Novak* carried a novel writing credit:

"The Senior Prom," airing next Tuesday over NBC, marks the TV writing bow of John Ryan, technical advisor on the series and a former English teacher at the San Marino High School. — *The Hollywood Reporter*, 4/9/64.

The stars of the *Mr. Novak* series appeared on their second *TV Guide* cover for the week of April 18–24, 1964. There was an extensive article on Dean Jagger's careers in both education and the acting profession.

Jagger's dedication to his television performances was observed by his wife: "Jagger takes himself and his work in Mr. Novak seriously. His wife says, 'Every performance he does on that TV show could be a major motion picture.' The result has been two-fold. Mrs. Jagger says, "The desire to do something outstanding every week takes its toll." The toll has been stomach ulcers and the first serious illness Jagger has ever suffered in his life. The

Mr. Novak appeared on the front cover of three issues of *TV Guide*, now considered collectable items today, sold on internet auction houses and web sites including Ebay

second result of his dedication, says a friend, is that "he is more Albert Vane than he is Dean Jagger." — TV Guide, April 18–24, 1964.

E. Jack Neuman's creative vision of his dramatic series about a high school had received primarily positive responses from viewers and critics. The approaching summer would be a time of further advancement and in some cases distressing changes.

Chapter Six

**Summer School —
Changes, Controversy
and Initial Production
of Second Season**

E. Jack Neuman addressed the Annual Representative Assembly of the Washington Education Association at their event in Olympia, Washington:

I can't please everybody with *Mr. Novak*. I don't even try. I do try and please the television audience. I don't believe they have twelve-year-old mentalities. I've never believed that there is a low common denominator for mass taste. I think that everything on that screen should be truthful and honest and complete. That doesn't always happen — with Mr. Novak — or anyone else. We've made mistakes I hope we won't make again because I feel my audience is sensitive, emotional, mature, adult and intelligent and that they deserve truth and honesty and completeness each week. Mr. Novak is not a perfect man — certainly not the perfect image of a teacher. But I wanted him to try for perfection — and keep trying — week in and out. If the volume of mail we receive is any indication, the audience identifies with this imperfect image — and this kind of effort. — 4/17/64.

In an interview, Neuman did mention some errors in the first season's episodes:

"We made 7 bad pictures out of the 30. And that kills me," he says. "Mainly they were badly written — two by me — but the press of time and my own stubbornness caused me to go through with them. One show looked good on paper but just didn't play. We did another about off-campus clubs and got so far "in" nobody knew what we were talking about. In another we tried getting Novak away from school, but it didn't work. Stories set in hotel rooms and cocktail bars you can get anywhere. Those eager, hurrying kids are the most attractive background I can get and I'm going to stay with it." — Paul Baessler, "The Man Behind Mr. Novak," *Los Angeles Herald-Examiner*, 4/19/64.

Leonard Freeman, the new producer for the next season, would unfortunately not follow Neuman's vision and would create several shows that would pull away from the campus. Bob Schultz observed the change in concepts and authority:

E. Jack had wanted to continue the scripts that focused on the high school and the kids like he had done in the first season. Freeman wanted to get away from the school in several stories. This may have been where Jack had his major disagreement. Freeman did what he was told by the MGM execs. He didn't associate with the crew and everybody ignored him. He basically worked on scripts and the budget in an office. To the crew and cast I don't think he made any difference where Jack *had* made a difference since he was the creator. Freeman had a big ego and started to consider the series his show. — Int.

The Academy of Television Arts and Sciences announced its Emmy Award nominations. The series was nominated for best Dramatic Program and Dean Jagger was nominated for Continued Performance by an Actor in A Series. Neither would win.

Photoplay was the biggest and most respected of the Hollywood fan magazines. While it too would use sensational titles on its covers, most of their articles contained factual content. There had been no adverse criticism of James Franciscus in previous issues. The rising attacks on the actor by other fan magazines prompted *Photoplay* to seek out the truth about the TV star:

What is the truth about Mr. Novak, the serious-minded, good looking young man who is causing all the talk in Movietown? Is he really a vain, obstinate actor who refused to take direction from a veteran director? Is it true that he fights with Dean Jagger, his co-star? Is it true he won't talk with magazine writers and is coldly self-centered? Or is he badly misunderstood? A "Photoplay" writer spent days gathering clues to the mystery, talked with his friends and co-workers, visited the set and finally decided that Franciscus deserves a better public relations break than he's getting; that he's really a darned nice guy being victimized by stories based on truth — but not the whole truth. Jim's reputation for being "exclusive, standoffish and conceited" has won him no friends. When the Hollywood Women's Press Club held its annual Television Night party, such renowned performers as Ralph Bellamy and Jeffrey Hunter attended, but Franciscus didn't. The network made the excuse that his wife was having a baby. But since the party was held in October and the baby due in December, the lady scribes considered the excuse rather thin. The truth is Franciscus thinks it's more important to learn his lines than to create a glamorous public image.

Jack Neuman, who created *Mr. Novak* and helped create *Dr. Kildare*, tells how Jim "gets to work at daylight, is never late, works until 7:30 P.M. and shows up next morning with all his lines memorized." As to interviews, he says, "Sometimes I think Jim had been interviewed by writers by every high school and college paper in the country. Co-operative? You never saw a more co-operative guy." And Jack Paladino, his publicist, adds that the time Jim gives to school papers leaves him small time for magazines. "He's dedicated to this role of Mr. Novak," says Paladino.

The origin of the story that he had been fighting with Dean Jagger is harder to track down than the other rumors. Maybe it rose from the fact that Jagger suffered a serious ulcer attack early in the fall. Jeanne Bal denies that there has been any friction on the set at all. She says, "I don't think I've worked on a show where people got along better together. We have a lot of fun, we even play jokes on each other." Jim makes his own admiration for Jagger clear when he's called the star of the show. "I'm not the star," he quickly interrupts. "Dean Jagger is. He's the most important member of this cast."

The final charge against Mr. Novak is his alleged failure to accept direction. Quite truthfully, in the early stages of production, he had a disagreement with a director who left the show. But a person close to all concerned says the director didn't leave because of the hassle but because he found a better job. Nevertheless, Jim did argue with him about the way Mr. Novak should be played. "The director was thinking in terms of Our Miss Brooks," a Franciscus adherent explains. "Jim couldn't see things that way, and as it turned out, he was right. R. W. Caveney, assistant principal at John Marshall High School, and technical advisor for *Mr. Novak*, says that Franciscus is actually less likely to question a line or an action than Jagger is. "Mr. Jagger used to be a teacher," Caveney says admiringly, "and sometimes with his personal knowledge of the education profession, he'll detect a way that the show can be improved. Occasionally he'll ask, 'Do you really think a principal would say that?'" But Mr. Franciscus only asks advice. "When a real teacher (there's always one on the set) says Franciscus is doing something wrong, he's eager to correct his mistakes. This doesn't happen often, but occasionally it does."

Jim Franciscus is a lucky young man with a loving wife, two beautiful daughters, talent and a bright future. But luck or no luck, Franciscus still stands in danger of being ground to bits by Hollywood's rumor mill. By presenting the full array of facts, the testimony of a battery of witnesses, "Photoplay" hopes to halt it. As every teacher welcomes truth, the public should welcome the truth about Mr. Novak, television's controversial teacher. — Andy Wood, "James Franciscus: Teacher with a Bedside Manner," *Photoplay*, 5/64.

This truthful coverage of the rumors concerning Franciscus was a rarity. Other fan magazines would continue to print lies and exaggerations since most would contain articles written by members of the offended Hollywood Women's Press Club.

Near the end of April the *Mr. Novak* series received one of its most prestigious awards. The George Foster Peabody Award recognized outstanding and commendable public service by the radio and television industries. The NEA's Henry S. Noerdlinger issued a publicity release which read in part:

The Peabody Citation, given to "Mr. Novak" for distinguished achievement in television entertainment, was read by Bennett Cerf, president of Random House, at a luncheon of Broadcast Pioneers in New York City, April 29. The program was honored, said Mr. Cerf, for "restoring dignity and honor to the popular image of the American school teacher, for reminding our young people that there is no grander pursuit of knowledge, and for daring to insist — without preachment or piety — that the uneducated man is an incomplete man. This series has assumed special importance in an age of lowered standards and school dropouts. It has sensed its responsibility and risen to it with courage and good taste."

E. Jack Neuman proudly holds the Peabody Award
during shooting of a 16mm promo film for high schools

James Franciscus had refused to take part in personal appearances. His heavy work schedule on the series and weekends with family precluded any travel. A rare exception occurred at the beginning of May when he agreed to appear at Christian College in Columbia, Missouri. He was to receive the first "Man of the Year" award during "Novak Night." This was given on May 2 as part of the Annual Alumnae Homecoming. Accompanying the star was his wife Kitty who was impressed by the reception:

> Since the series was on summer hiatus, Jim agreed to go to Columbia. He was a native of St. Louis and Missouri held a special appeal for him. We received a great welcome and he really enjoyed attending all the festivities. Since it was an all-girl college, there was no shortage of young admirers for my husband. They were darling young ladies and we really had the best time. Jim was so handsome in his tux at the banquet. His award was a golden apple and the whole banquet hall was decorated with golden apples. On the flight back to Los Angeles, Jim said that although he received a Sour Apple award from the Women's Press Club, he now had *two* Golden Apple awards. — Int.

Kitty and Jim Franciscus during their visit to Christian College

A change in the billing for the next season was announced in a syndicated piece:

> Last year, it was "*Dr. Kildare*" star, Dick Chamberlain, who got a promotion in jobs between seasons. This year it will be Jeanne Bal, assistant principal at "Mr. Novak's" school. She will be second star to James Franciscus next season. — Bill Ladd, "Television-Radio Almanac," Louisville, Kentucky, *Courier-Journal*, 5/3/64.

If this were to happen, Dean Jagger would be moved to third billing. Was this announced due to the producer's concern over the veteran actor's ability to continue? Did Bal's new contract with MGM include this billing change? There are no recorded reasons but perhaps this adjustment in billing would have a bearing on a revision that would soon alter the series.

Jeanne Bal's profile continued to rise and her enthusiasm for the role of the vice principal was showcased in a syndicated column:

> When Jack Neuman and Boris Sagal gave TV viewers "Mr. Novak" they included a fringe benefit of no mean value in the person of Jeanne Bal. As Miss Pagano, the assistant principal, Jeanne manages to generate just the right amounts of feminine

mystery and emotion to keep Jefferson High from looking too dully academic. Jeanne Bal is considerably more extroverted than she can allow Miss Pagano to become. She appears to be completely happy with her "Mr. Novak" connection. Jeanne married attorney Edward Lee last August, then answered a rush call to replace Gloria Talbott, who would have been the assistant principal if she hadn't broken her leg. "When I was hired, Jack decided to change the assistant principal from Miss Harvey to Miss Pagano. He liked the idea of my being of Italian extraction. I'm really French, of course." The Italian-French flavor exuded by Jeanne caused the storm signals to go up almost immediately at NBC. The network's keeper of standards and morals decided after a few episodes that Miss Pagano should not wear sweaters or full skirts ("too much movement"). — Hal Humphrey, "TV Comment," Hayward, California, *Daily Review*, 5/8/64.

E. Jack Neuman discussed the next season's changes in the Novak character and the importance of Jeanne Bal's participation:

"We will poke into the backgrounds of Mr. Novak and other principal actors. So no wonder that the dedicated teacher jousts against ignorance, smug colleagues and lethargic students with new-born confidence these days. His naivete has faded. He doesn't keep blundering in and out of difficulties with the Board of Education. And seldom any more does he find himself on the short end of a word-battle with principal Albert Vane — or worse, with some precocious student. He doesn't for the simple reason that the imaginary young teacher has been on the firing line long enough to achieve professional maturity. He's got a full semester under his belt. This is not to say that everything has gone along as scheduled with "Mr. Novak" and company. Jeanne Bal's role in the scheme of things was a modest one until one day she reported for work on the twelfth episode and was handed a new script. Every place the name "Albert Vane" had been written, it was crossed out and "Miss Pagano" inserted. Dean Jagger was in the hospital with ulcers, she was

Assistant Principal Jean Pagano

told — so would she please learn his lines? During Dean's three-week absence from the set, Jeanne came through magnificently, so that when he returned to work (at first on only a few-hours-a-day basis), her role didn't shrink back to its original size. Now, with Jagger back full time and Franciscus still operating under a full head of steam, Jeanne continues to command a big part of the show. Besides learning more about Mr. Novak as a person, Neuman says, "we'll learn more about where Mr. Vane (Did you know he taught math for 15 years?) and Miss Pagano (Did you know she had a bad marriage with the hero of her high school football team?) have been all their lives. We'll see a lot more of some other members of our faculty: Mr. Peeples, Miss Scott, Pete Butler, Miss Dorsey and the rest." — Edgar Penton, "Mr. Novak Passes with Flying Colors: Classroom Drama is promoted to Next Season," Bristol, Pennsylvania, *Daily Courier*, 5/9/64.

Mr. Novak appears at parade for Cerebral Palsy

Neuman's plans for expansion of the characters would not be implemented in the second season due to creative decisions by Leonard Freeman and MGM.

James Franciscus appeared in the First International Celebrity Parade for Cerebral Palsy which was televised on May 16. He was also active in the Foundation for the Junior Blind and the Arthritis Foundation. The actor would gladly donate his time to charity work.

By early June, E. Jack Neuman had completed a short promotional film for the NEA. It would be distributed to various schools, teacher's groups and other educational organizations. Neuman hosted the film from Principal Vane's office. He thanked the NEA for their advice and showcased Mr. Novak's growth as a teacher through clips from the first season's shows. Vane was also shown addressing a dropout and the civil rights issue as well as humorously scolding Miss Scott for being late to class. The lost battles, along with the triumphs, of Novak and Vane were showcased. Near the end of the film, Neuman proudly displayed the Peabody Award that had been given to the series and mentioned the other thirty awards the show had received. He declared that *Mr. Novak* had been honored for restoring dignity and honor to the image of the American School Teacher. The series' producer closed with an assurance of the NEA's continued advice and technical assistance. The upcoming second season would keep disclosing the story of Mr. Novak and would explore current problems in education. Neuman hoped to attract respect and response for education and educators everywhere. The 16mm one reel film was sent to the NEA on June 8.

A few days later, an announcement brought news that would be devastating to fans of the series. "Miss Pagano" would not be returning for the new season. Sometime later a columnist reported the events of this alarming cast change and the departing actress gave her side of the story:

> Is the TV viewer fickle or are the men behind the scenes, the producers and network executives, whose arbitrary decisions make it appear this way? Let's take the controversial case of lovely Jeanne Bal, whose impact as assistant principal Jean Pagano in this, the first season of "Mr. Novak," caused one film expert to exclaim: "She's the first combination of beauty, intelligence and grace to come along since Irene Dunne." Jeanne became such a viewer favorite in the series, no one dreamed

she'd become literally shrugged off when filming for a second season was about to begin several weeks ago. But that's exactly what happened, so quickly that it took Jeanne completely by surprise. One day I was talking to Jeanne and she was enthusiastically telling me she could hardly wait for the second season to commence filming the following week. The next day, Jeanne had "quit" the series. Whether she quit or was put into a position where she was forced to quit is a conclusion you can draw for yourself when you hear Jeanne's side of the story.

With refreshing candor, Jeanne told me: "My contract read that in the first year of the series, I was to receive $750 per episode for a minimum of 20 episodes. The following year, I was to have the same minimum number of episodes with a salary boost to $900 per each. I anticipated no trouble. The studio was so enthusiastic about

me my role was being progressively expanded. But then they hired a new producer (Leonard Freeman) who, I'm told, insisted on a change for the sake of technical accuracy. California High Schools have no assistant principals. They have a girl's vice principal and a boy's vice principal. All well and good, but I was made to understand that since they were hiring an additional actor for the boy's vice principal role, I should naturally not expect a raise to $900. I balked at this; the decision was not mine, so why should I be made to suffer because of a producer's whim? Then I was told, 'All right, we'll honor the raise but you'll have to sign for 14 episodes instead of 20.' On the surface, this may seem a reasonable request, but in the dog-eat-dog business one develops an intuition that has to be very keen for survival. I got the feeling they were trying to tell me I wasn't wanted. One thing I became convinced of, though everything was smiles and honeyed words, there was a definite 'take it or leave it' attitude in our discussions.

"Now, this is rather strange under the circumstances. I had given them (MGM-TV) more than they'd hoped when I originally signed the contract. And they told me so till the new producer came in. Frankly, I didn't care about the raise; this was only a matter of principal with me. What I did care about was that there was a calculated plan to minimize the importance of my role. Finally, when the chips were down, this was openly admitted. To go one step further, if the series hadn't been a success and I hadn't felt I made a strong contribution, I'd have kept my mouth shut and submitted humbly to a demotion. After all, I probably would have deserved it. But I couldn't see myself fading into insignificance which is what they wanted me to do, after I'd earned the right to at least maintain the importance I'd achieved in the first season.

"The strange part about this whole mess is that my very own agent knew what was going on weeks before and didn't even clue me. And when I decided to quit the series, my agent's ultimatum was 'if you quit, you might as well find a new agent!' Imagine that! I'm probably the only actress in history who's been fired by the man who's supposed to be working for her." — Hank Grant, "Jeanne Bal Dropped from Novak Series," *The Troy Record*, 6/11/64.

Producer Leonard Freeman offered his side of the dispute:

"It's true Miss Bal won't be with the series. There are a number of reasons. The first is because we're going to conventionalize the show's power situation." He explained high schools in California have a vice principal for boys and one for girls; that actually there is no overall assistant to the principal as the role played by Miss Bal. Consequently, series plans to intro veepees for boys and girls, as schools have in this state. Under this plan, Freeman conceded, there would be less for Miss Bal to do. "If MGM decided it wanted Miss Bal on her terms, it could have had her. Their feeling was that under her conditions, they didn't wish to exercise their option. We are not discontented with Miss Bal. We like her. But we have had a number of letters objecting to a pretty young girl in the role of disciplining young men. And we prefer to have a vice principal for boys and one for girls, as schools in this state have," said Freeman. — Unsourced article.

Series producer Leonard Freeman

Marian Collier had enjoyed working with Jeanne and regretted her departure:

We were all surprised when it was announced that Jeanne wouldn't be returning. I figured that her husband, who was a lawyer, had intervened in the contract dispute. I heard that his advice to her was a factor in her not returning. It was too bad because she was very good. Jeanne always had a very authoritative character. Whenever she came on the screen, you watched her. The loss of Jeanne was the first strike against the series. — Int.

Bob Schultz, a veteran of television production, was appalled at this loss to the show:

The fact that Freeman was in agreement with Jeanne leaving shows you who he was. Her departure involved a financial dispute and lesser hours but should have been worked out. She was an essential part of the show's appeal. The suits figured they had to cut costs as they figured it was too expensive a show. But it really wasn't that expensive. It was dumb to let her go. Freeman's citing the letters of complaint about Jeanne's attractive appearance was just an excuse. Apparently that was where this power thing came from the studio to put Freeman on... the execs wanted to run the show. It was a shame and there was worse to come. That's probably why, at some point, E. Jack said, "Just give me the money and you can do what you want. Here's a bunch of scripts I'm writing or rewriting and that's it." — Int.

When the second season would begin production, Freeman's plan for a male vice principal was not implemented. An actress would be hired to replace Jean Bal in a similar role at Jefferson High. It was an ominous shift just before initial filming of the second season was to begin.

Leonard Freeman was acquiring new stories for the upcoming second season. He was dedicated to conducting extensive research in his efforts to produce realistic scripts:

> Freeman visited a number of high schools to get a feel of his subject. He came away with respect for the teachers, and awed by the complex problems facing the high schooler of today. Despite what is termed our burgeoning economy, today's young student faces an almost hopeless situation wherein each year thousands graduate to the job market — where fewer jobs are available each year because of automation. Consequently, many have a sense of futility, and many of the male teenagers enlist in the armed services rather than face a jobless future, asserts Freeman. These and other problems of the high schoolers will be incorporated into next season's series by Freeman, who promises there will be no easy answers for what are very complex problems. It would be presumptuous to attempt any answer for some of these problems, he admits. — Dave Kaufman, "Freeman Schools Self for 'Novak,'" *Daily Variety*, 5/20/64.

Some of the new scripts would deal with such diverse topics as an attack by students on an aggressive shop teacher and the story of parental pressure to overachieve which drives an average student to attempt suicide. Another script would showcase the implementation of teaching machines. These primitive computers are sold with the promise that they will perform better than the actual teachers who might become obsolete in the future. In the *Daily Variety* article, Freeman discussed another story by the series' educational advisor:

> "Moonlighting" deals with teachers working on the outside to earn coin to supplement incomes. Being adapted by ex-teacher Mike Dolinsky, from an original by John Ryan, a teacher, yarn is based to a large degree on his own experiences. Novak (James Franciscus) works nights so he can earn more so that he can pay his ailing pop's medical bills. "We tell without a propaganda pitch what the teacher faces on $5,700 a year, and we're telling it in the most personal way, through John Novak," Freeman says. — *Ibid*.

Script advisor Dr. G. Keith Dolan found he was moonlighting and utilized the series to enhance his educational efforts:

I thought the show was very authentic and was an excellent program. James Franciscus was a nice-looking guy and I was impressed with his role as written. Dean Jagger was very good as the principal. When I watched *Mr. Novak* I felt that often the plotlines rang very true to issues that we dealt with at San Bernardino. I was moonlighting at Redlands University... teaching courses for beginning secondary teachers. My request for a print of "First Year, First Day" to be shown in my classes was granted. Many of the class members were impressed and we had good discussions as a result. — Int.

Vince Howard, who had played history teacher Peter Butler, had never acted before he was cast in the series. He discussed the help he received and his pride in playing the role:

"The wonderful help, support and advice I've received from everyone connected with the show, particularly Jack Neuman, James Franciscus, Dean Jagger, and Jeanne Bal, is remarkable and unusual. They've taken time out from their busy schedules to help me, to coach me on how a scene should or shouldn't be played, and given me the benefit of their wealth of acting experience." It is noteworthy and gratifying, Vince believes, that he is the first Negro portraying a continuing role of a professional man in a network series. — "Beach Club Singer Gains Part On 'Mr. Novak' Series," *Los Angeles Sentinel*, 5/28/64.

This was two years before Bill Cosby would be starred in the *I Spy* TV program. Franciscus' wife Kitty would witness a disturbing event as a result of her husband's popularity:

Jim and I were at the Ambassador Hotel in Los Angeles. We were on the way up to our room and a bunch of girls came in for their prom. They were all dressed up and looked so darling. They ran up to Jim and started screaming "Mr. Novak!" It scared me and they started to grab at his clothes. I called security and they sent a few guards to get us out of there. He had tried to smile and be nice but was very shaken by their attack on him. We then decided to use back entrances of restaurants and hotels to avoid the screaming fans. After a while we could only go to two special restaurants in Los Angeles because Jim knew they were private and he wouldn't be mobbed. — Int.

The first day of June brought the initial filming of "The People Doll: You Wind It Up and It Makes Mistakes." It was the story of a promising student who is in love and wants to drop out and get married. The script was the first one by writer John D. F. Black who had previously written scripts for *Have Gun, Will Travel*, *The Fugitive*, *The Untouchables*, and *Combat*. He would be pleased with the working arrangements on *Mr. Novak*:

Lenny Freeman called me and asked me to come over and work on *Novak* as a writer. I worked closely with Lenny on all of the episodes I wrote for *Novak*. He did give me a few pointers regarding the scripts but I was given complete freedom. I had a very Catholic upbringing and in "The People Doll" I felt the young man was really tormented by his own sensuality but wasn't giving it to it. — Interview.

There was a scene near the end of "The People Doll" that took place at a Polish wedding party. The script called for Miss Scott to dance with the groom's father and Mr. Novak to cut a rug with the bride. Marian Collier recalled an unscripted moment of spontaneity from her co-star:

> During a break in filming at the wedding party, the band continued to play. They started a lively polka and Jim came over and started dancing with me. I was taken by surprise but it was delightful of him to twirl me around the dance floor. The still photographer managed to get one shot of us dancing together and I requested a copy. — Int.

A replacement for Jeanne Bal had been found:

Phyllis Avery as Girls' Vice Principal Ruth Wilkinson

Phyllis Avery has been set by producer Leonard Freeman for continuing role in MGM-TV's "Mr. Novak" series starring James Franciscus and Dean Jagger. — *Daily Variety,* 6/2/64.

She was a veteran actress and had appeared in such motion pictures as *Ruby Gentry* and *The Best Things in Life Are Free.* Her television credits included continuing roles as the "wife" on *The George Gobel Show* and *Meet Mr. McNulty.* Avery would portray Jefferson High School girl's Vice-Principal Ruth Wilkinson, a new character added to the series.

Marian Collier felt that the choice of Jeanne Bal's replacement was an acceptable one:

Phyllis Avery was very nice and very competent. She wasn't very authoritative and went with the flow. Phyllis was very professional and was very good in an episode with Eddie Albert. She just didn't have Jeanne's presence. — Int.

"Born of Kings and Angels" went before the cameras on June 10. It was a strange story about a member of Novak's debating team, who searches for his past while on a field trip. Returning to the series for his second lead was Peter Helm:

After I had done the first episode, I began regularly watching the program. Every one that I saw was good and it was a show of high quality. "Angels" was an odd show for the series. It was kind of like a *Twilight Zone* episode with a strange mood. James Franciscus and I had an intense scene near the end where I ended up slapping him. He was great to play off of and he gave me a lot to work with. I think we did that heavy scene in one take. The episode was almost entirely shot on location. The fictitious city the debate team went to was Culver City. It was just a few blocks away from MGM. The diner and the hotel were real and gave the episode almost a documentary feel. There were even some tilted camera angles used while my character walked around Culver City. It was another great experience and a fulfilling role. — Int.

Verne (Peter Helm) searches for his past during a field trip in "Born of Kings and Angels"

Playing a small part in the episode was the former star of *Circus Boy*. Mickey Braddock had starred as Corky in the series which ran from 1956 to 1958. He had been out of the acting profession for some time and had attended college. Braddock would also appear in the "One Monday Afternoon" episode which was filmed some months later. In 1966, as Mickey Dolenz, he was cast in *The Monkees* TV series and would become a pop music superstar.

There had not been any merchandise issued in relation to the series except for the board game. A second product was released by the record division of MGM:

THEME FROM MISTER NOVAK. The first band of each side of this disk is pegged to the NBC-TV drama series, with all the rest being contemporary ballads. The TV theme and the pops are given richly styled and danceable instrumental work overs by studio orchestra directed by Nick Venet. — Weekly *Variety*, 6/17/64.

This was quickly obtained and appreciated by Laure Georges:

> In the Summer of 1964 I went to my favorite music hangout with my boyfriend — Wallichs Music City in Hollywood. I was hoping to get the new Dave Clark 5 album. As I turned down the aisle I saw something so epic that I thought I must be dreaming! I started shrieking and my boyfriend rushed over, thinking I was injured.
>
> Right on the shelf was a "Theme from Mr. Novak" album! I grabbed a copy and went to the cashier to purchase my treasure. I forgot about the DC5 album I originally planned on. I couldn't afford two albums and my mind was made up. The color picture on the cover of Principal Vane and Mr. Novak was so cool! The minute I got home I went to my bedroom to play the record. I was a bit disappointed because I thought JF would be singing just as Richard Chamberlain did on a 45 record I had. But the music was fantastic and the LP became a favorite. On the following Tuesday evening (Novak Night), my girlfriends came over per usual and before we watched the show, I told them I had a surprise. Do you want to talk major craziness, hilarity and envy? All of the girls were able to get a copy of the *Novak* album within the week and they loved it too. — Int.

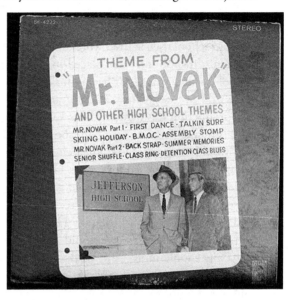

"Moonlighting," in which Mr. Novak must take a second job to help pay the medical bills for his ailing father, went into production. The teacher finds his previous abilities to be suffering and faces a loss of stature with his students. It was directed by Richard Donner:

> I thought it was a very interesting show in which Novak is demeaned. I discussed Jim's history as an actor and it got very personal. I had a conference with him as to whether he could draw on something from his personal life. Get a little deeper. His character was embarrassed by his students.... I wanted a little more depth... felt his portrayal was a bit surface. He listened and delivered a layered performance that was completely right for the story. — Int.

In a later syndicated interview, Franciscus discussed the unique qualities of his part in the episode:

> It was my most difficult role. You rarely get to see an actor you get to know on a series break down and weep with the panic of not being able to pay bills. It let me stretch my muscles a little. — Mary Anne Corpin, "Franciscus Calls Premiere His Most Difficult Role," *Baton Rouge Advocate*, 9/20/64.

Marc Wanamaker was a Hollywood resident and high school student who found himself a part of the series by chance:

> Everyone I knew watched *Mr. Novak*. It was a wonderful show and everybody loved James Franciscus. I went to Hamilton High in Culver City for summer school and was usually done by noon.
>
> One day I noticed they were filming and was approached to by a production person to be an extra. I had been an extra at Uni High on the *Billie* film. Every day I went to school then started work around one or two to six. We were coached by the assistant director and were placed in different seats in the classrooms. Outside the school we were placed for background. There were not more than ten extras and we were paid $25 a day. It was important to me because I watched and learned how a TV production was made. I think I was in about six episodes.
>
> Jim Franciscus was very handsome and wasn't very tall. He was very personable and would hang out. He seemed closer to our age and was "one of us." Dean Jagger seemed to us to be a movie star. He was very tall and personable but we were a little intimated because he was an adult. It was a warm set and everybody was part of something that was good. Director Richard Donner didn't seem that old to us and was very warm and friendly. He would tell us what to do and told us to have some fun. Donner said we could sign up at MGM to see some screenings and maybe get some more extra work. I went over and saw *The Haunting* and met its Director Robert Wise. He ended up hiring me to work on *The Hindenburg* feature and later sponsored me for a membership in the Motion Picture Academy. — Marc Wanamaker, Interview, 3/15/17.

During the first year of the show, there had been hints of a romance between Mr. Novak and Miss Scott. Nothing further had developed possibly because Franciscus had requested that his character not be tied down. He may have wanted to be free to have an occasional romantic encounter. "Miss Scott" discussed this frustrating situation:

> Actress Marian Collier has put on her running shoes, looking forward to another television season of chasing one of video's most eligible bachelors. For the past year she's been chasing Jim Franciscus, who plays the title role of the teacher. The young lady's luck hasn't been too good. The best she could do was to corner Franciscus for an occasional date, usually to attend some school function. "Nothing has really developed," said Marian of her make-believe chase. "I think he's got other things on his mind. All the kids are wondering when Mr. Novak and I will get together." — Joseph Finnigan, "Actress Plans to Keep Running After Bachelor," *Baton Rouge Advocate*, 6/22/64.

Veteran actor Eddie Albert was the guest star on the next episode to be created. "Visions of Sugar Plums" was the story of happy-go-lucky teacher who returns to work after many years as a vagabond. His unorthodox methods cause doubt about his abilities to educate. Featured in the show was young Beverly Washburn:

> I had been watching the series and liked it. It was an excellent show that was very well written. Jim Franciscus was quite the hunk and even though I was a veteran of

the acting profession, I was a teenager and had a crush on him. Eddie Albert was very friendly and really suited the part. You never thought he was acting. He had an infectious charm. Phyllis Avery was adorable and there was a beautifully done last scene with Eddie. It was a very harmonious shoot and both the crew and cast were first rate. I felt fortunate to work on such a classy show. — Interview.

Phyllis Avery was interviewed during the filming of the episode and expressed her happiness in becoming a regular on the series and discussed the acting freedom she was experiencing:

Eddie Albert serenades Marian Collier in "Visions of Sugarplums"

There aren't many good parts for women in television so I was surprised and thrilled that the offer came from "Mr. Novak," which is one of the few shows I watch. Dean Jagger is a dear man and a wonderful actor. He took me aside the first day of rehearsal and told me that we didn't have to follow the script absolutely stringently, to say something if we felt it. I did a scene with him and was amazed with his improvising talents. This isn't to say we take great liberties with the script, we don't. But it provides closeness in the relationship between an actor and the part. In the show we begin today, I become involved with a vagabond teacher who sings and plays the guitar. — Don Page, "A Faculty Change for 'Mr. Novak,'" *Los Angeles Times*, 8/9/64.

Franciscus was an intense, serious actor who was completely focused on his craft and career. The pressures of his continuing stardom on the series and the heavy workload were beginning take a toll on his nerves. Reporter Peer J. Oppenheimer found his interview subject to be somewhat difficult:

Franciscus' wife Kitty explained that there were two Jims: one at work — hard driving, dedicated, not always easy to get along with; the other away from his career — with a sense of humor to match his sincerity and intelligence. I found out the hard way about the Jim Franciscus-at-work. I have known Jim socially for four years and always found him friendly. Yet when I had lunch with him at MGM recently, he was distant and a bit curt — his mind apparently more on his role than the interview, which he obviously didn't enjoy. Later, when I expressed surprise at Jim's rather abrupt attitude, Kitty explained, "At the studio he's strictly work. That's the kind of actor he is, that's why he is so good. Outside the studio he's just crazy and wonderful. But he can't combine the two. Even at home, at times when he's given a rewritten script to study, his mind is consumed with it. I talk to him but I know he isn't paying any attention. I learned to accept him like this. Jim is delighted the way his career is going but resents playing the part of star off-screen. Because of his schoolteacher role on TV, people honestly think he is one," Kitty told me. "We recently spent a weekend in Las Vegas and everywhere we went, they brought him their educational problems. Jim just cringed and fled back to the hotel." — "James Franciscus — From Riches to Success," *Family Weekly*, 6/28/64.

The increasing demands on the actor's privacy and his intense concentration on his craft would result in occasional temperamental behavior that would erupt on the set. His hateful attitude toward the fan magazines would also increase with further antagonistic statements about their credibility. They would respond by printing more untruths to portray the actor in a negative fashion.

Marian Collier observed the star of the series withdrawing to his home and family:

> In the second season, the only time we ever saw Jim socially was at MGM on Friday nights. Next to the studio was the Retake Room bar. He'd hang out a little with us, have a drink, then go home. It was funny. Richard Kline was our cameraman and was most attractive. All of the girls in the Retake Room would go up to him instead of Jim. — Int.

On July 1, Franciscus and Neuman attended the National Education Association's Convention in Seattle. There was a presentation of the School Bell Award for "distinguished dramatic interpretation of education during the year ended April 1, 1964, through a series aired over a national television network: the 'Mr. Novak' series." The actor received a citation from the Classroom Teachers Association and the producer accepted the School Bell Award. While in Seattle, Neuman expressed regret at Bal's departure and promised a welcome change for one of the series' regulars:

NEA president Lois V. Edinger presents the School Bell Award and a bound copy of the September NEA Journal to James Franciscus

> We had such great plans for her this season! So what will we do? We're going to feature Marian Collier, who plays Miss Scott, our attractive blonde home economics teacher. We'll learn more of her family background and of another romance that antedates her sentimental attachment to Mr. Novak. — Francis Murphy, "Behind the Mike," *Portland Oregonian*, 7/2/64.

E. Jack Neuman proudly displays the School Bell Award for *Mr. Novak*

Marian Collier was very pleased with these plans to increase her prominence in the show:

> Although I was sorry to see Jeanne go, I was happy to hear from Jack that my part would increase, as would the other regular teachers. When this didn't happen, and I was used less than in the first season, I was very disappointed. We all were but we couldn't go to Mr. Neuman because he wasn't the producer anymore. It must have been Freeman's decision as he was the new producer and Jack had diminished his involvement. He didn't have the same ideas as Jack about the show. Somehow he didn't think we were that important. The successful first season had been about teachers and all of a sudden he cuts us down." — Int.

Marian Collier had obtained a larger than usual role in "The People Doll" and had been promised more screen time in the second season.

This was ultimately not to be done. The other teachers found their roles to be lessened. Bob Schultz assumed it was an economic situation that was shortsighted:

> In the second season, the regular cast of teachers who had appeared in the first season in small but steady parts were used a lot less. It was down to money and MGM not wanting to pay actors if they didn't do the full week. The studio also didn't want to pay larger syndication residuals for a lot of the actors who only had small parts. They had a contract with NBC for the second season and had to deliver the show at a certain figure. An increasing budget for the show was a big concern for the suits. The attitude on the lot was "It's just TV." The MGM execs were concentrating on their big features per year because they felt that was where the money was. Saving money on the series could be applied to the features. Even some of the big wheels who ran the departments on the MGM lot felt that TV was secondary. If a big feature needed something the TV show could wait.

Mr. Novak and Miss Scott enjoy a country outing in "The People Doll"

> MGM had a bunch of fuddle heads that still had their heads stuck in the 30's and 40's. It was a shame because it weakened a great show that had been so critically respected.
>
> At the time, I had a long conversation with Jim about his salary. We were talking about the forthcoming season and were looking forward to it. He said he had asked for more money. He said the suits were fighting him tooth and nail because he was wanted a little more money. I found out later he was making $5,000 a week which was six day's work. Apparently, in the second season, he had to continue to fight for the $5,000 a week. This was ridiculous as Jim was the main reason for the series' success. The execs didn't know what they were doing. — Int.

Work began the next day on "Beyond a Reasonable Doubt." This was the story of a girl who enrolls at Jefferson after having been acquitted of killing her parents. Suspicion follows her every move by teachers and students. The girl was played by Susan Tyrell and the episode was directed by Richard Donner. Marian Collier had a rare dramatic scene in this episode where she was required to cry. In a later interview in the February 1965 issue of *TV Radio Mirror* she recalled the assistance she received from the star of the series:

> The scene, doubtless viewed by now, had Miss Scott inadvertently setting fire to the school, and weeping hysterically in aftermath. Some actresses weep easily, others need a good reason. Marian Collier is one of the latter. Indeed, the only thing that seemed likely to move her to bona fide tears was the fear that nothing could move her to bona fide tears! "Jim took his whole lunch hour," she recalls now, "to show me how and give me the confidence. And he's not a man who likes to go without lunch. Heaven knows, he didn't have to. It was the director's job, and it was my problem. But he did, because that's how he is. And it worked."

The next show to be filmed starred Simon Oakland as an aggressive shop teacher who runs his class like a foreman. He is jumped by three students and causes injuries to the leader. The boys spread lies placing the blame on the instructor.

Directed by Allen Reisner, "With a Hammer in His Hand, Lord, Lord!" heralded the return of Walter Koenig:

Shocked teacher Simon Oakland confronts his attacker, Tim McIntire, in "With a Hammer in His Hand, Lord, Lord!"

I got the part of the insecure student after Joe D'Agosta called me in to read. I was not very present for most of the episode but had a big scene with Dean Jagger in his office at the end. After pressure from the principal, my character crumbles and admits his involvement in the fight. Dean was a total pro and worked well with me in the scene. Alan Reisner directed by omission. He said nothing about anything that I did. I came to think he wasn't happy with my work because he didn't say anything to me. I finally got mad and spoke up. I told him I was doing a lousy job and that he must be unhappy with me. He didn't reply and looked bewildered. After the scene was completed I stormed out thinking I'd done badly. It was later written up in an article that said I was a great actor. — Int.

The strong storyline was written by John D. F. Black who witnessed the power of Koenig's performance and opposition to the lead character:

> I saw the dailies of Walter's scene with Dean Jagger at the end of the episode. In it he breaks down under Principal Vane's interrogation. He broke out in a sweat from within as his character collapsed. I was absolutely stunned by his performance. They screened the finished episode for a group of shop teachers. After the screening

they threw a hissy fit. They found Simon Oakland's character coarse mannered and unpleasant. I wrote the character to be aggressive because he had to push his students to become proficient at manual labor. The job markets in those fields were declining and the teacher felt they had to be superior to compete. When I was an adolescent I worked with a cabinet maker. I wanted to show the respectability of manual labor. — Int.

James Franciscus was receiving increasing mail from teachers, students, and fans of the series. Many would connect him with the character he played on television. The actor responded by writing a column for the Associated Press:

Real students write us about how they gain inspiration from John Novak. Real teachers admit to finding new dignity and new purpose in their lives because of him and Principal Vane, who is played by Dean Jagger. The letters have a tendency to lump John Novak and James Franciscus into one big fuzzy package and praise me for my selfless devotion to education. But I'm not John Novak, the selfless, under-paid teacher. I'm James Franciscus, the well-paid actor. Through letters and daily personal contact with educators who work with the "Mr. Novak" show, all of us — the cast, the production crew, the writers — have a powerful new awareness of the educator's urgent role in our culture. The plaudits belong to John Novak — to the John Novaks and the Jane Novaks in big schools and little schools across the country." — "Actor Intimidated by Teacher's Role," Aberdeen, South Dakota, *Daily News*, 7/15/64.

James Franciscus signs an autograph for a stewardess upon arriving in Los Angeles Airport

"Little Girl Lost" was the story of a delinquent girl who is transferred to Jefferson High and has a disregard for authority. The lead was played by young Davey Davison:

I thought the script by Betty Ulius was particularly good. The character of Edie Currie allowed an amazing range for an actor to play which was unusual in episodic TV. I was thrilled to get the part. It's funny, director Paul Wendkos never called me by name. He always called me "the sparrow." Because I was in nearly every scene I worked many hours with the crew. One day is was eighteen hours. It was a great experience and one of my favorite shows in my career. — Interview.

The role of the delinquent girl's boyfriend was played by Buck Taylor:

I was glad to be cast on such a great series. It showcased a lot of young actors and was highly regarded. Davey Davison was an extremely good actress who was very realistic as the troubled girl. James Franciscus was very nice and laid back. A very focused actor. Dean Jagger was awesome. You never knew when he was acting. I was thrilled that I got to sing and play the guitar. A good shoot. — Interview.

JIM & DICK-FRIENDS OR ENEMIES? JIM TALKS ABOUT DATE!
DICK TALKS ABOUT GIRLS! SUPER PINUPS! EXCLUSIVE PHOTOS!
FAMOUS ASTROLOGER PREDICTS THEIR FUTURE EXPECTATIONS!

In mid-summer 'TEEN magazine published a one-shot special issue titled "Jim Franciscus & Dick Chamberlain: The Screen's Most Exciting Leading Men." It contained rare photos, interviews, astrological profiles, and pinup portraits. Interviewed prior to her leaving the show, Jeanne Bal expressed admiration for her co-star:

I think Jim is one of the finest actors in the business. It's been a pleasure working with him. I don't think I've ever worked on any show where people get along better. Jim is a lot of fun and sometimes we play jokes on each other. I admire Jim's desire to get the best performance possible and although it may take longer to do, it's the only way actors should work.

"Love Among the Grownups" went before the cameras and found Novak and an attractive French instructor to be victims of a poison-pen-letter campaign. The teacher was played by Geraldine Brooks. This episode featured the second television appearance of young Lane Bradbury:

Jagger and Lane Bradbury take a break during the filming of "Love Among the Grownups"

I was aware the show and got the part of the jealous student after doing a read. Director Abner Biberman allowed me to add my own interpretations to the part which was something I really enjoyed. Jim Franciscus was fine to act with. It was a good professional relationship and I felt we worked well together. Dean Jagger was an amazing actor. He and I had a wonderful and easy rapport in our scenes. It was a good experience and I was glad to be cast on such a prestige show. — Interview, 3/2/17

The month of August brought news that the teachers and the students of Jefferson High would soon be seen worldwide:

"*Mr. Novak*" will make debut in 12 overseas countries next season. Scheduled to meet "Mr. Novak" for the first time are Canada, Argentina, Australia, Brazil, England, Finland, Japan, Philippines, Mexico, Peru, Uruguay, and Venezuela. — *Los Angeles Times*, 8/4/64.

A syndicated piece described an ambitious undertaking by the prominent two TV series at MGM:

"*Mr. Novak*" and "*Dr. Kildare*" will tackle the subject of VD in a two-part episode shared by the programs next season. "It's not an easy subject to water down," Kildare's Dick Chamberlain said. "But they will," he added." — "Tricky Subject For 2 Programs," *San Antonio Express and News*, 8/9/64.

In a later interview, E. Jack Neuman recalled the genesis of the scripts:

The surgeon general's office approached David Victor, producer of *Dr. Kildare*, suggesting an episode calling attention to the V.D. epidemic among 14- to 20-year-olds. About the same time, the New York Department of Public Health wrote to E. Jack Neuman with a similar proposal for the *Novak* show. "I began fishing around, and visiting several high-school principals and some of the Los Angeles health-department workers," said Neuman. "To a man, they told me what a frightful thing this is, what a devastating effect it is having emotionally and academically on uncounted numbers of teen-agers. They began plying me with facts and material." Neuman discussed his findings with the executive personnel of the two shows, Norman Felton and David Victor for *Kildare* and Leonard Freeman of *Novak*. Like the vast majority of people who are other-wise well informed and knowledgeable about current affairs, Neuman and his colleagues at MGM had absolutely no idea of the magnitude of the V.D. epidemic.

"The really frustrating thing is that today, for the first time in history, total eradication of venereal disease is a practical possibility, because a quick and certain cure does now exist," said Neuman. He was particularly struck with the inadequacy of V.D. education in schools — in many areas nonexistent, in others spotty, and often sadly ineffective. "Too often it's left up to an embarrassed gym teacher, who shows a few slides," he said. "The only state with a competent system is Oregon, where they start in the sixth grade, and consequently the V.D. rate is extremely low. We all felt obligated by the nature of the subject to do something about it," said Neuman. — Jessica Mitford, "The Disease that Dr. Kildare Couldn't Cure," *McCall's*, 9/65.

Mr. Novak's Producer also expressed his commitment to the project in the same article:

Leonard Freeman emphasized the need to remove the social onus that is attached to this particular disease, "so a young person would feel free to go to a doctor at the beginning. People should realize it's not the victim that's abhorrent; it's the disease. The terror of syphilis is that the symptoms are so brief — and painless. The victim can sit it out for two weeks, and then the symptoms disappear altogether — but he becomes a carrier; he isn't really cured. The disease goes underground, but reappears in later life in the most deadly forms. The reasons for doing this show, to bring this to the light of day, seemed to us quite indisputable."

This challenging project would be the subject of much controversy in the forthcoming months.

A sports-orientated episode, "One Monday Afternoon," came next. It presented the story of a star quarterback on the Jefferson High football team who is accidentally killed during a scrimmage. Claude Akins guest starred as the football coach.

Brooke Bundy had a small role at the tragic athlete's girlfriend. She found one scene to be very traumatic:

Carol Walker (Brooke Bundy) mourns her deceased boyfriend in "One Monday Afternoon"

Paul Wendkos was a fine director. It was one of the great acting lessons of all time. I saw the helmet after my boyfriend had the fatal accident and that it didn't protect him. I was crying and really believed the scene. I couldn't stop crying even after they finished the scene. I went home that night after filming ended and tried to explain what happened. It was a very powerful acting experience. — Int.

The two-part script for the V.D. story, now called "The Rich Who Are Poor," had been carefully polished by its writer and advisors:

Neuman had submitted an extended, unusually detailed outline of the drama, so there'd be no surprises for the network — all the cards were on the table. The network considered the outline long and painfully, then gave the go-ahead, with a proviso that there'd be no carte blanche approval until they saw the finished script. The draft screenplay, having won this tentative approval, was next subjected to the searching scrutiny of various experts. It was vetted for medical accuracy by public health educators in Atlanta, Washington and Los Angeles; for English usage by a panel of the National Education Association (which acted in an advisory capacity to the Novak program); and for "taste and propriety" by NBC's own Broadcast Standards Department. — *McCall's*, 9/65.

By the first week of August, and after much refinement courtesy of the many advisors, the two scripts had been officially finished. The Promotional Film for the National Education Association had been distributed and was well received:

A special film on MGM-TV's "*Mr. Novak*," put together for the National Education Assn., has met with such enthusiasm that 55 prints have been ordered by the NEA for showing to teacher groups across the country. Film reviews John

Novak's first year as a teacher and introduces the NEA president, Dr. Lois Edinger. It was supervised by executive producer E. Jack Neuman. — *The Hollywood Reporter*, 8/11/64.

This 16mm one-reel film was also being shown at Future Teachers of America meetings and was another indication of the series' influence on the educational community.

In "'A' as in Anxiety" a student attempts suicide as a result of parental pressure to overachieve. The lead was played by young June Harding who found the star of the series to be difficult:

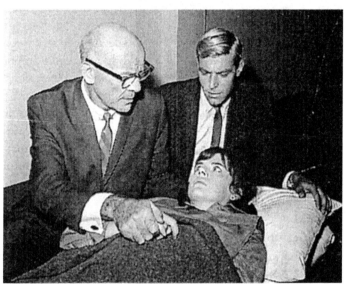

Principal Vane and Mr. Novak comfort a distraught Karen Parker (June Harding) in "'A' as in Anxiety"

Jim Franciscus seemed to be very tense and angry. He didn't speak to me at all except during a take. He appeared to be tired and at one point yelled at me to play a scene the way he wanted it done. He was scary to me. I became very disturbed and left the set only to quickly return and finish the scene. Dean Jagger was dignified but I felt Franciscus was very stressed. When filming was done I was glad to get out of there. It was not a happy incident for me. When my mother watched the episode, she cried and told me I had given an excellent performance. That somehow made the whole experience worthwhile. — Interview.

This display of temperament by the star of the show was a rarity but was an indication of the increasing pressure of his work schedule, fame, and studio interference. Bob Schultz observed firsthand the strain on Franciscus:

Shooting a series was a hard grind. Jim was on the set every day and worked hard to make the show work. He was under a lot of pressure and must have had a bad day. He never yelled at the crew who would do anything for him. He *was* the show. He had to have been under additional pressure entering the second season with all the changes going on. When E. Jack was running the show during the first season he let Jim do his thing. Now he was being told what to do. I knew him well. He was very reserved and came from a good background. He was a gentleman. If he lost his temper on the set it had to have been from additional pressure from somebody he didn't like. — Int.

Marian Collier had received requests for personal appearances. She traveled to East Chicago and arrived at her alma mater of Washington High School. The actress enjoyed the activities and the response of the students:

Marian Collier addresses the student body during her return to Washington High School

"It takes a homecoming like this to discover the real impact of the show on students and teachers alike," she said. "I appeared at three assemblies — scared to death. I goofed the first speech, did little better on the second — and was a smash on my third. I signed so many autographs my hand hurt for days. The students were interested in every detail," she said. "Naturally they wanted to know about Jim and Dean Jagger, but even more important, they talked of story points in the various episodes. And you know something," she said, flashing one of those smiles that has captivated John Novak on more than one occasion, "I didn't even mind when they called me Miss Scott. As a matter of fact, I liked it." — "Likes Her Role as a Teacher," *San Mateo Times*, 8/29/64.

Marian then traveled to Houston and made a series of appearances on September 10. She was featured on the *Chris Chandler* TV show and held a press conference with 50 high school journalists. While there, Marian lamented her limited exposure on the series:

"Would you believe it if I were to tell you I was in 25 or 30 episodes last year? Yet you probably

Marian Collier during an appearance on the *Chris Chandler Show* in Houston

can't even remember what I did. Actually I do quite a bit on every show, but most of it gets left on the cutting room floor. The motto is, "when in doubt, cut Miss Scott!" If I had all the clips they've cut, I'd have enough film to do Cleopatra," she declared with a shrug. "You see my lines don't really contribute to the plot. I'm just sort of along to see that Mr. Novak eats his dinner, or that he makes it to his next class," she explains. "But this season, they tell me things will change." — Ann Hodges, "Marian Puts Romance in Novak Scripts," *Houston Chronicle*, 9/11/64.

The last episode to be filmed before the second season began was "Let's Dig a Little Grammar." It was a musical effort that showcased two trumpet players at the school. Tommy Sands played an extroverted musician who is also a brilliant student. Novak attempts to stop him from dropping out to pursue a career in music. The other student, a shy introvert who is the superior musician, was played by youthful veteran Johnny Crawford:

"JoJo" Rizzo (Johnny Crawford) blows some hot trumpet in "Let's Dig a Little Grammar"

I was very familiar with the *Mr. Novak* series. It was a prestigious job to work on that. The scripts were good and highly regarded. They got a wonderful trumpet player for me to mime to. He laid down the music and I took a disc of it home to practice to. I knew how to hold a trumpet but had never studied. Tommy Sands was very professional and I enjoyed working with him. Comic Allan Sherman made his dramatic debut in the episode and was very funny. He was quick with the one liners and was breaking me up the whole time. He had me to where I had to sequester myself to concentrate on my dialogue. James Franciscus was a total pro and it was a joy to act with him. A rewarding shoot. — Interview by Ronald V. Borst.

Making his acting debut was popular singer Allan Sherman. The song parodist recalled getting cast and the rigors of television production:

Sherman, who had been in front of the cameras a comparatively short two years, admits that he never tried acting until Producer Leonard Freeman talked to him about being in the Novak episode.

"My agent called me and I didn't believe him," Sherman said. "So I called Leonard just to confirm it. I remember saying something like… "You are looking, maybe for Cary Grant?'

Freeman assured him that he was looking for Allan Sherman to

Vic Rizzo (Harvey Lembeck) and jazz-band leader Georgie (Allan Sherman) contemplate socks in "Let's Dig a Little Grammar"

play the role of a jazz musician trying to gather a combo for a Las Vegas stand. "Let me tell you, actors earn their money," Sherman declared. "I was on the set at seven in the morning — and I didn't leave until seven that night. I pulled a short day because I wasn't feeling well." At the present, there is only one thing on his mind — getting to a TV set Tuesday evening (Nov. 10) to watch his acting debut. "I'll be in New York at the time," he said, "but even if I'm in the middle of a performance, I'll walk out. This I gotta see." — *Mr. Novak* Publicity Release.

Syndicated television columnist Hal Humphrey gave the star of *Mr. Novak* a further opportunity to air his grievances towards the fan magazines:

Jim Franciscus, that nice young "Mr. Novak" from the TV series of the same name, is getting a lousy reputation with Hollywood's "in" group. He is insisting that publicity people write only facts about him. Nobody this square has landed around here since Lawrence Welk, who still has the same wife and accordion. In a town which overlooks that Lassie is a male and has already forgotten why Eddie Fisher left Debbie Reynolds, Franciscus hasn't a chance of getting his way — but he's still trying. And making a lot of people mad. The latest edict to the MGM publicity staff where "Novak" is filmed and likewise to the NBC network is that he will not submit to interviews for fan magazines. "Those magazines are trash, completely untruthful. When Dean Jagger was in the hospital last year, one of these magazines had me calling on him and saying, 'Please forgive me Dean for causing your ulcer.' It was ridiculous. I wasn't even at the hospital and of course said no such thing to Dean or anyone else," Franciscus maintains. The fan magazine editors' response to the Franciscus boycott is naturally quite violent and reflected in their pages with more untruths about the blue-eyed and blond TV hero. — "Franciscus Flunks Hollywood Aptitude Test," Beckley, West Virginia, *Post-Herald*, 9/14/64.

James Franciscus addressed reporters and educators during a close-circuit screening from Chicago at KTAR-TV. He outlined the policies for the new season's programs:

> "*Mr. Novak* will not be quite so interested in causes as last year, and it will be more personal. There will still be the same concern on real problems of education, but they will be submerged in the story line, and individuals will be more important." As for himself, he will not take the leading role as often as last season, but will share top spot with Dean Jagger, who plays Jefferson High's principal. "The stories this year will be quite strong. Three cause stories will be done on a very personal basis. Unless you personalize a story through one teen-ager, contact with an audience is lost, except for a riot, which we will do. If you don't personalize a child who becomes pregnant, or an individual who gets syphilis, which we are going to do, then the idea of the program becomes too generalized." But what was probably most revealing for this viewer was the concern the professional educators had in a television series. They spoke about how "Mr. Novak" had improved their image in their own communities, and of the many pupils who had been influenced by the show to become teachers. — "'Mr. Novak' to Be More Personal, Says Franciscus," *Arizona Republic*, 9/16/64; and Mary Anne Corpin, "Franciscus Calls Premiere His Most Difficult Role," *Baton Rouge Advocate*, 9/20/64.

As the new season was about to begin, there had been a major change with the departure of Jeanne Bal. A new producer had been assigned with his own ideas about the series' content. The star was under increasing pressure and had alienated many publicity outlets. While the show was still popular and critically respected, the second season would not be an easy one.

Chapter Seven

Sophomore Year —
Mr. Novak's Second Season
(First Half)

The *Mr. Novak* series' second season debuted on September 22, 1964. It was broadcast on the NBC network and returned to its previous Tuesday 7:30 to 8:30 P.M. timeslot. "Moonlighting" was directed by Richard Donner and received primarily good notices:

TONIGHT'S PREMIERE NIGHT ON NBC-TV!

7:30 Mr. Novak

Back for his sophomore year comes America's favorite teacher, played by James Franciscus. Tonight, an emergency forces John Novak to "moonlight" at another job. Co-star Dean Jagger, as Principal Vane, deals with the case.

> Summer vacation is over, and "Mr. Novak" is back for another semester. "Moonlighting," initial episode for the second season was a superior, qualitative, tee-off choice, a departure from past "Novaks" in that it centers on the personal problems of the teacher instead of the students. While the word "message" is one that is odious to most producers, Leonard Freeman had admirably succeeded here in not only presenting a strong and often moving story, but at the same time pinpointing the plight of the teacher who doesn't earn enough for more than his everyday needs. What does he do when an emergency arises? He turns to "moonlighting" — that's taking a part-time job at night to supplement his income. A well-written story by Meyer Dolinsky deals with Novak's sorry situation when his father becomes ill, and there is a great financial strain on the son to give his pop proper medical attention. He can only do this by taking a job parking cars at nights, and the long, long hours not only cuts into his efficiency as a teacher, it lowers his stature in the eyes of his students. Eventually, his principal works a way out of the unhappy dilemma facing Novak. James Franciscus turns in a highly sensitive and skillful portrayal of the idealistic teacher suddenly faced with the economics facts of life. Dean Jagger is, as always, most believable as the principal. Good support comes from Joe de Santis, Frank Ferguson, Bert Freed, Mabel Albertson. Richard Donner directs it very well, and all in all, it adds up to a very good show. — Daku, "Telepix Reviews," *Daily Variety*, 9/24/64.

Laure Georges and her girlfriends were also impressed with the first show of the new season:

> There were two new girls to our weekly Novak Night party which brought the number up to an even dozen. This first episode was especially poignant because of the seriousness of the theme. Mr. Novak's father was ill and JF portrayed a distressed, frazzled teacher trying to earn extra $ for hospital expenses. Both JF and Dean Jagger excelled at their emotional roles. During our discussion after the show, we talked about how hard it must be for teachers to earn a living. We knew for a fact that our science teacher was moonlighting because we had seen him at the local grocery store bagging groceries in the evening. — Int.

Original reviews of the second season's episodes can be found in the episode guide.

In the trade-magazine ads for the season premiere the billing read, "Starring James Franciscus and Dean Jagger with Phyllis Avery." This implied full co-starring status for the new regular in the series.

On the same day as the "Moonlighting" broadcast, it was announced that the censors had rejected a controversial script for the new season:

> NBC-TV censors have nixed a "Mr. Novak" script, "He Grabs a Train and Rides," on grounds it is not suitable for the 7:30 P.M. timeslot. Story, penned by Sterling Silliphant, deals with a Negro narcotics addict, and the problems that drove him to it. Series is produced by Leonard Freeman. Silliphant story was to concern James Franciscus and a Negro youth, bitter and hostile. Youth goes to college, and the high school teacher meets him when he's home for a visit. Teacher learns the youth has "two monkeys on his back"; that he feels he must succeed for his family and race, and that actually he doesn't want to go to college, because he is very good at working with his hands, etc. — *Daily Variety*, 9/22/64.

"The Crowd Pleaser" went into production and was the story of Principal Vane being talked into running for State Superintendent of Schools. He ultimately loses the election. This outcome would be changed when additional scenes were shot near the end of the year to accommodate a major shift in the series.

Phyllis Avery had two daughters who were most pleased that their mother was now a member of the faculty at Jefferson High School:

> When Mom suddenly becomes Girls' Vice-Principal at one of the best known high schools in the country, what do her daughters do? "The reaction was unbelievable," smiled petite and efficient Miss Avery. "Understandably enough, it was pointed not toward the fact that I would be working in a popular series, but that I would have a speaking acquaintance with James Franciscus." The girls, Avery, 15, and Anne, 14, are currently attending Westlake School in Los Angeles. "For the last year, they have been getting their co-educational kicks watching 'Mr. Novak' every week, and I do mean every Tuesday night," Miss Avery laughed. "You see — Westlake is an all-girl school." — Maureen James, "Daughters Delight in 'Mr. Novak' Role," *Boston Sunday Advertiser*, 9/27/64.

In the last week of September, production was due to begin on "The Rich Who Are Poor." The scripts had passed muster with all of the advisory boards as well as NBC's Department of Standards and Practices.

Dianne Lennon: GOD BLESSED US WITH 2 BABIES IN 10 MONTHS!

RADIO TV MIRROR

OCTOBER 35¢

The Woman Who Taught "Mr. Novak" To Love His Wife

Jim Franciscus ("Mr. Novak") with Kellie, wife Kitty and baby Jamie

Whose Wife Is Dick Chamberlain Kissing Now?

Why David Janssen Rejected His Father's Name

What Patty Duke Learned About Love — From A Stranger

As the new season got underway, James Franciscus continued to be annoyed by the fan magazines. His wife Kitty remembered a particularly irritating cover of *TV Radio Mirror*:

Jim hated the TV/ Movie fan magazines. They would take one teeny little thing... then build it up and make it something with innuendos where it wasn't right. He thought it was so dishonest and he couldn't stand that. An article that made Jim so mad was the one in *TV Radio Mirror* that said "The Woman Who Taught Mr. Novak to Love His Wife" and it turned out to be his mother. He felt these kinds of articles were insulting to his family. — Int.

The article in question was not really that bad and actually had some positive content, but Franciscus had built up a hatred for the magazines which would continue for the rest of the series' run. His chief objection seemed to have been the misleading covers that would promise scandalous articles.

September was ending and Franciscus gave an interview on the NBC lot to reporters and teachers:

"Scripts are submitted to the National Education Association committee, which tells the director 'this does or does not happen in school, and, this is or is not a problem.'" Mr. Franciscus is on the side of realism. We learned that he does some rewriting of the scripts to take the pomposity out of his role. "Do you believe that a teacher on TV should smoke and sip an occasional drink?" he was asked. "I believe that the average teacher does one or both," he said. "I think it's the truth, although it may tarnish the image somewhat. The NEA group agreed with me. It was the network that was a little worried." The show has received more than 30 awards from various educational and entertainment sources. — Robert Houston, "Hailed by Many Teachers — 'Mr. Novak' Tries to Be Human," *Omaha Sunday World Herald*, 9/27/64.

After so much sincerity and hard work by Neuman and Freeman, the NBC network had stopped the V.D. scripts from being produced:

> NBC-TV blue-pencillers have killed a two-part teledrama dealing with venereal disease, which was to have been on MGM-TV's "Mr. Novak" and "Dr. Kildare" series. Episode, "The Rich Who Are Poor," written by E. Jack Neuman, was to have gone before the cameras this week, when the word came the NBC-TV censor had won a heated argument, and the yarn was tabled. It was a 160-page screenplay by Neuman. Idea was to have the VD story originate on "Novak," involving a teen-ager, and on the second hour of the story, move over to the studio's stablemate, "Kildare," for the final unfolding. Although NBC-TV censors wouldn't permit the VD yarn, a telefilm dealing with venereal disease was seen last season on "The Nurses," which is on CBS-TV. — *Daily Variety*, 9/29/64.

Neuman and *Kildare's* producer Norman Felton were angered and frustrated by this last-minute rejection and valiantly tried to save the scripts:

> "We pulled out every stop to persuade them to change their minds," said Neuman. "I was on the telephone upside-down and backwards," said Norman Felton. "I believed in this project. But there was no recourse." — *McCall's*, 9/65.

Producer Leonard Freeman commented on the rejection of the controversial scripts on drug addiction and venereal disease:

> Two major Novak efforts this season written by two of the finest playwrights were scuttled by NBC's censors before they reached the sound stage. The first was a Stirling Silliphant drama on narcotics addiction, and the second a play by E. Jack Neuman on venereal disease. Novak producer Leonard Freeman says both shows are dead, that he received an absolute no form NBC to which there is no appeal. He said no reason was given for the rejection except that the scripts were unacceptable. I have read the Silliphant script which is a skillful and sensitive story of a young Negro who turns to drugs out of frustrations of his own existence in a white world. There is a powerful scene in which Novak puts the boy through cold turkey — a torturing experience not only to cleanse him of drugs but to create a link between the two men, to bridge the chasm in his life. Freeman says of the script; "If we did this right — and there's no guarantee — it could be one of television's most memorable shows, one of the great ones." The VD script came after investigation showed an alarming recent increase in incidence of venereal disease among teen-agers — "up to 700% in this age bracket," Freeman said. "CBS Reports," said Freeman, "might do a documentary on this problem which would be seen by maybe 8 million people. But on these two shows, it could have made as many as 60 million aware of the situation." — Cecil Smith, "The TV Scene," *The Los Angeles Times*, 11/10/64.

Although the scripts were rejected, their having been submitted to the network showed the progressive nature of the *Mr. Novak* television series and the writing skills of E. Jack Neuman.

"With a Hammer in His Hand, Lord, Lord!" aired and was well received.

Andy Towner (Frank Silvera) encourages
his son Frank (Wayne Grice) in
"Boy Under Glass"

LEO DUROCHER shows James Franciscus
how to throw a knuckle ball in "Mr. Novak"
at 7:30 this evening on Channel 3.

In "Boy Under Glass," Mr. Novak becomes unpopular because he is failing a poor student who is a promising baseball player. The boy, who is African American, and his father believe that prejudice will prevent the youth from making better money except as a professional athlete. The student was played by Wayne Grice and the father by veteran character actor Frank Silvera. Baseball manager Leo Durocher appeared as a guest star. There was some location filming at Culver City High School which had a full-sized baseball diamond.

Series' regular Vince Howard had never acted in his life prior to being cast. He acknowledged help that he had received, dispelled a rumor that had plagued the star and expressed satisfaction with his developing acting skills:

> Howard says credit for his improvement as an actor should go to Dean Jagger. "Dean frequently goes out of his way to give me tips. I think everyone on our show has learned a lot from him." Howard denied rumors of a feud between Jagger and co-star James Franciscus. "The (feud) was started by the fan magazines, which really have it in for Jim. Actually, Jim is one of the nicest guys in the world. Ironically, many of his problems started because he is such a devoted husband. During last television season Jim discovered he didn't have much time to be with his wife, Kitty, who whenever he had time, he wanted to have it without interruptions, especially for interviews with those silly fan magazines... you know, those magazines with stories like, 'What Haley Mills Father Told Her About Sex.' Well it didn't take long for the magazines to go after Jim. They began to print ugly and distorted stories about him. They capped the year by voting Jim 'the most uncooperative star of the year.' He didn't mind that. I think he relished the award." Howard appeared in nearly two thirds of the *Novak* shows last year, but seldom played a major role. One of the exceptions was an episode in which he had a 20-minute scene — one of the longest scenes for any performer during the TV season. "I completed that scene in one take," he said with a proud grin, "and I knew then I had come a long way." In all, the program will have about 10 performers in semi-regular status. — Jack Major, "He Escaped to Show Biz — Many of Vince's Friends Wound Up in Jail," *Akron Beacon-Journal*, 10/4/64.

"Visions of Sugar Plums" aired and was a showcase for new cast member Phyllis Avery.

A major magazine described reactions to the series by educators and the NEA's advisory panel. There had been criticism from teachers about Mr. Novak's social drinking, romantic encounters and an off-campus fight with a student. These protests were in the minority of the nation's teachers. The series was warmly endorsed by the NEA and all scripts would be reviewed in advance by a rotating advisory panel. Henry S. Noerdlinger, manager of the NEA's Los Angeles information center, would also review the scripts. In some cases, requests were made to alter the scripts prior to filming. Sometimes this would be done and at other times the scripts would be filmed as originally written. A case in which the panel agreed with E. Jack Neuman's script yielded a positive outcome:

> The teachers stood staunchly by Neuman in approving a downbeat ending to *The Exile*, the story of a dropout. This episode involved a student who had left high school and stayed out until he was over-age. When he wanted to reenter day school, because he wanted no part of adult evening classes, Principal Vane turned him away. This ending worried Dan Schreiber, director of the NEA's Project Dropout, who felt it was wrong to show a school rejecting anyone who wanted an education. Wires and phone calls flew back and forth between Washington and Hollywood. In the end, the script was filmed as originally written. "The panel members were convinced the story needed a tragic ending to shock youngsters and their parents," says Henry Noerdlinger. "As it turned out, the film was so effective in dramatizing the plight of the dropout that educators and sociologists everywhere asked for prints of it, and the Nassau County, N.Y., jail requested it as an educational film for prisoners." — Stanley Gordon, "Can Mr. Novak Keep the Teachers Happy?" *Look*, 10/6/64.

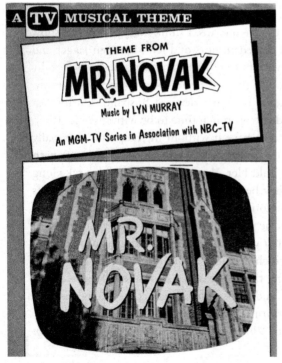

Tony Dow returned for his fourth role in the series with the filming of "Johnny Ride the Pony: One, Two, Three." He did not reprise his previous role of George Scheros but instead played a member of an off-campus club that carries out a dangerous initiation hazing.

October also brought a different kind of honor to the *Mr. Novak* series. Issue No. 91 of *Mad* magazine featured the satiric story "Mr. Nudnik." It was written by Arnie Kogen and illustrated with brilliant caricatures by Mort Drucker. Many of the students at Jeffyson High School have crushes on the handsome teacher including boys and the janitor. Mr. Vay, the principal,

literally has patience and wisdom written all over him. The yarn spoofed Dean Jagger's eccentric way of line delivery and featured "Miss Paganini." The climax of the story found Mr. Nudnik passing a poor student whose brother is the show's sponsor. It perfectly captured the look and feel of the series in a humorous way.

Dean Jagger gave a syndicated interview in which he recalled the moment that he realized the effect of the series' popularity:

Last season he underwent some corrective surgery and for some time after was on a rather strict diet which banned, among other things, alcohol. One evening, however, when his wife and child were away visiting relatives, Jagger dropped by a popular Sunset Strip restaurant for dinner on his way home from the studio. "I was waiting for a table, and sat down at the bar and had a glass of club soda to pass the time," he said. "And all of a sudden I was aware that every person in the room was looking at me in shocked silence — Mr. Vane, the high school principal, was sitting at a bar, drinking! They didn't approve at all, but the reception was most gratifying." — Cynthia Lowery, "'Mr. Novak' Show Presents Realistic School Scenes," Baton Rouge, Louisiana, *State-Times*, 10/8/64.

"Little Girl Lost" aired to good reviews for Davey Davison's performance.

Mr. Novak, Shahri Javid (Claudine Longet) and Principal Vane in "The Silent Dissuaders"

"The Silent Dissuaders" was the story of an Iranian exchange science teacher and her efforts to convince a gifted student to pursue further education instead of being forced to marry. Pressure was being put on the girl by her mother, boyfriend and society's expectations. The teacher was portrayed by Claudine Longet and the student was Kim Darby. Her boyfriend was played by Buck Taylor in his second appearance. He was impressed by his co-stars:

Claudine was very beautiful with a French accent. She was a graceful lady and very good. Kim was a very sensitive, thinking actress and I knew she was going to go far in the business. Franciscus and Jagger were just as good as before and I liked the part of the boyfriend. — Int.

Broadcasting published an Arbitron ratings chart for mid-October. *Combat* led the Tuesday 7:30 to 8:00 P.M. slot with a 17.2 rating and a 33.0 share. *Mr. Novak* placed third with a 14.5 rating and a 28.0 share. *Combat* also led the 8:00 to 8:30 slot with a 20.4 rating and a 35.0 share while *Novak* lagged in third place with a 16.2 rating and a 28.0 share. *Novak's* ratings would slightly improve over the course of the second season but *Combat* would always lead the time slot.

In mid-October Marian Collier traveled to New York to receive her own award from the Niagara Falls Teacher's Association:

Marian Collier, James Woelfle, and Dr. Lois V. Edinger at the Niagara Falls Teachers Association event

Dr. Lois Edinger, who was president of the NEA, was there and they were all so great to me. They were so happy to see me and said I was so perfect in the part of the Home Ec. teacher. I didn't dare tell them about my background in school. I was proud to get the silver serving tray award from actual teachers. I still have it and still use it. I told them that all of us in the series hoped to entertain, but also hoped to teach something. We were serious about trying to capture the teaching profession on the screen. I also told them that 25 percent of letters to the show were from teachers who often offered suggestions on how to do our job. I presented a cake from the students of Jefferson High School to the head of the NFTA. It was a great experience. Jim and Dean were so busy that they didn't want to do personal appearances. There were many requests of both of them. Jim did very few and I think Dean did a couple... sometimes with Jack. — Int.

"One Monday Afternoon" aired on October 27 and on the same day production began on "An Elephant is Like a Tree." It starred Tony Bill as a student who had been blinded in an accident. Celeste Holm portrayed his overprotective mother. The script was written by John D. F. Black who based the story on experience and was impressed by the actors:

> I had a blind Uncle and I wanted to write an episode based on him. He sold newspapers on a corner. I wanted to do something about blindness. When I told Lenny (Freeman) I wanted to write a script about a blind student he said... "Do it." Celeste Holm was marvelous as the mother. Tony Bill was outstanding and completely believable in the role of the blind boy. — Int.

The rejected two-part script by E. Jack Neuman, concerning a youth who had contracted VD, received support from a high-ranking member of the medical community:

U. S. Surgeon Luther Terry has appealed to NBC to reconsider its nix on two MGM-TV telefilms dealing with venereal disease. Before the NBC blue-pencilling, the vidpix had been scheduled for MGM-TV's "Mr. Novak" and "Dr. Kildare." In a letter to NBC prexy Robert Kintner, the Surgeon General stressed public interest points in a dramatization of the social problem. Dr. Terry pointed out VD rate has been jumping at a shocking rate, particularly among teenagers. With TV chary on the subject, because of the intimacies involved, Terry and the Public Health Service have had tough going alerting the public and juves about the alarming VD trend. A presentation in good taste on programs such as "Novak" and "Kildare" would greatly benefit the government in warning the citizenry of the growing problem, Terry said. The VD two-parter was nixed last month after a reportedly heated wrangle between NBC censors and MGM-TV. The nix came one week before episode, "The Rich Who are Poor," was scheduled for filming. — *Daily Variety*, 10/28/64.

One of the leading newspapers in the country commented further on this appeal for the controversial scripts:

The National Broadcasting Company, which declined to present a two-part television drama about a high school boy who contracts a venereal disease, had been asked by the American Public Health Association to reconsider its decision. Dr. John D. Porterfield, president of the association and also coordinator of medical affairs at the University of California, made the request in a letter. In urging N.B.C. to give "serious consideration" to televising the drama, Dr. Porterfield said it might be helpful in combating a social problem, especially among teen-agers. It was learned that N.B.C. also had received six or eight similar letters from other persons associated with health groups or social welfare. In a formal reply to Dr. Porterfield, N.B.C. explained the reasons for its position but did not indicate it would reopen the matter. It was understood that N.B.C. officials held to the opinion that if the drama were to be valid it would have to contain certain passages and dialogue, including a discussion of sexual intimacies, which they did not consider appropriate for television and especially the "Mr. Novak" show. It was said, however, that N.B.C. did not consider the subject of venereal disease to inappropriate for television. — Val Adams, "N.B.C.-TV Urged to Review Ban on Youth Drama," *New York Times*, 10/29/64.

Ironically, the finished scripts contained very little discussion of sexual intimacies and were presented in good taste by Neuman.

Photoplay magazine interviewed the two stars of *Dr. Kildare* and *Mr. Novak*. They had diverse reactions to the banning of the scripts by N.B.C. Richard Chamberlain felt the studio had made the right decision:

"I think there are better places for dealing with venereal disease than on the *Kildare* show," he stated. He admitted that he had not read the script by Jack Neuman, but he knew the general outline and subject manner. While he conceded the worthiness of the intentions, he didn't feel the show should be filmed. "After all," he remarked, "*Dr. Kildare* is an entertainment show. I wouldn't presume to tell people what to do about syphilis. If this particular script fit into our pattern of entertainment, then

I would have no objection to doing it. But I don't see how it could be, when the subject is syphilis. I don't see how a show about syphilis can really be informative unless it gets right down to the clinical facts. And how are you going to do that on prime-time television? My basic comment is that there are other agencies, dispensing information about syphilis," he said. "Departments of the government, public health offices and schools have the responsibility for telling people the facts about venereal disease and its treatments." — Jay Richards, "Dick Chamberlain vs. Jim Franciscus: Should V.D. Be Discussed on TV?," 6/65.

James Franciscus gave an entirely different point of view to *Photoplay*:

"I think it's a pretty frightening thing when networks can dictate what can and what cannot be seen on television," he said. "Here is a subject — venereal disease-that is vital to the public interest. Yet NBC is afraid to talk about it on the one show where the problem should be discussed — *Mr. Novak*. It would do much more good to have venereal disease discussed on our show than to put it on a documentary at 10 o'clock in the evening. Most teenagers wouldn't see it at that time, and they must be given the facts." He laid the blame for the ban of the two-part show directly on network officials. "They claim they wouldn't allow it because they were afraid sponsors wouldn't want their products associated with a show about syphilis," said Jim. "I think it was just timidity on their part. At least one of our sponsors said he had no objection at all, for any reason, to going ahead with the show. If a network is going with a show, it should go all the way. It shouldn't dictate what we can put on the air. They say the public is behind the artistic development, but I think that's wrong. I think artistic development is behind the public's progress in thinking. Television was floating along, putting out innocuous fluff until a show like *The Defenders* came along to demonstrate that ideas could be dealt with entertainingly. People are ready to accept thoughtful material-if only the networks would realize it." — 6/65.

Photoplay also heard from E. Jack Neuman, who had written the controversial scenario:

"My script raised two very valid questions: What is education doing about VD and what is the medical profession doing about it? The usual form of instruction on venereal disease is for a very embarrassed and awkward teacher to run a half-hour film on the subject and ask students afterward, 'Any Questions?' This happens once or twice a year. I'm not unaware that *Kildare* and *Novak* are entertainment shows. But I think you can entertain people with information that is vital to them. People must learn that syphilis is intolerable, not the victims of it." However, when he was asked if there was any chance that NBC would reverse its decision, he responded sadly, "No." — 6/65.

The rejection was unfortunate but did show that E. Jack Neuman had real foresight and integrity in writing the scripts. The *Mr. Novak* series was a progressive program and had brought many cutting-edge stories to the airwaves.

In the midst of this controversial publicity, it was announced that for the second time, a leading player in the show would be withdrawing:

> MGM-TV's "Mr. Novak" series has a dropout problem. Last season, Jeanne Bal, who played the vice principal in the series about high schoolers, exited the show on grounds there wasn't sufficient meat in her role to warrant her staying in it. Yesterday, Phyllis Avery, who portrays vice principal for girls in the series, said she has renegotiated her exclusive pact with producer Leonard Freeman, because she has been "disappointed" in the development of her role. Miss Avery now will work on a non-exclusive basis. Previously her pact called for her to be in 7 out of 13 episodes produced. Producer Freeman confirmed Miss Avery's statement, explaining it was difficult to find scripts with robust roles for her part. — *Daily Variety*, 10/30/64.

Bob Schultz observed this second cast change that was to be detrimental to the show's continuing success:

> Freeman saying they couldn't find enough roles for Phyllis was bullshit. It probably was for the same reason to cut costs and save on residual payments. It was another dumb decision. She had been given third billing when the season began and was the third lead on the show. To lose two leads is suicidal for a series. There were too many changes going on. After this happened, Jack must have really thrown up his hands and realized that the ship was sinking and that he should develop other projects. After this he would just stay in his bungalow and work on his script rewrites. — Int.

This was a very distressing and damaging situation. The irony is that Phyllis had appeared to good advantage in episodes which had aired up to that time. She was establishing a rapport with the viewing audience that started to overcome the departure of Jeanne Bal.

The beginning of November brought the release of the feature film *Youngblood Hawke*, which starred James Franciscus. This Warner Bros. motion picture had been filmed before the *Mr. Novak* series had begun and gained much pre-release publicity due to Franciscus's popularity as the television teacher. The film was based on a popular novel by Herman Wouk and the main character was an uneducated aggressive young writer who claws his way to success. The film was only a modest success at the box office. His wife Kitty recalled the film:

> Jim loved the book but felt he was wrong for the part. The main character is an uneducated big tough guy... a punk. There was nothing you could do to Jim's face to make him look unintelligent. Jim did his best but he wasn't the character from the popular book. The movie didn't do very well at the box office. — Int.

"From the Brow of Zeus" went into production and was the story of a ten-year-old genius who enrolls at Jefferson High and is taunted by some of the older students. The boy was played by Michael Petit and returning for her second stint was Beverly Washburn:

Blonde Beverly Washburn (top left) and
Michael Petit (center) in
"From the Brow of Zeus"

Since my previous appearance I had seen some episodes and was really impressed with the quality of the show. I was glad to be cast again. Even though I had worked with him before, and was a veteran of the acting profession, I was star struck to work with James Franciscus. There was something about him that was so sexy. He was soft spoken, impeccable and charismatic. He really fit the bill in the role of Novak. Michael Petit was fabulous... and an incredible young actor. Vince Howard was very good in our scene and a nice man who was fine singer. The whole shoot was a joy. — Int.

A syndicated column lamented the high rating for the *Combat* series over *Mr. Novak*:

It is a shame, besides a blow against civility, that a line sergeant in Combat is a bigger hero to most of us than a dedicated high school teacher. The Nielsen rating service, the standard upon which TV networks base their programming decisions, recently ranked ABC's Combat series as No. 9 in its hit parade of top 50 shows. Mr. Novak, which appears opposite Combat, hasn't even enough points to place among the top 50. Some may try to seek solace for this rupture in our cultural taste by claiming that the kids control TV sets at the early hour of 7:30 on Tuesday when both shows are on. If that should be true, then it is time we told our kids to watch Mr. Novak that evening, or turn off the TV. The values induced by an hour of Combat have little or no bearing on what our kids must face up to later. Mr. Novak, on the other hand, is a show with some substance. It may not have the emotional impact generated by the business of killing, but Novak's fight to make this a better world is certainly more vital and contemporary than the one being waged by the weary line sergeant in Combat. Technically, Combat is a good enough series, and were it winning against some inane comedy or variety show, there would be no cause for alarm. The fact it is beating out Mr. Novak proves how lazy and undiscriminating we are. — Hal Humphrey, "With Nielsen Help: Bury Us? We'll Do It Ourselves," *The Los Angeles Times*, 11/6/64.

"Let's Dig a Little Grammar" aired and Allan Sherman's dramatic debut received good notices.

The introduction of primitive computers was the subject of the next episode to be produced. They were called teaching machines and a trial run was being implemented at Jefferson High. Nehemiah Persoff played a teacher who feared they will put human teachers out of their jobs. Returning for his second appearance on *Novak*, and playing the aggressive salesman of the teaching machines, was Martin Landau:

Robert Coolidge (Martin Landau) instructs a student in the application of a teaching machine in "Enter a Strange Animal"

This episode was about a teacher and a machine. By adding the machine the teachers will fade. The concept was progress... and was it progress? In an early scene where I'm explaining the teaching machines to students, I decided to play it like a machine. I was very rapid in my dialogue delivery. There was a lot of dialogue and I learned it the night before. Nicky Persoff was an actor that I had many a cup of coffee with. When I heard he was in the episode, I knew that his pedantic style would be a good contrast to my aggressive salesman.

The final scene, which is a confrontation between Nicky's teacher and my salesman, was added at the end of a Friday's filming. Word came from Jack Neuman's office that we were short on time. He gave us some new pages of dialogue that he had written. We had to do another five or six minutes and we had to learn and film the scene before we could leave. Nicky's teacher confronts the salesman and says he is not interested in experiments in teaching but is only interested in profits. The salesman doesn't give a damn about the students. It was a powerful scene and nicely capped the episode. It was a prophetic story as computers are now doing as much or more teaching than the human educators. Director Alvin Glaser left me alone. Jim Franciscus was always there. He was always present in the moment. I could look in his eye and see a person. The *Mr. Novak* series was head and shoulders above most of what was on the air at that time. — Int.

Randy Kirby was a young actor who had worked for several years in theatre on the east coast. He had been a member of Equity and came to California in the fall of 1964. Shortly after arriving he was cast in a major television series:

I had watched a few episodes of *Mr. Novak* and liked it. In my first week in California I was cast in "Enter a Strange Animal." The script was very powerful and I was looking forward to my first role in television. Director Alvin Ganzer was deeply committed to getting everything right and that was a comfort to me. I thought James Franciscus was a classy guy. I got a feeling of professional warmth and accessibility from Dean Jagger. With those guys a high bar was expected. I did notice Franciscus and Jagger off camera and they were talking. They seemed to enjoy each other's company and were laughing at some private joke between them.

Martin Landau was very intense in a good way. There was never even a half a second of a lack of focus. He had a power of character that made him a real person in the role of the aggressive computer salesman. Nehemiah Persoff scared me at first with his intensity but as soon as he opened his mouth he was nice. When I saw the primitive computers on the set I was very intrigued and thought they would end up being used in the future. The storyline of the teachers being worried about being replaced was a genuine concern. The show's concept of computers being used in schools was prophetic. My being on a prestige show like *Novak* really helped my career. I was with the William Morris Agency and it got me in good with them. — Randy Kirby Interview, 10/12/16.

There were many times when the hours were long and arduous. Bob Schultz would find that his last weekday would often go into the late hours:

On Fridays there were always a lot of pick up shots to do in the evening. We would wrap late around 7 P.M. and then they would announce that we had a lot of pickups to do. Sometimes they would bring food in. I remember coming home at 11:30 on Friday nights. Those Fridays were killers. — Int.

E. Jack Neuman had not been featured in any articles or publicity as the second season progressed. He continued to work on script rewrites and for the most part remained in his bungalow on the lot. Bob Schultz recalled changes in the former producer and creator of the show:

In the second season, I had a lot more scotch and waters in the evening at Jack's bungalow. He would be working and would stop and we would have some drinks. We'd have some laughs but didn't talk about the show at all. We would just blow our steam off for an hour and then we'd go home. In the first season, when we'd gather, we'd have the laughs but he would talk a lot about the show with us. — Int.

Marian Collier observed changes in the principal of Jefferson High:

Dean Jagger hadn't been like he was in the first season. He just didn't give what he used to give. He was always professional but he'd just stand there and say his lines. I think it might have been partially because Jeanne wasn't there. I think Freeman messed him up. — Int.

"The People Doll: You Wind It Up and It Makes Mistakes" and "Boy Under Glass" were broadcast in the later part of November.

In a promotional description for "Born of Kings and Angels," which aired on December 1, the series was described as having ratings trouble and might not make it to a third semester. There are had been cast changes and different approaches to story content and *Combat* continued to trounce *Mr. Novak* in the Nielsen ranks. The show's ratings had continued to be respectable but low.

Burgess Meredith would be appearing on an upcoming two-part episode. It would be titled "Faculty Follies" and would feature the regular cast in musical and comic performances as part of a show to raise funds for the school. Filming began on December 1 and was a long shoot of twelve days to complete the two-part episode. Franciscus's wife Kitty recalled a prank played by her husband on the episode's director:

In the episode the cast performs comic songs in the school auditorium. Jim appeared in a Beatle wig carrying a guitar, along with Vince Howard and Bill

Kitty Franciscus subs for Jim during the "Droppity Dropouts" number
in the "Faculty Follies" episode

Zuckert, who also wore wigs. They were to lip sync to a song called "Droppity Dropouts." Jim loved director Joe Sargent. During a rehearsal for the "Dropouts" number, Jim suggested I put on the wig, carry the guitar and go out with Vince and Bill. He wanted to see how long it would take for Joe to notice. I went out and for quite a while he didn't notice until Jim came out behind the three of us. Joe screamed with laughter and we all had quite a chuckle about it. Jim did love to play pranks sometimes. — Int.

L-R, André Phillipe, Marian Collier, and Larry Thor bring down the house with the "Workshop Annie" number in "Faculty Follies"

Marian Collier, who had formerly been a dancer in Las Vegas, would enjoy working on the episodes:

I loved performing my "Workshop Annie" number. Larry Thor, who appeared with me, was a great radio actor. André Phillipe, who also appeared, had been a professional entertainer and was great. It was so much fun to do. I loved that episode so much and I think the whole cast of regulars were happy to have more to do than usual. They were all wonderful in their stage performances. It was funny to see Jim in his Beatle wig during his number. He was so good in that. — Int.

David Sheiner returned in the two-parter as music teacher Paul Webb. He recalled a difficult scene and an impression of Burgess Meredith:

In "Faculty Follies" I had a long speech on the stage. It took six or seven takes. I had to say, "These young people who are studying music have all become magicians... the word was musicians. Finally I got it and everyone applauded. Burgess Meredith was a very pleasant man. He had difficulty with his dialogue which surprised me as he was a major talent. Television can be very tricky for people who are used to film. The quicker pace and amount of dialogue can be a difficult change. I thought he was slightly slower than he should have been. It was a great shoot and I really enjoyed the cast performing the musical numbers. Marian was great when she sang "Woodshop Annie" and Jim was funny in his Beatle wig. — Int.

During early filming of these musical episodes came devastating news for fans of the show. Principal Vane was leaving Jefferson High School:

> Dean Jagger has asked for and been granted release from his co-starring role in MGM-TV's "Mr. Novak" series on advice of his physician. Jagger, who portrays Principal Albert Vane in the series, has suffered recurrence of an ulcer that bothered him last season. He has been ordered to take a complete rest until full recovery of the ailment. Jagger has not worked on the show for the past two weeks after doing six episodes in advance. No replacement yet has been set. — *Daily Variety*, 12/4/64.

Chapter Eight

Second Midterm —
Mr. Novak's Second Season
(Continued)

The loss of Dean Jagger was a major blow to the series, which was in real trouble with low ratings and changes in content and personnel. He had been a large part in the show's critical success and was very effective playing against Jim Franciscus's Mr. Novak. In the days following this startling announcement, many columnists hinted at another reason for Jagger's departure other than his ulcers:

> Dean Jagger quits his school principal Mr. Novak click in Jan. blaming it on ulcers. But there's been a big feud. — Herb Lyon, "Tower Ticker," *Chicago Tribune*, 12/4/64.

A feud *was* part of the reason but it had not occurred with Jim Franciscus. There was another member of the *Novak* production team who had been at odds with the veteran actor for some time.

James Franciscus was shocked by this decision and realized Dean Jagger's importance to the series:

> It was a jolt because Dean was so much a part of the show, equally as important as Novak. He was the rock of Gibraltar and wonderful. — *The TV Collector*, 11–12, 89.

Franciscus's wife Kitty recalled her husband's reaction to the news that his co-star was leaving the show:

> When Dean had to leave the show due to ulcers... Jim didn't want him to go. He really liked and respected Dean and felt they worked very well together. There was never any feuding between them during the run of the series. Along with being angry at the fan magazines and their salacious lies about his personal life, Jim was very upset by repeated references to the feuding. They were professionals who were always cordial to each other. — Int.

Marian Collier lamented the departure of Jagger:

> We were all stunned when Dean left the show. I knew he hadn't been happy for a while but as far as I was concerned, when he was gone, the show as gone. As the second season had progressed, we all knew the show was declining. All of us teachers had little or nothing to do and there were too many changes. — Int.

A syndicated columnist reported this unfortunate cast loss and recapped several discouraging facets of the show's history:

> Things are never stagnant at Jefferson High. That's where "Mr. Novak" teaches in case you are not a fan of the weekly NBC Tuesday-night

series. In fact, more of the faculty leaves each year than the students. Last season Jeanne Bal, who played the assistant principal at the high school, left the show because her part was growing smaller each week. This season, Phyllis Avery came on to assist Dean Jagger, who plays kindly old Mr. Vane, the wise and sincere principal. Miss Avery was also dissatisfied with her duties on the series and would not be around when graduation time arrived. Now comes the most disheartening news of all. Dean Jagger has been forced to quit the show due to a recurrence of an ulcer condition. Jagger's doctors are said to have told the veteran actor to withdraw from the series immediately. Since the show has several episodes already filmed, it will be at least five weeks before a new principal is needed. — William E. Sarmento, "Dean Jagger Forced to Quit," Lowell, Massachusetts, *Sun*, 12/8/64.

Dean Jagger had been at odds with Leonard Freeman for most of the second season's filming. Freeman's, and possibly MGM's, new concept was to lessen the involvement of the other teachers who had been peripherally and regularly involved in most episodes. There were several shows which focused on their specific plots with Novak and a guest star primarily featured. An issue of *TV Guide* which came out in late February discussed changes under Freeman's regime and dissatisfactions with Jagger's established persona:

> The character of Albert Vane ran more to the sweet. Consequently the problems arose from outside sources, and Vane's solutions were perforce too steeped in the milk of human kindness to always make for sharp drama. Already the show had shown the telltale signs. The scripts had been aired dealing with suicide and parricide to name a couple of the obvious concessions for more "excitement" in the series. Dean Jagger was uneasy with the tendency toward melodrama which the scripts had begun to display. Periodically he was unhappy with the writing. — Dwight Whitney, "Adding Curry to the Curriculum," 2/20–26/65.

The "outside sources" were an indication of Freeman's desire to move the stories away from the school, which had been a critically praised facet of the first season. There may have directives from the MGM execs to boost the previous season's low ratings with more sensationalistic plotlines. This approach had not significantly improved the ratings and the departure of Jeanne Bal and lessening of Phyllis Avery's roles had hurt audience identification. The character of Albert Vane and his interplay with Mr. Novak had been one of the major strengths of the first season which had been produced by E. Jack Neuman. Dean Jagger's side of the conflict was presented in a syndicated piece:

> Fans of the Mr. Novak series appreciated the fact that Albert Vane was not a black-and-white character facing into the sunset at the close of each episode. Probably no one on TV has received more thoughtful laudatory viewer mail than Jagger. It was not by accident that the character of Albert Vane registered with this impact. When the producers hired Dean Jagger they got a package deal. Besides getting an experienced actor who knew his craft, they soon found that Jagger had a conscience about his work and was duty-bound to it regardless of how many waves he caused. What might be called this conflict of interest between Jagger and his employers

naturally led to many hotly debated conferences over what direction a given episode should take. Jagger was always on hand to see that a guest star or a new writer did not corrupt or distort the principal and or his relations with Jefferson High's faculty and students. The attack of ulcers which took Jagger out of a few episodes last season no doubt was repeated early last fall when a new producer put more "message" episodes into the schedule. Jagger's artistic soul was offended. He believed, with some justification, that too much hard moralizing would mean sacrificing the series' humanness, a department where the Vane character shone. Not being the vindictive type (or the type to hire a press agent), Jagger never aired his feeling beyond the studio set. When the doctor finally ordered him to the hospital for ulcer surgery last December, Jagger left the series quietly. — Hal Humphrey, "TV Flunks the Mr. Novak Test," *The Los Angeles Times*, 2/24/65.

The loss of Dean Jagger would be lamented by both journalists and viewers. Bob Schultz observed this regrettable departure of Albert Vane:

Freeman was a stooge for the studio. When Jagger complained about sensationalistic stories that got away from the humanness of the second season, he was right. The original concept by E. Jack had brought critical respect to the series. Freeman must have gone to his superiors at MGM and said that the old man is a pain in the ass and that they should get rid of him. Being a stupid producer, he didn't realize the negative impact on the show with Dean's leaving. Especially after the departure of Jeanne Bal and the lessening of Phyllis Avery's role. Freeman and the studio didn't know what they were doing. The brass couldn't see ahead of their noses. Those guys were all back-stabbers. — Int.

Mr. Novak producer Leonard Freeman

Laure Georges and her friends were also saddened by Principal Vane's departure:

My friend Sue had some shockingly bad news for the Novak Night group. Her uncle worked at NBC and found out that Dean Jagger was leaving the show. Oh No!!! We all admired him so much and enjoyed the way he and Mr. Novak complemented each other. We even began to worry that JF might also leave; the actors were dropping like flies! But relief came swiftly when we were reassured by Sue's uncle that Jim would continue with the show. We vowed to watch the remaining new episodes still featuring Dean Jagger with close interest and appreciation. — Int.

The "'A' as in Anxiety" episode, which featured June Harding as the pressured student, aired on December 8.

The next day brought news that a new principal had been selected for the series:

> Burgess Meredith is replacing Dean Jagger as principal of Jefferson High in NBC's "Mr. Novak." Appearing as Martin Woodridge, Meredith commenced co-starring (opposite James Franciscus) this week in the show's first two-parter, "Faculty Follies." Jagger bowed out recently in an assorted "doctor's orders" exit, but reports had him dissatisfied with the often-minimal import of his role. — *Daily Variety*, 12/9/64.

Burgess Meredith was born in 1907 in Cleveland, Ohio. He later attended Amherst College in Massachusetts. In 1929 he became a member of Eva Le Gallienne's Civic Repertory Theatre in New York. Meredith made his Broadway debut as Peter in Le Galliene's production of *Romeo and Juliet* in 1930. He achieved stardom in the 1935 production of Maxwell Anderson's *Winterset* and the following year made his film debut in an adaptation of the play. After appearing in several quality theatrical productions in the late 1930's, Meredith focused his attention on Hollywood. He received favorable notices for his role of George in the 1939 adaptation of Steinbeck's *Of Mice and Men*. After a few more films, he enlisted in the United States Army Air Forces and was discharged in 1944 with the rank of Captain. The following year he starred as war correspondent Ernie Pyle in *The Story of G.I. Joe.*

In the late 1940's Meredith continued to appear in several motion pictures and made his television debut in 1949 on *The Ford Theatre Hour.* In the 1950's he appeared on such dramatic anthology series as *Robert Montgomery Presents, Lux Video Theatre, Omnibus,* and *The Dupont Show of the Month.* In 1959 he starred in his first of four *Twilight Zone* episodes. "Time Enough at Last" was the story of a frustrated bookworm who is not allowed to read by his shrewish wife. He survives a nuclear holocaust and can now read all he wants except for a tragic event which renders him without clear vision. This was an excellent episode of Rod Serling's series and remains a favorite with its fan base. Meredith also appeared in "Mr. Dingle, the Strong," "The Obsolete Man," and "The Printer's Devil." In the early 1960's he appeared on such TV series as *Ben Casey, Wagon Train, Burke's Law,* and *Rawhide.* He had achieved much success as a popular guest star on many TV shows but had never worked as a regular on a series.

Burgess Meredith had been initially hired for the two part "Faculty Follies" episodes. His character was in a cantankerous state because of his slow advancement and was a bit bitter because he was entering middle age and felt he had not done well. The new educator opposed a musical performance by the teachers in comic roles because it was demeaning to the profession. He eventually relents and performs a comic song about sports. Leonard Freeman discussed his being chosen and the personality of the new principal of Jefferson High:

> The character Meredith played in "Faculty Follies" was startling. Woodridge is an academic and social misfit of the sort that is supposed to curdle an agency man's blood. His trouble is that he hates people. In "Follies" he is, to quote producer

Leonard Freeman, "not only a rigid traditionalist but an estranged human being." The script was originally written for another actor, Donald Pleasance (who was unavailable) and was already being shot with Meredith in the Pleasance role — when the doctor's call came through. The idea of picking up Meredith grew out of happy desperation — Meredith's presence made it too obvious to miss. Freeman discussed this wild notion with MGM executive Alan Courtney and E. Jack Neuman, executive producer and co-creator of *Novak*. Both were pessimistic about how Meredith might receive the idea, but that same afternoon Freeman cornered Meredith on the set anyway. "He had a sinister look," recalled Meredith. "I thought he had come to fire me." Meredith mulled the matter over the weekend and accepted. The men from MGM were waving real money and such attractive side inducements as a piece of the action, limited hours and a car to pick him up at the Beverly Wilshire every morning. "There were a couple of factors," Meredith explained. "I've always carried the main burden. This way Jimmy (Franciscus) would take it. And it's a little easier to jump aboard an established hit."

Freeman and Meyer Dolinsky, a schoolteacher-turned-writer, immediately went to work on changes. The Woodridge character, once a misogynist with a mother problem, suddenly acquired a home life and an understanding wife in the person of actress Anna Lee. The focus changed from a deep psychological estrangement to a temporary hang-up over his career, setting the stage for his transformation to what Freeman calls "the delightful pixy with the Yankee Shrewdness" which he hopes will transfix audiences. — Dwight Whitney, "Adding Curry to the Curriculum," *TV Guide*, 2/20-26/65.

Burgess Meredith's nickname was "Buzz." James Franciscus would be impressed by his new co-star's abilities as the new principal:

> In came Buzz and he was just terrific and delightful, and he knew he was picking up and filling shoes that were hard to fill, but he did, by God, he filled them wonderfully. He was magnificent in it. — *The TV Collector*, 11–12/89.

Bob Schultz was also impressed with Jefferson High's new principal:

> Burgess came in when everything was going downhill. However, after a few shows, he became very good as Martin Woodridge. He was a great talent and a total pro. His looks helped since he had to be an authoritarian figure. Buzz played the role differently than Dean did and soon fitted in. — Int.

Marian Collier respected the actor who replaced Jagger but to her it wasn't the same:

> Burgess was a wonderful actor and actually grew into the role but I just couldn't imagine him as "our" principal. Dean had been so perfect in the role and had been a major part of the show's success in the first season. — Int.

"Johnny Ride the Pony: One, Two, Three" aired in the middle of December.

"Beat the Plowshare" went into production. It was the story of an ex-convict, played by Harold J. Stone, who houses four students who are living under illegal conditions without direct adult supervision. One of the students was played by youthful acting veteran Jimmy Hawkins:

L-R, Jimmy Hawkins, Stephen Mines, and Harold J. Stone in "Beat the Plowshare, Edge the Sword"

> I had friends who worked on the first season and said it was a good experience. I was known for doing comedy and liked the fact that the show was dramatic. I was looking forward to a serious role. Part of the episode was shot on the MGM back lot on what was called the Andy Hardy street. I'd worked with Harold J. Stone on Elvis's *Girl Happy*. He was a very classy guy who would often speak of his family. Harold was very good in the lead. A memorable shoot. — Interview.

Near the end of December production began on "Where is There to Go, Billie, but Up?" which starred Lois Nettleton as a substitute teacher who enjoys skydiving. She enters in a romance with Mr. Novak that has turbulent consequences. Making her TV debut on the show was 14-year-old Alison Mills. The young African-American actress found the experience to be both exciting and rewarding:

> I had seen the show and liked it. It was very popular and my whole family liked James Franciscus. I'd joined an acting group called the Theatre of Being. It was headed by actor Frank Silvera and was a mixed group but contained most of the African-American actors in LA. It was the only one in Hollywood where there were known black actors. The *Novak* company called Frank and requested a young actress of color for the part. I got a call from MGM to read and was ecstatic. There hadn't been any opportunities in two years and I was grateful for the chance. I really liked the character of Billie. MGM soon called and said I had the part and I screamed with happiness.
>
> When I arrived on the set Lois complimented me on getting the role. During the actual filming, we stayed and related in character. After we finished the takes to do the big scene, there was a deep silence and the crew applauded. Lois told me I was

Alison Mills (Billie) with Jean Corcoran (Lois Nettleton) and Mr. Novak in
"Where Is There to Go, Billie, but Up?"

wonderful and I told her she was wonderful and we hugged. It was beautiful. After I worked with Jim, he came over to my mother and said I did a great job. He was a nice man who made me feel comfortable. He was so handsome and I think I even had a crush on him. Everyone was so kind to me that I felt respected as a young actress.

We told everyone to watch the show when it aired because there were so few chances for black actors at that time. Nichelle Nichols, Kyle Johnson, Frank Silvera, Bea Richards, Juanita Moore, and most of the troupe all watched the episode's broadcast from my house. Everybody was screaming and crying and proud of me. I don't think I even got to sleep that night because I was so excited. Being on *Mr. Novak* was an amazing credit to my resume and it gave me much credibility. I ended up on the *John Forsythe Show* as a result of being on *Novak*. It was a beautiful experience that I have never forgotten. — Alison Mills (Newman) Interview, 1/16/17.

Marian Collier was amused by an article in an issue of *TV Radio Mirror*. "Fair Warning from an Ambitious Blonde: 'I'm Planning to be Jim Franciscus' <u>Second</u> Wife" hinted strongly of an affair between the two stars of *Mr. Novak*. The article actually discussed Marian's desire for a bigger part in the second season's episodes. There had also been some discussion of Miss Scott getting married to John Novak. This was the kind of scandalous introduction to unrelated stories that so infuriated Franciscus. Miss Scott never did marry Mr. Novak and Marian's part didn't increase for the rest of the second season.

"Beyond a Reasonable Doubt" and "Love Among the Grownups" aired in the latter half of

"*Jim planning to be Jim Franciscus Second Wife!*"

MGM were in the final stages of assembling a series having to do with the problems of a high-school English teacher. They had, as their title-star for "Mr. Novak," a young man named James Franciscus, not unknown to national audiences but selected here mainly because of his startling facial resemblance to Richard Chamberlain—who, as *Dr. Kildare*, already had the cane-brake burning out of control.

Now this was no more than fair, since Chamberlain, in his turn, had been selected as *Kildare* largely because of *his* resemblance to James Franciscus. But it did little to pacify Jim—who, ever since *Kildare's* entry into orbit, had grown increasingly thin-skinned over well-meant ecstasies beginning with the words, "You know who you look like?"

Indeed he did! His resentment at the comparison was *not* due to any personal feeling toward Dick, whom Jim likes and admires. It was owing to a well-founded idea that "seniority," in this case, had been reversed. It was (as MGM knew very well) Chamberlain who looked like *him*. Franciscus had been a figure (*Please turn the page*)

December. During the closing weeks of 1964 the previously filmed episode with Dean Jagger was reformatted to introduce Jefferson High's new principal. The new producer revealed his new strategy:

Mr. Novak appeared on the front cover of three issues of TV Guide, now considered collectable items today, sold on internet auction houses and web sites including Ebay

Then Freeman delivered his master stroke. It happened he had previously shot a script called "The Crowd Pleaser," which had once been scheduled at election time. In this story, Vane runs for state superintendent of schools and loses. Freeman had withdrawn it on the grounds that viewers were surfeited with politics. It was lucky he did. Now he put on the show, retitled "Mountains to Climb," in for retakes. Instead of losing, Vane wins, and in a dramatic last-scene (performed by telephone since Jagger is not around to act in it) it is Vane who appoints the greatly misunderstood Martin Woodridge Jefferson High's new principal. "It is our little plus," explains Freeman. "Now we can bring Dean back from time to time in his new role of state superintendent." — *TV Guide*, 2/20–26/65.

On the first day of January Capitol Records released a single by pop-music duo Jackie and Gayle. Titled "Why Can't My Teacher Look Like Mr. Novak?" it was an up-tempo tune extolling the virtues of the handsome television educator. The singers complained about their own ugly and harsh instructors. Industry publication *Billboard* printed a publicity photo of Franciscus and the two singers examining the disc. There is no record of his opinion of the song.

The first episode to air in 1965 was "From the Brow of Zeus" which was broadcast on January 5.

On the following day, two shows aired that had a connection to the *Novak* series. The first was the popular music show *Shindig*. Jackie and Gayle appeared in a production number singing "Why Can't My Teacher Look like Mr.

Novak?" as the Shindig dancers swirled around them. There were blowup photos of the show's producer Jack Good as a school marm and as several stuffy teachers. Despite this promotion the record failed to chart.

On the same night there was a spoof sketch on *The Danny Kaye Show*. Guest star Peter Falk played a shabby teacher who works in a gas station at night and Kaye played his father. It was sort of a takeoff on the "Moonlighting" episode which had begun the second season of *Novak*.

Two nights later, *The Jack Benny Program* aired a sketch that kidded the *Novak* show. Benny played the principal at Benedict Arnold High School and guest star Jack Jones played an idealistic young teacher. Benny was upset with his teachers working extra jobs to supplement their low incomes. In the finale, it turned out that the principal was also working a night job. This satiric sketch was also based on the "Moonlighting" episode.

"An Elephant is Like a Tree" aired next to good notices for Tony Bill's portrayal of the blind student. The next show to be filmed had a political theme which promised a dramatic and timely installment:

> A mock United Nations session is underway at MGM this week — for a "Mr. Novak" seg which pulls no punches — shows Bircher's attempts to Commie-tinge "Novak" and the tv school for the "U.N." session in which kids tackle typical assembly problems. The script concludes for educators: "Our job is not to make ideas safe for young people — but to make young people safe for ideas." Bob Culp, guesting in the above mentioned "U.N." seg ("The Tender Twigs") of "Novak" thesping with right arm in a cast — busted bone resulted during karate wood-breaking exercises for his upcoming "I Spy" series. — Army Archerd, "Just for Variety," *Daily Variety*, 1/18/65.

Returning for his fifth and final episode was Tony Dow. He portrayed the U.S. representative and was impressed by the UN set and Robert Culp:

> There was a huge set for the U.N. Assembly scene. It filled most of a sound stage. Usually a show would try and get by with as few extras as possible. In this case, there were a lot of us and it was an impressive scene. I was friends with Peter Helm and Johnny Crawford, so it was a fun show to do. Robert Culp was a terrific actor and was very good as the conservative radical. He appeared to be quite calm at first then gradually became his real self of the extremist. His emotion ruled his reason. Burgess Meredith in taking over from Dean Jagger portrayed the principal as more of a soft-spoken intellectual type. It was an excellent episode and a good example of the progressive nature of the series. — Int.

L-R, Robert Crawford, Tony Dow, and Johnny Crawford; &
Robert Culp with E. Jack Neuman during filming of "The Tender Twigs"

Peter Helm once again appeared on the series in the role of the Assembly President:

Tony Dow and Johnny Crawford were all in the Assembly scene and it was like hanging out with school chums. Director Joseph Sargent really handled the huge crowd of actors and the scenes went very smoothly. Robert Culp had a bit of an ego and it was a bit negative, but he was a pro and did a good job. I thought the episode was kind of unique. The United Nations was very big in the news and it was a timely subject. — Int.

Randy Kirby returned to the program and was cast as the Assembly Representative of Lebanon:

After I had been in "Enter a Strange Animal," I caught several *Novak* shows and continued to be impressed by the series. I didn't consider the show to just be entertainment but instead was life because it was so real. I was stunned when I walked on to the huge Assembly set. I kept watching the director and camera which had to cover all those people. It just flowed in lengthy takes and I felt I was learning more about production. Although it was just a one-day shoot it was both enjoyable and illuminating. Robert Culp was very professional and was very good as the fascist father. Burgess Meredith had a brief scene and was totally believable. He was a fine actor who had real authority. — Int.

L-R, Franciscus, Randy Kirby, and others during filming of "The Tender Twigs"

Walter Koenig had played a Russian exchange student in an earlier installment of the series. He was approached to appear as the Russian Assembly Member but passed on the role:

I was asked to be in the episode as the Russian student. I looked at the script and saw that it was a very brief role. By this time I had acquired important parts on *Mr. Novak, Ben Casey*, and the *Alfred Hitchcock Hour* and wanted to move on with my career. I refused to appear. Bob Stambler was furious and said I would never work again in Hollywood. It's funny, I would later return to *Mr. Novak* for a third time in "The Firebrand," episode. — Int.

"Enter a Strange Animal," with Martin Landau as the teaching-machine salesman, was the next show to air. So far all of the new episodes had featured Dean Jagger in his familiar role of the principal. "May Day, May Day" was produced next with a script by John D. F. Black. It was the story of a teacher who is convinced that he'll be let go during an evaluation and dares Woodridge to fire him. It turns out that there is a potentially scandalous reason for his wish to be discharged. As the month of January was ending, "Beat the Plowshare, Edge the Sword" was broadcast with Harold J. Stone receiving positive notices.

"Honor and All That" was made next and starred Beau Bridges and Michael J. Pollard as a pair of student agitators. They stir up their classmates at a basketball game under the guise of protecting the honor of Jefferson High. Bridges enjoyed returning to the series and working with his co-star:

The *Novak* series was respected and I really looked forward to appearing on it again. My part of the instigator was multi-layered and was a challenge to me as a young actor. Michael J. Pollard was fantastic and a contemporary of mine. He could be sensitive but also very funny, almost in the same breath. Burgess Meredith became a lifelong friend and getting to work with him early on was a blessing, almost like working with a fun uncle. I learned so much from him, mostly by observation. — Int.

An ominous warning was carried in a syndicated piece:

Next fall's tentative schedules are expected to be made public in about two weeks and there are at least 19 programs which will be retired at season's end. Another 18 may — or may not — survive another season. On the dubious list are such

Beau Bridges and Burgess Meredith during down time while filming "Honor and All That"

programs as "*Mr. Novak*," "*The Alfred Hitchcock Hour*," "*International Showtime*," "*The Man from U.N.C.L.E.*," and even "*The Jack Benny Show.*" Death of course, comes to most television entertainment shows from a single cause — low Nielsen ratings. Some programs with low Nielsens but other important qualities, notably involving prestige and image-making for the network, survive in spite of ratings. — Cynthia Lowery, "At Least 19 Programs May Drop from View When Spring Arrives," *The North Adams, Massachusetts, Transcript*, 2/4/65.

The *Novak* series had a low Nielsen rating but was still receiving awards and critical acclaim. Would this continued recognition be enough to grant the faculty and students of Jefferson High another semester?

June Lockhart had played many roles on TV as a kindly mother. She was cast in "Once a Clown" as a confrontational lawyer and mother of a failing student. Her son, played by *My Three Sons'* Don Grady, is the class clown. He feels that he can't live up to high expectations of him. June welcomed this change of character and was impressed by her youthful co-star:

> I had seen some episodes of *Mr. Novak*. It was literate and I enjoyed it. It had a charm to it with incidental humor. A very fine piece of television... thoughtful and interesting. I enjoyed playing a more sophisticated and arrogant character. Don Grady was a nice young man and a very experienced actor. In the car-convertible scene, I told him he did a good thing with his character and gave a very ballsy performance. He made it a strong character. He laughed at me saying this and didn't expect to hear that from me. However, he was glad to hear it. Jim Franciscus was cool... not much sense of camaraderie. He was remote and was running lines all the time with a script clerk. I was warmer with Burgess Meredith as we were both from New York and he knew my father. I wore my own wardrobe. It was a positive shoot with no bad memories. — Interview.

The second part of "Faculty Follies" aired on February 9th and there was large ad in the *Hollywood Reporter* promoting the episode.

Laure Georges and her friends found the two-part segments to be very entertaining:

> The Novak Night girls watched "Faculty Follies" with great joy and interest. We all loved the musical numbers. Miss Scott's "Workshop Annie" number was terrific fun. We went completely crazy seeing Jim and the other two teachers in their Beatle wigs. Their performance of "Droppity Dropouts" was so clever and hilarious. A few shrieks could be heard in my living room that night! — Int.

Two days later *Daily Variety* published a list of the next season's schedules. These were in line as far as the sales departments of the networks were concerned. The Tuesday 7:30 to 8:00 slot for NBC was marked open. The 8:00 to 8:30 slot announced the telecast of *I Dream of Jeannie*. There had been no official announcement of *Mr. Novak's* cancelation but this was a forbidding sign of the show's precarious position.

Burgess Meredith gave a syndicated interview in which he talked about accepting the role and his impressions of the production:

> Meredith is acting in his first television series, although he did the narration for one some years back. He had been reluctant to take a regular series role, not caring to get involved in the long, tedious and often frustrating spadework. "I've been fending them off," he said. "They all said five-year contracts and I kept thinking of myself as an old man being carried out on a stretcher." He took the role on NBC-TV's

Novak because the series is established and the "invitation came when I didn't have something in the immediate future. I thought it over for a few days and snooped around a little bit," he said. "I found the atmosphere was very nice; no problems that I could see would come up. They've given me a pretty good break as far as hours are concerned. I'm so proud of the series. I like the things they try to do. That story about the boy genius in high school a few weeks ago was beautiful." — Joseph Finnigan, "Meredith: He's New Boss for Novak," unsourced article from Neuman archives, 2/10/65.

A Nielsen ratings report of mid-February showed *Mr. Novak* at number 31 with a rating of 21.0. This was in the bottom half of the top 40 and was distressing news for both the production and NBC.

"The Silent Dissuaders," with Claudine Longet and Kim Darby, aired on February 16.

Some other participants of the show had also been unhappy with the way the second season had progressed. An article perpetuated a myth and revealed additional dissention:

> A note about "Mr. Novak." It seems the show has been having personality problems for a long time now. The two top stars have not seen eye-to-eye since the middle of last season and other members of the cast have problems with directors, producers and writers. This may have led to the show being folded by NBC and the producers, MGM. — Bob Foster, "TV Screening," *San Mateo Times*, 2/18/65.

There was more than an element of truth in this assessment. Along with precarious ratings and cast changes, turmoil on the set may have been the deciding factor in the cancelation. Bob Schultz would reiterate his belief that there was never any feuding between the leads:

> When Dean left the show, there were some things in the press about him having a feud with Jim. It was implied that a main reason Dean left the show was due to his ulcers flaring up from all the conflicts with his co-star. There wasn't any feud and they had good chemistry. The feud was with Leonard Freeman and the MGM brass. — Int.

Dick Sullivan (Robert Walker) contemplates his hopes in "The Student Who Never Was"

"The Student Who Never Was" went into production on the same day and featured Robert Walker as the guest star. He played a student who perpetrates a hoax on Jefferson High by creating a fictitious transfer student.

A few days later there appeared to be a glimmer of hope for the ailing *Mr. Novak* series:

> Looking at the fall's skeds, we note a total of 40 new series being offered by the three webs, five more than last year at this time, but don't let the figure fool you because quite a few currently airing series that do not appear on the fall skeds — most notably "Rawhide," "Mr. Novak" and "Tycoon" — could well be given second life come lock-in time. — Hank Grant, "On the Air," *Daily Variety*, 2/19/65.

In the next day's *TV Guide* there was a feature that covered the Dean Jagger's departure and the hiring of Burgess Meredith. A disdainful quote regarding Jagger's attitude prior to leaving was on display:

> "I think it got to the point where he thought he *was* Albert Vane," an insider said. "He did a lot of impromptu writing which brought him into conflict with the management. Poor Dean. There was always somebody down there trying to smooth things out. — 2/20–26/65.

The insider was undoubtedly Leonard Freeman. This condescending attitude would guarantee that Albert Vane would not be returning to the series as a guest star which Freeman had desired. Jagger would respond to this attack at a later date.

The final episode with Dean Jagger, "Mountains to Climb," aired on the 23rd. After some revision, he wins the election as School Superintendent and appoints Burgess Meredith as the new principal. The loss of the first principal of Jefferson High was lamented by a columnist:

ALSO TONIGHT: Dean Jagger bows out of the Mr. Novak series by running for the post of state superintendent of schools. Although Burgess Meredith is a commendable replacement for the ailing Jagger, the series suffers a distinct loss at his departure. As Jagger interpreted Albert Vane, the school principal emerged as a disciplinarian who sometimes made mistakes and who sometimes was gripped by indecision. In short, a somewhat complex individual and a rarity in the stereotyped series of television. — C. J. Skreen, *Seattle Times*, 2/23/65.

Burgess Meredith discussed his becoming the principal and his acclamation into the series:

> In a newly shot ending, Jagger wins the election and disappears from the show. "That's done with a phone call from Jagger," explains Burgess. "His first action in his new job is to appoint me as principal. The following week, I'll be going full blast, dealing with a half-dozen complex problems." Will Meredith continue the sweet, understanding look of Jagger? "My approach will be whatever the writers

decide. Due to my nature, they seem to be making it more varied and complicated. I'll be a more witty, controversial-but-brilliant-type. I'll be capable of being severe, lenient, compassionate — whatever the occasion calls for. The scripts have been quite good so far." What about rumors that NBC-TV is prepared to axe the series for next season? "Well, I just got a call this morning from MGM telling me not to make any other plans for next season. So how do you take that?" But in addition to everything else, Meredith is a firm believer in the series. "One of the reasons I took the role is that I have two kids, and *Mr. Novak* is one of the very few programs on television that I would like them to watch." — Francis Murphy, "Behind the Mike," *Oregonian*, 2/23/65.

Dean Jagger replied to the *TV Guide* article and (Freeman's) condescending comments in a syndicated piece:

> Last week he came close to losing his temper after reading quotes in a magazine by a so-called "insider" on the *Mr. Novak* series, who was belittling Jagger for his "impromptu rewriting" and getting "to the point where he thought he *was* Albert Vane." "That is the kind of thing," said Jagger, "you get from people who never made it big. How unfortunate for this man, and I know who he is, who now finds it necessary to twist everything I said or did so that he can protect himself. The really sad part of it for him is that I have survived quite nicely, but his series has been canceled." He was referring to what at present seems an almost certain scrapping of *Mr. Novak* by NBC from next season's schedule. If the series should happen to survive cancellation, it then faces the problem of surviving the loss of Principal Albert Vane. — Hal Humphrey, "TV Flunks the Mr. Novak Test," *The Los Angeles Times*, 2/24/65.

This adverse publicity would not help the precarious position of the ailing series.

MGM Records released a 45 rpm single from the "Faculty Follies" show. The A side contained "Droppity Dropouts" as sung by James Franciscus, Vince Howard and Bill Zuckert. The B side featured Vince Howard singing "Oh Friday Day." The cover featured a publicity portrait of James Franciscus. The record did not chart.

"There's a Penguin in My Garden" began filming the 24th of February. It starred Vera Miles as a nun who leaves the convent to consul her irresponsible nephew before he inherits his father's millions. Allan Hunt appeared again on the series in the supporting role of Red:

> "I had a small scene with Bob Random, who played the nephew. He was very brooding and subdued in his characterization. I asked director Alvin Ganzer if I

could chew gum and be very effervescent in my scenes. He said okay and I played the part of Red as a hyper, happy-go-lucky teenager. Vera Miles was excellent as the ex-nun. She bought a dignity to the character that was very authentic. — Int.

Hunt's brief scene would later lead to his being cast as a regular on a top-rated television series.

John D. F. Black was impressed with Leonard Freeman's willingness to fight for content in his scenarios:

> I came from a very Catholic background and had nuns in my family. "Penguin" was a hissy fit situation. A guy from Standards and Practices took umbrage that the Catholic Church was going to be offended by the presentation of the nun and the title of the episode. He enlisted Mother Superiors from somewhere and got them to criticize the habits as being ridiculous and the nun character leaving the order. Lenny got on the phone to the network and smoothed things over. They already had the episode in the can so there wasn't going to be any revisions. — Int.

Leonard Freeman had made errors in judgement but also had achieved considerable quality in many of the episodes of the second season.

The next day several syndicated stories carried the news that NBC had abandoned the *Mr. Novak* series. This wasn't officially cancelation, but was very close to it:

> If *Mr. Novak's* uncertain future on TV concerns you, here's a skull-duggering development. In New York yesterday NBC cryptically announced that "at MGM's request," it was relinquishing its interest in the series so that the studio might negotiate with another network. On the face of it, it sounds hopeful. It would seem to mean that NBC, in the beau geste of the season, had decided not to stand in the way of the series' continuance elsewhere, whereas what it really means, I'm afraid, is that the network is giving up on the show. Goodbye and lots of luck. We got on the long-distance phone yesterday to check it out, just for the heck of it. "Positively not interested," an ABC spokesman said. "Never heard of it," a CBS spokesman said. "This is news to me, and I was talking to the producer this morning," the press girl at MGM who handles the show said. She said she'd find him and call back. Never did. Judging from past experience, a series that is unsalable on one network is rarely picked up by another. Whatever the truth of the gesture by NBC, the fact remains that *Mr. Novak* — despite the trials and story problems of the past two years, trials that may have aggravated the ulcers of the fictional "principal," Dean Jagger — is a series that seems a bit more deserving of another season's extension than any 15 or 16 sure holdovers you can name. While I'm not sure actor Burgess Meredith wouldn't lose the same fight Jagger did, to keep the stories out of the melodramatic vein and in the area of reality, I've a hunch the new man might have been a far more persuasive off-stage advocate for a subtler, more responsible approach. At this juncture, it doesn't seem as if Meredith is going to have a chance to take it down before the schedules are set and sold for next season. NBC's bulletin yesterday was an ill omen. — Bernie Harrison, "Whither 'Mr. Novak' — A TV Mystery," *Washington Evening Star*, 2/25/65.

It seemed as if the ending of the series was a sure thing. There had still been no official announcement but the lack of *Mr. Novak* on the fall schedule and the release by NBC seemed to be a tacit admission of cancelation.

There were no further developments for the rest of February. Leonard Freeman and E. Jack Neuman gave no interviews on the state of the series.

In the midst of almost certain cancelation, the *Mr. Novak* series continued to receive awards. One of the second season's most prolific writers was recognized:

> John D. F. Black has received citation from Braille Institute of America for his script, "An Elephant is Like a Tree" on "Mr. Novak." — *Daily Variety*, 3/2/65.

The episode had featured an outstanding performance by Tony Bill as a blind student.

"May Day, May Day" aired on the same day.

There still continued to be a sliver of hope for the show. A columnist suggested an unlikely but possible solution to the specter of cancelation:

> Although it is no reflection on his acting talent, Burgess Meredith is likely to have a short contract as the new principal of TV's Jefferson High on the *Mr. Novak* show. There is no official word yet, NBC's tentative schedule for next season does not list *Mr. Novak* as returning. Considering the present state of television, this "dropout" by *Novak* almost constitutes a crime. By any standards, the *Novak* series is one of the more commendable offerings on the air. At times, the program concentrated on the melodramatic at the expense of reality, but fundamentally came to grips with problems that could confront any high school official. In all probability it is not too late to save the series, but it would require an avalanche of letters to 30 Rockefeller Plaza, New York. More effective, perhaps, would be a concerted effort by high-school newspaper editors throughout the land. — C. J. Skreen, "Novak Series Rates Renewal," *Seattle Times*, 3/3/65.

The King Family Show was a musical series featuring the familial singing group. On the March 6th show daughter Cathy King sang "Why Can't My Teacher Look like Mr. Novak?" It didn't help the sales of the record but indicated the continuing popularity of James Franciscus.

Walter Koenig returned for his third and final performance on the series with "The Firebrand." He played a brilliant captain of the debating team, who stirs the students to demonstrate on behalf

Paul Ryder (Walter Koenig) confronts Mr. Novak during a student protest in "The Firebrand"

of a school bond issue. Koenig called upon personal memories in his portrayal and also recalled a disruption during filming:

> Director Michael O'Herlihy and Joe D'Agosta called me in for the part of the campus agitator. The role was patterned after a student at the University of California in Berkley named Mario Savio. He organized the students to go on strike. My father was an iconoclast and was into activism. The part was an homage to him. Michael let me do my thing on this episode. We were filming on location in front of John Marshall. There was a scene where I jumped on top of a car. One of the extras made cross-eyes at me during a take. I blew my top and stopped the camera. Michael removed the kid and we reshot the scene.
>
> Jim Franciscus and I got along fine in our scenes. He was very professional in his approach to acting. The *Mr. Novak* group was a very good set of actors. Burgess Meredith played the principal after Dean Jagger left the show. I had a big scene with him in a hallway and it went well. I was thrilled to work with him as I was a fan of his performances. — Int.

Julie Sommars made her first and only appearance on the series as a member of the debating team:

> I was always thrilled to get cast in any show and *Mr. Novak* was an especially happy time because it was so early in my career. Michael O'Herlihy was a fine director and a real gentleman. I had been a high school debater in South Dakota so I could relate to playing the debater, Ellen Cable. Tisha Sterling, who appeared in the episode, was a good friend. Burgess Meredith was excellent as the principal and Walter was suitably intense as the agitator. — Julie Sommars Interview, 10/25/15.

"Where is There to Go, Billie, but Up?" with Lois Nettleton as the sky-diving teacher was broadcast.

Even though the series appeared to be canceled, in an ironic twist, awards continued to be presented to participants:

> Burgess Meredith will receive a 1964 Communication Award from California Teachers Assn. — Southern Section next Friday (19). Meredith's is for his role in "Mr. Novak" vidseries. Public Relations Advisory Committee of CTA–SS will present Communications Awards to "Mr. Novak" as top net vidseries about teachers and Leonard Freeman, series producer. — *Daily Variety*, 3/12/65.

The same day brought production of the final episode of the second season. "And Then I Wrote" starred Tommy Sands as a brilliant student who turns down a scholarship. His father, who has no business sense, needs the boy's help in running the family music store. Appearing in a small role was acting newcomer Louise Latham:

> Tommy Sands was pleasant to work with a real professional. Mike Kellin and Norman Fell were great character actors and I learned a lot from observing them. James Franciscus was very nice and very good-looking. Burgess Meredith was always

trying to do the best with the material. He brought great authority to the part of the principal. I enjoyed working on the show. — Interview.

A column by Walter Winchell which was issued the same day brought an air of finality to the series:

> Talented Burgess Meredith in a daze over the cancellation of TV's "Mr. Novak." He had just moved his family to Palm Springs. — "The Broadway Lights," *Lebanon Daily News*, 3/12/65.

Winchell was one of the most powerful and influential columnists in Hollywood. He had contacts in all of the studios. If he were to report something it was more than likely a truism.

A few days after this revelation, "The Tender Twigs" aired and would later be taken to a prestigious organization as an example of the outstanding quality of the series.

A sarcastic column item lamented the uncertainty of the series continuing:

> There is considerable doubt that "Mr. Novak" will return. Not surprising, since it concerns itself neither with war, James Bond, fugitives nor witches. — Bill Ladd, "Television and Radio Almanac," Louisville, Kentucky, *Courier-Journal*, 3/14/65.

The official industry notice of the cancelation came in its premiere publication:

> Approximately 40 teleshows are being guillotined this season on the three networks, in an upheaval about on par with the casualty rate of the past few semesters. The 1964–65 casualties, by network, include, NBC-TV: "90 Bristol Court," "Bill Dana Show," "That Was the Week That Was," "The Alfred Hitchcock Hour," "The Jack Benny Show," "Mr. Novak," "Kraft Suspense Theatre," "Mr. Magoo," "The Rogues." In some instances producers of shows involved haven't yet been notified, but that's simply a formality because their option dates haven't come up as yet. Shows involved are not on the skeds for next season, and web spokesmen make clear they won't be. — "40 Shows Being Dropped by the Webs," Weekly *Variety*, 3/17/65.

The *Mr. Novak* series had lasted for two seasons and 60 episodes. It had won many awards for excellence and was a show that had resulted in artistic progression in the TV medium. A high level of quality had been maintained for both seasons with the majority of programs to be of a superior level. The show's positive depiction of teachers had made a real impact on academia and many viewers would be inspired to become educators. James Franciscus had become a popular television performer and had elevated the image of high school teachers in America. E. Jack Neuman's vision of his series had been achieved and recognized. The sophomore year of Jefferson High School had been interrupted by news of its forthcoming closure. All that was left was the rest of the semester and a final session of summer school.

Chapter Nine
Expelled:
Mr. Novak Canceled

The last day's filming on the final episode, "And Then I Wrote," concluded on March 18. A huge wrap party was held on the MGM lot that evening. Bob Schultz was part of this farewell celebration:

> I remember one hell of a party after the show was canceled. On the last day of filming... everyone was so close... we had a great buffet. They lit the set with colored filters. Jack was a great host and showed a blooper reel of outtakes. He came on at the beginning in place of the MGM lion and roared. It was very funny and we all screamed with laughter. It was a great party and a nice send off after two years. The *Novak* cast and crew were like a family. — Int.

Marian Collier attended the wrap party with mixed emotions:

> It was a tremendous party and everyone was there except for Dean and Jeanne. There was a big photo of Jack as the MGM lion. He also showed a reel of bloopers and came on at the beginning again as the MGM lion. We all laughed. It was a good time but it was also sad to me because it was the end of a great thing. — Int.

A syndicated article that was issued on the same day offered another possible reason for the cancellation of the series:

> Gloomy outlook on tubes: TV operations in Hollywood were never running so hysterically as at this moment. Everybody is waiting, frightened to make a move toward next season's programming — all due to the FCC threat to divest the three major networks of much of their sponsorship.... The situation is all the more desperate since this is the dead-line time of year for networks and sponsors to come together on coming-season offerings. The spirit of wholesale indecision is indicated by the number of shows being cancelled and then reinstated — among them "Perry Mason" and "Mr. Novak," both of which were killed off and now hurriedly resurrected in the wake of tremors from Washington. "If you think television quality took a nose-dive this season," observed one show planner, "wait until you see what's apt to be coming into living rooms next fall and winter!" — Harold Heffernan, Bluefield, West Virginia, *Daily Telegraph*, 3/18/65.

Perry Mason was indeed added to the fall's schedule, though the writer had been in error about *Mr. Novak* being resurrected. The main reasons for its cancelation had been low ratings, cast changes, and turmoil on the production. Perhaps the FCC's threats were the final nail in *Novak's* coffin. The *Mason* series had incurred no cast changes and was still very popular in the ratings. The final quote about the scheduling of lesser-quality series in the fall would become dramatically true with the series that would replace *Novak* in September.

Although the show had been canceled, the awards would continue:

"Mr. Novak" producer Leonard Freeman and Burgess Meredith will be honored today at a luncheon of California Teachers Assn., southern section, at the Statler-Hilton. — *Daily Variety*, 3/19/65.

That night, James Franciscus appeared on television as part of the America's Junior Miss Pageant:

Its girl watching time again as 50 pretty teen-age high school seniors compete for $14,000 in scholarship grants in the national finals of America's Junior Miss Pageant, live from Mobile, Ala. James Franciscus, the durable teacher of the Mr. Novak TV series, will crown the winner, who succeeds Linda Felber of Colfax, Wash. — "Mr. Novak Crowns Miss Junior Miss," Edwardsville, Illinois, *Intelligencer*, 3/19/65.

Publicity photos showed Franciscus being given apples from some of the contestants. He was also pictured with the winners.

Protests had begun to arrive at newspapers concerning the series' cancelation:

From Mrs. Donald M. Hurd, 6605 Tanglewood Road, San Diego: "Once again I must drop a line and argue in favor of 'Mr. Novak.' It is an excellent program and always informative, sometimes controversially welcome. It makes me so mad to have all good dramatic shows get taken off the air. We want excellent dramatic TV. 'Mr. Novak' is this type of show. Burgess Meredith is growing strong in his new role as the principal. Jim Franciscus as Mr. Novak has matured this last year to become a believable English teacher — one I'd be proud to have for my teen-age daughter. That's why I like this show — it is presented as our schools should be. There are always two sides to a problem, or question, and this show always shows both and in a genuine informative way...." (The cancellation of "*Mr. Novak*" seems inexplicable and inexcusable. — D.F.) — Donald Freeman, *San Diego Union*, 3/22/65.

Another paper issued a report on reaction of the viewing audience for the canceled show:

Viewers are still expressing amazement at NBC-TV's decision to drop Mr. Novak, which — no matter what the ratings may say — invariably has scored high in personal popularity polls. The post-season cancellation is also a tough break for Burgess Meredith, who has been turning in a slick characterization of the new high school principal. Burgess and his family moved to the West Coast for the unexpectedly short-lived assignment. — Anthony La Camera, "Best TView in Town," *Boston Record American*, 3/19/65.

"Honor and All That," with Beau Bridges and Michael J. Pollard, aired on March 23.

The series had been canceled and Jagger had been gone for several months. The network was still receiving voluminous protests from the viewers about Albert Vane's departure:

> NBC's getting bags of mail about missing Dean Jagger on "Mr. Novak." — Ted Green, "Mister Mainstream," *Backstage*, 3/26/65.

While Burgess Meredith had achieved growing approval from some viewers, many still resented the change in the cast.

"The Student Who Never Was," which starred Robert Walker, aired on March 30.

A columnist had previously suggested that high school newspaper editors band together and promote efforts to save the *Mr. Novak* series. One such editor had picked up the challenge:

> Acting on a suggestion in this space, the staff of the West Seattle Chinook high-school paper ran an editorial plea for NBC to retain the Mr. Novak series. Unfortunately, the program appears doomed unless some other network picks it up. — C. J. Skreen, *Seattle Times*, 4/1/65.

Other high school newspaper editors also published pleas for the show's continuation. Unfortunately, these noble efforts had no effect on the network's decision.

"There's a Penguin in My Garden," with Vera Miles, and "The Firebrand," with Walter Koenig aired in the first half of April.

A syndicated column bemoaned the idiocy of the television industry. It also revealed the identity of the show which would replace the first half hour timeslot of *Mr. Novak* in the fall:

Walter Koenig and Julie Sommars in "The Firebrand" (photo courtesy of Walter Koenig)

> The theatre of the absurd is intentional. Television of the absurd is not. In other words, what television really needs is some creative absurdity — say, for instance, a beauty pageant for "Miss Divorcee America" to go with other absurd contests, and to keep up with the times. NBC-TV's *Mr. Novak* series, about a teacher, is being cancelled. Whether or not one cares for the show is irrelevant to a statement the network is reported to have issued to some state education associations that contacted NBC-TV about the matter. According to "The Report Card," a newspaper published monthly by the Ohio Education Association, part of the statement said: "The program development process is a continuing one. Seasonal revision of our programs enable the network 'to meet the developing tastes of our audiences.' Sounds beautiful. But hold! What about these 'developing tastes'? Well — One of the situation comedies that will replace 'Novak' this fall is 'My Mother the Car,' in which a young fellow's dead mother 'returns' to give him advice through the radio of an old car." — Rick Du Brow, "TV Gets Absurd... Not Intentionally," *Trenton Evening Times*, 4/14/65.

My Mother the Car has gone down in history as one of the worst, if not *the* worst, situation comedy of the 1960's.

There were further expressions of displeasure with the network's attitude to *Mr. Novak's* cancelation:

> More banana oil is poured over the TV industry by its own members than one is likely to find in any other business. Network executives have become so expert at kidding the public and those around them that they will say almost anything now. In a form letter sent out by NBC's "coordinator of corporate information" to a viewer lodging as complaint with the network canceling "Mr. Novak," the "coordinator" said, "We, too, recognize the value of the portrayals of those in the teaching profession and this, in fact, was a guiding consideration in our decision to present it on NBC for two seasons — which is, as you know, a long run by any entertainment standard." But not so long as six years of "Bonanza," is it, Mr. Coordinator, or three years of "The Virginian" (with a fourth coming up), eh? — Hal Humphrey, "TV Comment," Hayward, California, *Daily Review*, 4/18/65.

"And Then I Wrote," starring Tommy Sands, was broadcast on April 20. There would be one more original episode of the series to air and then the reruns would begin.

Dean Jagger had recovered from his ulcers and was enjoying his ease:

It's been about three months since his operation forced him to leave *Mr. Novak*. Most of his stomach was cut away; for a time they feared cancer. But he's O.K. now and he can eat almost anything. But he won't do anything, at least not for a while. He says he enjoys loafing and his plans are to loaf through the summer. By then, maybe he'll want to work. He'll have no trouble finding a job. Already, the offers are flooding in. It is no secret that he didn't find *Mr. Novak* as fulfilling as he expected. Dean told me all about his troubles there, but now that he's had a brush and with death and now that it's all in the past, he says he'd rather I didn't print anything which sounds vindictive. And I'll respect his wishes. Suffice to say that Dean sums up his experiences with the *Mr. Novak* company this way: "It was a mishmash of unbelievable amateurishness." — Dick Kleiner, "Show Beat," Port Arthur, Texas, *News*, 4/21/65.

Jagger's remark was surely in regard to his conflict with Leonard Freeman during the tumultuous second season.

Although the series was finished, it still continued to receive awards:

> The television series "best portraying America," according to an award it has just received, is NBC's "Mr. Novak." The series, starring James Franciscus as a high school teacher, is being dropped by the network at the end of the season. The award came from the Thomas Alva Edison Foundation, which each year cites "distinguished contributions" in the mass media to science, education and youth. — Richard Doan, "Between Channels," *The Salem, Ohio, News*, 4/22/65.

The final new episode of *Mr. Novak*, "Once a Clown," aired on April 27. It starred Don Grady and June Lockhart and officially brought the series to an end.

> **DON GRADY** portrays the son of a politically influential attorney in "Once A Clown" on Mr. Novak. June Lockhart, who plays the boy's mother, threatens Novak with his job after the boy is denied a diploma because he failed in his studies.
>
> **7:30 p.m., Chls. 10, 4.**

Laure Georges viewed the final show of her favorite series with deep feelings:

> My Novak Night girlfriends and I gathered to watch the last episode. Each of us was completely devastated to see our favorite show ever come to this sad ending. The tears flowed yet we felt a certain joy that we had experienced the thrill of being on the series as extras and viewing such wondrous episodes together. We tried to analyze our mixed bag of emotions and to calm the anger we felt toward the powers that be-mainly TV executives and fate in general for allowing this travesty to occur. None of us could grasp why some really *dumb* shows would continue while the highest quality TV series on the air would be taken away from us. We were crushed by the turn of events. — Int.

NBC-TV had begun an odd policy which had resulted in cancelation of several shows. These series had achieved ratings which would have previously resulted in their renewal:

> "There was a time when a 30 share of an audience would almost automatically insure the renewal of a network program for the ensuing season. There were other factors involved, but usually the 30 or over share would give the established show the nod — over the gamble of a new untried property. Now see this at NBC-TV: "Alfred Hitchcock," with a 40.4 share of audience, axed; "Mr. Novak," with a 31.7 share, out of next season's schedule; "Kraft Suspense Theatre," close to a 34 share, suspended; "The Rogues," with a 35.6 share, suspended. A closer examination turns up mitigating circumstances, although the new property gamble remains. There are other factors, such as lead-in share, the competition in the time slot, program balance, availability of scripts, etc. It's more than a passing interesting to note, though, that

neither CBS-TV or ABC-TV has pursued the NBC-TV course. Not one nighttime entertainment show on either CBS-TV or ABC-TV, which has an over 30 share in the April Nielsens, has been axed. Only NBC-TV has taken such steps and here are some of the reasons: "Mr. Novak" is another case of two-network competition, at least for the first half, in its Tuesday 7:30 to 8:30 p.m. slot. From 7:30 to 8:00 p.m., CBS-TV doesn't program, with "Joey Bishop" coming in from 8:00 to 8:30 p.m. Although the Metro property does run second to ABC-TV's "Combat," "Novak's" 31.7 share isn't considered imposing. — Murray Horowitz, "No Guarantees in 'Magic' 30 Share: 'Hitchcock,' 40.4 Share & Others On NBC-TV With Over 30, Axed," Weekly *Variety*, 4/28/65.

NBC-TV's new policy, cast changes, tumultuous production and the feared FCC crackdown had all contributed to the removal of *Mr. Novak* from the broadcasting schedule.

James Franciscus discussed the cancelation of the show and his pride in its accomplishments:

School is out for Mr. Novak — Permanently. James Franciscus, who starred in the series, refuses to be too upset over the demise of the show. "We were very fortunate to get two years out of it," commented Franciscus the other day. "It was a difficult show to do. Actually, two years was just about right as far as everybody doing a good job. If we had gone into a third year, we would have had more of a repetition problem with the stories. Viewers might have had their fill. This way we leave them wanting more." Franciscus said that though *Novak* gained in the ratings this year, it consistently lost out to *Combat* which is on ABC at the same hour. "*Combat* was always near the top. We finished in 31st place, which isn't bad. It's interesting though, that the shows below us, 32 through 40, were all picked up for next year — and they're all comedies. I think the time slot hurt us more than anything. I don't want to take anything away from *Combat*. It's a fine show. But you can tune in anytime and the guns are still going off and it only takes two minutes to find out who's in trouble. With ours, you need to get in at the beginning and at that hour, especially 6:30 p.m. central time, you're not ready to put your mind to a show like *Novak*. It's like watching *The Defenders* that early. I couldn't do it either." Franciscus mentioned that *Novak* departed some-what this season from the original idea of the series. "It was a bit more melodramatic, but the producer felt it was necessary and our ratings did improve, so maybe it was a good move. I'm still amazed that when you're turning out 30 episodes a year you can get even 10 that are good, under that kind of pressure. But it's over and done with and I enjoyed it thoroughly. We had something to say and we said it. We pictured teachers as human beings, Not Eve Ardens, not Wally Coxes, not buffoons." — Aleene Macminn, "'Mr. Novak' Is a Dropout and It's All NBC's Doing," unsourced article from the Neuman archives, *circa* 4/65.

HELP SAVE MR. NOVAK'S LIFE

TS Readers To The Rescue

James Franciscus had been featured in several articles in *Teen Screen* magazine. An issue from late April contained a request for readers to get signatures on a petition that was to be sent to Robert Kintner, president of NBC in New York. The magazine stressed that the ratings had been the main reason for the demise of the series and petitions with many signatures might convince NBC to reverse its decision. Laure Georges was a regular reader of *Teen Screen* and immediately began to organize the petitions:

> I called all my Novak Night friends and urged them to purchase as many copies of *Teen Screen* as possible. They did and we gathered at my house for an important "signing" of the protest petitions and tried our best to state our case for saving the finest TV show ever! We all then went around to all our friends and ended up with many signatures. Being young and optimistic, we truly felt our voices could be heard. We mailed a large packet of coupons to the president of NBC in New York. Alas, our efforts never came to fruition. But we felt satisfied that we had given the project our very best. Life and TV would go on-but not quite as joyfully as before. — Int.

Despite being dropped by NBC, the excellent quality of the series was still being acknowledged. Recognition had come from a prestigious institution on the east Coast:

> Producer Leonard Freeman flew to New York at the invitation of the United Nations to attend a screening of "The Tender Twigs" episode of *Mr. Novak*, the first TV film to be shown in the Dag Hammerskjold Auditorium. Freeman will address the UNICEF representatives at their annual meetings this week. — Cecil Smith, "Inside TV," *Los Angeles Times*, 5/19/65.

Franciscus gave a final interview of the time concerning the series' impact and reasons for cancelation:

> When the award-winning "Mr. Novak" was cancelled by NBC-TV earlier this season, James Franciscus, the star who erased the ivory-tower image of the high school teacher and made him human and vulnerable, received an offbeat letter.
> "It came from a teacher," Jim said in a telephone interview from Hollywood. "I got a terrific charge out of it. He wrote, 'Thank you for what you have done for the teacher's image. This Christmas I received a copy of "The Carpetbaggers" and a bottle of scotch.'
> "I don't know if the show did that," Jim laughed. "But I think its greatest contribution was to give the trained, responsible teacher a more realistic image."...
> While Jim is justifiably proud of "Mr. Novak" which won a Peabody Award its first year out, an Emmy nomination and a long string of other honors, he feels television is no longer the medium for a specialized audience.
> "The nature of the beast is that it's geared to the masses. The pendulum has swung back to the escapism-type of show. Comedy is king now and everyone who knows the business is well aware that a show like 'Mr. Novak' is a victim of the trend.
> "Its demise was due to a combination of network commitment to other shows, network percentage of ownership, and the network position in the 1965–66 season. That position is quite clear — a large number of situation comedies are on the schedule.
> "It's a little like drinking," Jim laughed. "They don't care about the quality —only the quantity. It's a tragedy because there's a good market for selective shows and the networks couldn't care less about the selective audience. They're involved in a wild race for the mass audience where even a fraction of a point in the ratings assumes tremendous proportions in their eyes....
> "Financially, I'm in good shape, thanks to television. I have an interest in *Mr. Novak* on a residual basis. At this point in my career I want to concentrate on movies." — Eleanor Roberts, "Jim Has No Regrets at 'Novak's' Demise," *Boston Herald*, 5/23/65.

Two respected institutions, meeting in Chicago, praised the canceled series and pleaded for its return:

> The American Medical Association and a joint committee of the National Education Association today commended the National Broadcasting Co. for its

production of "Mr. Novak." NBC was encouraged to continue the series by the AMA and NEA joint committee. — *Tucson Daily Citizen*, 5/28/65.

Although the show had been finished for some time, a few letters of protest continued to be sent to the newspapers:

> "Ernie: Following last night's broadcast, I cannot understand how Mr. Novak can be taken off the air. It is one of the very best programs to have come into our homes in many years for young people and adults, dealing with problems and bringing some action to bear on them. Can't something be done to keep it on the air for the following year? We have so many programs that just fill the time."   MRS. K. O. EATON
>   Sepulveda.
> Having collected literally dozens of national awards and citations for carrying Mr. Novak, NBC has apparently milked the program for all its public relations value and decided to strive for ratings. Yes, you guessed it. My Mother the Car is scheduled for Tuesday evenings at 7:30. That means audience and sponsors and profits, all of which are more important than awards and citations. No, there's nothing we can do to save Mr. Novak. — Ernie Kreiling, "A Closer Look," Van Nuys, California, *Valley News*, 6/6/65.

Allan Hunt appeared several times in the *Mr. Novak* series. He had a one scene role as "Red" in "There's a Penguin in My Garden." In early summer, this brief appearance would jumpstart him into a high-profile part on a popular TV series:

> I had played my scene in the *Novak* episode in a very animated, boyish fashion. Bob Random, my co-star, had been very low key as was the nature of his character. In the spring of 1965 the word was out that the producers of *Voyage to the Bottom of the Sea* were going to add a character. They were looking for a young surfer-type named Stu Riley. I went to see a casting director named Frank LaTourette. He talked to me... thanked me for coming... and said goodbye. Two months later my agent called and said, "You have an interview at 20th Century Fox for *Voyage*." I went to Joe Augusta's office and he and said, "Allan, we have to move fast... do you know what's happened?" They had settled on Bob Random who had been in the *Novak* episode with me. The final vote went to the ABC executives who had come for a screening of the *Novak* show. By sheer chance the scene they had rolled up was the scene between the two of us. Joe told me that the executives thought they were supposed to be watching me. They all turned to series' producer Irwin Allen and said, "OK, we want him." My lively acting in the scene caught their attention. I ended up playing Stu for two seasons. Ah, the magic of show business! — Int.

There were still some institutions that recognized quality television programming. In Columbus, Ohio, an award was bestowed on the cancelled series:

> NBC prexy Bob Kintner won the "First Person" Ohio State Award, sponsored by the University's Institute for Education by Radio-Television. Other 1965 awards were made in the categories of tv network, informal and formal instruction, and tv

local, again formal and informal instruction. In category of tv network, informal instruction, winners included NBC and Metro-TV for "The Exile," a segment of "Mr. Novak." — Weekly *Variety*, 6/9/65.

In mid-June, the National Academy of Television Arts and Sciences announced the nomination for September's Emmy Awards Show. Dean Jagger was nominated for his role as principal Albert Vane in the *Mr. Novak* series. Although he would not win, this second nomination was once again recognition of his acting excellence as the principal.

The following month the show won another award from the NEA's convention in New York:

National Education Assn., in convention here, awarded "School Bell" citations to three NBC shows. Acclaimed were "Profiles in Courage," "Mr. Novak" and "The Eternal Light." — *Daily Variety*, 7/2/65.

The airing of the *Mr. Novak* series was nearly over. There were to be reruns during August and then oblivion. A newspaper columnist neatly summed up the end of the landmark television program:

Nothing I say here will make any difference, but it must be said, nevertheless.

The dropping of Mr. Novak from the NBC schedule is an important loss to network television. True, Mr. Novak didn't run high in the ratings. True, it was scheduled opposite ABC's Combat and the sound and fury of World War II makes for more exciting viewing than the problems of a high school teacher.

But many programs with intrinsic merit have been sustained in network schedules long after they've ceased to be rating-getters because they served the network's image or, possibly because they were simply good television....

Mr. Novak has been on just two seasons and NBC continued to accept awards and citations for it from educational groups until the bitter end. So it continued to have value to the network, image-wise, and it had rich value to the viewing public....

I didn't watch Mr. Novak much this past season and it's possible that if I and other columnists had devoted more attention to it, it might have survived. But I have watched its re-runs much of late and rediscovered the fact that it is a fresh, challenging, entertaining, well-made program of notable high quality....

It's refreshing to see a program revolving around education where students are thought of as individual human beings, rather than test scores.

Naturally, this fine program was among several lame-ducks to earn nominations for Emmys from the TV Academy. They went to both the series and to Dean Jagger for "Outstanding Achievement." What's wrong then? Obviously Mr. Novak was too good a program to endure on television today.

Mr. Novak's time period on NBC next season will be occupied by two comedies, Please Don't Eat the Daises and My Mother the Car. Television, Ever Onward and Upward!" — Ernie Kreiling, "TV Week: A Closer Look," Pasadena, California, *Independent Star-News*, 8/8/65.

E. Jack Neuman had been in pursuing efforts to keep the *Mr. Novak* series available in alternative outlets. A letter to Neuman outlined the potential plans:

> Dear Jack: As you know we have been vigorously pursuing the matter of keeping *Mr. Novak* alive in non-theatrical distribution through as many channels as possible. It looks as if our best bet will be through Associated Films, a uniquely diversified organization. They propose the series for non-theatrical sponsorship, to place it in their regular school rental library, and also to make it available for long-term lease for teacher training institutions and others who want permanent retention prints. They propose to release ten per year and to announce a five- or six-year release schedule. I recommend that we use the pilot as the sample since this has been screened and approved by so many groups.
>
> Associated plans to make up a presentation to be submitted for our approval and for this purpose we need a complete list of all awards won by the series as well as any other ammunition which you may have from schools and others asking for the series. If it is not too much trouble I would appreciate it if you would nominate the ten programs which you recommend for the first year's release. As we discussed their list of prospects will include 3M, Xerox and Bell & Howell. If you have any other ideas since we were together I would appreciate your sending them along. Best regards always, Sincerely, Haven Falconer.
>
> P.S. For your file I am attaching the turn-down from Eastman Kodak in case anyone asks you why we went to 3M which is such an ardent competitor of the most important supplier of motion picture film." — 8/9/65. Courtesy of Marian Collier Neuman.

This was a progressive concept. The show had received much approval from institutions of learning. If it could be used in actual schools as part of the curriculum, then the series would continue to inspire and educate. Neuman replied to this projected distribution with his list of 10 excellent episodes:

> Dear Haven: Naturally, I would be delighted to see *Novak* going in a non-theatrical distribution situation and as the last of the awards filtered through I have learned that there is no immediate plan to syndicate the series because of the high price competition of other available products. Burns has advised me that they intend to make a package of *Kildare* and *Novak* for daytime syndication which would just about sign the death knell on any healthy syndicated contract. In, short, as far as syndication goes we are flogging a dead horse and therefore I am most eager to see the film get exposure in non-theatrical distribution. Please let me know if there is any other information you will need to accomplish this. Best regards, E. Jack Neuman. — 8/16/65. Courtesy of Marian Collier Neuman.

Neuman's list of the 10 episodes chosen for outstanding quality were (1) "First Year, First Day," (2) "To Lodge and Dislodge," (3) "X Is the Unknown Factor," (4) "The Risk," (5) "A Single Isolated Incident," (6) "A Feeling for Friday," (7) "The Exile," (8) "Sparrow on the Wire," (9) "Death of a Teacher," and (10) "Day in the Year."

There would be economic factors that would prevent syndicated reruns of the show in the 70's and 80's. There is no known evidence of any success with the non-theatrical proposal but a similar circumstance would occur several decades later. It was an admirable attempt to use the proven quality of the series to teach and inform in actual classrooms.

The final rerun of *Mr. Novak*, "And Then I Wrote," aired on Tuesday August 31st.

Laure Georges and her friends were on hand to say goodbye to their favorite TV series:

> Over the summer, we had watched the reruns — sometimes as a group when our schedule allowed it. On this last night, all of the Novak Night girls made an effort to be there for the final hurrah of our show. We had somehow accepted the fate of the phenomenal, ground-breaking program and it was a night to celebrate more than to grieve. Mom served a special cake in honor of *Mr. Novak* (school house theme) and it was a sweet effort to cheer us up. We had a serious, cross-your-heart vow to remember *Mr. Novak* forever and to follow Jim Franciscus in every role he played from then on. — Int.

After the Freshman and Sophomore years, Jefferson High School was closing its doors for good.

Chapter Ten

School's Out — Aftermath

September of 1965 brought pre-show publicity for the next Emmy Awards. Among the festivities would be an ironic musical production:

> As a kind of prologue to an orgy of self-indulgence (premiering all its new shows the same week), the TV industry gathers this Sunday evening (via NBC) to award Emmys for the period between April 13, 1964, and April 30, 1965.... A sad ballad for those shows that did not survive is to be sung by a quartet of cancelled stars — James Franciscus (Mr. Novak), Robert Reed (Defenders), Shirl Conway (Doctors and Nurses), and Robert Coote (Rogues). — Hal Humphrey, "Emmy Streamlined for 17th Edition," *Los Angeles Times*, 9/8/65.

The series had been canceled for a year and there was still an additional award to come:

> Fifteen writers received Writers Guild of America Script Awards at ceremonies last Wednesday (23) night held concurrently in New York and Hollywood. Best dramatic episodic script, any length: John D. F. Black for "With a Hammer in His Hand, Lord, Lord!" (Mr. Novak). — Weekly *Variety*, 3/30/66.

John Ryan was a real-life teacher who had served as an advisor on both seasons of the series. He reflected on his admiration for the production and its actors:

> "Mr. Novak IS dead. The television show was discontinued a year ago. But I'd hate to think all that that show stood for is dead. A teacher, I left a high school classroom to join Mr. Novak as technical adviser. I stayed to write three of the stories and parts of many others, and to appear in about 20 of them. For two years I was about as close to Novak, I suppose as anyone besides Jim Franciscus and Dean Jagger and the show's creator-producer, E. Jack Neuman. For me it was a revelation.
> I found Neuman absolutely sincere about wanting to portray teaching authentically. Under a mountain of pressures, the man flogged himself daily to get the show right.... I was in and out of Neuman's office constantly as he nursed the show along. "Make it honest, Ryan," he'd bark at me as I analyzed a script. That was the Novak theme — make it honest. Educators of course, must fret and stew about bond issues and school boards and good public relations and intra-faculty harmony and disgruntled parents and a hundred other things. "Make it honest, Ryan!" How he would cut through it all to the heart of the story. Neuman should superintend a school district, or at least be principal of a high school. The kids would worship him.
> Jim Franciscus wouldn't speak a dishonest line if the world were going up in flames. "We've got to do something to get teachers' salaries up," Jim would say to me. Hollywood is the alleged home of selfishness and superficiality, but in it, from men like Jim, I heard more honest concern expressed for my profession than I hear most anywhere else.
> I don't remember that Jim blew a single line in two years of daily shooting. No doubt he did but I don't remember when. His slips were very infrequent despite constant, grueling late-night script study. Exactly twice I heard him raise his voice in anger on the set, in two seasons, yet the daily pressures on him were enormous. If James Franciscus ever really taught a high school English class, he'd be magnificent.

Dean Jagger once called a young director by phone the day after a scene had been shot and apologized — with total, healing honesty — for earlier criticizing him. Typical.... Dean and I came to work closely together. He deliberately, patiently absorbed my amateurishness while we worked on his lines to make them authentic. On screen, principal Albert Vane was a man who could be indignant, but one who could understand and forgive. I found Dean Jagger to be like that. I would gladly teach for Dean if he was principal of a high school, and it would be a heck of a fine high school, if it were his!

Mr. Novak wanted to be like teachers really are. It agonized, weekly, as it came to see that teachers themselves often can't decide how they really are. There are vastly too many different kinds of them! Mr. Novak wanted to do teaching a good turn. It did. Some people astutely talk about promoting teaching, and the sound of their own voices sounds good in their ears. But Mr. Novak from Hollywood, U.S.A., acted, and with a sincerity and persistent tenacity that I, a veteran teacher, was eye witness to.

Mr. Novak was television that was not pap. It was not moronic or pitched to imbeciles.... — John Ryan, "Mr. Novak: Apple for the TV Teacher," unsourced article from Neuman archives, *circa* 9/66.

Walter Koenig had appeared three times on the *Novak* series. In "The Boy without a Country" he had played the tormented Russian exchange student. In the spring of 1967 he received a call that would lead to his most iconic role:

"Joe D'Agosta asked me to come in and read for a role on the *Star Trek* show. Joe had helped me get the part of Aleksei in the *Novak* series and knew I could do a convincing Russian accent. He would be there when I read for the part. I had done an episode of *The Lieutenant* which had been produced by Gene Roddenberry who was at the interview. Director Joe Pevney, who was also present for the audition, had directed me in an episode of *The Alfred Hitchcock Hour.* Writer-Producer Gene Coon was the only other person there who I had not previously worked for. I felt the character of Chekov seemed like a distant cousin to Aleksei. I read in a stern fashion and everyone was quiet afterward. They asked me to make the character funny. I gave a bizarre reading and they broke up. They asked me step outside and I thought it was a done deal. I was waiting in an outer office when another actor showed and went inside to read. A few hours went by and I was still waiting in the office. Finally, the door opened and a wardrobe man came in. The others had left and I went to the wardrobe department. A young man on the effete side dropped to his knees and put his hand on my crotch. I said, "What the *hell* are you doing?' He replied that he was measuring me for my costume. I had the part. I'm sure the others had seen the *Novak* episode or had been told about it by Joe. I thought it was ironic. My first starring role on television had been as Aleksei on *Novak* as a Russian and now I was going to be appearing as a Russian on the show that would catapult me into being a cult icon. — Int.

By the end of 1967 the series had been off the air for over two years. For some canceled programs there could be an option for a syndicated package of reruns. Yet some series might never return to the airwaves:

There are some shows even a crack salesman can't put into syndication. He won't even try. The shows come off the networks every year and they're piled up in the vaults, serving no one. There are enough of them to supply programming for a fourth, fifth and maybe even a sixth network. Looking back over two decades of TV film series, the distributor can and must weed out all but the wild successes for the syndication market. Those that fall by the wayside do so for a number of reasons, but primarily because they cannot get a price high enough to meet reuse costs. A show that doesn't make it for at least three years on the network has two strikes against it in the syndicated market. It has already proven itself to be without sufficient appeal. The best guarantee of successful syndication is a long network run. Yet many shows that enjoy long and successful lives aren't syndicated because they have passed out of fashion. One distributor termed *Mr. Novak* as valueless in the syndication market. It ran for 60 hours on the network, but the viewer seems to have lost his appetite for high-school English teachers, and the teen-age problems he solved several seasons ago have been made passé by today's flower children. — "Why Some Off-Network Series Can't Be Syndicated," *Television Magazine*, 12/67.

The *Mr. Novak* series had featured many cutting-edge stories that contained universal themes. The argument that the show would seem dated in the Age of Aquarius was a weak one. The real reasons for the lack of future syndication would be financial. A letter to *Television Magazine* from MGM Television appeared in the next issue in the form of a rebuttal to the reason given for *Mr. Novak*'s failure to be rerun. It was not a case of dated material:

Just when I get enthused about the new "Television" I hit page 40 in the December issue and I can hardly believe what I'm reading. There is a point in the "off network" article that MGM-TV would like to take issue with. Our *Mr. Novak* is not in syndication for reasons that have been stated previously in the press, and that is its high residual costs involving the two lead characters. There has, in fact, been continual interest from stations inquiring about possible release of this series in syndication. Keith A. Culverhouse, director of advertising, MGM Television, New York. — *Television Magazine*, 1/68.

Bob Schultz felt the limited number of episodes was a factor in the non-syndication:

For a series to be successfully syndicated it usually had to have three to five seasons for the package. *Novak* only had two seasons of 60 episodes so there wouldn't have been enough shows for a five-day-a-week or even weekly rerun schedule. I felt this was the main reason. Jim and Dean took a staggered or lesser than normal salary while the show was in production to make more money later. When they would have later sold the block of episodes for rerun syndication, they would have received larger payments than normal. This would have made the show more expensive for the syndicated stations. These were the two reasons for there being no reruns. It's a shame because there was still interest in the series for quite a few years after it stopped. — Int.

Franciscus's wife Kitty recalled her husband's view as to why the series wasn't rerun:

> Jim told me later that the reason *Mr. Novak* wasn't syndicated was that it was too expensive to pay the appropriate royalties. There was apparently a 100% royalty rate that no network wanted to pay. Jim thought it would have been fun to have the show back on the air. He in no way killed any syndication possibilities as some rumors have said. — Int.

The *Mr. Novak* series, not ever being rerun, eventually faded in the memories of the viewing audience. In the late eighties there would be an odd but welcome resurrection.

In a wonderful twist of fate, the first year of the seventies brought about a marriage between the series' producer and Miss Scott:

The happy newlyweds out to
dinner in Beverly Hills

> In 1970 Jack was separated from his wife and I had gone through a divorce. He called me... he always called me "Miss Collier"... and asked me if I'd like to have dinner. I said okay and took my friend Maggie Banks along. I thought, "I'm probably going to get fired." Then I realized that the show had been over for five years. We started seeing each other and ended up getting married. — Int.

Starting in the late seventies there would be an occasional book or magazine article on classic TV series. If any mention was made of the *Mr. Novak* show, it was usually very brief with perhaps a photo of Franciscus and Jagger. There was no full-length coverage of the television series. James Franciscus was very active in the first two decades after the show ended and sometimes there would be a scant reference to the series in articles about the actor.

(Above) MR. NOVAK: Other professions were not entirely neglected in the sixties. Schoolteachers got a hearing in this Norman Felton series, with James Franciscus as an English teacher at Jefferson High and Dean Jagger as his principal.

(From an unsourced history of television book. Norman Felton was the producer of *Dr. Kildare*!)

Marian Collier shared her husband's pride in having done the series:

In later years, Jack would often say how proud he was of all the awards to *Mr. Novak*. It was his baby and everyone had acknowledged it. He was thrilled. We had a lot of the awards at the house and I would see them and feel so proud to having done the show. It was one of the greatest things I ever did. It was a great time and the show really meant something. Not just to Jack and myself but to the public and the teachers. I did keep in touch with Vince Howard after the show ended and he would comment on how great the series was. He also would thank Jack for getting him started as an actor. — Int.

In 1985, media mogul Ted Turner arranged for the purchase of the biggest and best known motion picture studio in Hollywood's history:

Turner Broadcasting System Inc., agreed Wednesday to acquire MGM-UA Entertainment Co. for $29 a share. The MGM-UA deal calls for Turner to pay $1.5 billion up front for the entertainment company. Immediately afterward, the United Artists Corp. film-production company would be sold to Tracinda Corp. for $470 million. Tracinda is a holding company controlled by financier Kirk Kerkorian, currently MGM-UA's largest shareholder, owning 50.1 percent of the stock. TBS operates WTBS-Superstation, a nationwide distributor of sports, movies, regular commercial programming and news and cable television systems, and Cable News Network.

In Metro-Goldwyn-Mayer, symbolized by its roaring lion, Turner would get a studio rich in Hollywood History and acquire a vast library of 2,200 titles, including such classic gems as "Gone with the Wind" and "The Wizard of Oz" that analysts said would bolster programming at WTBS. Other assets of Culver City-based MGM that would remain after the United Artists divestiture include the MGM film studio, and distribution and syndication operations." — Associated Press, "Turner Plans to Acquire MGM, Drops Bid to Buy CBS," Doylestown, Pennsylvania, *Intelligencer*, 8/8/85.

The following year, Turner sold the Culver City based Corporation:

> Ted Turner ended his brief career as a movie-making mogul Friday, announcing that Turner Broadcasting System Inc. has agreed in principal to sell its recently acquired MGM Entertainment Co. to United Artists for $300 million. Turner also announced the intended sale of MGM's 44-acre production facility and Metrocolor Film Laboratory to Lorimar-Telepictures Inc. for $190 million. Turner is keeping the vast MGM film library, which had been his chief objective in buying MGM. UPI, "Turner to Sell MGM Except for Film Library," Marietta, Georgia, *Daily Journal*, 6/7/86.

Two years later there was the premiere of the media mogul's new cable TV station:

> Ted Turner, who gave cable TV its first superstation, launches his latest broadcasting venture Monday night with the debut of Turner Network Television. Designed, in the words of the TBS Chairman, to "inform, educate and entertain," TNT will have a lineup of original specials, classic films, and exclusive television series. — John A. Bolt, Associated Press, "New Turner Channel Ready to Debut Tonight," Marietta, Georgia, *Daily Journal*, 10/3/88.

The "exclusive television series" would be first-run repeats of classic shows from the past. One of the series would be *Mr. Novak* which premiered on October 30 at 4:00 A.M. For the first time in 23 years the respected show would now potentially be seen by over an estimated 17 million homes. Most of the publicity about the new station focused on the broadcast of *Gone with the Wind* and the *Novak* series received no prominent advertising in either newspapers or *TV Guide*. There was only a notification of the title and time slot in the evening's schedule. However, there was some publicity in the TNT guides which had been sent to subscribers of the new network. The *Mr. Novak* series would air on an irregular basis, usually at 2:00 or 4:00 A.M., for the next two years.

4:00 AM
11 MOVIE: ☆☆☆ "My Name Is Nobody" (1974)
BET Video Vibrations
CBN MOVIE: ☆ "Big Calibre" (1935)
CNN Sports Review
DSN Walt Disney Presents
LIFE Investment Advisory
PTL Changed Lives
TNT Mr. Novak
USA Night Flight (R) (In stereo.)
WTBS (4:05) Night Tracks (In stereo.)

Series return, October 30, 1988

2 A.M.

- **3** News
- **12** CNN News
- **21** Praise the Lord
- **39** Profiles
- **45** To be announced
- **CNN**—Crossfire
- **FAM**—Paid programming
- **MAX**—Movie: (2:20) 'The Witches of Eastwick' (2:00)
- **NICK**—Car 54, Where Are You?
- **SHO**—Movie: (2:15) 'Dead
- **TNT**—Mr. Novak
- **USA**—Madame's Place

Series end, October 22, 1990

Reruns often depended on the length of the late-late movie: If needed, a *Novak* episode would be used to fill in the time. Fans of the show who subscribed to TNT or received word of the repeats, would set their VCRs to record the episodes. Those that viewed the shows again, who were original fans or had merely heard of the show by reputation, were delighted by the quality of the program. A fan who was amazed by the videotaped shows was a writer and co-publisher of a publication that covered vintage TV series. Diane Albert recalled her reactions to the reruns and her desire to produce the first comprehensive article on the *Mr. Novak* show:

> I had not watched the original run of the show in the sixties. We watched *Combat* in our house and I was too young to care about a high school series. As I grew up all of sixties TV was ingrained in my psyche. I collected old *TV Guides* and had become more aware of the show and that the leading character was a teacher. Before I met my future husband Steve, he was doing *The TV Collector* as a fanzine which he had started around 1976. When we met in 1978, my being a writer wanted to take over the fanzine and make it a real magazine with interviews. In 1982 we launched it as a real magazine with interviews from veteran actors. Our goal was to chronicle long-lost and short-lived TV series from our childhood. We always included episode guides in our articles. We developed a substantial number of subscribers and were pleased with the magazine's success.
>
> By 1988 we had a regular column listing upcoming shows that would be of interest to collectors so that they could watch or tape them. We got the first monthly mailing from the new TNT Network for October and noticed that in the middle of the night *Mr. Novak* would begin airing. I got very excited and knew my readers would go berserk about seeing this show after its never being rerun. I made sure to set my VCR to tape it when it was being broadcast.
>
> I was very happy to finally see the show and was fascinated and amazed at how well it held up. How well written, directed, and acted it was. How gorgeous Jim Franciscus was. The controversial subjects they tackled at such an early time in TV history. It was very authentic. I loved the way Jim underplayed Mr. Novak. I thought he projected a character who had a lot of insight into the teenage psyche and his portrayal was of a teacher who I would have liked to have had. I really liked Dean Jagger's subtle wit. He had an ability to know when to close his eyes to something he should not have allowed to happen if it should have. He infused a quirkiness into the character that was fascinating. All of the other faculty members including Jeanne Bal, Marian Collier, Vince Howard, and the others were always excellent support for the leading men.
>
> Some months later we decided to do a two-issue article on the show so we got as press kit from TNT. Eventually I found Jack Neuman. Marian, his wife, hit it off with me right away. When I first got Jack on the phone I was surprised to know that he was married to the former "Miss Scott" of the show. She was so excited about the upcoming issues and was very helpful. Jack was very open, honest, and agreeable. Marian gave me Jim Franciscus's phone number.
>
> He was extremely receptive to talking about the show. We established a good, chummy rapport from the beginning. He answered all my questions without hesitation. He made it clear he was extremely proud to have been associated with a TV series of such high quality. Many of our readers gave enthusiastic responses

to the *Novak* issues. I was especially proud to go so in depth on the series because there hadn't been anything substantial written about it prior to *The TV Collector*. — Interview, 9/10/16.

Issue #44,
September–October 1989

Around this time Marian Collier was also surprised to be seeing episodes of her old series:

I didn't know that TNT was rerunning the series. My sister-in-law taped some episodes off the air and sent me VHS copies. Seeing the shows again, I couldn't believe how good it was and how well it held up. I loved seeing them again. It was a great series, especially for its time. In those days, there were some really good shows on, but nothing like this. It was so good and honest. Jack felt the same way. — Int.

The two issues featuring the *Mr. Novak* articles were nos. 44 and 45 and were published in Sept–Oct and Nov–Dec of 1989. Numerous quotes from Neuman and Franciscus have been used in this book courtesy of Diane Albert.

The final episode of *Mr. Novak* as broadcast by TNT aired at 2:00 A.M. on October 22, 1990. It was ironic that the original run was for two years and these repeats also were shown for the same amount of time. Although there never was any major publicity about the reruns, many fans were able to tape the majority of the 60 episodes. As a result of this, as the nineties began, sets of VHS copies of *Mr. Novak* began to make the rounds among tape collectors. Most people who saw them either on TNT, or on tape, were amazed at the high quality of the series.

One person who was amazed by acquiring a videotape of the show was veteran teacher John T. Taylor:

I was, and still am, a science teacher who now educates on the college level. I began my teaching career in the fall of 1963 and was a high school teacher for the first three years. In my first year, I watched about half of the episodes of *Mr. Novak*. I caught the rest in reruns and enjoyed all of them. The topics were serious and real about what went on in all schools. It was like I was in a classroom. I learned more from the interaction between Vane and Novak than in the education classes

First-year high school teacher
John T. Taylor during a class in 1963
(photo courtesy of John T. Taylor)

that I had to take in the university. I also learned a lot about being a teacher from watching Mr. Novak make mistakes then progress.

"Jim Franciscus… if he had been in my school would have been a fine teacher. He was an idealist and always dressed in a suit and tie. I thought Jim made a better teacher than Dick Chamberlain did as a doctor on *Kildare.* Dean Jagger was a perfect principal who was wise and understanding. I wish my first principal had been more like him. I deliberately made myself available to watch most of the second season and continued to admire the show. I liked the fact that Novak became a wiser teacher as I had done. Vane also continued to be the wise and understanding character. I didn't like Burgess Meredith coming in as the new principal. He played a rough educator and it was such a contrast to Vane. He became more human in the last episodes. I was angry when the show was canceled. In watching the two seasons I learned a lot, was entertained and became a better teacher.

I didn't know that the show was rerun on TNT in the late eighties. Around 2000 I acquired a VHS tape with the "Moonlighting" episode. I myself was working an extra job while teaching and it really hit home. I was so impressed that I started looking for other shows. I eventually acquired a full set of VHS tapes with many episodes. It really held up as a great dramatic show. I kept my admiration for Jagger as Vane. He was as great in the role as I remembered him. Franciscus seemed to be a little Hollywood perfect but did a great job as the idealistic teacher.

In the late nineties as a college professor, I was teaching education technology to pre-teachers. I called the course, "T6: Teaching Teachers to Use Technology to Teach." Every week I asked the students to bring a video clip to be used in the classroom. I didn't like what they brought in so I started use *Mr. Novak* clips as well as other education-based TV shows. After the success of using the clips I started to do presentations at conferences called "How Hollywood Treats the Classroom." I would use segments of *Novak* episodes to show a first-year teacher and how they make mistakes. The *Novak* show provided perfect answers to a teacher's mistakes. Most of my audience, after viewing the clips, wanted to know how to get copies. I told them to look around the internet. I would sometimes give a student a whole episode and ask them to critique it. They would show a clip with their report.

I was in Long Beach, California, at an international conference and presented some clips of *Novak.* I received a lot of interest about the show so I made my *Mr. Novak* website around 2004. The address is fccj.us/MrNovak/mrnovak.html. The purpose of the web site was for teachers to be able to learn about the show. Sometimes I would make free copies of my tapes for those that were interested. A lot of people, including many teachers, requested sets of tapes. The reaction was very positive to seeing the show again.

John T. Taylor, still an educator in 2017 (photo courtesy of John T. Taylor)

Over the years many elderly teachers, who saw the show in its original run, told me that it inspired them to become better teachers. Some had even become teachers as a result of the series. *Mr. Novak* had a real impact. I've found out that Warner Home

Video owns the show and I really hope they will release DVD sets on both seasons. They have already done 4 seasons of *Dr. Kildare* so let's hope it happens. The *Mr. Novak* program helped me to become a better teacher when I was young. It could still be both entertaining and informative. It's a classic television drama and really should be seen by more people. — Interview.

John Franciscus also had started collecting various episodes of *Mr. Novak*. He too was pleased with the quality of the series and his brother's performances:

"I hadn't been aware of the TNT reruns in the late eighties. In the following decade I began to collect my brother Goey's movies and TV works. I would write or get in contact with various collectors and managed to get a lot of the *Novak* episodes. In watching them again I felt they held up beautifully. Each one had a message and the writers were wonderful. Goey did a fine job in the leading role and all the accolades from teachers and educational organizations were well deserved. Dean Jagger played the principal with authority and intelligence. As I watched the episodes I felt that each had a moral message. The majority of them were excellent and the moral lessons were integrated into the entertainment. I felt that modern schools could possibly screen episodes to inform their students. If a school had problems of a similar nature to the moral of each story, then they might use the shows to teach in an assembly. I think it would be great if the program were officially released by Warner Home Video. Then more people would become aware of the genuine quality of the series. *Mr. Novak* was one of the first adult approaches to defending the teachers and the educational system. It was a much-needed progression at the time." Int.

Laure Georges, now married as Laure Gonzalez, also found herself reviewing the show after many years:

When I was six years old, I started lining my huge doll collection up in rows so I could "teach" in my little classroom. My interest in teaching grew from there. As I entered high school at John Marshall and began to consider college options, teaching seemed more enticing than ever. I needed an impetus to push me into a solid direction and *Mr. Novak* couldn't have happened at a better time. I watched JF in his ground-breaking role as a teacher who deeply card about his students and wasn't afraid to take an unpopular stance when necessary. He always did the right thing, not the easy one. *Mr. Novak* definitely inspired me to lofty goals. I started teaching a kinder/first-grade combination class in Farmer's Branch, TX, where I taught private kinder for 17 years. My last round of being an educator occurred at Lamar Middle School in Irving where I was an inclusion assistant in special education. After 10 amazing years in that career, I retired in 2010 with 30 years of teaching under my belt. I never lost sight of why I wanted to educate children — and the love of learning I desired to pass on to them. Mr. Novak was more than a dreamboat; he was a teacher to emulate and a sweet inspiration to me.

I wasn't aware of the TNT reruns in the eighties. I didn't have cable TV and had no idea that my favorite show was being aired. About a year and a half ago, my daughter's friend Susie came across some DVD episodes of *Novak* and sent them to me. She had no idea what a rush of nostalgia and joy would occur when I received them. I was enthralled to see the series again and a wave of memories flooded my mind with details about being on the set and seeing my friends and myself on TV. I simply adored each episode and ended up viewing them twice. My husband Alex vaguely remembered watching *Novak* and was excited to see the shows with me. I recalled the Novak Nights at my house in the sixties with my girlfriends — giggles and tears included as we drooled over the dreamy Jim Franciscus and analyzed each episode after watching it. What an impact *Mr. Novak* had on all us! Alex and I were amazed that the show held up so well and was appropriate for modern times due to the life lessons and relevant subject matter. At a later time, I shared the Novak DVD's with my daughter and she couldn't help but notice that JF was a hottie! She really appreciated the meaning of the shows too and wants to share them with her sons when they get a bit older.

"All this came to a head in September of 2015 when I saw Chuck Harter's request in the *John Marshall Alumni Newsletter*. I was jubilant to see that he wanted feedback from anyone who was an extra or had memories to share. Chuck interviewed me by phone and it was so much fun to reminisce. He has been so wonderful about keeping me updated on the book's progress. I'm honored and overjoyed to have been even a teeny part of this nostalgic, epic story. I went through some boxes in the attic and found my *Novak* game, album, scrapbook and even a framed photo of JF. I am using these items

Laure Georges (Gonzalez) today, with her treasured mementos of the Mr. Novak Nights

now with a new respect and reliving the golden times they represent. *Mr. Novak* was a timeless, top-quality, trend-setting TV show that will never be surpassed. It was a glorious showcase for JF, who was perfect for the role. Dean Jagger was a great principal. Many other stars shone in *Novak* episodes also. To this day, *Mr. Novak* is my most-loved TV series of all time. It may be 50+ years later but the glow never fades. I hope fervently that a DVD-reissue company will see the light and bring the show back to life for other generations to love and admire just like we did! After all, it is as timeless as my heartfelt memories of JF-the epitome of a great teacher and a beautiful man. — Int.

Marian Collier reflected on this important part of her professional life:

Jim was perfect as Novak. I can't imagine anyone else in the role. He was a good actor, was focused and was very present in his scenes. Dean was brilliant. When he played Principal Vane and was on the set, you couldn't look at anyone else but him. Jeanne Bal was perfect and a strong woman but not overly so. When I saw myself as Miss Scott, I thought, "My God, I'm not that bad." I never thought of myself as a great actress but I saw the shows and thought I was good in my scenes. It was great seeing the other regular teachers, especially Vince. They were all very good and professional even if they only had a brief scene. It brought back many happy memories of how well we all got along when filming the series. Everyone on the production was so interested in doing good work. I could hardly wait to get to the studio in the morning. The show was an

Marian Collier and Chuck Harter at a Heritage House Auction in Beverly Hills, 2016

excellent production with great writing. It was filmed beautifully by Dick Kline and his work really helps it so stand up. Even the kids who just had a few lines were good. It was an honor and a privilege that I was chosen to be part of such a ground-breaking show. I'm so thrilled about this new book. I know that Jack is up there looking down and he's smiling. It would be so great if Warner Home Video, or some other reissue company, would officially release the series on DVD. If more people could see the shows they would realize what a classic series it was. *Mr. Novak* leaves a legacy of quality entertainment. — Int.

In the draft of a speech after the show had been canceled, the program's creator and producer expressed his views on the series:

Mr. Novak has been an honor, a pleasure, and an eye-opener for me. I hope Mr. Novak has inspired some teachers; I hope he will attract future teachers; I hope he has provoked respect for teachers and education everywhere. I hope Mr. Novak's remark about being trusted with the most precious thing in a parent's life — but not being trusted with money — rings a bell on the salary issue. I hope that Mr. Novak has whet some ambitions, stirred some brains and excited people about education. — E. Jack Neuman, 3/6/65.

The last word should go to Mr. Novak himself. James Franciscus recalled his pride in the series during an interview for *The TV Collector* two years before he passed. His comments were published posthumously in the September/October 1991 issue:

> I liked the scenes that dealt and interacted with Novak and the students, in which Novak was not all-knowing, but trying his best, and vulnerable; and that the kids were not treated as someone that should be ruled by an authoritative teacher figure, but rather from someone who's lived longer and has more experience by the very nature of that, and has a better perspective, perhaps, on some of the same hurdles the student's facing, because the teacher's faced them before. Not that he knows it all, but he sure can ease the way. Those are the ones that meant the most to me, I think.
>
> The part meant a lot to me because I had seen teachers portrayed up to that point as sort of buffoons and people that we give our kids to — to not only educate, but to rear — but wouldn't allow them at our cocktail parties. They were, in essence, second-class citizens. And up until that time teachers had been portrayed by *Mr. Peepers* and *Our Miss Brooks*, which were fine shows, but no one had ever tackled a teacher as a heroic image, who was a valuable member of our community, one of THE most. So, I had a great feeling for that and that's what we set out to do, and I think it helped a little. I was really dedicated to the concept because I thought it was fair and right, and I recall saying to myself when I graduated from college that if I didn't make it as an actor, I'd want to teach. So it fit in nicely with my outlook anyway.

James Franciscus in *Longstreet* — ABC-TV — 1971–1972

Chapter Eleven

Alumni — Later Careers and Memories of *Mr. Novak*

The principals involved with the series all went on to other projects after the show's cancelation. In some cases greater triumphs would happen in their future. Here are the subsequent activities of the class of 1965:

E. Jack Neuman: He created *A Man Called Shenandoah*, which ran for one season on ABC. Airing from 1965 to 1966, it starred Robert Horton as a cowboy with amnesia in search of his real identity. Neuman then wrote the screenplay for the MGM feature *The Venetian Affair*, which was a spy thriller released in 1966. It starred Robert Vaughn in the lead. In 1970, he married Marian Collier and remained with her until his passing. After several projects in the early seventies, he wrote *The Blue Knight*, which was a TV movie about the police and featured William Holden in the lead. Produced by Lorimar, and airing in 1973, it was well received by critics and viewers. Neuman then created the long running *Police Story* TV series. It began in 1973 and ran for five seasons on NBC. It was an anthology series with an ever-changing cast. His next success was the TV series *Petrocelli*, which starred Barry Newman as a Harvard-educated lawyer who practices law in Tucson, Arizona. The program aired for two seasons from 1974 to 1976 on the NBC network. Neuman then created an adaption of *The Blue Knight* TV movie which became a series starring George Kennedy. It aired from 1975 to 1976 on CBS.

In 1982 Neuman wrote the teleplay for the TV movie, *Inside the Third Reich*. The five-hour film was a dramatization of the life of Albert Speer, who had been Adolph Hitler's architect and confidant. The movie, which starred Rutger Hauer as Speer, aired to much critical acclaim and later won two Emmy Awards. One was presented to Marvin J. Chomsky for direction and a multi winner award given for the sound editing. Neuman had been nominated for Producer but did not win. However, he did win a Writer's Guild of America Award for outstanding script, television long-form, for the mini-series. Neuman would spend time teaching writing courses at UCLA and USC during the eighties into the nineties. His next writing project was *A Death in California*, which was a two-part TV miniseries in 1985. The film starred Cheryl Ladd and was the story of a Beverly Hills socialite who ends up on trial after her psychopath boyfriend is accused of murder. It was produced by Lorimar and was a ratings success. Neuman won a Writer's Guild Award for his screenplay. *Courage*, a TV movie released in 1986 came next. Neuman's last work was *Voices Within: The Lives of Truddi Case*, a two-part TV miniseries which aired in 1990 on ABC. Neuman co-wrote the script with Truddi Case who was portrayed by Shelley Long. During his long career, Neuman was the recipient of numerous writing awards, particularly from the Writers Guild of America. He was nominated six times for WGA awards, winning four times. He was awarded, cited, and nominated more than 53 times, including several Edgar Allen Poe awards from the Mystery Writers of America, the Peabody Award for *Mr. Novak* and the President Eisenhower Freedoms Award for *The Scott Machine*. E. Jack Neuman passed away on January 15, 1998, in Los Angeles, California.

James Franciscus: In the year following the demise of *Mr. Novak*, he appeared as a guest star on *Twelve O'Clock High* and *Combat*, both of which aired on ABC. In 1968 he acted in *Judd for the Defense* and *The F.B.I.* series, which were also broadcast on ABC. He then starred in his first TV movie. *Shadow over Elveron* was the story of a doctor who confronts a corrupt sheriff as played by Leslie Nielsen. The film received good notices and a solid rating. Franciscus would go on to do many TV movies in his career. In 1968 he formed Omnibus Productions and produced the TV movie *Heidi*. Controversy occurred when an American League football game between the New York Jets and the Oakland Raiders ran long. NBC broke away to begin the broadcast of *Heidi*. Sports viewers complained and a new rule was instigated that required networks to broadcast any games in their entirety. The next year he starred in two theatrical features which were well received by both critics and audiences. *The Valley of Gwangi*, as released by Warner Brothers/Seven Arts, was a science-fiction thriller and featured special effects by Ray Harryhausen. *Marooned* found Franciscus cast as one of three astronauts who were trapped in a capsule during reentry. The attempts to rescue the spacemen provided suspenseful entertainment and the Columbia Pictures film was a success. After a few more guest appearances on TV series, he was cast in *Beneath the Planet of the Apes* for Twentieth Century-Fox. This 1970 sequel to the popular *Planet of the Apes* was popular and is considered the best of the sequels. Franciscus also starred in the TV Movie *Night Slaves* for the "ABC Movie of the Week." He then founded the James Franciscus Celebrity Tennis Tournament to help raise money for multiple-sclerosis research. The matches would continue for many years. Omnibus produced its second TV movie with an adaptation of *Jane Eyre* starring George C. Scott, which was a well received. In 1971 he journeyed to Italy to star in Dario Argento's giallo thriller, *The Cat o'Nine Tails*.

In the same year Franciscus began filming his most popular series after *Mr. Novak*. *Longstreet* would air for two seasons on the ABC network. The lead was a blind insurance investigator and Franciscus received positive reviews by critics and organizations for the sightless. Martial-arts legend Bruce Lee appeared in several episodes of the first season. In the early seventies he appeared on the *Circle of Fear* TV series and starred in the comedic TV movie *The 500 Pound Jerk*. In 1973 Franciscus provided the voice of the star of *Jonathan Livingston Seagull*. The film was based on the very successful novel by Richard Bach. Although it was not well received by critics it was a success with audiences. Omnibus Productions released *The Red Pony* which starred Henry Fonda and was a successful TV film. Franciscus then acted in his next TV series. *Doc Elliot* was the story of a doctor from New York who relocates in Colorado to practice medicine. This ABC-based show was not a success and folded after fifteen episodes. For the next few years Franciscus appeared in several TV movies including *Aloha Means Goodbye*, *The Dream Makers*, *The Trial of Chaplain Jensen*, *Insight*, and *One of My Wives Is Missing*. The quality of the films was uneven but he generally received good notices for his performances. In 1976 he co-starred with Fred Astaire in a sequel to *The Doberman Gang*. This comedy-crime movie, *The Amazing Dobermans*, was distributed by Golden Films. He rounded out the year with the lead in *The Man Inside*. This TV film co-starred Stefanie Powers and was a police drama. The following year found Franciscus appearing in his final TV series. Linda Evans co-starred in *Hunter* which was the story of two US government special agents. It aired on the Syfy network and was canceled after 13 episodes. In 1978 Franciscus had a supporting role as the president of the United States in *The Greek Tycoon*. This theatrical feature starred Anthony Quinn as a character very similar to Aristotle Onassis. In the late seventies Franciscus appeared in TV movies *Secrets of Three Hungry Wives*, *The Pirate*, and *Puzzle*. He also acted in several theatrical features including *Concorde Affaire '79*, *City on Fire*, and *Killer Fish*.

The beginning of the eighties brought roles in the theatrical features *When Time Ran Out*, *Nightkill*, and *The Last Shark*. In 1981 he starred as John F. Kennedy in the popular TV Movie *Jacqueline Bouvier Kennedy*. Jaclyn Smith appeared in the title role and she and Franciscus received critical praise for their performances. The respected actor then had a supporting part in the controversial Pia Zadora vehicle *Buttlerfly*. His last starring role was in the theatrical film *Veliki Transport* which was released in 1983. This was a WW II drama that was filmed in Yugoslavia. It told the true story of a great transport of Partizans from Vojvodina to Bosnia in 1943. James Franciscus's final acting appearance was in the 1985 TV movie drama *Secret Weapons*. He was cast as a Russian colonel involved with espionage. The actor was financially secure but was dissatisfied with his roles of recent years. He then turned his attentions to writing and became somewhat of a recluse. Franciscus had always been a three-pack-a-day smoker and by the late eighties had developed emphysema. In his final years he reflected on an honorable career in both acting and producing and was generally at peace with himself. He also took pride in his many charitable efforts. James Franciscus passed away on July 8, 1991, in North Hollywood, California.

Dean Jagger: After a year and a half of rest to completely cure his ulcers, Jagger returned to television with a role on *The F.B.I.* in late 1966. He also appeared on *The Fugitive* with David Janssen. Both of these series aired on ABC. In the following year he acted in the British WW II drama *First to Fight*. He then appeared in two western features. *Firecreek*, was released by Warner Brothers/Seven Arts and co-starred Jimmy Stewart and Henry Fonda. MGM's *Day of the Evil Gun* followed and featured Glenn Ford. The last year of the sixties saw Jagger's participation in two films. The first was the Disney Studio's *Smith!*, which starred Glenn Ford as a western rancher. *The Lonely Profession* was a TV movie for Universal that featured Harry Guardino as a detective. Jagger had a busy year in 1970 with roles in Commonwealth United's *Tiger by the Tail* and *The Kremlin Letter*. This Twentieth Century-Fox spy thriller had an international cast including George Sanders, Max Von Sydow, and Orson Welles. Jagger returned to television with the TV movie *The Brotherhood of the Bell* for CBS. He also guest starred on an episode of *The Name of the Game* series as a senator. His next part was as the father of the title character of the short-lived *Matt Lincoln* series. This ABC show featured Vince Edwards in the lead. In most of his appearances Jagger received positive notices by the critics.

The next year brought a role in the cult classic *Vanishing Point*. This low-budget adventure feature for Cupid Productions starred Barry Newman who races a Dodge Challenger from Colorado to San Francisco. The early seventies brought roles on *Bonanza*, *The Partridge Family*, *Columbo*, and *Kung Fu*. Jagger's skill as a character actor was shown to good effect in these appearances. He continued to appear on many series including *Medical Center, The Delphi Center, Shaft,* and *Love Story.* The veteran thespian also acted in TV movies *The Stranger, The Lie, I Heard the Owl Call My Name,* and *The Hanged Man.* At this point in his career Jagger was not interested in doing a weekly TV series and was content to do regular guest shots. In the mid-seventies he acted in *The Lindberg Kidnapping Case* TV movie, the *Harry O* series, and the *Evil Town* horror feature. In 1977 he was reunited with his *Mr. Novak* co-star James Franciscus with two guest appearances on the *Hunter* TV series. Jagger followed this with a supporting role in *Game of Death.* This was a feature that used footage of the late Bruce Lee with a double to create a new film. The last year of the seventies saw Jagger appear on *The Waltons.* This series was very popular and he received good reviews.

There were three appearances in 1980. The first was on the *This Is the Life* religious TV series. He then had a small supporting role as a Supreme Court judge in the *Gideon's Trumpet* TV movie. It was based on a true story and starred Henry Fonda as Clarence Gideon who fought for the right to have publicly funded legal counsel for the needy. The movie aired to critical acclaim. His third appearance of the year was the horror feature film *Alligator.* In 1985 the thespian was cast in his final acting role on the popular *St. Elsewhere* TV series. He had a small role as a doctor. The veteran of the acting profession had worked steadily in the twenty years after the demise of *Mr. Novak.* He had a reputation as a respected character actor and always performed to the best of his ability no matter what the quality of the production. Dean Jagger passed away on February 5, 1991, in Santa Monica, California.

Jeanne Bal: Jeanne's first role after leaving *Mr. Novak* was on *The Fugitive.* In the same year of 1964 she also appeared on the NBC's *Karen* TV series. The following year she had a supporting role on an episode of the sitcom *McHale's Navy* and guest starred twice on *The Perry Mason Show* for CBS. She received praise from the critics for these dramatic performances on the successful lawyer series. Her next appearance was her most iconic and popular guest stint after *Mr. Novak.* Jeanne guested on NBC's popular *Star Trek* series. In "The Man Trap" she played Nancy Crater who was an old flame of Captain Kirk. The actress was well received and the episode remains a favorite with *Star Trek* devotees. She then had a supporting role on the short lived *Hey Landlord* sitcom which starred Will Hutchins and Sandy Baron. Jeanne was inactive in 1967 and returned to television the following year with as a guest star on NBC's *I Spy* series. In "Happy Birthday Everybody" she portrayed Shirl Mathews and received good notices. Her next appearance in the same year was on the Roman Catholic religious-themed *Insight* series for CBS. She played the leading role. The following year was another one of inactivity. In 1969 she was cast in an episode of the *Matt Lincoln* series. Dean Jagger had appeared in two segments but did not appear in the episode with Jeanne. In 1971 the actress obtained her final acting opportunity with a small role in the *Company of Killers* TV movie. The stars were Van Johnson and Ray Milland. It was somewhat of a *Mr. Novak* reunion as the script had been written by E. Jack Neuman. Among her costars were Marian Collier, Vince Howard, and Larry Thor. After this role, Jeanne retired from the acting profession. She led a private life and made no public appearances or gave any interviews. Jeanne Bal passed away on April 30, 1996, in Sherman Oaks, California.

Phyllis Avery: Phyllis's first appearance after the *Mr. Novak* show ended was in the sitcom *O.K. Crackerby!* The star was Burl Ives and she had a small supporting role. The next year the actress was cast in the *Bob Hope Presents the Chrysler Theatre* dramatic series. In the western-themed "Massacre at Fort Phil Kearney" the stars were Richard Egan and Carroll O'Connor. The year of 1967 brought a supporting role on NBC's *Daniel Boone*. Fess Parker starred as the frontier hero and the series was a popular one. Three years of inactivity followed. Phyllis returned to television with a small part in the sci-fi TV movie, "The Last Child." This "ABC Movie of the Week" starred Michael Cole, Van Heflin, and Harry Guardino. Her next role was that of a nun on the popular *All in the Family* series. In the 1973 episode "Edith's Conversion," Phyllis played Sister Theresa who explains aspects of the Catholic Church to Archie Bunker's wife. Four years later the actress returned to television with a small role in the *Maude* sitcom. This Norman Lear-produced comedy starred Bea Arthur and was very successful. In 1977 she appeared in an episode of the popular *Charlie's Angels* show. "Angel Trap" found Phyllis sixth-billed in a small part. The next year saw her final acting job for some time. "Baretta" was a very successful show for ABC and starred Robert Blake as a New York City detective. She had a small role in the "Just for Laughs" episode. Realizing that her career had become an erratic series of small parts, Phyllis left the acting profession and became a successful real-estate agent in Los Angeles. She returned to performing with a bit part in the 1993 Warner Brothers feature *Maid in America*. The stars of this comedy were Whoopi Goldberg and Ted Danson. Two years later the actress came back to television with a small role on the *Coach* series which featured Craig T. Nelson. Her final appearance was in the 1999 teen comedy *The Secret Life of Girls*. She had a funny scene as the Owl Lady and received much laughter for her performance. Phyllis Avery passed away on May 19, 2011, in Los Angeles, California.

Burgess Meredith: (Note: Since the actor had such a large number of roles in the remainder of his career, only highlights will be examined.) In the year of *Mr. Novak's* cancelation, Meredith guest starred on series *Laredo*, *The Wild, Wild West*, *The Trials of O'Brien*, and *The Loner*. He was in demand as a character actor and usually received positive reviews for his performances. In 1966 he returned to films with a supporting role in the United Artists feature *Madame X*. This soap opera starred Lana Turner and was a popular film. Meredith continued to make guest appearances in the *Please Don't Eat the Daises*, and *Branded* TV shows. He then landed what would become his most iconic role. He was cast as the Penguin in the extremely popular *Batman* TV series for ABC. The stars were Adam West as the Caped Crusader and Burt Ward as Robin the Boy Wonder. The show was a pop-culture phenomenon and Meredith proved to be a fan favorite as the arch-villain. He would make several appearances on the series and would repeat his role in the *Batman* film which was released late in the year. He did not neglect other feature film work and appeared in the western comedy *A Big Hand for a Little Lady* and the dramatic *Hurry Sundown* with Michael Caine. In the late sixties Meredith would guest star *on The Invaders, Bonanza, The Monkees,* and *Daniel*

Boone. There were film roles in *Torture Garden*, *Skidoo*, and *McKenna's Gold*. Meredith possessed a great work ethic and was always pursuing his craft.

The first half of the seventies brought many appearances on television which included *The Bold Ones*, *The Name of the Game*, *Room 222*, and *McCloud*. Feature film work included *Such Good Friends*, *A Fan's Notes*, and *Beware the Blob*. His performance in *The Day of the Locust* was nominated for Best Supporting Actor by the Academy of Motion Picture Arts and Sciences. In 1976 he appeared in the popular *Rocky* feature as Mickey, the manager of the prizefighter. Sylvester Stallone starred as Rocky Balboa and Meredith was again nominated for Best Supporting Actor. He returned to the part of the manager in *Rocky II* which was released in the last year of the seventies. In the early part of the next decade the actor appeared on a couple of episodes of the *Archie Bunker's Place* TV series. He made his third appearance as the manager in *Rocky III*. Meredith had not been cast as a series' regular since *Mr. Novak*. His recurring role of Dr. Willard Adams in the *All in the Family* spinoff *Gloria* kept his profile high with viewers. The show starred Sally Struthers as Gloria Stivic. The performer acted in several TV movies during the rest of the decade. These included *Wet Gold*, *Outrage!*, *G.I. Joe the Movie*, and *Mister Corbett's Ghost*. In 1990 he appeared for the final time as the manager in *Rocky V*. There were roles in the TV movies *Night of the Hunter*, *Mastergate*, and *Lincoln*. He acted in a few episodes of the *In the Heat of the Night* TV series and was cast as a Judge. He appeared with Jack Lemmon and Walter Matthau in the feature *Grumpy Old Men*. Meredith was cast as Grandpa Gustafson and reprised the role in the *Grumpier Old Men* sequel. Meredith's final performance was as a voice actor in the *Ripper* video game which was produced in 1996. He had been pursuing his craft for over sixty years and was an accomplished and respected member of the acting community. Burgess Meredith passed away on September 9, 1997, in Malibu, California.

Leonard Freeman: The former producer's next project after the end of the *Mr. Novak* series was to co-author the script for the 1968 feature *Hang 'em High*. The other author was Mel Goldberg and it was released by United Artists. Clint Eastwood starred in the western movie which received critical acclaim. In the same year he created the *Hawaii Five-O* television series. This detective show, which aired on the CBS, network was primarily filmed on location in Hawaii. It starred Jack Lord as Detective Steve McGarrett with James MacArthur and Kam Fong as supporting regulars. Freeman wrote the pilot and would eventually pen four more scripts for the program. *Hawaii Five-O* proved to be very popular and would go on to air for twelve seasons in total. In 1973 Freeman co-wrote, with Will Lorin, the script for the TV movie *Cry Rape*. This dramatic film starred Andrea Marcovicci and was broadcast on the CBS network. Leonard Freeman passed away on January 20, 1974, in Palo Alto, California.

Marian Collier: After *Mr. Novak's* demise, Marian appeared in three TV series in 1965. She was featured in ABC sitcoms *The Farmer's Daughter*, and *Gidget*. The actress was also seen in the wartime dramatic series *Convoy* for NBC. She was inactive during 1966. In the following year she acted in MGM western feature *The Last Challenge*, which starred Glenn Ford. She also made an unbilled appearance in the Trident Films feature comedy *Doctor, You've Got to Be Kidding!* Marian had two roles in 1968. The first was in the Universal feature comedy *Nobody's Perfect*, which starred Doug McClure and Nancy Kwan. This was followed by a role on CBS's *Mannix* series. This popular show featured Mike Connors as a detective. Another year of inactivity occurred in 1969. The first year of the seventies saw the actress in two made for TV movies for Universal Television. *A Clear and Present Danger* was a dramatic story that starred Hal Holbrook and E. G. Marshall and dealt with the effects of pollution. Her second role was in the *Berlin Affair*, which was a spy drama starring Darren McGavin. She had three parts in 1971. Marian appeared in *The Hunting Party* feature with Oliver Reed and Candice Bergen. The actress was featured in *Company of Killers* with Ray Milland for Universal Television. This was followed by *Crosscurrent*, which was released by Warner Bros. Television and starred Robert Hooks. In 1972 she was appeared in an episode of the *Emergency!* series for Universal Television. Three TV movies followed in the next year. They were *Incident on a Dark Street* for 20th Century-Fox, *Stat!* for CBS and *Egan* for Paramount Television. Marian had her next role in 1974's *Three the Hard Way* feature which was a blaxploitation release by Allied Artists. She also appeared as a nurse in the popular *Police Story* anthology series. This Columbia Pictures Television program had been created by E. Jack Neuman.

The year of 1975 was a busy one for the actress with roles in *Sarah T. — Portrait of a Teenage Alcoholic*. This Universal Television TV movie starred Linda Blair and was very successful. Marian acted in episodes of *Lucas Tanner* for Universal Television and *Kate McShane* for Paramount Television. She ended the year with another role as a nurse on the popular *Marcus Welby, M.D.* series. This Universal program starred Robert Young in the lead. In the year of the bicentennial there were roles the *Law and Order* TV movie in which she played a nun and the *Delvecchio* detective series. In the next year Marian was featured in the *Rafferty* series for Warner Brothers Television. This short-lived medical show starred Patrick McGoohan. The year of 1978 brought another nurse role ABC's popular *Welcome Back, Kotter* sitcom. After a few years of inactivity, Marian returned to acting in the prestigious *Inside the Third Reich* TV miniseries. This 1982 production earned critical acclaim and several awards. It was written by E. Jack Neuman and was based on the book by Nazi Albert Speer. The last year of the eighties saw Marian featured in the Richard Donner directed *Lethal Weapon 2*. This Warner Bros. release starred Mel Gibson and was very successful with audiences. The actress would also appear in two sequels which included *Lethal Weapon 3* in 1992 and *Lethal Weapon 4* in 1998.

In 1990 she acted in the TV movie *Voices Within: The Lives of Truddi Chase*. This intense drama was adapted by E. Jack Neuman form the autobiography of the title character. The nineties saw Marian acting in *Under Investigation* which was a 1993 video release for New Line Cinema. She followed this role with an appearance in the Sylvester Stallone vehicle *Assassins*, which was issued in 1995. Two more roles followed as the decade came to a close. She had a part in 1997's *Conspiracy Theory*. This thriller feature starred Mel Gibson and was directed by Richard Donner. In the new millennium Marian acted in 2003's *Timeline*. This sci-fi feature was released by Paramount. She next appeared in the video short *A Golightly Gathering*. Sparkhill Productions released this in 2009. In the same year she gave her final performance to date in the *iCarly* TV series. The program was a popular family show on the Nickelodeon Network. Marian continues to live in Hollywood and enjoys singing with two music groups. The Verdi Chorus and the Santa Monica College Chorale regularly perform concerts to wide acclaim. She also maintains the E. Jack Neuman archive. Marian has made her first appearance at the Hollywood Collectors Show. The actress enjoyed autographing photos and meeting fans of *Some Like It Hot* and *Mr. Novak*.

Bob Schultz: The property master's first major project after the end of *Mr. Novak* was the MGM released Elvis Presley vehicle *Spinout*. He did not receive a credit in this 1966 release. A few years later he was put under contract with director Mike Nichols. Bob was the property master for the epic *Catch-22* feature which was issued by Paramount in 1970. This all-star feature, based on the critically acclaimed novel by Joseph Heller, was a popular success. In the same year he worked on *They Call Me Mister Tibbs*. This Mirisch Corporation film starred Sidney Poitier as a police lieutenant with support from Martin Landau. His next project for Mike Nichols was the controversial *Carnal Knowledge*, which was released by Embassy Pictures. This adult-themed film starred Jack Nicholson, Ann Margret, Art Garfunkel, and Candice Bergen and was a major release in 1971. *The Cowboys* was issued in the following year and starred John Wayne. It was directed by Mark Rydell and was a popular motion picture. In the same year Bob was the property master for *The Life and Times of Judge Roy Bean*. This First Artists production was directed by John Huston and starred Paul Newman and Ava Gardner. The industry veteran's next project was the TV movie *The Killer Bees* which was broadcast on the ABC network in 1974. The stars were Edward Albert and Kate Jackson with a strong support from screen legend Gloria Swanson. His final completed assignment was *W. W. and the Dixie Dance Kings*, which was a 20th Century-Fox vehicle for Burt Reynolds. This popular film of 1975 also starred Art Carney and was directed by John G. Avildsen. Bob worked on several projects after this, but unfortunately they were not completed. He eventually retired from the industry and lives in Encino California.

Final Memories

In the course of interviewing various people for this book, I asked them to finish two statements. Here are the results along with a retrospective reflection from the leading man.

THE MR. NOVAK SERIES WAS…

"pretty revolutionary for its time. The fan mail I received from teachers showed they appreciated being depicted as the intelligent, hard-working professionals most of them are." — James Franciscus (John Novak) — entire series. (Mobile Register, 11/6/71.)

"a great show that really holds up very well. I loved playing Miss Scott. It's so much fun to see the episodes again. The show is still very good and can apply to modern times." — Marian Collier (Marilyn Scott) — entire series.

"a great step in advancing an area of respect and dignity to TV shows." — Richard Donner — (Director) — "X is the Unknown Factor," "A Thousand Voices," "The Private Life of Douglas Morgan, Jr.," "The Death of a Teacher," "One Way to Say Goodbye," "Moonlighting," "Beyond a Reasonable Doubt."

"gratifying." — John D. F. Black (Writer) — "With a Hammer in His Hand, Lord, Lord!," "The People Doll: You Wind It Up and It Makes Mistakes," "An Elephant Is Like a Tree," "Mountains to Climb," "May Day, May Day," "There's a Penguin in My Garden."

"probably the best series of the series I did. It was a good experience." — Bob Schultz (property master).

"had a bunch of wonderful actors and was a triumph for Producer E. Jack Neuman. It was an interesting and enlightening series about school." — Ed Asner (Harmon Stern) "First Year, First Day," (Paul Berg) "An Elephant is Like a Tree."

"very cutting edge back in the day and really holds up well all these years later. Seeing my episode again, I thought I was pretty good. Richard Donner's direction was excellent with his use of extreme close-ups. It was a good hour of TV." — Frankie Avalon (David Muller) "A Thousand Voices."

"a wonderful production about a teacher who was a hero with his ethics. I enjoyed viewing the episode again but didn't like the way my character was so flippant to Mr. Novak at the end. The direction and acting was first-rate and I think it holds up very well." — Diane Baker (Mildred Chase) "A Feeling for Friday."

"a very good experience. Excellent cinematography by Richard Kline." — Barbara Barrie (Mary Smith) "How Does Your Garden Grow?"

"a groundbreaking series and I was so fortunate to be a small part of it. The show took on some really tough subjects; among them, religious persecution, bullying and teacher's rights. These were subjects that up to this time were not seen on network television." — Beau Bridges (Mike) "Pay the Two Dollars," (Pat Knowland) "Sparrow on the Wire," (Jay Bartlett) "Honor — and All That."

"my second part on TV with all the excitement and trepidations of being a young actress and bringing what I could to it. After seeing it again, I liked some of my performance especially the scene with Mr. Novak while I'm sitting at the desk. It was a well-written script with the twists and turns of a well-written script." — Lane Bradbury (Ellen Westfall) "Love Among the Grownups."

"new and fresh and different. It holds up very well. It was great to see the episodes again. "X Is the Unknown Factor is a lot of food for thought. The terrible pressure put on students to overachieve was shown in a quality fashion. It was a nourishing and interesting segment. I thought "The Song of Songs" was very provocative and filled with many layers of innuendos." — Brooke Bundy (Patrice Morgan) "X Is the Unknown Factor," (Shirley Whittier) "The Song of Songs," (Carol Walker) "One Monday Afternoon."

"a great experience for me. The scripts were good and it was highly regarded." — Johnny Crawford (Jojo Rizzo) "Let's Dig a Little Grammar," (USSR Assembly Member) "The Tender Twigs."

"one of the best series on television — week after week. I had never seen my episode and after viewing it was amazed at how ahead of its time the series was. I

was very proud of the writing, direction, production and acting." — Pat Crowley (Ariel Wilder) "Love in the Wrong Season."

"a wonderful series filled with good scripts and fine talent both in front and behind the camera." — Davey Davison (Silverman) (Edie Currie) "Little Girl Lost."

"progressive and very much ahead of its time in its subject matter and production values. After seeing the episodes again, I feel the show holds up today as quality television. Most old shows don't hold up. The writing is complex and the actors are terrific. The writers created a great atmosphere for the school because they didn't scrimp on the kids." — Tony Dow (George Scheros) "To Lodge and Dislodge," "The Death of a Teacher," "Fear Is a Handful of Dust," (Mike Kenyon) "Johnny Ride the Pony: One, Two, Three," (United States Assembly Member) "The Tender Twigs."

"a rewarding experience for me. It was a classy series and got the ball rolling in my acting career. As a result of my exposure on Novak, I started to work on just about every TV show on the air in the '60's. Seeing my episode again I was impressed by Richard Kline's excellent photography and the story line." — Richard Evans (Charlie Payne) "The Exile."

"very well done, as much as I've seen. It still plays well in current times." — Richard Eyer (Jeff) "Day in the Year."

"...can't really say." — June Harding (Karen Parker) "'A' as in Anxiety."

"a very classy show. Viewing the episode again, I thought there was warmth where the kids had to say goodbye to the gangster. Harold J. Stone was very good in the lead." — Jimmy Hawkins (Peter Beatty) "Beat the Plowshare, Edge the Sword."

"an excellent show about teenagers. After watching the episodes again, I was amazed at how good they were. Not dated at all and the plotlines could work in modern productions." — Peter Helm (Douglas Morgan, Jr.) "The Private Life of Douglas Morgan, Jr.," (Vern) "Born of Kings and Angels," (President UN Assembly) "The Tender Twigs."

"a bit of a groundbreaking series that put the focus on a time in all our lives when we're going through the teen years. It gave the writers great opportunities and some of the stories were very sophisticated for that time." — Allan Hunt (Dick Elerton) "Hello, Miss Phipps," (Unbilled) "A Thousand Voices," (Jerry Donan) "One Monday Afternoon," (Albania Assembly Member) "The Tender Twigs," (Red) "There's a Penguin in My Garden."

"ahead of its time. It was entertaining and intellectual. It wasn't just out to make a buck and be a hit show and was very well thought out and professional. Seeing it again I thought I looked like a woman and felt I did a good job as the

young wife. The show absolutely holds up to the present day. I was proud to be on the series." — Sherry Jackson (Cathy Ferguson) "The Risk."

"my first experience with Hollywood acting and writing at its highest level. It was great to see the episodes again and they held up beautifully. I showed 'Enter a Strange Animal' to my son Spencer who's a computer software designer. He's 28 and when he saw the teaching machines he jumped up and paid attention. He was shocked that they had primitive computers that long ago." — Randy Kirby (Phillip) "Enter a Strange Animal," (Lebanon Assembly Member) "The Tender Twigs."

"an emotional and hard experience." — Tommy Kirk (Todd Seaton) "Love in the Wrong Season."

"integral in propelling my career. It was a nice experience for my first starring role on TV." — Walter Koenig (Aleksei Dubov) "The Boy Without a Country," (Jim Carsey) "With a Hammer in His Hand, Lord, Lord!," (Paul Ryder) "The Firebrand."

"special, intelligent, deep and ahead of its time. After viewing 'Pay the Two Dollars' again I felt that there was nothing archaic about it." — Martin Landau (Victor Rand) "Pay the Two Dollars," (Robert Coolidge) "Enter a Strange Animal."

"well done." — Louise Latham (Adele) "And Then I Wrote."

"the only one of its kind. It was thoughtful, provocative and intelligent drama and still is." — June Lockhart (Mrs. Nelby) "Once a Clown."

"a well-written and -acted television series, which attempted to show a realistic teacher in truthful situations. I found watching the segment again to be a pleasure. Martin Landau is very good and the whole story is still relevant." — Tom Lowell (Carl Edwards) "Pay the Two Dollars."

"a quality show... producers, writers and all involved tried to produce something that would cause people to think about serious matters yet still be entertained. The actors and production values were the best. It was a mind provoking show that one was proud to work on. It deserves more attention and exposure." — David Macklin (Mike Daniels) "X Is the Unknown Factor," (Fred) "Love in the Wrong Season," (Charles Stoddard) "Enter a Strange Animal."

"full of meaningful human stories that I loved. It was so special seeing it again. Jim was really good and very dashing in the romantic scenes. Lois was amazing... she was kind of quirky... very captivating and very real. I was humbly and tenderly impressed by my young self as the troubled girl. I was in awe of myself as a young focused actor." — Alison Mills (Newman) — (Billie) "Where Is There to Go, Billie, but Up?"

"entertaining. I liked seeing the episode again and thought it was a very good show." — Brenda Scott (Sue Johnson) "Fear Is a Handful of Dust."

"beautifully done. It was well cast and the scripts were good." — David Sheiner (Paul Webb) "Faculty Follies: Part 1," "Let's Dig a Little Grammar" (Dr. Wexler) "Day in the Year."

"an intelligent show and a departure from most of the western shows popular in the 60's. Seeing it again, I was struck by Walter's excellence in the lead." — Julie Sommars (Ellen Cable) "The Firebrand."

"a realistic show of its time. The scripts were provocative and truthful. As a beginner in the acting profession, it was a good experience for me. Seeing the episode again I realized that it had an interesting script, somewhat before its time." — Tisha Sterling (Myra) "The Firebrand."

"a great series showcasing a lot of young actors. I had a good time working on the show. I wish more people could see the series. It was great to see the episodes again and I think the show really stands up." — Buck Taylor (Nick Bradley) "Little Girl Lost," (Scott Lawson) "The Silent Dissuaders," (Don) "Honor — and All That."

"a fond and grateful memory for me. It was an excellent show and very well written. After watching 'Visions of Sugar Plums' I was surprised at how well it held up. Eddie Albert really suited the role and Phyllis Avery was adorable." — Beverly Washburn (Ruth) "Visions of Sugar Plums," (Edith) "From the Brow of Zeus."

"a very well-constructed series that helped a lot of people and that's what my husband wanted it to do. His performances as Mr. Novak are still wonderful all these years later." — Kitty Wellman (Mrs. James Franciscus).

"an excellent show that made my brother Goey a big star. He was great as Mr. Novak and I think the series really holds up today in all departments." — John Franciscus (brother of James Franciscus.)

"innovative, top quality, meaningful and phenomenal! It's been great watching the shows again and it remains my favorite TV series of all time." — Laure Georges (Gonzalez) (extra) "First Year, First Day."

"a pivotal show that I related to be in and it was a privilege for a Hollywood kid. There were interesting stories about current issues relating to young people." — March Wanamaker (extra on series)

"a breakthrough showing that teachers and administrators were human beings." — Dr. G. Keith Dolan (principal of San Bernardino High School/script advisor.)

"an exciting discovery 25 years after it had been on and that it exceeded all expectations." — Diane Albert (writer for *The TV Collector* magazine.)

"the absolute best drama about teaching ever produced by Hollywood. It was not only the first, but the finest and still is." — John T. Taylor (veteran teacher and owner of *Mr. Novak* website)

JAMES FRANCISCUS WAS...

"very good looking and a very professional actor. He was perfect as John Novak." — Marian Collier.

"excellent and knew the character and was good in the role. He was very shy... withdrawn... protective. He was the kind of guy... when you found a sense of security with him was very delightful... funny and a pleasure to be around." — Richard Donner.

"blond and the perfect center for a television series." — John D. F. Black.

"a great guy... very quiet... very humble. He was gracious. As an actor he never flubbed his lines... Jim was always there." — Bob Schultz.

"a very nice man. A good performer. I liked him." — Ed Asner.

"a terrific actor... very professional and intense." — Frankie Avalon.

"a gentleman who was very smart and I respected him." — Diane Baker.

"very low key and very talented." — Barbara Barrie.

"a total professional, but approached his work with a great sense of joy. He was very kind to me and inspired me to give my very best." — Beau Bridges.

"a fine actor and a true Yaley." — Brooke Bundy.

"cool." — Johnny Crawford.

"a joy to work with!" — Pat Crowley.

"a very generous actor, talented and handsome. It was a pleasure to work with him." — Davey Davison.

"really just a nice guy and unlike most stars of the day. It was like he was your best buddy. He was just like he was on the show." — Tony Dow.

"a very serious guy, quiet, reserved. He was a gentleman." — Richard Evans.

"easy for me to work with. A classy guy." — Richard Eyer.

"rude... yelled to have his way —. He was — never mind." — June Harding.

"a nice guy... very professional... no star attitude." — Jimmy Hawkins.

"a good actor and a good guy. He really looked the part. He hit his marks and knew his lines." — Peter Helm.

"focused and high-strung. He was good looking and it was the perfect part for him. His eyes always seemed to be impressionable... taking in things around him. He was curious and learning the role of the young teacher." — Allan Hunt.

"a true gentleman and a method actor." — Sherry Jackson.

"perfect for the show. His temperament was a good temperament for the series and he acquitted himself admirably." — Randy Kirby.

"a tough, hard man." — Tommy Kirk.

"totally professional and a pleasure to work with. He was a nice guy... not too personal. All the girls were swooning over him but he took it with a grain of salt." — Walter Koenig.

"steadfast, hard-working, professional and talented." — Martin Landau.

"good to work with." — Louise Latham.

"a splendid, dedicated and serious actor who didn't take his work lightly." — June Lockhart.

"a wonderful actor and a gentleman." — Tom Lowell.

"the best. He was an excellent actor who listened and was great to work with because he gave you the freedom to go for it and you knew he would go with you. He was friendly, guileless, open, approachable, cooperative and generous." — David Macklin.

"the heartthrob of everybody. Adorable. He was kind and a good actor." — Alison Mills (Newman).

"kind, nice and very polite in a friendly way." — Brenda Scott.

"excellent. One of the most professional actors I ever saw. His ability to learn lines was amazing because he had a lot of dialogue and didn't have much time to prepare. He was always letter perfect." — David Sheiner.

"not a very nice person." — Julie Sommars.

"easy for me to work with and a gentleman." — Tisha Sterling.

"always good and a gentleman. He went on to do several series." — Buck Taylor.

"a wonderful and consummate actor who was very professional and very nice. He was quite the hunk." — Beverly Washburn.

"Mr. Novak... the man I married." — Kitty Wellman.

"my brother Goey... and I remember him with admiration." — John Franciscus.

"dreamy, adorable, handsome, intelligent and a terrific actor. He made the series shine." — Laure Gonzalez.

"a kind, personable and friendly guy. All of us were pulling for him to do a good performance because we liked him so much and he always did." — Marc Wanamaker

"a model for teachers. I think he epitomized what young teachers should be like." — Dr. G. Keith Dolan

"the teacher I wanted to be." — John T. Taylor.

"such a great actor that he took a character and with his underplaying turned him into someone so real that it was hard to believe he was just playing a part." — Diane Albert.

**Afterword
by Walter Koenig**

I was in the eighth grade. I was still writing on my Spanish exam when time expired. A couple of the better pupils handed in their tests and began comparing answers. One of the blank spaces on my paper could be filled in by their discussion. I didn't hesitate. When I returned to my seat the teacher was staring at me. She knew what I had done and it left me feeling incredibly guilty. That feeling never went away. In 1964 I was cast as a student in an episode of the *Mr. Novak* series called "With a Hammer in His Hand, Lord, Lord!" A scene in which the school principal interrogates the character I was playing instinctively brought back my experience in that Spanish class. The raging humiliation was still there and I knew exactly how to play that confrontation. John D. F. Black, the writer of the episode, was evidently impressed with my performance and so, I was told, was Dean Jagger, the series' co-lead who was playing the principal. I was informed that he thought my work "memorable." It just goes to show that cheating works.

Reading this book by Chuck Harter brought back many satisfying memories. You don't have to have been an actor... just a student to appreciate the skillful way in which he unfolds the stories behind the cameras. If the series is ever reissued, and I've heard rumors to that effect, this tome should be in your lap. What a perfect way to enjoy the series and, at the same time, reference how it was all put together.

By the way, I ran into James Franciscus, the other lead on the show, at a gas station a few years after making my last of three appearances on the series. He had no idea who I was.

Walter Koenig — 1/15/17.

MR. NOVAK

4 NBC
WRC · TV
WASHINGTON, D.C.

TUESDAY ★ 7:30 P.M.

Episode Guide — Season One

MR. NOVAK

Metro-Goldwyn-Mayer

for

NBC (Tuesdays 7:30 P.M. EST)

60 Minutes.

First Season — 1963–1964

Created by E. Jack Neuman and Boris Sagal.

Starring:

James Franciscus as John Novak.

Dean Jagger as Albert Vane.

and

Jeanne Bal as Jean Pagano.

Crew:

Music .... Lyn Murray.
Director of Photography .... Frank Phillips.
Art Direction .... George W. Davis and McClure Capps.
Supervising Film Editor .... John Dunning.
Film Editor .... Robert J. Kern, Jr.
Assistant Director .... Al Westen.
Set Decoration .... Henry Grace and Hugh Hunt.
Recording Supervisor .... Frank Milton.

We wish to thank the Advisory Panel of the National Education Association for its invaluable assistance.

(Note: Different crew members will be noted in the episodes they worked on.)

🍎 🍎 🍎 🍎

Episode One — **First Year, First Day**
Broadcast September 24, 1963

Synopsis:

Mr. Novak's teaching career gets off to a rocky start when the school's outstanding student quits school to devote full time to an auto-body shop which he ran during summer vacation. Novak's unorthodox approach to the problem draws strong criticism from Principal Albert Vane and Novak's reputation — both with the students and with the faculty — hangs in the balance.

Guest Star Lee Kinsolving as Paul Christopher.
Co-Starring Ann Shoemaker as Miss Rose.
Edward Asner as Mr. Stern.

with

Steve Franken .... Jerry Allen.
Marian Collier .... Miss Scott.
Donald Barry .... Mr. Gallo.
Paul Genge .... Mr. Christopher.
Shirley O'Hara .... Mrs. Clyde.

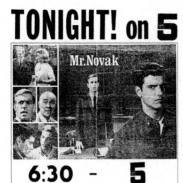

TONIGHT! on 5

Mr. Novak

6:30 – 5

And

Gloria Talbott as Miss Harvey.

Reviews:

This looks like a winner. It features a handsome young high school teacher and easily might be called "Dr. Kildare Goes to High School." Dean Jagger is superb as the ever-present older adviser (naturally he's the principal), and James Franciscus is quite good as the teacher. Before the opener gets too involved in a flimsy storyline, there are some wonderful scenes where the principal welcomes the new teachers and introduces them to the students. If the series can maintain even part of the excellence of those scenes, it may make teaching as appealing as neuro-surgery. — *Steven H. Scheuer, King Features Syndicate,* San Diego *(CA)* Union, *September 24, 1963.*

Mr. Novak is a product of MGM Studios, where Dr. Kildare serves as the model for every young hero used in the series. The difference in the show is that Novak can tell his mentor, the principal, where to get off. Kildare doesn't dare do that to Gillespie. A high school is a good place to base a drama, and a teacher is something of a mysterious character to most people, sort of a cross between a doctor, minister and a lawyer. This series attempts to show a teacher as a human being, and for the most part, succeeds. — *Bob Hull, "TV Talk,"* Los Angeles Herald Examiner, *September 24, 1963.*

Mr. Novak, a series set in a high school, makes a promising start. The characters involved are real and the story makes a strong point against drop-outs. The best part — aside from a good climatic scene between Franciscus and guest Lee Kinsolving — comes as the teachers meet the students the first day at school and the principal makes a slip of the tongue that causes an attack of the giggles. It's an irresistible scene. Clever music is used, with a rock-'n'-roll theme sneaking in whenever students appear on the scene. — *"The TV Scout,"* Kenosha *(WI)* News, *September 24, 1963.*

Mr. Novak deals with a young English teacher (James Franciscus) in a metropolitan high school, and is Dr. Kildare all over again. Franciscus even looks like him, and there is the usual older colleague. The show is straight out of NBC's happy Hollywood fairyland of the professions. The show stank. — *Rick Du Brow, "Television in Review,"* Baton Rouge *(LA)* State-Times, *September 25, 1963.*

Mr. Novak, the series that's supposed to hold teachers, parents and students enthralled, checked in last night with a formula script about a dropout that might have been done on any series. It left us unmoved. James Franciscus, as the "dedicated" English teacher was not very forceful and the most believable performance was that of Dean Jagger, as the high school principal. — *Eleanor Roberts, Traveler Television Editor,* Boston *(MA.)* Traveler, *September 25, 1963.*

In the first episode, the series took a firm grip on a topic of deep national concern today. Mr. Novak's teaching career got off to a challenging start when a straight-A pupil (guest Lee Kinsolving) deserted the classroom for a body-repair job. Franciscus was in fine dramatic form as he conjured up ways of reselling the dropout on the values of education. He was genuine as a man devoted to the science of learning. Kinsolving seemed to have boned up to gain firsthand knowledge of what a dropout feels, what he thinks and desires. He was credible in his portrayal. Academy Award-winner Dean Jagger (movie *Twelve O'Clock High*) played his role as principal of Jefferson High with the assurance that came from the long acting successes he's enjoyed. He looked like a principal, acted like a dedicated man who loved his work. He seemed a human type, but one possessed with a hidden temper that commanded respect from those associated with him. The weekly use of 1,000 students of John Marshall High School (Los Angeles) as guest stars in the new series provided authenticity of its settings. — *Bert J. Reesing, Television-Radio Editor*, Cleveland *(OH)* Plain Dealer, *September 25, 1963.*

The hour-long production has an excellent cast. Everyone who has had difficulty or enjoyment in high school will like this show. You can even identify yourself with some of the characters. In the opening story, Mr. Novak's teaching career gets off to a rocky start when he has an argument with the school's most outstanding student who wants to quit school. Mr. Novak shows the boy why he should stay in school, and the reason is one that should stick with all viewers, especially teenagers. — *Bill Shelton, "TV Tonight,"* Cullman *(AL)* Times, *September 25, 1963.*

The hero is James Franciscus, a handsome, blond young man not unlike Richard Chamberlain. He plays an idealistic teacher in a large urban high school. Where Kildare has his Gillespie, Novak has his Mr. Vane, the mature wise school principal, played by Dean Jagger with understanding and wit. The production was glossy and the sentiments expressed about education were valid, if sometimes a bit high-flown. The high school pupils shown seemed like fine, high-spirited kids. There was not juvenile delinquent among them. — *Cynthia Lowry, AP Television Radio Writer,* Danville *(VA)* Bee, *September 25, 1963.*

Mr. Novak, a believable school teacher, is superbly played by James Franciscus. The principal is equally well interpreted by Dean Jagger. Television has had other school teacher shows — Eve Arden in Our Miss Brooks and Wally Cox as Mr. Peepers, among them. However, the teachers were only comics in those series; people to kid about. Learning was only something to spoof. Mr. Novak is a dedicated teacher. He believes in leading, guiding, stimulating youngsters, and making learning exciting. There are some wonderful moments when the principal introduces the new teachers and explains their jobs to them. These are moving scenes, depicting in thrilling fashion the worth and rewards of teaching and learning. I hope, and almost believe, that this show will be a great success. It surely deserves it. — *Larry Wolters,* Chicago Trib., *September 25, 1963.*

GOOD OLD GOLDEN RULE DAYS — According to the last head-count in America there are 13 million high school students versus 607,462 high school teachers. They meet face to face five days of the week. It is difficult to fool either faction — particularly the students. NBC's *Mr. Novak* is an attempt to capture some of the dramatic elements of these daily encounters and put them together in an hour-long weekly television series. Last night's opening program was completely successful and scored one of the first bull's-eyes of the new season. James Franciscus is an excellent choice for the role of the dedicated new teacher. He has the good looks to attract the women and the masculinity to make him acceptable to the men. If television is to create a new teacher "image" to replace Our Miss Brooks they couldn't have made a wiser choice. His Co-Star, Dean Jagger, plays the high school's realistic yet sympathetic principal. His informal instruction to the new teachers in the opening drama was one of the high pints of the hour.

"This morning, you will meet your students for the first time and believe me, ladies and gentlemen, they are going to size you up. They will watch you and make their first judgment of you. They may not like you at first. A simple thing like a moustache could do it.... Don't hang a sign on your face that says 'PAL' and above all don't become personally involved with any of your students."

A fine scene in the high school auditorium followed where Principal Jagger introduced his new teachers to the student body. The dramatic ingredients were simple but to them was added the ominous figure of a cocky, belligerent honor student who openly defies Novak. By the time Novak goes before his class for the first time, I found that a tension had been built up that was equal to any created by a shoot-out at Gold Gulch. Much of this was due to the skill of Lee Kinsolving who played the surly student. The showdown comes when Kinsolving after challenging Novak to give one good reason why he should continue his education. That the show succeeded in sustaining its mood and maintaining its dramatic pace is a measure of the success of director Boris Sagal and writer Joseph Stefano. Contrary to the rules, Novak becomes involved personally with the student in an effort to give him a reason for staying in school. He finds it in the boy's father who is a building contractor. Like one I have known personally, he is wealthy, successful, shallow, uneducated, unpleasant and a terrible failure as a human being. He drives himself ten hours a day because his lack of education has narrowed his horizons of interest. The young man takes a closer look at his old man and there, behind the aggressiveness and the gold cuff-links and the power that money buys, he finds nothing but a pitiful slob. He's back in school the next day.

Viewing the results, Principal Jagger says, "He's a born teacher." "How do you know?" says an assistant. "He knows when to break the rules."

Last night's show as filmed at L.A.'s John Marshall High with 1000 student extras. The campus will continue to serve as a location. The opening show received standing ovations when shown to audiences of high school teachers — none of whom looked like James Franciscus. — *Terence O'Flaherty*, San Francisco Chronicle, *September 25, 1963.*

It's the first day of school in this high school themer and the series promises to be as realistic as the 1000 actual students (John Marshall High) used in the debut. And it's a very promising sample of continuing strength. The script by Joseph Stefano was colorful, exciting and keyed with probing intensity the plight (psychological, not psychiatric, praise be!) of a problem student, excellently played by guest star Lee Kinsolving. James Franciscus and Dean Jagger co-star, Franciscus in the title role and Jagger as the principal, both giving their continuing roles a colorful dimension of sincere reality that does not negate their abilities to display a thoroughly professional range of emotions. The series, created by E. Jack Neuman & Boris Sagal, with Sagal directing the debut, was given a rich sendoff with this initial episode. No bets were missed — it will draw teenage viewers (the most critical TV audience) as well as adults with its promise of eschewing shock values for dramatic moral messages that are neither pretentiously preachy or dull. In important support were Ann Shoemaker, Edward Asner, Stephen Franken, Gloria Talbott and Jeanne Bal. William Froug, who's since left the series, produced this one and six others. — *Hank Grant, The Hollywood Reporter, September 26, 1963.*

"Earlier in the evening we saw the premiere of another show, NBC's Mr. Novak, which has as its central hero a handsome high school English teacher, and playing the title role with much sympathy and understanding was James Franciscus. If you were expecting another Our Miss Brooks look at the inside of a classroom, then you were probably disappointed. This new hour show took an honest, straight-forward approach, and you felt that this was an actual high school. Actor Dean Jagger was excellent as the principal, a man of professional experience and much wisdom dealing with students and faculty. You didn't find any schoolteacher stereotype in his characterization. And this was true, generally with the entire show. For the first time in a tv series, we're being given an unvarnished look at modern high school. — *Emmet Weaver, "TV Notebook,"* Birmingham *(AL)* Post Herald, *September 26, 1963.*

CLASSROOM SERIES A TELEVISION PRODIGY — "Mr. Novak" turned in a straight-A report card Tuesday night on NBC. The hour-long series about a young high school teacher on his initial assignment emerged as one of the best of the new season. James Franciscus stars as Novak with Dean Jagger as principal Albert Vane. Both gave outstanding performances. The premiere episode carefully avoided the dangerous dramatic traps that a series of this nature might encounter. It was not preachy and did not attempt to deliver a great moral message. In "First Year, First Day," Novak arrived at Jefferson High (filmed at John Marshall High School) eager to impart wisdom and knowledge to his "eager" students — so he thought. His first problem concerned the school's leading student (Lee Kinsolving) who decided to drop out and return to the profitable auto-body shop which he ran during summer vacation. Novak's sensitive but firm treatment of the boy persuades him to resume his education. Franciscus' deportment was so exemplary, the Board of Education should make Mr. Novak part of its curriculum. Dean Jagger's speech at the beginning, outlining his teach-conduct code was a masterpiece of acting (and script writing). Jagger and Franciscus fought a cold war of teacher-student philosophy throughout the opening show and it was resolved without saccharine dialogue, or a contrived ending. "Mr. Novak" faculty members include Steve Franken, Marian Collier, Gloria Talbott and Jeanne Bal. A fine staff. It is an adult show. If the teen-agers like it, "Mr. Novak" will be the hit of the season. — *Don Page, Los Angeles (CA) Times, September 26, 1963.*

It's regrettable that "Mr. Novak" is stamped with some of the clichés that trademark those link sausage telefilm series, because it is otherwise a promising new entry for NBC-TV, one that could give that network a fast start on Tuesday nights. Presumably the creators, E. Jack Neuman and Boris Sagal, feel they are playing it safe by passing up all the avenues to a distinctive television series and relying instead upon the formula devices that give it a similarity to all other vidseries about professional people. The debut show had all its winning moments in the first half, when it seemed as though "Novak" might become a serious version of "Mr. Peepers," with some of the same charm and low key stories about earnest tyros learning the teaching game. But it soon became clear that this was going to be another conventional melodrama showcase and that the title character was going to have more in common with detectives and urbanized cowboys than with Mr. Chips. From the looks of things Novak is going to be busier looking after his wayward flock outside the classroom than in it. In the preem chapter, he's initiated to extra-curricular teaching by a high school senior who drops out to go into business for himself. Novak feels obliged to save him from free enterprise, first, because the kid has the best grade average in the school's history and, second, because Novak knows that winning the boy back will earn him the confidence of the rest of the class. Novak pursues the kid and, using the boy's dad as an object lesson, predictably captures the game. Lee Kinsolving does well as the young dropout. In James Franciscus, the series has a prepossessing hero who fills the prescription for Novak with just the right amount of candor and innocent idealism. The character of Novak is an interesting conception and the series' strongest point thus far. Next strongest is Dean Jagger, who is cast perfectly as the school principal (and correlative of Dr. Zorba, Dr. Gillespie, et. al.). Two good looking gals are introduced who promise future romances angles and there are other faculty members who will have running and perhaps significant parts. — *Les, "Television Reviews," Weekly* Variety, *October 2, 1963.*

Grade A: This is an excellent episode which sold the series to NBC. The use of location filming at John Marshall High School adds an air of authenticity. Dean Jagger registers strongly as Principa Vane and is excellent in his orientation speech to the new teachers. When first seen, James Franciscus as Novak appears awkward and naïve. A strong dramatic scene with the difficult boy in the teacher's first class further reveals Novak's inexperience. His confrontation with the Principal showcases the character's growing strengths and Franciscus' genuine rapport with Jagger. He is very good in his final encounter with the troubled student and his defiant father. By the end of the episode Franciscus has made Novak an idealistic character to be admired. There is good support from Marian Collier, Steve Franken and Ed Asner. Guest star Lee Kinsolving as the arrogant student is believable. Joseph Stefano's script contains realistic dialogue and delivers the moral lesson with a minimum of sentiment.

🍎 🍎 🍎 🍎

Episode Two — **To Lodge and Dislodge**
Broadcast October 1, 1963

Synopsis:

A 16-year-old blind student falls deeply in love with her English teacher, John Novak. Campus gossip flares, and Novak, with an assist from Principal Albert Vane, presses frantically for a humane solution to the delicate problem.

Guest Cast:

Kim Darby.............................Julie Dean
David Kent ....Joe Flavio
Tony Dow..............................George

Jimmy Baird............................Billy Gee
Vicky Albright........................Barbara
Michael Winkelman................Charlie.

Executive Producer: E. Jack Neuman
Producer: Joseph Calvelli
Writer: E. Jack Neuman
Director: Boris Sagal
Recording Supervisor: Franklin Milton, John D. Dunning
Supervising Film Editor
Music: Lyn Murray.

Reviews:

Kim Darby portrays a blind student in this week's chapter of 'Mr. Novak' (Channels 6, 7 and 11 Tuesday at 7:30). James Franciscus is cast in the title role, that of a high school teacher.

Good show. Not only does a student have a crush on Mr. Novak but to complicate matters further, the lovesick girl is blind. The subject matter is so sensitive one wonders whether the author will be able to write himself out of the corner but he does it with style and with such an adult, sensible approach, that the potentially corny drama becomes believable. Newcomer Kim Darby scores as the blind girl, and regulars James Franciscus and Dean Jagger are fine. Judging by the first two shows, the TV academy can engrave Jagger's Emmy. — Hammond *(IN) Times, October 1, 1963.*

Kim Darby makes an auspicious debut. — Appleton *(WI)* Crescent, *October 1, 1963.*

Last Tuesday, *"Mr. Novak"* offered the story of a blind girl with a crush on her teacher and Kim Darby as the sightless child, her face glowing with puppy love, touched the heart. The confusion of James Franciscus as the handsome teacher, his inner terror at the thought of the problem, the refusal of Dean Jagger, the principal, to help the situation, all seemed right to me. And the kids, who were everywhere, were certainly right, make no mistake about that. — *Cecil Smith, "The TV Scene,"* The Los Angeles Times, *October 7, 1963.*

Rerun Review:

Young Kim Darby established herself as quite an actress in this repeat episode. Some touching moments during this impossible situation. — Greensboro *(NC)* Daily News, *April 28, 1964.*

Grade A: (This episode was not available for viewing.) Kim Darby was excellent in her portrayal of the blind student who has a crush on Mr. Novak. Tony Dow, Marian Collier and contemporary reviews mentioned her distinction in the role. In the script there was a good segment in Novak's class where he inadvertently failed to recognize Julie's blindness. Vane and Novak had an intriguing scene where the principal ordered his young teacher to confront the girl's crush. It was undoubtedly well played by the series' leads. The other blind students were portrayed with a realism that was inspiring. The final scene where Novak and Julie discuss her romantic feelings was honest and beautifully written with no false sentimentality. Franciscus and Darby must have been outstanding in this delicate incident. The young actress's portrayal really helped her fledgling career and led to better roles. E. Jack Neuman considered this one of the ten best episodes of the first season.

🍎 🍎 🍎 🍎

Episode Three — **I Don't Even Live Here**
Broadcast — October 8, 1963

Synopsis:

English students who made A's in the classroom of Harold Otis become C students with Mr. Novak. Novak suspects that Otis, the school's wittiest, most popular instructor, fed his class a steady diet of funny jokes and answers to the midterm and final exams. Novak sets out to expose Otis, but as he nears success, he suddenly fears it's a campaign he will regret.

Produced by William Froug.
Written by Milton Rosen.
Directed by Abner Biberman.

Guest Star Herschel Bernardi as Mr. Harold Otis.
Co-Starring Shelley Fabres as Dani Cooper.

With

Steve Franken	Jerry Allen.
Diane Ladd	Mrs. Otis.
Trudi James	Jane.
Pamela Baird	Gloria.
Rickie Sorensen	Carol.
Glenn Perry	Phil.
Marian Collier	Miss Scott.
Roy Glenn	Mr. Pichot.
André Phillipe	Everett Johns.

Kathaleen Ellis ....Mrs. Floyd.

Associate Producer...................Robert E. Thompson.
Music......................................Lyn Murray and Leith Stevens.
"Mr. Novak" Theme................Lyn Murray.
Director of Photography ....Richard H. Kline.
Art Direction...........................George W. Davis and LeRoy Coleman.
Assistant to Producer...............Robert Stambler.
Recording Supervisor ....Frank Milton.
Supervising Film Editor...........John Dunning, A.C.E.
Film Editor ....Robert J. Kern, Jr.
Set Decoration ....Henry Grace and John MacNeil.

Reviews

Interesting study of a teacher we all had somewhere along the line. He's the funny man who always had a joke, saw to it we passed the exams, and was one of the school's most popular teachers. Here, he comes face to face with Mr. Novak and his jokes begin to fall flat. As played by Herschel Bernardi, he's quite believable, and you'll be glad you

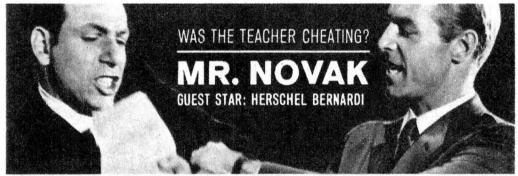

got through his class before he met Mr. Novak. — San Antonio Light, *October 8, 1963.*

This series continues to impress. Credit Herschel Bernardi with a fine sensitive performance as a teacher who is so afraid of his talent to instruct that he hides behind a façade of glib patter. What's worse, he supplies the students with answers to test questions ahead of time. This raises the issue of a teacher's ethics. Dean Jagger again provides stalwart support as the high school principal, but star James Franciscus is far too dour to be accepted as anything but a glum young man. — Rockford *(IL)* Morning Star, *October 8, 1963.*

Tuesday night's story about a teacher desperate for popularity with the youngsters was totally believable. It touched on a universal dilemma: The conflict of professional standards and personal popularity. Herschel Bernardi (remember him in the old "Peter Gunn" series?) performed splendidly as this well-disposed but shallow man. — Pittsburg *(PA)* Press, October 14, 1963.

Rerun Review:

Repeat of a winner in its first outing, and justly so. — Hayward *(CA)* Daily Review, *June 23, 1964.*

Grade B+: The best part of this segment is guest star Herschel Bernardi's excellent performance as the teacher. In the early part of the episode he is jovial and flippant and seems impervious to Mr. Novak's concern about his teaching methods. When caught by Novak apparently giving answers to his students, he becomes angry and defiant. Later when evidence has been brought before the principal and he is called in for a conference, the previously humorous teacher becomes a tragic and insecure figure. Bernardi colors his transitory performance with shade and nuance. Diane Ladd is good in a brief bit as the teacher's long suffering wife. Franciscus also scores in his dramatic encounters with the wayward educator. His expressions of anger, confusion and sympathy are believable Dean Jagger is quietly authoritative in his scenes with both Novak and Otis and the sentiment of the teacher's downfall is never excessive or false. The cautiously optimistic ending is dramatically affecting.

🍎 🍎 🍎 🍎 🍎

Episode Four — **X Is the Unknown Factor**
Broadcast — October 15, 1963

Synopsis:

TV's noted real-life educator, Dr. Frank Baxter, guest stars in a drama which probers the perennial problem of cheaters. Dr. Baxter portrays an industrialist who comes to Jefferson High to test the school's most brilliant science student for a coveted scholarship. One boy passes the test with flying colors, but an English test crib-sheet threatens to ruin the boy's chances.

> Produced by E. Jack Neuman.
> Teleplay by Preston Wood.
> Original Story by Milton S. Gelman.
> Directed by Richard Donner.
>
> Also Starring Dan Macklin as Fred Daniels.
> Co-Starring Anne Seymour as Dorothy Vreeland.

And

Dr. Frank Baxter as Dr. Gagan.

With

Steve Franken	Jerry Allen.
Brooke Bundy	Patrice Morgan.
Ross Elliot	Ray Daniels.
Vince Howard	Mr. Butler.
Ruth Packard	Clerk.
Music Score	Leith Stevens.

"Mr. Novak" Theme ....Lyn Murray.

Reviews:

BEST BET — Mr. Novak continues the high standards set by this very worthwhile series with "X Is the Unknown Factor." Dr. Frank Baxter, television educator, appears and there are several references to his and Dean Jagger's baldness. — *"The TV Scout,"* Kenosha *(WI)* News, *October 15, 1963.*

An interesting study of a student scientist, under pressure to win a scholarship, who resorts to cheating and short cuts to get through "unimportant" courses like Mr. Novak's class. Except for a cliché segment in which the lad's father tries to bribe our hero, it's a well done though hardly gripping story. A cute sidelight plays up Dr. Frank Baxter's startling resemblance to Dean Jagger, particularly around the hairline. — *"TV Key,"* San Antonio *(TX)* Light, *October 15, 1963.*

Rerun Reviews:

A story about an honor student who is being pushed toward a scholarship in science so hard he attempts to shortcut on his "nonessential" English course. The pressures of trying to make good in his specialized field are his excuses for cheating, but we have a hunch that if Mr. Novak (as portrayed stolidly by James Franciscus) were a bit less self-righteous, the boy might have been spared a lot of trouble. Interesting, but slow pacing deprives the story of its full dramatic impact. *"TV Time Previews (Bell-McClure Syndicate),* Baton Rouge *(LA)* State-Times Advocate, *June 2, 1964.*

MR. NOVAK — James Franciscus, Dr. Frank Baxter and Dean Jagger probe the perennial problem of high school cheaters. Timely, poignant, searching.

Grade A: A first-class episode that explores the consequences of cheating. David Macklin gives a superior layered performance in the lead as the student who is pressured to overachieve. He is especially good in the climactic scene where he breaks down and confesses his transgression, knowing it will cost his scholarship. Brooke Bundy provides good support as the helpful girlfriend. Dean Jagger is excellent both in his initial address to the students, and a later scene where he urges the pupils to get help with any problems. Franciscus is especially fine in a scene with the student's arrogant father. Vince Howard shines in a brief scene with Novak and the other regulars expertly play a comic vignette where they note the similarity between Vane and guest star Dr. Frank Baxter. The theme of excusing a cheating student who is otherwise brilliant is handled with taste. Richard Donner's direction is very effective with excellent framing and good use of forced perspective. This was one of Neuman's top ten episodes of the first season.

Episode Five — **A Single Isolated Incident**
Broadcast — October 22, 1963
Synopsis:

A racial incident threatens to erupt into major trouble at Jefferson High School. Negro student Marcy Desmond is pelted with garbage and insults, and other Negro students receive anonymous phone calls warning them to stay home. The story revolves around Principal Vane's handling — sometimes clumsy, sometimes brilliant — of the potentially explosive situation.

Written and Produced by E. Jack Neuman.
Directed by Abner Biberman.

Also Starring Joe Mantel as Jack Parkson.
Co-Starring Tige Andrews as Lt. Charles Green.

With

Steve Franken..........................Jerry Allen.
Gloria Calomee........................Marcy Desmond.
Charles Lampkin.....................Robert Desmond.
Keg Johnson............................Jimmy Sergeant.
Frances Karath ....Thelma.
David Saber.............................Toby.
Dennis Joel.............................Bill.
Steve Talbot.............................Steve.
James Houghton ....Jim.

Faculty

Vince H., Stephen R., Marian C., Donald Barry as Mr. Gallo, André P.

Reviews:

Viewers should watch "Mr. Novak" on NBC Tuesday for one of Neuman's nobler achievements in the TV realm. He has written and produced a well-thought-out and researched story about "A Single Isolated Incident" in a racially integrated high school. *Hal Humphrey, The Los Angeles Times, October 20, 1963.*

Here's another sensibly handled, realistic story detailing one day at Jefferson High, when an incident involving Negro students threatens to erupt into racial battle. Values are not sacrificed for drama here, and the feeling is that everything is resolved the way decent people — adults and teenagers — would do it. — *"TV Tonight,"* Monessen *(PA)* Valley Independent, *October 22, 1963.*

Commendable story. Fortunately, it's Dean Jagger's show and he, as principal, makes the hour believable. — *"TV Key Previews,"* Washington *(DC)* Evening Star, *October 22, 1963.*

Rerun Review:

Mr. Novak (James Franciscus) takes a back seat here and Jagger is particularly good with human reactions that run from indignation and confusion to clear thought. — *"TV Previews,"* Rockford *(IL)* Morning Star, *April 21, 1964.*

TENSION — "A Single Isolated Incident," the Tuesday episode of NBC-TV's "Mr. Novak" series, tells the story of a Negro high school student who is pelted with garbage on her way to school, and of other Negro pupils who are warned to keep away from class. Gloria Calomee plays the student and series star James Franciscus portrays the teacher, Mr. Novak.

GRADE A: Another outstanding episode with a script by E. Jack Neuman that confronts racial prejudice. Dean Jagger is in magnificent form throughout. He is compassionate comforting the abused girl, authoritative when he addresses Novak's class to find the assailants and indignant in a final assembly where he talks of equality. Semi-regular Gloria Calomeé registers strongly as the frightened victim with big close-ups that really register her pain. There is solid support from Tige Andrews as a police lieutenant and Joe Mantell as an aggressive reporter. Keg Johnson is also good as an African American student who is outraged by the attack. The regular teachers all have effective supporting roles and Jeanne Bal makes an initial appearance as the vice principal. Abner Biberman provides excellent direction and the moral lessons are delivered with honesty and integrity. This was one of Neuman's top ten episodes.

🍎 🍎 🍎 🍎 🍎

Episode Six — **The Risk**
Broadcast — October 29, 1963

Synopsis:

A high school teacher and his young bride share a common problem—alcoholism. Guest star Alexander Scourby portrays Allen Ferguson, who applies for a teaching position at Jefferson High, but admits to Principal Vane that he once had a drinking problem. Mr. Novak, who once studied under Ferguson, gives him a strong recommendation. His new career is threatened, however, when his young wife staggers onto the campus drunk.

Produced by E. Jack Neuman.
Teleplay by E. Jack Neuman.
Story by Theodore Apstein.
Directed by Michael O'Herlihy.

Guest Star Alexander Scourby as Allen Ferguson.
Co-Starring Sherry Jackson as Cathy Ferguson.

With

Steve Franken .... Jerry Allen.
Lurene Tuttle .... Mrs. Grange.
Reba Waters .... Amy.
Kim Charney .... Frank.

Faculty

André P., Kathaleen E., Marian C., Stephen R., Vince H.

Film Editor .... Ira Heymann.

Reviews:

"The Risk." Alexander Scourby is perfect as the teacher referred to in the title. Hardly a gripping hour, but Scourby makes the teacher so believable you actually want to see how he makes out. Besides, did you ever have a teacher who could recite "The Raven" like Alex Scourby? — *"Best Bets,"* San Antonio *(TX)* Light, *October 29, 1963.*

A depressing theme presented in thoroughly adult manner, unsweetened by sticky sentimentality that cues a happy solution. — *"TV Time Preview,"* Baton Rouge *(LA)* State-Times, *October 29, 1963.*

Realism and lack of hysterical writing makes this an absorbing hour. — *"Highlights by The TV Scout,"* San Antonio *(TX)* Express, *October 29, 1963.*

Mr. Novak   6:30

Alexander Scourby and **Sherry Jackson** share the guest star spotlight with series stars **James Franciscus** and **Dean Jagger** in tonight's poignant chapter of **MR. NOVAK.** For fine dramatic entertainment, see **MR. NOVAK** at 6:30.

Grade B+: The chief virtue is Alexander Scourby's outstanding performance as the reformed alcoholic. He handles the role with sensitivity and dignity. The actor is especially good when he recites "The Raven" in class and subtly draws a parallel of Poe's difficult life and his own. Scourby also displays great tenderness and understanding of his young wife's disease. Franciscus is good when expressing confidence to his mentor. The story lags in the middle but picks up with Sherry Jackson's drunken appearance at the school. The actress underplays to great effect with subtle use of a twitching hand to express her loss of control. A scene in an office when Vane and Novak confront the teacher and his wife is tense and touching. Neuman's script handles the issue of alcoholism with taste and honesty. The finale where Novak reassures his mentor contains a low-level sentiment and is all the more effective because of it. One of Neuman's top ten.

🍎 🍎 🍎 🍎 🍎

Episode Seven — **Hello, Miss Phipps**
Broadcast November 5, 1963

Synopsis:

Screen and stage star Lillian Gish plays an outspoken social hygiene teacher who triggers a community controversy on sex education in "Hello, Miss Phipps." When Miss Phipps permits a student to turn in a paper that frankly discusses sex, the boy's father, a newspaper editor, makes public charges demanding her resignation.

> Produced by William Froug.
> Written by John T. Dugan.
> Directed by Don Medford.
>
> Guest Star Lillian Gish as Maude Phipps.
> Co-Starring David White as Ralph Morrison.

And

Arch Johnson as Robert Elerton.

With

Steve Franken	Jerry Allen.
Pat McNulty	Mrs. Donzie.
Claudia Bryan	Mrs. Harrison.
Steve Gravers	Coach Gallo.
Allan Hunt	Dick Elerton.
Peter Brooks	Peter Mulley.
Sherry Alberoni	June Harrison.
Assistant Director	Ted Butcher, Jr.

Reviews:

TEACHER'S CAREER THREATENED. A hygiene teacher's career is threatened because of her frank attitude toward sex education in NBC-TV's Mr. Novak series Tuesday. Lillian Gish portrays Miss Phipps, the veteran teacher whose resignation is demanded by parents. Dean Jagger, who plays principal Albert Vane, supports the teacher's stand.

If you have to write a show about an outspoken spinster who teaches sex education to high school students, it would help to get Lillian Gish to play the part. Well, they did, and Miss Gish, aided by Dean Jagger and James Franciscus, makes this a warm and entertaining hour topped off by the inevitable speech to the outraged parents. — *"TV Previews,"* Hammond *(IN)* Times, *November 5, 1963.*

Lillian Gish plays a controversial teacher who numbers sex education among her subjects. Abounding in earnestness, the script fails to ignite dramatically despite its incursions into such worthy areas as sex and academic freedom. — *"TV Time,"* Decatur *(IL)* Herald, *November 5, 1963.*

Hope you didn't miss Mr. Novak this week. It was by far the best of the series. I'll bet the old timers couldn't believe their eyes when they recognized the unmistakable features of Lillian Gish (shades of "Way Down East") — this great star of the silents was a revelation in the role of the controversial school teacher. Age has certainly not dimmed her talents. Lillian came through with a superb performance. — *Francis Murphy "Behind the Mike," Portland Oregonian, November 9, 1963.*

GRADE B+: Veteran actress Lillian Gish carries this episode to superlative effect. She is by turns forceful, intelligent, sympathetic and has real presence. Dean Jagger is very good in scenes with his former teacher. They range from amusing subservience to intelligent discussion of her damaging accusations. Franciscus displays a fine rapport with Gish. Jagger and Franciscus's increasing chemistry is shown to good effect. Regular Steve Franken provides good support as does Pay McNulty as a pregnant married student. Her scene with the hygiene teacher is beautifully played. Allan Hunt shines as a troublesome student. Gish's final scene in which she confronts the parental accusers is magnificent and never becomes over sentimental. The several mentions of sex are tastefully handled. There is a charming coda at the end with Gish, Franciscus and Jagger that neatly tops this exceptional effort.

🐫 🐫 🐫 🐫

Episode Eight — **To Break a Camel's Back**
Broadcast November 12, 1963

Synopsis:

John Novak tries to tame a young and beautiful hellion in "To Break a Camel's back." Holly Metcalfe, a daughter of migrant workers, arrives at Jefferson with a record of having attended 11 high schools previously. When Principal Vane predicts a grim future for her, Novak sets out to bring the girl within reach of conformity.

Produced by E. Jack Neuman.
Teleplay by E. Jack Neuman.
Story by Mike Adams.
Directed by Michael O'Herlihy.

Also Starring Joey Heatherton as Holly Metcalfe.
Co-Starring Royal Dano as Harry Metcalfe.

With

J. Edward McKinley ....Paul Stockton.
Connie Davis ....Ethel Metcalfe.
Sharyn Hillyer ....Betty.
Rich Murray ....Frank.
Tom Curtis ....Herbert Small.
Frank Gardner ....George.

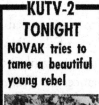

KUTV-2
TONIGHT
NOVAK tries to
tame a beautiful
young rebel

James
FRANCISCUS
Dean
JAGGER
star in

TO BREAK
A CAMEL'S
BACK
on the most-honored show
of the new season
MR. NOVAK

1st Run **6:30**
KUTV-2

Reviews:

Some scenes in Mr. Novak's very good episode are so realistic you'll feel you are eavesdropping, as Principal Dean Jagger runs his school, learns of the illness of an old friend, turns down a job. These scenes are expertly staged and directed. Our hero (James Franciscus), meanwhile, is trying to straighten out insolent, sexy Joey Heatherton. — *"TV Scout,"* Abilene *(TX)* Reporter News, *November 12, 1963.*

There are some fascinating moments which reveal what a high school principal has to contend with and they are beautifully played by Dean Jagger. The main story, unfortunately, is an overwritten, overacted account of a rebellious 17-year-old girl. Joey Heatherton does the best she can as the recalcitrant teen and there's a nice, although brief, performance by Royal Dano as her father. — *"TV Previews,"* Rockford *(IL)* Morning Star, *November 12, 1963.*

Novak has his hands full with problem student Joey Heatherton. We should all have problems that look like Joey Heatherton. — Akron *(OH)* Beacon Journal, *November 12, 1963.*

Rerun Reviews:

Mr. Novak repeats the episode, "To Break a Camel's Back," which almost broke James Franciscus's will to go on teaching. Jefferson High has not been the same since Joey Heatherton, the wildest teen ever to study Chaucer, enrolled. Jim wants to break her rebelliousness but not her spirit and it's scratch-and-go all the way. — *"TV Scout,"* Appleton *(WI)* Post Crescent, *May 26, 1964.*

Grade B-: Dean Jagger is the major strength of this installment. Neuman's script makes several good points about the pressures that face school administrators. Jagger's reaction to the death of a fellow principal is underplayed and effective. Jeanne Bal has her biggest exposure to date and is very good. She has real rapport with Jagger and carries a hint of closeness between them. Joey Heatherton has a somewhat over-written part in a partially clichéd script. However, she acts effectively in several scenes with Franciscus and her breakdown and reformation at the end is both emotionally satisfying and believable. Franciscus emerges as a more assured teacher and displays authority in his clashes with the rebellious coed. Royal Dano is good in a brief scene as the girl's confused and concerned father. Marian Collier is charming in some brief scenes that hint at a romance between herself and Mr. Novak. A good episode if not an outstanding one.

Episode Nine — **A Feeling for Friday**
Broadcast November 19, 1963

Synopsis:

High School teacher John Novak slips out of town to court an old flame but his trip leads to comical adventures in "A Feeling for Friday." At the invitation of Mildred Chase, Novak plunges into a weekend of private merriment on the family's secluded estate. His troubles start when the butler mistakes him for a delivery boy. Matters grow worse until a frustrated Novak breaks up a posh cocktail party by wrangling with a romantic rival, but not before he gets in a few well-spoken phrases on the subject of teacher's pay.

Written and Produced by E. Jack Neuman.
Directed by Michael O'Herlihy.

Guest Star Diane Baker as Mildred Chase.
John McGiver as Charles Edward Chase.
Also Starring Peter Breck as Jerry Allen.

And

Steve Franken	Jerry Allen.
Edward Platt	Bernard Perry.
Patrick O'Moore	Mr. Spencer.
Tom Curtis	Mr. Duncan.
George Takei	Walter.

Faculty

Stephen R., Larry Thor as Jim Hendricks, Marian C., Nice H., Kathaleen E., Anne Loos as Mrs. Danfield.

Story Editor	James Menzies.
Music Coordinator	Malcolm Beelby.
Assistant to Producer	Donald Leonard.
Assistant Director	John Bloss.

Reviews:

It's a nice, realistic show with some good comic touches. — *"TV Tonight,"* Monessen *(PA) Valley Independent, November 19, 1963.*

Tonight they get Novak (James Franciscus) out of the classroom and into a weekend romance which turns out to be a comical misadventure. One of the best shows this season. — *"Preview of Today's TV,"* Los Angeles Times, *November 19, 1963.*

For a show that has been paid so much favorable lip service, "Mr. Novak" shouldn't be languishing in Nielsen's back 40. But, as with any show, it doesn't always come up smelling like a rose and the lookers may be eyeing other channels or waiting for Red Skelton to come on while James Franciscus is extricating himself from another embarrassment in the back stretch. Last Tuesday's issue written by E. Jack Neuman, who also produced and shares screen credit with Boris Sagal, was certainly not his best effort and lacked

OLD FLAME—Diane Baker portrays an old college sweetheart who makes a dramatic reentry into the life of teacher John Novak (James Franciscus) in "A Feeling for Friday," "Mr. Novak" episode Tuesday, Nov. 19 at 7:30 p.m.

the vigor or action or sparkle of dialogue. While not a romantic figure as such, he delineates well the role of a high school teacher who never lets his high principals bog down his love life's pleasures. In this gambit he takes the epistolary bait from an old girl friend and finds himself enmeshed with some stuffy country clubbers, who look down their noses at a high school teacher. If he's so smart why isn't he teaching in college? This lights the fuse and he sails into all of them, not physically, but it would have helped to give the play some life. There would have been a "better feeling for Friday" if he had socked a few of his traducers. Director Michael O'Herlihy didn't pick up the pace fast enough and let the camera linger too long on incidental passages. Franciscus was well supported by Jeanne Bal, who seemed to have more professional polish than the others and should be cut in for bigger roles. Diane Baker wasn't too impressive as the unspoiled and unstable sassiety belle. John McGiver gave a good account as the bloated aristocrat who was big enough to admit "we're all venal" and the only one to send Franciscus away with a better feeling for Friday. — *Helm, "Telepix Follow-Up Reviews,"* Daily Variety, *November 21, 1963.*

Rerun Review:

Diane Baker, who invites Mr. Novak out for the posh shindig, is especially appealing and so is her father, John McGiver. — *"Television Tonight,"* Monessen *(PA)* Valley Independent, *May 19, 1964.*

Grade C-: This episode's plotline of social snobbery is somewhat forced and unrealistic. The main part of the hour is spent away from Jefferson High School and contains dialogue that is too forced and preachy. The story drags during scenes as the mansion and the wealthy snobs are presented as clichés. There is a good performance by Diane Baker as Novak's former flame who ultimately reveals her shallow existence. John McGiver is also good as the girl's father who is the only member of the privileged group to reveal any humanity. Franciscus gives his all during a speech defending his career choice as a high school teacher but is defeated by the forced dialogue. The best part of this subpar episode is a depiction of Novak's being overworked at Jefferson in the opening scenes. There are some charming hints at a romance between Novak and Miss Scott who displays a bit of jealousy toward her fellow teacher. A lesser effort.

🕯 🕯 🕯 🕯 🕯

Episode Ten — **Pay the Two Dollars**
Broadcast November 26, 1963

Synopsis:

Teacher John Novak attempts to break up three scuffling students and finds himself accused of breaking a boy's arm, in "Pay the Two Dollars." When one of the boys falls backwards, pinning and breaking his own arm, the boy's father files suit against Novak for deliberate bully tactics. When the Board of Education's appointed attorney attempts to settle the case out of court, Novak balks and threatens to fight the case himself.

Produced by E. Jack Neuman.
Written by Milton Rosen.
Directed by Walter Doniger.

Guest Star Martin Landau as Victor Rand.
Special Guest Star MacDonald Carey as Mr. Edwards.

Tom Lowell ....Carl Edwards.
Paul Lambert...........................Arnold Brecker.
Adrienne Marden ....Mrs. Edwards.
Todd Bingham ....Gary Kemp.
Beau Bridges ....Frank Stoller.

Faculty

Stephen R., Marian C., André P., Kathaleen E., Larry T., Vince H., Marion R.

Reviews:

An expected storyline that's reasonably well done. Just as Kildare had to face malpractice, Mr. Novak must come to grips with the accusation that he deliberately injured a student. He parallels Kildare's attitude by refusing to take the easy way out and settling the case. Needless to say, idealism saves the day. — *TV Previews,"* Hammond *(IN) Times, November 26, 1963.*

GRADE A: This is a great episode concerning the vulnerability of teachers to unjust accusations. There is superior dialogue throughout. Martin Landau delivers an excellent performance as Novak's attorney. Initially the lawyer wishes to settle but is forced to engage his skills in the teacher's defense. Landau transitions from amiability to intense fortitude with complete believability. Tom Lowell as the injured boy is very good, as is MacDonald Carey as his indignant father. Franciscus registers strongly in all his scenes and works well with Landau and Lowell. This is an explanatory episode on the legal aspects of the school system, but it remains dramatically sound. Regular André Phillipe has a nice bit consoling the accused teacher. Doniger directs with apparent skill and uses extreme close-ups of Landau and Novak to great effect.

🍎🍎🍎🍎🍎

Episode Eleven — **Love in the Wrong Season**
Broadcast December 3, 1963
Synopsis:

Interested in a glamorous young teacher, Novak is puzzled by her hot and cold attitude toward him. Then he inadvertently discovers that he has a rival — the woman is falling in love with one of her students with the resulting gossip endangering two reputations. Novak seeks to unravel the strange romance.

Produced by William Froug.
Written by Richard deRoy.
Directed by Ida Lupino.

Guest Star Patricia Crowley as Ariel Wilder.
Special Guest Star Tommy Kirk as Tod Seton.

With

Steve Franken ....Jerry Allen.
Tim McIntire ....Chris.
David Macklin ....Larry.
June Vincent ....Mrs. Wilder.
Mike Winkelman ....Mark.

Reviews:

A tender, understanding love story, nicely played by James Franciscus, Patricia Crowley, Tommy Kirk and Dean Jagger. The entire story is handled realistically. — *"TV Tonight,"* Monessen *(PA)* Valley Independent, *December 3, 1963.*

There are several touching moments, all arising out of the pupil-teacher relationship. The boy is well played by Tommy Kirk. — *"TV Previews,"* Milwaukee *(WI)* Journal-Sentinel, *December 3, 1963.*

GRADE A-: This episode is a love story about student crushes on teachers that is presented with sensitivity and taste. Pat Crowley is excellent as the frightened teacher who finds herself falling love with a student. Her performance is full of nuance and shade. Tommy Kirk is very appealing as the awkward youth who has a crush on his instructor. There is great chemistry between them and all their scenes are beautifully played. June Vincent is good as the teacher's domineering and insensitive mother. Franciscus is superlative and ranges from boorish aggression in early scenes, to jealousy and eventual sympathy for the confused teacher. Jagger is both compassionate and authoritative towards the frightened teacher. Ida Lupino's directs the actors to superb effect with frequent use of shadowy lighting and extreme close-ups. There is a charming tag at the end between Novak and Vane showcasing their palpable rapport.

ǔ ǔ ǔ ǔ

Episode Twelve — **The Boy Without a Country**
Broadcast December 10, 1963

Synopsis:

A hero's welcome is prepared by Vane and Novak for a new student, a Russian defector, who's quick to show that he's not so easy to get along with, giving them an insight into the ideologies of youth from another nation. The boy's misunderstanding of kindness for weakness comes near to ruining his life in his new land where freedom of choice is a principal difficult for him to understand.

Guest Cast:

Walter Koenig ....Aleksei Dubov.
Jeanne Cooper.........................Louise Sargeant.
James Chandler ....Mr. Sargeant.
Mary Lynn Gary ....Mary Lynn.
David Saber............................Tony.
Mike Winkelman ....Don.
Rickie Sorensen ....Clay.
Laird Stuart ....Erik.

Executive Producer: E. Jack Neuman
Producer: Joseph Calvelli
Story: Richard DeRoy
Writers: E. Jack Neuman/Richard DeRoy
Director: Michael O'Herlihy
Recording Supervisor: Franklin Milton
Supervising Film Editor: John D. Dunning
Composer/Theme Music: Lyn Murray.

Walter Koenig, left, and Dean Jagger in a scene from the "Mr. Novak" series episode on KSD-TV at 6:30 p.m. Tuesday.

Reviews:

It's a good show with almost a documentary quality. The National Freckle Champion, Mary Lynn Gary, appears and does quite well with her dialogue. — *"TV Scout,"* San Antonio *(TX)* Express, — *December 10, 1963.*

This episode brings a new student to Jefferson High, a brilliant, if somewhat withdrawn, boy from the Soviet Union. Walter Koenig is sensitively sullen as the youth and there are good performances from Jeanne Cooper, Dean Jagger and Jeanne Bal. — Des Moines*(IA)* Register, *December 10, 1963.*

Producer E. Jack Neuman teamed with Richard DeRoy to pen the teleplay "The Boy Without a Country," and what they came up with was an interesting concept, but blurry in its telling. Story dealt with a young Russian who defects to the West, and enters high school in this country. Weakness of the Neuman-DeRoy script was that the motivation of the youth was never clearly spelled out, then it's wrapped up with a hurried, too-pat ending in which the Russian sees the light. Not at all convincing. The Russky youth is bewildered by the freedom he encounters in the American school, which is understandable, but he's also surly most of the time, which isn't understandable. At one point, in an argument with his schoolmates, he cries out he didn't escape to the U.S., he escaped from Russia. This doesn't exactly clarify his motives, although the writers toss in an apology for this later on. What happens to a youth raised in a totalitarian state, when he comes to a free society, could have made for a fascinating story, but it didn't here. Despite the inherent weaknesses of the script, there are uniformly good performances from Walter Koenig, as the young Russian; Jeanne Cooper, and regulars James Franciscus and Dean Jagger. Michael O'Herlihy's direction is okay. One distracting factor is over-production. Principal actors are in a number of corridor scenes, but there is such a frenzy of activity around them with youngsters racing to and fro, as they say, some of the dialog is inaudible. *Daku, "Telepix Follow-Up Reviews," Daily Variety, December 12, 1963.*

GRADE A: This winning episode concerns acceptance and different cultural influences. There's a great scene in Novak's class where the students discuss American freedoms and Russia's programming of youths. Some real points are made without heavy moralizing. Walter Koenig is very good as the Russian student. He underplays with a stoic intensity and has genuine presence. Jeanne Cooper is fine as the boy's concerned foster mother and is featured in several emotional scenes with Jagger. Franciscus interacts well with Koenig and their encounters are well played. Jeanne Bal's growing rapport with the principal is showcased to good effect. André Phillip and Marian Collier have an amusing bit where they are late to an assembly. The high point of the episode occurs near the end where there is a lengthy two-shot scene between the boy and the principal. Jagger and Koenig are excellent in this honestly emotional finale.

🍎 🍎 🍎 🍎

Episode Thirteen — **A Thousand Voices**
Broadcast December 17, 1963
Synopsis:

Singer Frankie Avalon turns dramatic actor, and Glenn Ford's 18-year-old son Peter makes his television debut in "A Thousand Voices." Avalon portrays the leader of an off-campus car club, which teacher Novak attempts to aid — until it almost costs him his career.

Produced by E. Jack Neuman.
Written by Anthony Wilson.
Directed by Richard Donner.

Guest Star Frankie Avalon as David Miller.

With

Steve Franken............................Jerry Allen.
Robert F. Simon ....Ben Kailey.
Rita Lynn ....Rita Muller.
Bill Alan Bloom.......................Alan Corey.
Maxine Stuart..........................Angie Kailey.
Peter Ford..............................William Kress.

Faculty

Marian C., Stephen R., Kathaleen E., Vince H.

Music Coordinator.................Malcolm Beelby.

Reviews:

Mr. Novak makes a conscientious effort to examine the plight of a lonely student who sees his one claim to fame disappearing. Frankie Avalon heads the Templars, an automobile club needing a sponsor to function off-campus. Novak (James Franciscus) tries to help, but doesn't have the time. He tries to find a sponsor, only to learn people regard the gang as juvenile delinquents. It makes a good story point. — *"Best Bet,"* The Norfolk Virginian-Pilot, *December 17, 1963.*

Maladjustment, Sickness Shown — The home screens were full of sickness, maladjustment and unhappiness Tuesday night. "Mr. Novak" struggled nobly for an hour trying to help a disturbed boy from a broken home. At the end, he sadly abandoned his salvage operations — the boy ran away and Mr. Novak went back to his classes. — *Cynthia Lowry (AP television-radio writer), "New York,"* Indiana *(PA)* Evening Gazette, *December 19, 1963.*

GRADE B: This episode features a student's alienation and desire for identity. Guest star Frankie Avalon gives a sincere performance that ranges from angry rebellion to desperation. The script, which occasionally presses the juvenile delinquency angle too strongly, is redeemed by strong dialogue. Jagger is quietly authoritative in several scenes where he confronts the alienated youth and his gang. His underplaying is most affecting. Franciscus is very good in his scenes with both the student and the principal. His earnest desire to help the lost teen is formidable. Rita Lynn registers as the boy's uncaring mother. Jagger is superlative in a scene near the end where he tells Novak that not all students will succeed. There is excellent direction from Donner who often uses extreme close-ups to great dramatic effect. The quietly downbeat ending is both tragic and emotionally moving. A secondary episode redeemed by acting and direction.

🍎 🍎 🍎 🍎

Episode Fourteen — **My Name Is Not Legion**
Broadcast December 24, 1963
Synopsis:

High School teacher John Novak and Principal Albert Vane try to bring a brilliant student back from a world of fantasy in "My Name Is Not Legion."

Produced by William Froug.
Written by Robert E. Thompson.
Directed by Bernard Girard.
Guest Star Peter Lazar as Arnold Frazer.
Co-Starring Shelley Fabres as Dani Cooper.

With

Steve Franken	Jerry Allen.
Eddie Applegate	Swish Leher.
Ricky Klein	Greg Sikes.
Connie Gilcrest	Mrs. Jensen.
Rex Ingram	Shields.
Steve Groves	Coach Harman.
Noel Drayton	Sam Klauser.
John Washbrook	Chief Justice.

Review:

Mr. Novak examines the problems of a gifted student whose inabilities to adjust make him a problem child. According to his background, the boy has lived everywhere from Saudi Arabia to South America. His attitude is defiant and neither he nor the other students get on. This is an eloquent plea for understanding these children. — *"TV Scout,"* Abilene *(TX)* Reporter-News, *December 24, 1963.*

GRADE D: A rare misfire for the first season. Almost nothing works in this episode. Barney Girard's direction is weak and fails to establish any dramatic mood of substance. His use of fantasy sequences is not only wrong for the series, but fails to impress. The script is full of clichés and the theme of the brilliant-but-awkward student never really registers. Peter Lazar portrays the lead with no appreciable skill and therefore generates no sympathy. Jagger, Franciscus and Bal make a professional attempt with the weak dialogue but fail to bring the script to life. Franciscus in particular gives his all in some crusading speeches but is beaten by the banal dialogue. The only redeeming aspect is a winsome performance by Shelley Fabres as a sensitive coed.

ẽ ẽ ẽ ẽ

Episode Fifteen — **He Who Can Does**
Broadcast December 31, 1963
Synopsis:

Teacher John Novak brews a king-size potion of unexpected trouble when he invites Rand Hard, a Pulitzer Prize-winning novelist, to address the Jefferson High School literary club. In addition to flaunting some orthodox views on education, hardy turns out to be a man from assistant principal Pagano's past. Hardy attempts to renew his old courtship of Miss Pagano, to hire Novak as his secretary and to sell Jefferson's brightest students on the advantages of quitting school and going to sea at an early age.

Produced by William Froug.
Written by Roland Wolpert.
Directed by Irving Lerner.

Guest Star Edward Mulhare as Rand Hardy.

With

Steve Franken.........................Mr. Allen.
André Phillipe ....Mr. Johns.
Vincent Howard......................Mr. Butler.
Kathaleen Ellis ....Mrs. Floyd.
Mike Winkelman ....Mark.
Vicky Albright.........................Helen.
Charles Irving..........................Room Clerk.

Reviews:

Good emotional conflicts on several different levels make this absorbing entertainment. Very colorful as the odd-ball novelist is Edward Mulhare. — *"TV Previews,"* Rockford (IL) Morning Star, *December 31, 1963.*

An unconventional novelist comes to Jefferson High at Mr. Novak's (James Franciscus) invitation. The man, well-played by Edward Mulhare, believes in living life to the fullest. He began by leaving high school, bumming around the world, loving it up, and becoming famous. Now he runs into an old love (but can't remember her name), offers Novak a job, and is generally a bad influence on the students.

7:30 p.m.—**4**—Mr. Novak: Prize-winning novelist, Edward Mulhare, advises students to quit school and go to sea.

It's the old good vs. evil tale with a twist. Our hero may be the one corrupted. — *"Best Bet — TV Scout,"* Lima *(OH) News, December 31, 1963.*

A prize-winning novelist is the villain of tonight's drama and fans will spot him as a bad guy right off. Nicely played by Edward Mulhare, the novelist is a jaunty soul, something of a lover, with ideas you'll disagree with quickly enough, but you'll hang on to see what the fellow will be doing next. — *"Best Bets on TV,"* San Antonio *(TX) Light, December 31, 1963.*

Grade A: An intriguing episode that features an excellent performance from Edward Mulhare as the sophisticated British author. His acting ranges from arrogance to a tragic weakness of character. Mulhare dominates a great scene in which he addresses Novak's class on the subject of following their hearts and possibly leaving school. The actor is also effective in a scene after his breakdown when he encounters Miss Pagano, a former flame, and is rejected by her. Franciscus is superior in his incidents with the novelist and his ultimate refusal of Hardy's job offer is beautifully played by both. Jagger is moving in a segment where he offers assurance to a distraught Miss Pagano. Bal is in superb form throughout. Her initial concern upon hearing of her former lover's arrival to her strength in spurning his attempts at reconciliation showcase Bal's considerable dramatic skills. A first-rate script and direction yields a great installment.

෫ ෫ ෫ ෫

Episode Sixteen — The Song of Songs
Broadcast January 7, 1964

Synopsis:

Teacher John Novak faces charges of teaching pornography and religion in "The Song of Song." Ray Whittier, influential father of student Shirley, demands Novak's dismissal after protesting certain reading assignments given by Novak. When principal Vane supports his teacher, Whittier removes his daughter from school — and the Board of education begins an investigation of Novak.

Produced by E. Jack Neuman.
Teleplay by E. Jack Neuman and James Menzies.
Story by Emmet Lavery.
Directed by David Alexander.

Guest Star Edward Andrews as Ray Whittier.

With

Brooke Bundy ....Shirley Whittier.
Robert Brubaker......................Wayne Kelton.
Bill Hamilton.........................Frank Temp.
Barry Brooks ....Mr. Wilson.

Faculty

Marian C., Vince H., Kathaleen E., André P., Hollis Irving as Miss McGuire, Anne Loos as Mrs. Danfield.

Reviews:

6:30-7:30 (5-NBC) MR. NOVAK. James Franciscus is accused of teaching lewdness when one of his stuoents (Brooke Bundy) chooses an excerpt from the Bible's "Song of Songs" for her poetry project.

A parent wants to have Novak dismissed because he disapproves of our English teacher's reading assignments. The script brings up the age-old controversy on how much influence a parent should have over teachers, and the performances of Edward Andrews, Dean Jagger and James Franciscus do it justice. — "*TV Key Previews,*" Waterloo *(IA)* Daily Courier, *January 7, 1964.*

If you can accept the fact that an overly-possessive father hysterically brings charges that Mr. Novak is teaching pornography in his class when a young girl recites "The Song of Songs," then you may enjoy this episode. It makes some valid points about teaching ethics, but the story would have been stronger had the basis of the charge been stronger. Anyway, Edward Andrews does a good job as the narrow-minded father. — "*TV Tonight — TV Scout,*" Kenosha *(WI)* News, *January 7, 1964.*

GRADE C+: The primary strengths of this episode are the strong performances of Edward Andrews, Brooke Bundy and the series' leads. The script begins as an examination of what could be considered objectionable material for students. It veers off into a character study between the over possessive father and his daughter. The initial theme becomes lost in the presentation. Andrews is very good as the aggressive parent and his true insecurity after being confronted by his daughter is convincingly played. Brooke Bundy is very appealing in a performance of vulnerability and she works very well in her scenes with both Franciscus and Andrews. Franciscus registers strongly in his passionate defense of his teaching. Jeanne Bal has a large part and is heartfelt in her interactions with Novak when the teacher is upset by the accusations. Regular André Phillipe had a funny bit with Miss Pagano. An average segment.

🙢 🙢 🙢 🙢 🙢

Episode Seventeen — **The Exile**
Broadcast January 14, 1964
Synopsis:

The dilemma of a dropout who wants to get back into high school is explored in "The Exile." The dropout (Charlie Payne) — immature and miscast in an adult world — comes to the attention of Vane and Novak when he begins loitering around the school grounds. Novak manages to talk Charlie into enrolling again, only to be frustrated by regulations governing the reentry of students.

Written and Produced by E. Jack Neuman.
Directed by Michael O'Herlihy.

Co-Starring Richard Evans as Charlie Payne.

With

Les Treymane ....Mr. Bates.
Virginia Christine....................Alice Payne.
Gale Gerber...........................Pat Kelly.
Nicky Blair...........................Mr. Morganti.

Faculty

Stephen R., Marian C., Larry T., Kathaleen E., André P., James D., Marjorie C.

Reviews:

Any teen-agers dropping out of school are advised to watch this powerful look at a dropout a few years later. Richard Evans makes this fellow a tragic figure, neither kid nor adult, not suited to any job, and rejected by the Army. Drama is heightened by the fact that the show takes place on one school day, during which young Evans' world is reduced to a microcosm of misery. — *"TV Tonight,"* Monessen *(PA)* Valley Independent, *January 14, 1964.*

A thoughtful examination of some aspects of the school dropout problem. The most interesting scenes provoke Mr. Novak into questioning whether a teacher has boxed a disturbed youngster in without giving him some face-saving way to stay on. The most moving scenes involve the boy himself, lost, disintegrating and despairing. Worthwhile. — *"Best Bets on TV,"* San Antonio *(TX)* Light, *January 14, 1964.*

"Mr. Novak" only skimmed the surface of the current high school drop-out problem by focusing its plot on 20-year-old who wanted to but couldn't (according to rules) return to school after three years of playing hooky. Rather than proposing remedial action, the plot point served mostly as a warning to teenagers that they could become vegetables without high school diplomas. In short, a lecture on the effect rather than the — more important — cause. Nevertheless, a fine and sensitive performance by Richard Evans as the tragic youth, and very good as a guiltily unstrung teacher Stephen Roberts. — *Hank Grant, "On the Air — BLOODSHOT SQUARE EYEBALLS DEPT.,"* The Hollywood Reporter, *January 16, 1964.*

If the intent here was to strike a blow for the crusade against drop-outs it fell wide the mark. What turned up was a surly, rebellious punk, who left school because he wanted

'EXILE' — Richard Evans plays the part of a high school dropout who wants to re-enter school in tonight's 'Mr. Novak' episode. Channels 6, 7 and 11 at 7:30.

to be his own boss, wandered aimlessly for three years and when he wanted to get back the door was slammed in his face. It is doubtful if even a psychiatrist could do much with him. What the producer-writer hoped to accomplish to head off drop-outs got lost somewhere in the telling. The dialog was strong enough. Said drop-outer Richard Evans: "I was a damn fool to leave school and a damn fool to try and get back." Replied Dean Jagger: "Yes, you're a damn fool." He was too old, not yet 20. His credits wouldn't get him into a reform school. If the script threw E. Jack Neuman, executive producer and producer, he must shoulder the blame. It was his own. Evans played it to the hilt, with strength and feeling and scarred with hatred for those who tried to straighten him out. Franciscus, his patience tried, couldn't do it and Dean Jagger gave it the good old high school try and came up short. Both performances exuded their customary competence, as did as did supporting roles by Les Treymane, Jeanne Bal and a cluster of others but were all auxiliary to the incorrigibility of Evans.

Next week: anti-Semitism in school. — *Helm, "Telepix Followup,"* Daily Variety, *January 16, 1964.*

GRADE A: This excellent episode examines the consequences of a school dropout. Neuman's perceptive script is without sensationalism or overt moralizing. Richard Evans delivers a superior performance as the disillusioned dropout. He generates genuine sympathy despite his initial arrogance and his final desperation is tragic. Jagger is outstanding in a scene where he tells the boy that he cannot come back to school. He is both sympathetic and stern. Regular Stephen Roberts has a longer scene than usual and registers strongly. He makes his character an unpleasant cynic. Marian Collier is good in a dramatic bit where she is frightened by the dropout's attention. Virginia Christine effectively portrays the boy's concerned mother. A low-key final scene where a distraught Evans slowly walks across the campus for the last time is very effective. An eloquent plea for students to complete their schooling. One of Neuman's ten best.

Episode Eighteen — **Sparrow on the Wire**
Broadcast January 21, 1964
Synopsis:

Jefferson Hi's debating team star makes some anti-Semitic remarks which snowball into trouble for teacher John Novak in "Sparrows on the Wire." As debate team sponsor, Novak suspends Pat Knowland (Beau Bridges) from the club. His action causes three other team members to resign in protest. Another teacher joins the critics of Novak's methods and sets out with a contradictory line of strategy.

Produced by E. Jack Neuman.
Teleplay by E. Jack Neuman and Lionel E. Siegel.
Story by Lionel E. Siegel.

Guest Star Mike Kellin as Samuel Cohen.
Co-Starring Beau Bridges as Pat Knowland.

With

Neil Nephew	Arnold Gottlieb.
Shirley Bonne	Susan Hotchkiss.
Patrick Waltz	Mr. Fitzgerald.
Clive Clerk	Monty.
Warren White	Phil.
Jim Barringer	Roger.
Music Coordinator	Malcolm Beelby.

Faculty

Marian C., Stephen R., Vince H., André P., Anne Los as Mrs. Danfield.

Reviews:

Mr. Novak tackles anti-Semitism in a conscientious script which is unfortunately unresolved. Beau Bridges is a brilliant member of the debating team whose tactics include upsetting the opposition through racial slurs. Novak (James Franciscus) throws him off the team, a move which bothers Jewish teacher Mike Kellin, a man who has become resigned to anti-Semitism. Some good points here, but no solutions. — *"TV Scout,"* Lima *(OH)* News, *January 21, 1964.*

Tuesday's "Mr. Novak" crackled with provocative dialog on a touchy theme, anti-Semitism, but with sensitive handling to make it a think-piece instead of a shocker. Beau Bridges was so convincing as the junior-size bigot, wouldn't be surprised if papa Lloyd tanned his hide after seeing the show. — *Hank Grant, "On the Air,"* The Hollywood Reporter, *January 23, 1964.*

GRADE A: This is a sincere and effective examination of anti-Semitism from both a victim and perpetrator viewpoint. Mike Kellin is superb as a Jewish teacher who has experienced prejudice and doesn't wish to stir up additional conflict. His strength in confronting the young bigot at the end of the story is very powerful and uplifting. A youthful Beau Bridges is believable as the young racist and his final conflict with Kellin displays real acting skill. Franciscus is dramatically strong in his scenes with Kellin in which he convinces the teacher to confront the youthful zealot. Arnold Gottlieb shines as the Jewish student on the debate team who is insulted. His confrontations with Kellin, in which he refuses to back down, are beautifully acted by both of them. Marian Collier has some charming scenes where she is jealous of a pretty reporter's attentions to Mr. Novak. First-class all the way and one of Neuman's ten best.

🦗 🦗 🦗 🦗 🦗

Episode Nineteen — The Private Life of Douglas Morgan, Jr.
Broadcast January 28, 1964

Synopsis:

Jefferson High's "Campus Clown" takes extreme measures to gain recognition, in "The Private Life of Douglas Morgan, Jr." To cover his embarrassment because of his clumsiness, he plays the part of a buffoon until he realizes his classmates are laughing at him, not with him. When he resigns from ROTC and turns pacifist, trouble really brews.

Produced by William Froug.
Written by Paul and Margaret Schneider.
Directed by Richard Donner.

Guest Star Peter Helm as Douglas Morgan, Jr.

With

Steve Franken	Jerry Allen.
Frank Maxwell	Douglas Morgan, Sr.
Cheryl Holdridge	Betty
Hal Gould	Joe Garson.
Joan Tompkins	Mrs. Morgan.
Glen Vernon	Sgt. Otis Canfield.
Bob Diamond	R.O.T.C. Student.

Reviews:

A good portrait of a sensitive young man who covers up his feelings by acting the campus clown gives Mr. Novak a good episode. Peter Helm, a winning actor, plays the lad. He feels he is flunking R.O.T.C., so one day he announces he is sitting out the compulsory course because he is a "conscientious objector." The actions of Dean Jagger, and the reactions of the boy after the incident, are realistic and sensible. Viewers are left with a good feeling about the basic sensibility of people. — *"TV Scout,"* Abilene *(TX)* Reporter News, *January 28, 1964.*

GRADE C-: This installment is marred by an indecisive script that has contrived comedic scenes which are contrary to the show's premise. The conflict of the youth

CAMPUS COURTING — Peter Helm, as Jefferson High's campus clown, forgets his sometimes obnoxious sense of humor as he gets a touch of spring in his system and goes courting coed Cheryl Holdridge in a scene from Mr. Novak, Tuesday at 7:30 PM on KMJ-TV, 24.

being a conscientious objector is presented more intensely than required. Richard Donner's direction is only adequate and doesn't enhance the presentation like his previous efforts. Peter Helm tries very hard with an awkwardly written character but at times is presented too flippantly to generate audience sympathy. In a scene on the school grounds where there he confronts bullies, Helm rises to the occasion and is very good. The young actor is also on form in the finale where he sticks to his decision. Jagger registers in a scene chastising the young upstart. Frank Maxwell is good as the father encouraging his rebellious son. The happy ending is somewhat superficial as there had been insufficient build-up. A misfire redeemed by Peter Helm's performance.

ॐ ॐ ॐ ॐ ॐ

Episode Twenty — **Death of a Teacher**
Broadcast February 4, 1964

Synopsis:

The death of veteran Jefferson High School teacher triggers conflicting reactions from students and faculty members. English instructor James O'Neil collapses in Novak's arms as the pair ascend the school stairs. The editor of the school paper writes an editorial tribute to the dead teacher, but his faculty advisor denounces the article as inaccurate because it failed to mention that he was "murdered by his heavy work load."

Written and Produced by E. Jack Neuman.
Directed by Richard Donner.

Guest Star Harry Townes as Mr. Frank Deaver.
Co-Starring Tony Dow as George Scheros.
Phyllis Hill as Mrs. Doris O'Neil.

With

William Sargent ....Dr. Tyler.
Frank Albertson.....................James O'Neil.

William Swan..........................Father Servi.
Marc Rambeau........................Eddie.

Faculty

Stephen R., Marian C., Vince H., Marjorie C., André P., Kathaleen E., Larry T.

Review:

The reactions of teachers and pupils are examined when a well-liked, dedicated teacher suddenly drops dead. It's not exactly cheerful entertainment, but it makes strong points about the overly-burdensome work load carried by teachers. Harry Townes gives a sensitive performance as the dead teacher's good friend. — *"Tonight's Previews,"* Newark *(NJ)* Star Ledger, *February 4, 1964.*

GRADE A: A powerful and dramatic hour of television with an excellent script by Neuman. Frank Albertson is good in a brief appearance prior to his sudden death. The heart attack is handled by Donner with subtlety, taste and cinematic imagination. His direction of the episode contains his great use of framing and he sensitively

DEATH ON THE CAMPUS — Jeanne Bal comforts Frank Albertson after he suffers a fatal heart attack on the steps of Jefferson High School in this week's segment of **Mr. Novak, KMJ-TV, 24, Tuesday at 7:30 PM.**

handles the strong emotions throughout. Harry Townes is very good as the cynical veteran teacher who fears for his own health through overwork. His return to optimism in the finale is subtle and convincing. Franciscus and Bal are strong in their dramatic incidents. Jagger shows great compassion and strength when consoling the widow of the stricken teacher. Tony Dow is fine in a supporting role as the editor of the school's paper. Phyllis Hill is appealing as the widow who returns to teaching. Instead of the usual opening theme a more somber musical piece is used. One of Neuman's top ten.

🍎 🍎 🍎 🍎

Episode Twenty-One — **I'm on the Outside**
Broadcast February 18, 1964

Synopsis:

A young Mexican-American accuses teacher John Novak of prejudice in "I'm on the Outside." When Mr. Novak sends the student to the principal's office for sleeping in class, the boy tells Mr. Vane that Novak picks on him because he is of Mexican descent. When Novak tries to disprove the charge and win Steve's friendship, his good intentions backfire.

Produced by E. Jack Neuman.
Teleplay by Preston Wood.
Story by Preston Wood, Boris Ingster, and Leonard Brown.
Directed by Abner Biberman.

Co-Starring Teno Pollick as Steve Acero.

With

Argentina Brunetti ....Mrs. Acero.
Adelina Pedroza......................Luisa Acero.
Phillip Terry ....Lewis Clinton.
Rusty Lane ....Lt. Comerford.

Faculty

Marian C., Vince H., Larry T., Marjorie C., Anne L.

Reviews:

THERE'S more trouble brewing for "Mr. Novak" tonight (KYW, 7:30-8:30). Jefferson High's popular English teacher (James Franciscus) is charged with prejudice by a Mexican-American student (Teno Pollick).

A moving performance from young Teno Pollick makes this show's study of an underprivileged kid a good exercise in compassion. Pollick is sent to the principal's office when Novak finds him sleeping in class. The boy, tired and frustrated, accuses Novak of picking on him because he is Mexican. The real reason the boy is in this state makes you root for him all the way. — *"Television Tonight,"* Monassen *(PA)* Valley Independent, *February 11, 1964.*

Another laudable attempt by this series to treat a sensitive subject, and it comes off reasonably well. This time it's a Mexican student with a chip on his shoulder who's so convinced Mr. Novak is prejudiced against him, he actually has Mr. Novak believing it's true. The program sustains interest and two scenes, one between the boy and his Spanish-speaking counselor, and another with Novak directly, are exceptionally good. — *"TV Key Previews,"* Charleston *(WV)* Gazette, *February 11, 1964.*

Well-acted by the regulars (notably Dean Jagger) and guest star Teno Pollick, but this just adds up to another Hollywood effort to delve into racial prejudice (real and fancied) on a superficial level. Tonight's victim is a Mexican boy and, for balance, his faculty advisor is Negro. — *"TV Time,"* Decatur *(IL)* Herald, *February 11, 1964.*

Tuesday's "Mr. Novak" had a goodly number of cliché sermons, but the kind that warm rather than cool interest. Tano Pollick impressed highly with a sincere portrayal of a Mexican youth who presumes discrimination against him when there isn't any. — *Hank Grant, "On the Air,"* The Hollywood Reporter, *February 13, 1964.*

GRADE B: This is an above-average episode that explores misperception of racial prejudice. Teno Pollick delivers an excellent performance as the Mexican-American student who feels harassed by Mr. Novak. He is angry, defiant and adds considerable realism to the role. Franciscus displays depth in his initial misunderstanding of the youth's falling asleep in class. His scenes with Pollick crackle with emotional intensity. Jeanne Bal offers fine support and is authoritative when interacting with the puzzled Novak. Jagger in particular is effective when chastising the teacher for assuming an improper action. Regular Vince Howard has his biggest part to date and is very good. He displays genuine sensitivity in a lengthy scene where he counsels the troubled youth. Marian Collier acts well in a few dramatic bits with Novak discussing how students get along with their teachers. The positive ending is nicely done.

🍎 🍎 🍎 🍎

Episode Twenty-Two — Chin Up Mr. Novak
Broadcast February 18, 1964

Synopsis:

British actress Hermione Baddeley guest stars as a spirited 75-year-old exchange program teacher in a comedy episode — rare for this series. Vane assigns Miss Mumsley to take over a particularly troublesome English literature class of Mr. Novak, against the younger teacher's wishes. With her colorful teaching methods, Miss Mumsley deals most effectively with the class's chief disruptive influence, Joey Carter.

Written and Produced by Joseph Calvelli.
Directed by Michael O'Herlihy.

Guest Star Hermione Baddeley as Miss Margaret Anne Mumsley.
Co-Starring Don Grady as Joey Carter.

Faculty

Marian C., André P., Stephen R., Kathaleen E., Vince H., Larry T., Marjorie C.

Reviews:

HERMIONE BADDELY (right), English character actress, discovers being a Pom Pom girl is not as simple as Stardedt Kaaua makes it look on "Mr. Novak" at 7:30 tonight on Channel 3.

Another "integration" episode, this involving an aged English teacher in a minor conflict with Novak. Hermione Baddeley, one of the best and liveliest of Broadway's recent importees from England (here to do the original version of "The Milk Train Doesn't Stop Here Anymore"), has a field day as the teacher whose foreign methods both solve and create problems. Baddeley is such a delicious old pro that it's little wonder Mr. Novak, as played by James Franciscus, comes off second-best, even when he's right. Don Grady is tonight's specific problem pupil. — *"TV Previews,"* Rockford *(IL)* Morning Star, *February 18, 1964.*

Hermione Baddeley, a goodly English actress, and an amusing script, make a bright show. She plays an elderly British teacher who believes rules were made to be bent. She comes to Jefferson High as an exchange teacher to observe. But she pleads for a class and Vane (Dean Jagger) gives her one of Novak's. It contains Don Grady, a bright, sensitive pupil who acts the class clown. The role of the teacher was written for Margaret Rutherford, who would have been a delight. But you can't fault Miss Baddeley's fine acting job. — *"TV Tonight,"* Monessen *(PA)* Valley Independent, *February 18, 1964.*

A thoroughly delightful hour in spite of obvious, corny and sentimental story. Hermione Baddeley as a 75-year-old teacher sent over from England as an exchange teacher. Her performance is a rare treat. Don Grady of "My Three Sons" does quite well with the second lead. — *"Tonight on TV,"* Lumberton *(NC)* Robesonian, *February 18, 1964.*

Tuesday's "Mr. Novak" was distinguished by a warm, sensitive, nobly genteel and humanly appealing portrayal of a 75-yr.-old exchange teacher from Blighty. A simple, script, uncluttered by artificial conflict devices. — *Hank Grant, "On the Air,"* The Hollywood Reporter, *February 20, 1964.*

There has been no more moving portrayal this season than Hermione Baddeley's 75-year-old English Schoolteacher on last week's edition of "Mr. Novak." — *Cecil Smith, "The TV Scene,"* The Los Angeles Times, *February 25, 1964.*

GRADE A: This is a beautifully written and played story that has both laughter and tears. Hermione Baddeley is wonderful as the aged British exchange teacher and she becomes a character with much depth and substance. The actress is marvelous in a funny scene where teaches one of Novak's classes and wins over the problem students. In a later part of the episode, her heartbreak in reaction to a student's mockery is palpable. Don Grady as the sarcastic student adds considerably to the show's quality. The realization of his hurtful actions and apology are delivered with true grace. Franciscus works well with Baddeley and is warm and gallant when he consoles the depressed teacher with a dinner date. Jagger and Ball have their best rapport yet and balance beautifully. This is a different kind of installment which is very effective.

🍎 🍎 🍎 🍎

Episode Twenty-Three — **Fear Is a Handful of Dust**
Broadcast February 25, 1964

Synopsis:

Shy student Sue Johnson emerges from obscurity at Jefferson High when her talent at caricature is discovered by Novak. The teacher urges her to submit some of her satirical drawings of faculty members to the editor of the school paper. Growing campus fame sends Sue retreating to her small, personal world, but discovery of some her drawings described as pornographic forces her into a showdown.

Produced by E. Jack Neuman.
Written by Carol O'Brien.
Directed by Abner Biberman.

Co-Starring Brenda Scott as Sue Johnson.
Tony Dow as George Scheros.

With

Steve Franken ....Jerry Allen.
Cece Whitney ....Miss McGuire.
Steve Stevens ....Steve.
Gloria Calomeé ....Marcy.
Clive Clerk ....Eddie.
Peter Brooks ....Freddie.

Faculty

Marian C., Vince H., Larry T., Marjorie C.

Reviews:

"Fear Is a Handful of Dust," on Mr. Novak, is the first teleplay for 24-year-old Carol O'Brien, who has been writing public affairs scripts for a Cleveland station. She has

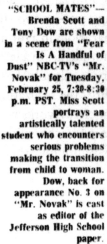

"SCHOOL MATES"— Brenda Scott and Tony Dow are shown in a scene from "Fear Is A Handful of Dust" NBC-TV's "Mr. Novak" for Tuesday, February 25, 7:30-8:30 p.m. PST. Miss Scott portrays an artistically talented student who encounters serious problems making the transition from child to woman. Dow, back for appearance No. 3 on "Mr. Novak" is cast as editor of the Jefferson High School paper.

turned in an absorbing, compassionate study of a square peg — a timid, shy and talented 16-year-old-girl. Brenda Scott is good in the role, although she is prettier than the script indicates. Novak (James Franciscus) discovers her talent as a cartoonist and tries to get her to work with Tony Dow, the editor of the school paper. But she is skittish as a fawn, until Novak explains some facts of life to her. — *"TV Scout,"* Abilene *(TX)* Reporter News, *February 25, 1964.*

An absorbing tale for adults and teenagers, but keep your youngsters away. Mr. Novak finds himself challenged by the rebellious withdrawal of a talented girl in his English class, until he learns of her fear about her morbid preoccupation with sex. — *"Tonight on TV,"* Lumberton *(NC)* Robesonian, *February 25, 1964.*

GRADE B+: This well-written script by young Carol O'Brien realistically captures a teen girl's angst. Brenda Scott's portrayal of the withdrawn artist is the high point of the hour. She elicits genuine sympathy for her vulnerability. A scene where Scott tries to look pretty in a mirror, then breaks down, is emotionally powerful. Franciscus displays superior acting skills throughout the episode. The final confrontation with the insecure student is excellent and he is both forceful and sympathetic in regaining her confidence. Scott and Franciscus work well together in all their scenes. Tony Dow is good in his encounters with Scott and is most sincere when encouraging her. The implication that the girl is curious about sex and produces some scandalous drawings is handled with subtlety and taste. Her newfound confidence at the finale is beautifully underplayed. An above-average show with a delicate atmosphere that is never false.

🍎 🍎 🍎 🍎

Episode Twenty-Four — **How Does Your Garden Grow?**
Broadcast March 3, 1964

Synopsis:

A pert substitute teacher comes to Jefferson high with impressive degrees, but no comprehension of how to communicate her knowledge in "How Does Your Garden Grow?" Mary Smith joins the faculty during a flu epidemic, but panics in her first class. When her ineptitude becomes apparent, Vane orders her dismissal, but reconsiders and places her as an observer in Novak's class.

Written and Produced by Joseph Calvelli.
Directed by Michael O'Herlihy.

Guest Star Barbara Barrie as Mary Smith.

With

Patricia Morrow ....Gloria.
Pamela Baird ....Claudia.
Teri Garr ....Lisa.
Karen Green...........................Sarah.
Linda Marshall ....Irene.

Faculty

Steve F., Marian R., Vince H., James Dawson as Coach Dawson, Marjorie C., Larry T., André P., Stephen R., Marian C.

Reviews:

"How Does Your Garden Grow?" is a character study vignette of a delightfully addle-pated, sensitive young lady who wants to be a teacher but cannot communicate. She comes to Jefferson during a crisis caused by a flu epidemic, and the one day the script follows sends her through comedy, frustration and blooming love. Barbara Barrie is a bit too introspective for the role. — *"TV Tonight,"* Monessen *(PA)* Valley Independent, *March 3, 1964.*

On a plodding "Mr. Novak," Barbara Barrie's performance as a bumbling, bewildered schoolteacher and her doe-eyed visual appeal grabbed me right by the throat. — *Hank Grant, "On the Air,"* The Hollywood Reporter, *March 5, 1964.*

GRADE D+: Another rare misfire from the first season. This episode, for the most part, is played for whimsy but a weak script and direction fail to deliver. The humorous tone depicting Barrie's flighty character in the early part of the installment is too obvious and lacks charm. Barrie gives her all as the insecure teacher and manages to raise whatever interest can be found. She is especially good in a scene at Vane's office as he tries to find the source of her insecurity. Jagger and Franciscus work well together as usual. There is a well-played but rather pointless scene where Novak has dinner in the addled teacher's apartment. It is nicely played by both of them but adds little to the plot. The ending is both tragic and poignant but after so much lackluster material it fails to be very moving. Barbara Barrie is the main appeal of this one.

🍎 🍎 🍎 🍎

Episode Twenty-Five — **The Tower**
Broadcast March 10, 1964

Synopsis:

Former leading lady Heather Angel returns to Hollywood after two decades to portray an unstable 65-year-old retired schoolteacher, in "The Tower." After 20 years spent in raising a family, Miss Angel launches a show-business comeback as Alfrieda, a geometry teacher whom Vane retires following numerous complaints about her classroom ability. Lost in a strange world, a confused Alfrieda reappears in her old classroom one morning, scribbling geometry problems on the blackboard.

Guest Cast:

Heather Angel as Alfrieda "Chalky" White.
Gilbert Green as Coleman.
Bernadette Hale as Miss Kroner.
Robert Ball as David.
John Ryan as John.
Charles Briles as Ken.

Executive Producer: E. Jack Neuman.
Producer: Joseph Calvelli.
Writer: James Menzies.
Director: Michael O'Herlihy.
Recording Supervisor: Franklin Milton.
Supervising Film Editor: John D. Dunning.
Composer/Theme Music: Lyn Murray.

Reviews:

Heather Angel, absent from the Hollywood scene since 1943 (Except for a Perry Mason Show two seasons ago), returns to play an about-to-be-retired school teacher on Mr. Novak. It's a sad tale about a lonely old lady who dreads retirement. The tragedy of the story is not lightened by any pat answers. — *"Highlights Tonight,"* San Antonio *(TX)* Express, *March 10, 1964.*

GRADE A-: (This episode was not available for viewing.) Based on the script, this must have been a dramatic and well-acted episode. The issue of competency and suggested retirement for an elderly teacher was presented with taste and compassion. There appear to have been several outstanding elements to this scenario. A tragic scene of the teacher's sparsely attended farewell party at the school was a highlight. The confused educator shows up to again teach her class and was gently escorted out by the principal. There was beautifully written dialogue. Jagger and Angel must have been superb. Near the end, when the ashamed teacher moves to the top of the school, the script was very dramatic but never strays into melodrama. Jagger and Angel must have been excellent when he gently talks her into coming down and going to her home.

Jagger's dialogue is magnificent when restoring order to the school. It's a first-class humanistic episode.

🕊 🕊 🕊 🕊

Episode Twenty-Six — **One Way to Say Goodbye**
Broadcast March 17, 1964

Synopsis:

A beautiful brunette with romance on her mind, and a boy on the verge of becoming a hoodlum, complicate the day for teacher John Novak in "One Way to Say Goodbye." When alumnus Jenny Peterson (Kathryn Hays) visits her old school and runs into Mr. Novak, it's love at first sight for both — but a secret from Jenny's past upsets the romantic apple cart.

Written and Produced by E. Jack Neuman.
Directed by Richard Donner.

Guest Star Kathryn Hays as Jenny Peterson.

With

Tom Nardini ....Tony Sinclair.
Glen Kramer ....Robert Peterson.
George Petrie...........................Charles Sinclair.
Toni Basil ....Randy.

Faculty

Marian C., Larry T., Stephen R., Kathaleen E., Vince H., André P., Marjorie C.

COMPLICATION—John Novak finds that romance with an alumnae of Jefferson High, played by Kathryn Hays, leads to complications in his career as a teacher on Mr. Novak, Tuesday at 7:30 PM on KMJ-TV, 24.

Reviews:

Good show for regular female viewers. Kildare hasn't been nipped by Cupid in a few weeks, so his teaching counterpart takes the plunge and he has excellent taste (Kathryn Hays). But, alas, while a TV series hero is loving, his script writers are figuring a way for him not to win fair lady. — *"TV Key Previews,"* Washington *(DC) Evening Star, March 17, 1964.*

Love comes to Mr. Novak (James Franciscus) in the mink-coated presence of beautiful Kathryn Hays, a graduate of Jefferson who returns to enjoy some "impulsive memories." Their romance is set against a background of the school's Open House, and Novak's problems with a near-delinquent. And, of course, there's something about the girl that

Novak doesn't know. Recommended for romantics. — *"Television Tonight,"* Monessen *(PA)* Valley independent, *March 17, 1964.*

GRADE B: This atypical and romantic story is very good and never slips into a soap-opera level. Neuman's script has realistic dialogue and the emotionally strong scenes are all well played. Kathryn Hays delivers an appealing performance and her character has a great chemistry with Mr. Novak. Franciscus is effective in a scene where he tells his new love of a decision to become a teacher. In fact, he is excellent throughout. Jagger is charming when he addresses the faculty about an upcoming parent's night. Tom Nardini offers good support as a punk student who gets in a fight with Novak. Their resolution is realistic and underplayed. Donner's directorial skill is evident throughout with his fine use of close-ups. A romantic scene between the leads is filmed in a shadowy profile that is very effective. The bittersweet ending in which Novak must let her go back to her husband is very moving. A love story that engages.

🍎 🍎 🍎 🍎

Episode Twenty-Seven — **Day in the Year**
Broadcast March 24, 1964

Synopsis:

The Jefferson High School campus is stunned by the narcotics death of a 15-year-old-girl, in "Day in the Year." Pretty quiet Martha Hyland collapses after being sent from Mr. Novak's class for giddy behavior. Her boyfriend, Jeff, cannot explain her actions, but a doctor suspects narcotics. When Martha dies, Narcotics Bureau investigators comb the campus for the pusher.

Produced by E. Jack Neuman.
Written by Sidney Marshall.
Directed by Ida Lupino.

Co-Starring Malachi Throne as Medford.
Richard Eyer as Jeff Yorker.

With

Mark Slade ....Ralph Bachett.
Patricia Hyland ....Martha.
David Saber............................Toby.

And

David Sheiner as Dr. Wexler.

Faculty

Marian C., Stephen R., Marion R., Marjorie C., Vince H., Kathaleen E., André P.

Reviews:

Producer Jack Neuman feels that "Day in the Year" by Sidney Marshall, is perhaps the best show they've done. He was so proud of it that he asked the press to take

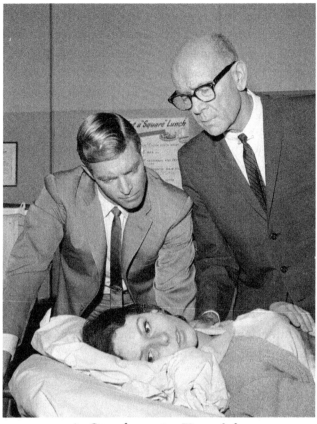

A Student in Trouble

James Franciscus (left), in the title role, and Dean Jagger, who plays the principal of the school, are seen at the bed-side of a student, Patricia Hyland, who has taken an over-dose of barbiturates in tonight's "Mr. Novak" episode. The program will be on Channels 11, 6 and 7, at 7:30.

a preview look at the film. I approached it with some hesitancy because it deals with the use of narcotics by teenagers, a theme that has been explored in scores of TV melodramas and documentaries. However, Marshall's script skipped the melodrama. It's a quiet and sensitive play that holds the fury beneath the surface, a rational, intelligent approach to a grimy problem. It was beautifully directed by Ida Lupino and contains some extraordinary performances, particularly the soft-voiced restrained cop of Malachi Throne, the solemn, factual doctor of David Sheiner and the 15-year-old addict of young Patricia Hyland in her debut performance. — *"The TV Scene,"* Los Angeles Times, *March 24, 1964.*

The tragedy of addiction is pinpointed in a dramatic script. When one of Novak's (James Franciscus) students collapses, a doctor diagnoses an overdose of narcotics. It's up to Malachi Throne, as a seemingly cold-blooded narcotics investigator, to find the pusher who supplied the girl. Throne is very good, particularly in a climactic scene with Novak. Ida Lupino's direction keeps the story moving. — *"TV Tonight,"* Monessen *(PA)* Valley Independent, *March 24, 1964.*

Though a narcotics problem has been treated more forcefully on TV than it is here, considering the show's early telecast hour and the audience it aims for, it's presented in good taste. A student becomes violently ill from an overdose of drugs and the authorities suspect the pusher may also be in school. — *"Tonight on TV,"* Lumberton *(NC)* Robesonian, *March 24, 1964.*

Rerun Review:

The cast, including Patricia Hyland as the student, Richard Eyer as her boyfriend, and David Sheiner as a doctor, does very well. — Washington *(DC)* Evening Star, *July 28, 1964.*

GRADE B+: This grim warning of the dangers of drug use is an effective installment. The girl's overdose, which is presented in the beginning of the show, is both realistic and dramatic. Partricia Hyland is believable as the tragic coed. Lupino's use of a distorted lens to show the overdose is economical and effective. There is an eerie jazz score for this episode that enhances the story. All dialogue discussing drug use is pragmatic. Malachi Throne, as the narcotics investigator, produces a shaded performance. He is initially cynical but later reveals his anguish at the drug problem among students. Franciscus's concern about a possible pusher on campus is impressive. David Sheiner is authoritative as a doctor who has experienced previous overdoses. Richard Eyer registers as the doomed girl's boyfriend. There is a fine closing scene where Novak and Vane question how to warn students about drugs. A very good episode.

🐦 🐦 🐦 🐦 🐦

Episode Twenty-Eight — **Moment Without Armor**
Broadcast March 31, 1964

Synopsis:

School grounds are quiet in the evening, and darkness was the accomplice of the unknown assailant who attacked assistant principal Jeanne Pagano.

Produced by E. Jack Neuman.
Written by Margaret Armen.
Directed by Michael O'Herlihy.

With

Michael Walker ....Bill Russell.
Robert Sampson......................Sgt. Holcolmb.

And

Oliver M. McGowan as William Russell, Sr.

Faculty

Marian C., Stephen R., Marjorie C., Larry T., Kathaleen E., Vince H.

Reviews:

This episode is more a mystery story than a customary lugubrious education vignette. Miss Pagano (Jeanne Bal) is assaulted and then, as a stand-in for the principal (Dean Jagger) has to discipline a boy who looks perilously like the one who attacked her. Is he the one and how can she handle the situation? Luckily, Mr. Novak (James Franciscus) is on hand to help. Miss Bal is excellent (as she invariably is) and late Robert Walker's son Mike is effective as the boy. — *"TV Previews,"* Rockford *(IL)* Morning Star, *March 31, 1964.*

A switch in emphasis from student-teacher problems, to a student-assistant principal conflict, heightened by the temporary absence of Principal Vane. Miss Pagano loses her confidence and composure when she's attacked outside school grounds in the dark, and it takes a gambling move on Mr. Vane's part to restore her judgment and her

MIKE WALKER, second son of the late Robert Walker, makes his guest-star debut as a troublesome high school student in "Moment Without Armor" on Mr. Novak, Tuesday, 7:30 p.m., NBC-TV.

faith. Fairly suspenseful. — *"TV Key Previews,"* Richmond *(VA)* Times-Dispatch, *March 31, 1964.*

Mike Walker, the second acting son of Jennifer Jones and the late Robert Walker, is the guest star. He made his debut earlier as a student in a classroom. He is very good as an insolent troublemaker who so riles the school's vice principal that she slaps him. And that's against the rules. An absorbing hour, with realistic character reactions. — *"Television Tonight,"* Monessen *(PA)* Valley Independent, *March 31, 1964.*

GRADE B: Jeanne Bal's excellent performance carries this suspenseful show. She ranges from fear after her attack to loss of confidence. Her regaining strength in the conclusion is never falsely melodramatic. The script effectively portrays the shattering effect an attack can have on a woman. Jagger, as usual, has a great rapport with her. Some scenes where he gently encourages her and expresses his admiration are both poetic and moving. Michael Walker is suitably evil as the punk student and proves to be a significant adversary. The script occasionally veers into melodrama, but Bal and Jagger easily carry the day. There is a cute scene where the principal dresses down Miss Scott for being chronically late. Marian Collier and Jagger play it for genuine humor. The happy ending is underplayed. A solid episode which is really a showcase for Bal.

🍎🍎🍎🍎🍎

Episode Twenty-Nine — **Fare Thee Well**
Broadcast April 7, 1964

Synopsis:

Noreen Corcoran guest stars as an unwed senior facing motherhood, in "Fare Thee Well." Teacher John Novak learns that one of his students, Cathy Williams, is pregnant and sets out to make the girl's final days before graduation as free from extra pressure as possible. To Cathy's juvenile mind, graduating with her class is the most important thing in the world. However, Cathy and Novak run head-on into opposition from Mr. Vane and school regulations that require immediate dismissal.

Produced by E. Jack Neuman.
Written by Carol O'Brien.
Directed by Abner Biberman.

Co-Starring Noreen Corcoran as Cathy Williams.
Doug Lambert as Jack Putney.

Special Guest Star Kevin McCarthy as Philip Williams.

With

Marc Cavell............................Boris.
Phil Bonnell ....Freddy.
Lori Fontaine ....Jane.

And

June Dayton as Emma Williams.

Faculty

Marian C., Stephen R., Vince H., Marjorie C., Marion R.

TUESDAY: Noreen Cor-
coran guest-stars as an
unwed Jefferson High sen-
ior facing motherhood in
"Fare Thee Well," a Mr.
Novak drama to be seen
Tuesday evening at 7:30
o'clock on Channel 5.
When Novak finds out
that the girl is pregnant,
he sets out to make her
final days before gradua-
tion as free from pressures
as possible. The teacher
encounters heavy opposi-
tion from the principal
(Dean Jagger), who cites
school regulations which
require the pupil's imme-
diate removal from school.

Reviews:

Mr. Novak is awash in a sea of tears as Noreen Corcoran portrays an unwed, pregnant student whose big regret is that she will not be allowed to graduate. In the show's favor: a conscientious effort to present honest reactions to a situation from the girl's parents, the boy who fathered the child, and Novak and Vane. But Miss Corcoran does cry a lot. — *"Highlights Tonight,"* San Antonio *(TX)* Express, *April 7, 1964.*

GRADE A-: This script by young Carol O'Brien is a moving exploration of the consequences of a teen's pregnancy. It is a show of strong emotions but never becomes overdone. The script brings up the issue of a pregnant teen afraid to tell her parents. It also explores the rule that a girl can't graduate if too far along in pregnancy. There is excellent acting overall. Noreen Corcoran is very good as the vulnerable coed and her anguish at the predicament is very effective. Bal expresses concern and a scene in her office with the teen is underplayed but heartbreaking. Franciscus has a good rapport with the girl and brings a realistic view to the terrible situation. Jagger is good when talking about the continual problem of teen pregnancies. Kevin McCarthy as the girl's supportive parent and Doug Lambert as the father of her child provide superior support. There is a poignant finale when the girl leaves school for the very last time.

🍎 🍎 🍎 🍎

Episode Thirty — **Senior Prom**
Broadcast April 14, 1964

Synopsis:

When Principal Vane and Mr. Novak threaten to remove a student official, Gail Andrews, from the chairmanship of the senior prom because of her light and inefficient attitude, she decides to shape up. Before the dance takes place, she learns that leadership can also invoke sacrifice.

Guest Cast:

Marta Kristen as Gail Andrews.
Kay Stewart Mrs. Andrews.
Ray Montgomery as Mr. Andrews.
Lesley-Marie Colburn as Vicki.
Jim Henaghan as Walter.

Executive Producer: E. Jack Neuman.
Producer: Joseph Calvelli.
Writer: Sidney Marshall.
Director: Michael O'Herlihy.
Recording Supervisor: Franklin Milton.
Supervising film Editor: John D. Dunning.
Composer/Theme Music: Lyn Murray.

Reviews:

JEFFERSON HIGH'S favorite English teacher (James Franciscus) has problems with a scatterbrained student (Marta Kristen) in tonight's episode of "Mr. Novak" (KYW, 7:30-8:30).

Mr. Novak, in its final new show of the season, is a primer on how to arrange the Senior Prom. Marta Kristen is the student in charge, a girl who wanted the job so she would be popular. But she evades responsibility, then reverses her field and buckles down so hard that she becomes unpopular. This makes the big night a sad one for her. The actual prom scene is pleasant. — *"Highlights Tonight,"* San Antonio *(TX)* Light, *April 14, 1964.*

Nice episode for students. As the title suggests, it's all about the trials and tribulations or organizing a prom, and centers around the frustrations of the young lady who heads the committee. Our hero is conveniently given the job of faculty adviser of the big event, so he's very much in evidence tonight. — *"TV Tonight,"* Greensboro *(NC)* Daily News, *April 14, 1964.*

The "Novak" had a thin but wistful plot that gave Marta Kristen a chance to shine as a timid student who develops backbone when given a prom chairmanship. Also gave "French Teacher" André Philippe a chance to display the good vocal pipes that provided his income before he turned actor. — *Hank Grant, "On the Air,"* The Hollywood Reporter, *April 16, 1964.*

GRADE B: (This episode was not available for viewing.) Marta Kristen's performance as the elected prom organizer was the highlight. She was initially frivolous and avoided getting things done. The coed becomes assertive with her committee after being threatened with removal by Novak. She even goes over the heads of the faculty to get some things done. There was a good scene where she successfully negotiated with the head of a hotel where the prom was to be held. Unfortunately, she became unpopular with some students due to her aggressive manner. Jagger had a funny scene where he addressed a student assembly concerning a small dog that was smuggled through several classes. The girl had been so busy that she hadn't a date. She didn't attend the prom that she worked so hard on. There was an emotional finale when Franciscus goes to her house after the prom and praises her newfound maturity and accomplishment.

"We will return to 'Mr. Novak' following a brief recess."

"I used to watch 'Mr. Novak,' but I'm a dropout."

Episode Guide —
Second Season

MR. NOVAK

Metro-Goldwyn-Mayer

for

NBC (Tuesdays 7:30 P.M. EST)

60 Minutes.

Second Season — 1964–1965

Created by E. Jack Neuman and Boris Sagal.

Starring:

James Franciscus as John Novak.

Dean Jagger as Albert Vane.

and

Burgess Meredith as Martin Woodridge.

Crew:

Associate Producer...................Robert Stambler.
Music......................................Leith Stephens.
"Mr. Novak" Theme................Lyn Murray.
Story Editor ....Lou Morheim.
Director of Photography ....Richard H. Kline.
Art Direction...........................George W. Davis and LeRoy Coleman.
Supervising Film Editor...........John Dunning, A.C.E.
Film Editor ....Ira Heymann.
Assistant Director....................John Bloss.
Set Decoration ....Henry Grace and Charles S. Thompson.
Recording Supervisor ....Frank Milton.

We wish to thank the Advisory Panel of the National Education Association for its invaluable assistance.

🍎 🍎 🍎 🍎

Episode One — **Moonlighting**
Broadcast September 22, 1964

Synopsis:

A second job to supplement his teacher's salary becomes a jeopardy rather than an asset to Mr. Novak in "Moonlighting." He takes a job as parking-lot attendant to help pay his father's doctor bills, but finds his work plays havoc with his teaching efficiency and at the same time lowers his stature in the eyes of the students.

Co-Starring in Alphabetical order

Mabel Albertson......................Mrs. Ring.
Joe deSantis............................Dr. Wolinsky.
Frank Ferguson ....Stanley Novak.

Bert Freed ....Lorimer.
Joe Sirola.................................Nelson.
Maxine Stuart..........................Miss Gardner.

With

K.T. Stevens ....Holly Bradwell.
Pat Morrow.............................Jan.
James Henaghan......................Richard Griffith.
Jim Barringer..........................Fred Lowell.

Faculty

Bill Zuckert............................Mr. Bradwell.
Shirley O'Hara ....Miss Gladstone.
Stephen Roberts ....Mr. Peeples.
Marjorie Corley......................Miss Dorsey.

Reviews:

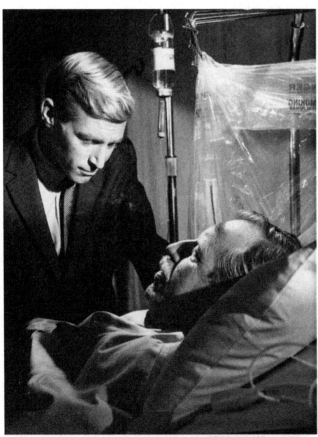

FINANCIAL PROBLEM—James Franciscus, as teacher Novak meets financial problems when his elderly father (played by Arthur O'Connell) becomes ill, in "Moonlighting," the new season's premiere drama of NBC-TV's "Mr. Novak" series, Tuesday, Sept. 22. The teacher, beset by medical bills takes a part-time job that affects his teaching duties.

"Moonlighting." An appropriate opening show for this program's second semester. Because of expenses incurred by his father's illness, Novak is forced to take a job parking cars at night which begins to affect both his efficiency as a teacher and his peace of mind. The script is a bit top heavy with stock statistics on the plight of teachers, but James Franciscus is at his best and makes the hour believable and touching. The finale, with Dean Jagger hearing him out, could easily have taken the story overboard, but Jagger and Franciscus make it the best scene of the play — *"TV's Best Bets for Tonight,"* Madison *(WI)* State Journal, *September 22, 1964.*

As long as "Peyton Place" is being seen after dark, there's no reason to be annoyed by the faint aroma of soap that comes from this episode. Clean-cut

Mr. Novak finds himself in deep financial water and takes a menial job to cover his father's medical expenses. Maybe the situation does occur in real life, but his choice of outside occupation stacks the deck a little too heavily, giving the episode too pat an opportunity to moralize on the sad state of teaching salaries and on the responsibilities of the profession. — *"TV Previews,"* Rockford *(IL)* Morning Star, *September 22, 1964.*

It must be disconcerting for educators to hear a TV teacher pronounce "Thoreau" as in "Zorro" (the mark of), but it must also be gratifying to see propaganda for higher teacher's pay presented as cogently and tastefully as it was on this season's premiere of "Mr. Novak." To initial its second season, the NBC-MGM series had Novak forced to moonlight a job parking cars in a garage in order to handle extra medical expenses in the critical illness of his father. The Meyer Dolinsky script (from a story by John Ryan) provoked excellent performances from James Franciscus (Novak) and Dean Jagger (Principal Albert Vane), the young-old tandem of the series. Director Richard Donner paced the hour nicely and got a lot of mileage in atmosphere out of the roar and speech of the garage setting. Production values and support throughout were top notch, but it will be the strength of the Franciscus-Jagger team that should win for "Novak" again in the Nielsen sweeps. — *Bill, "Television Reviews," Weekly* Variety, *September 30, 1964.*

GRADE A: The initial episode of the second season proves to be a success. John Ryan's fine script brings up the problems of teacher's low salaries. The stress of having to moonlight and the ensuing fatigue are presented in a realistic manner. Franciscus is excellent and delivers a performance of much depth and emotion that is the highlight of the story. The actor is particularly good in a scene where his class discusses the meaning of death. His embarrassment at being caught by his students parking cars is also expertly played. There is another fine scene in Vane's office where Novak breaks down and says he cannot continue. Jagger provides expert support and it is an emotional incident that is very affecting. Frank Ferguson is good as Novak's father. Richard Donner use of expert framing, powerful close-ups and tasteful presentation are very much in evidence. A great beginning to the sophomore year.

ฮ ฮ ฮ ฮ

Episode Two — **With a Hammer in His Hand, Lord, Lord!**

Broadcast September 29, 1964

Synopsis:

Simon Oakland guest stars in "With a Hammer in His Hand, Lord, Lord!" Industrial arts teacher Carl Green (Oakland) conducts classes like a shop foreman, which provokes student Lee Daragh into taking violent action.

Produced by Leonard Freeman.
Written by John D. F. Black.
Directed by Allen Reisner.

Guest Star Simon Oakland......Carl Green.
Co-Starring Tim McIntire.......Lee Daragh.
Walter Koenig ....Jim Carsey.
Arthur Franz ....Sol Moss.

With

Graham Denton......................John Majestic.
Skip Torgerson ....Vince Summers.
Peter Brocco ....Dr. Brown.
Tom Nardini ....Joe Costanza.

Faculty

Stephen R., Vince Howard as Mr. Butler, Marjorie C., Larry Thor as Jim Hendricks.

Reviews:

Good show. The shop teacher is attacked by three of his students, and there's a chance the lies of the boys will be accepted. The episode gives teachers who work in trade areas and have to cope with probable dropouts, their day in the spotlight. Our hero doesn't dig the get-tough-with-the-students manner of the shop teacher, forcefully played by Simon Oakland. — *"Tonight on TV,"* Lumberton *(NC)* Robesonian, *September 29, 1964.*

Give this series credit for attempting to follow the news headlines. Tonight's episode concerns an attack against a teacher, but the script doesn't deal entirely deal in black and white. The teacher (Simon Oakland) isn't exactly a paragon of the educational world himself. — *"TV Previews,"* Rockford *(IL)* Morning Star, *September 29, 1964.*

GRADE A: This well-written, literate episode by John D. F. Black features an outstanding performance by Simon Oakland as an aggressive shop teacher. The script is powerful but is never forced or overdone. Oakland has a long scene with Franciscus in which he informs his fellow teacher of the need to be tough on his students. The job market for industrial arts majors is tough and they must become proficient to survive. It is expertly played by both actors and Oakland's explanation adds depth to his character. Jagger is fine and lends his usual air of authority to all his scenes. Tim McIntyre is good as the punk student who attacks his teacher. In a closing scene in Vane's office, Walter Koenig delivers a superior performance as a guilty student who crumbles under the principal's interrogation. There is a subtle tag at the end where Vane is praised by a former student. It is a moving moment and Jagger's emotional reaction is very realistic. Reisner directs to great effect with interesting framing. A second-season winner.

Episode Three — **Visions of Sugar Plums**

Broadcast October 6, 1964

Synopsis:

Guest star Eddie Albert portrays a freethinking rover whose unorthodox teaching methods captivate his students but alienate the school board and the PTA, in "Visions of Sugar Plums."

Produced by Leonard Freeman.
Written by Joseph Calvelli.
Directed by Paul Wendkos.

Guest Star Eddie Albert as Charlie O'Rourke.

With

Adrienne Hayes......................Marian.
Beverly Washburn ....Ruth.
Robert Diamond....................Gus.

Faculty

Marian Collier as Miss Scott, Stephen R., Vince H., Marjorie C.

And

Phyllis Avery as Ruth Wilkinson.

7:30—Mr. Novak
Eddie Albert portrays a wanderer hired as a temporary teacher at Jefferson High. His unorthodox methods captivate his class but alienate the school board and the P.-T.A. N.B.C.—3

Reviews:

One scene here in which Principal Vane (Dean Jagger) is forced to teach a class is a gem. The episode is an absorbing, though slow-moving character study of an irresponsible but likable non-conformist, effectively portrayed by Eddie Albert, who tries his hand at teaching after a 15-year vagabond hiatus. — *"TV Key,"* Oneonta *(NY)* Star, *October 6, 1964.*

Eddie Albert is charming as the kind of teacher most students would enjoy having, but regulations and educational stuffed shirts being what they are (and my we include TV budgets in that) we know his assignment is only temporary. Albert paints a poignant picture of the character. — Dover *(OH)* Daily Reporter, *October 6, 1964.*

"Mr. Novak's" Jefferson High School has a new vice principal for girls. Like her predecessor Jeanne Bal who co-starred as Miss Pagano, Phyllis Avery is the brightest thing in the series. She made her debut last night sparring with guest star Eddie Albert while James Franciscus, who has the title role, took what amounted to a walk-on part. Miss Avery's characterization is one of spunk sprinkled liberally with sugar. — *Patricia Costa, "poinT of View,"* Rochester *(NY)* Democrat and Chronicle, *October 7, 1964.*

Tuesday's "Mr. Novak" had a wistfully warm plot about a guitar-strumming folk-singing teacher, sincerely etched by Eddie Albert. Although the finish confused his altruism with fear even an abhorrence of penned-in responsibility. Albert got across the idea that he wanted to live his life as most of wish we could. — *Hank Grant, "On the Air — BLOODSHOT SQUARE EYEBALLS DEPT.,"* The Hollywood Reporter, *October 8, 1964.*

GRADE A-: Eddie Albert's vivid portrayal of a non-conformist educator is the primary strength of this whimsical installment. He is initially frivolous to Novak and Vane but later reveals, with superb acting, his fear and insecurity. There is a great scene where he teaches a class of problem students and wins them over with unusual methods. A further incident by a lake, where he and the students discuss a poem by Robert Frost, is expertly acted by all. Albert also plays guitar and sings several folk songs and is very charming. Jagger is wonderful in a comic scene where he bluffs his way through teaching a math class. Phyllis Avery makes her first appearance and is a warm and sympathetic presence. She is admirable with Albert in a romantic scene where he tells her of his need to wander. Adrienne Hayes is fine as a shy student who blossoms under Albert's encouragement. The bittersweet ending is beautifully played.

🍎 🍎 🍎 🍎 🍎

Episode Four — Little Girl Lost
Broadcast October 20, 1964

Synopsis:

Mr. Novak tries to cope with problem student Edie Currie who has been kicked out of several schools and seems destined to meet the same fate at Jefferson High. He gets her the lead in the school play and she responds beautifully — until she gets involved in a stolen-car incident.

Guest Cast:

Davey Davison as Edie Currie
Jean Engstrom as Mrs. Currie
Buck Taylor as Nick Bradley
Arthur Franz as Det. Sgt. Sol Moss
Jim Bates as Warren
Karen Green as Judy.

Associate Producer: Robert Stambler
Assistant to the Producer: Don Leonard

Writer: Betty Ulius.
Story Editor: Lou Morheim.
Director: Paul Wendkos.
Recording Supervisor: Franklin Milton.
Supervising Film Editor: John D. Dunning.
Composer/Theme Music: Lyn Murray.

Reviews:

PROBLEM PUPILS: Guest star Davey Davison takes a between-classes break with her boyfriend (Buck Taylor), who leads her into trouble with the police, in "Little Girl Lost," a Mr. Novak drama to be seen Tuesday evening at 7:30 o'clock on Channel 5.

Mr. Novak last night centered around a wild student who fell for the teaching charm of Jim Franciscus and in the end was trapped in a theft case. Davey Davison gave a strong portrayal of the girl who suddenly changed her erratic ways after being given the lead in a school play. There was nothing wrong with the continuity — except the plot continued to make a mountain out of a mole hill. When it finally did end, it was rather weak and left Jefferson's school charmer looking rather meek. — *"Television by Sandy Gardiner,"* Ottowa *(ON)* Journal, *October 19, 1964.*

Davey Davison handles the challenging role of the problem child who's been shifted from school to school, and finally finds herself when she meets Mr. Novak. — *Steven H. Scheuer (King Features Syndicate), "TV Key Previews,"* San Diego *(CA)* Union, *October 20, 1964.*

GRADE B+: (This episode was not available for viewing.) According to the script, the best part of this installment must have been Davey Davison's performance. She is given several opportunities for a wide range of emotional aspects to her character. The student is initially sullen and rebellious and challenges Mr. Novak's efforts to encourage her. She later begins to soften when becoming involved in the school play. A chance of getting the leading role finds her happy and confident. Franciscus must have been very good in his scenes with the young actress. There is a well-written moment when there is almost a romantic incident between them. Jagger was undoubtedly very good when lecturing the defiant coed. Buck Taylor had several chances to portray her lying boyfriend. A lot of well-done scenes showcased the play's rehearsal. There was a poignant ending where Novak and the girl reach an understanding. A vivid character piece.

☕ ☕ ☕ ☕ ☕

Episode Five — **One Monday Afternoon**

Broadcast October 27, 1964

Synopsis:

The tragic death of Jefferson High's star quarterback during a practice session spurs Albert Vane and head coach Lou Myerson (guest star Claude Akins) to make a critical analysis of Myerson's quest for a championship team. The victim's father, maintaining his son was injured before the fatal accident, threatens to sue the school if the medical report verifies his claim.

Guest Cast:

Claude Akins as Lou Myerson.
Brooke Bundy as Carol Walker.
Simon Scott as Ralph Donan.
Allan Hunt as Jerry Donan.
Ross Elliot as Milliard Wright.

Associate Producer: Robert Stambler.
Assistant to the Producer: Don Leonard.
Writers: Mel Goldberg/Herman Groves.
Director: Paul Wendkos.
Story Editor: Lou Morheim.
Recording Supervisor: Franklin Milton.
Supervising Film Editor: John D. Dunning.
Composer/Theme Music: Lyn Murray.

Reviews:

ALAN HUNT plays Jefferson High's star quarterback whose sudden death saddens Coach Claud Akins and the school on "Mr. Novak" at 7:30 tonight on Channel 3.

"One Monday Afternoon" is a disturbing drama of a football hero, the golden boy of Jefferson High, who dies during a scrimmage. We see the grim, tragic consequences on his fellow players (who have been coached to "Hit, hit, hit!"); his best girl; his sorrowing parents and the devastated coach, skillfully played by Claude Akins. It's an off-beat heart-wringer that unfortunately loses much of its punch by turning into a routine sermon. — *"Highlights Tonight — TV Scout,"* San Antonio *(TX)* Express, *October 27, 1964.*

Good show. It's a character study of a high school football coach and his reactions when his star player dies in a scrimmage. Nothing unexpected happens, but Claude

Akins is letter perfect as the coach. — *"TV Key Previews,"* Charleston *(NC)* Gazette, *October 27, 1964.*

"Mr. Novak," NBC's weekly dramatic tribute to the schoolteachers, took up the delicate subject of high school football fatalities Tuesday night — but walked cautiously all around it without touching the core of the matter. The plot centered on a tough coach whose star player was killed in a scrimmage. The story then backed away from the problem of injury or death in connection with the sport and concentrated on the coach's reaction. — Waco *(TX)* Tribune-Herald, *November 1, 1964.*

GRADE B: (This episode was not available for viewing.) Based on the script, this was a better-than-average show. It seemed that at least 16 high school athletes died every year from football injuries. Guest star Claude Akins had many chances to explore his character of an aggressive coach. His attitude of winning at any cost results in the accidental death of the star quarterback during a practice scrimmage. In a later scene in Vane's office, the coach reveals that he was injured early on and couldn't pursue a career in football. He then channeled his energies into coaching. There is excellent dialogue in this exchange. Brooke Bundy had several scenes of strong emotions concerning the death of her boyfriend. Allan Hunt enjoyed a nice encounter with Brooke before the accident. Franciscus also had some well-written scenes with Akins. There was a realistic and upbeat ending with the emergence of a new star quarterback. A good installment.

ɮ ɮ ɮ ɮ ɮ

Episode Six — **Let's Dig a Little Grammar**
Broadcast November 10, 1964

Synopsis:

Tommy Sands and Johnny Crawford guest star in "Let's Dig a Little Grammar," a drama in which Novak arranges an unusual "test" to prevent a gifted student from quitting school to join a band.

Produced by Leonard Freeman.
Written by Mel Goldberg.
Directed by Joseph Sargent.

Guest Stars

Tommy Sands as Ray Wilson.
Johnny Crawford as Joel "JoJo" Rizzo.
Co-Starring Harvey Lembeck as Vic Rizzo.
David Sheiner as Mr. Webb.

With

Judith Morton..........................Lois.
Stephen Roberts ....Mr. Peeples.
Jon Silo ....Emillo.

Special Guest Star Allan Sherman as Georgie.

Film Editors ....Ira Heymann and Marvin Adelson.

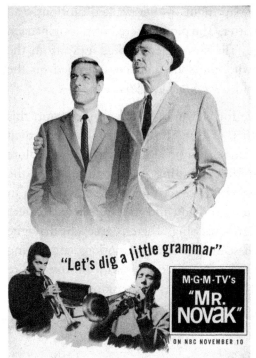

"Let's dig a little grammar"

M·G·M-TV's
"MR. NOVAK"
ON NBC NOVEMBER 10

Reviews:

Great Show for teenagers. The plot about two fledgling trumpeters is so obvious, it's like nowhere, but the music, particularly in the last act, is real cool and the cast has a ball. On tap are Tommy Sands, Johnny Crawford, Harvey Lembeck and, in an amusing bit, Allan Sherman. — *"TV Best Bets,"* San Antonio *(TX)* Light, *November 11, 1964.*

Even those viewers who don't dig jazz must have found this warm, sometimes extremely compelling drama to their liking. Aside from the plot conflict, there was a most interesting musical appreciation lesson for viewers that was as simplified as one of Leonard Bernstein's "Young People's Concerts." Mel Goldberg, who scripted the teleplay the teleplay, evidenced either inherent knowledge of music or admirable research to fashion a musical plot hook that could not be faulted by even an extreme jazz buff. The music hook served to demonstrate teacher efforts to guide students towards careers best suited to their talents. In this case, the "aptitude test" was a jam session, which served as a rousing climax. Mr. Novak (James Franciscus), in his capacity as student advisor, has on one hand a brilliant mathematics student (Tommy Sands) whose prime goal leans in another direction; he wants to become a professional horn player of the stature of Miles Davis or Dizzy Gillespie. College? Forget it, fellas, and he may even quit high school in his senior year to take a six-week job with a jazz band. On the other hand, there's an introverted student (Johnny Crawford) who demeans his own trumpet-playing prowess, though Novak is convinced he can cut Sands to pieces in a challenging session, if only the shy lad will come out of his shell. For Novak, in arranging the contest, he can win a daily double, since Sands must be convinced he'll never make the greatest trumpeter in the world, while Crawford must be convinced that this is where his future lies. Sands is no dummy, realizing in the final test he's been cut to size, and the fadeout promise is he'll be another Einstein, perhaps. Joseph Sargent directed briskly for producer Leonard Freeman, pointedly giving the jazz interludes a toe-tapping ride without diminishing the real crux of the plot, which lay with the provocative dialogue. Acting was fine all round. Allan Sherman cameo'd a good opening bit as a goatee'd but otherwise unhip jazz band leader and Harvey Lembeck scored a sincere effort as the shy lad's ex-musician brother. Good also was stellar star Franciscus, Stephen Roberts as Prof. Peeples, David

Sheiner as music instructor and Judith Morrison as Sand's fiancée. Needless to add, Sands and Crawford were solid in their key roles. In sum, 'twas a worthy dramatic effort, and the music — like crazy, man! So, also give music scorer Leith Stevens some skin for his yeoman assist. Not seen were 10 of this country's best jazz instrumentalists who were actually blowing up a storm: Keith Mitchell, Shelly Manne, Artie Kane, James Zito, Donald Farquist, R. W. Cooper, Richard Noel, Ted Nash, C. E. Shank and James R. Gibbons. — *Hank Grant,* The Hollywood Reporter, *November 12, 1964.*

GRADE A-: This musically themed episode has the benefit of strong performances by all concerned. There is a well-written script with honest conflicts and emotions. The musically based dialogue is very realistic. Tommy Sands contributes a vivid characterization as a gifted math student who opts to pursue music. Johnny Crawford is equally as appealing in his vulnerable portrayal of an insecure musician with great potential. Franciscus is fine in his scenes counseling each of the boys. Harvey Lembeck offers exceptional support as Crawford's older brother who is a bitter ex-player. Allan Sherman contributes an effective cameo as a swinging jazz band leader. Davis Sheiner is fine as a music teacher who understands the boys' potentials. He works well with Franciscus. The concluding jazz concert and cutting contest is beautifully directed by Joe Sargent and is an exciting climax to the hour. An episode that is a winner in every area.

🍎🍎🍎🍎

Episode Seven - **The People Doll:
You Wind It Up and It Makes Mistakes**
Broadcast November 17, 1964

Synopsis:

Mr. Novak tries to stop a promising student who wants to quit school and marry, in "The People Doll: You Wind It Up and It Makes Mistakes."

Guest Cast:

Burt Brinckerhoff as Joe Keenan.
Bonnie Franklin as Gina Czarnecki.
Malachi Throne as Frank Czarnecki.
Bob Random as Prinz.
Christopher Riordan as Student.

Associate Producer: Robert Stambler.
Assistant to Producer: Don Leonard.
Writer: John D. F. Black.
Story Editor: Lou Morheim.
Director: Herschel Daugherty.
Recording Supervisor: Franklin Milton.
Supervising Film Editor: John D. Dunning.
Composer/Theme Music: Lyn Murray.

'Mr. Novak' chaperones an off-campus party, 7:30 p.m., Ch. 4

Reviews:

"The People Doll: You Wind It Up and It Makes Mistakes." A rather cluttered title, but it has one great asset. Burt Brinckerhoff, one of the most sensitive and talented young actors in the business, plays a high-school dropout who'd rather marry and get a job than remain in school to fulfill his rather promising educational destiny. It's Novak's problem and there is no solution, but Brinckerhoff is always worth catching. Other worthwhile performances are given by Bonnie Franklin as the girl and Malachi Throne as her father. — *"TV Time Previews,"* Baton Rouge *(LA)* State Times, *November 17, 1964.*

GRADE D+: This is a lesser episode that is marred by a melodramatic script and lackluster direction. Franciscus and Jagger try their best but are let down by the writing. Burt Brinckerhoff as the student who wishes to marry gives his all as does Bonnie Beecher as his intended bride. They bring a little life to the overall dismal proceedings. One good aspect of the script is that it hints at the boy's sexual frustration in wanting to hurry the marriage. It is tastefully done but fails to ignite the storyline. Phyllis Avery is good in a scene in which she counsels Beecher in her office. Malachi Throne adequately registers as the girl's father in an underwritten part. Near the end there is a lively wedding party scene that features Marian Collier who energetically dances with Throne. She is charming with Franciscus and they add a touch of energy to the hour. This is an installment that just doesn't work despite the well-intentioned performances of the principals.

🦃 🦃 🦃 🦃

Episode Eight — **Boy Under Glass**
Broadcast November 24, 1964

Synopsis:

John Novak becomes the most unpopular teacher at Jefferson High School when he flunks star pitcher Frank Towner just before an important game. Novak offers the boy a re-exam and he accepts — but his father, fearing that his son's cramming will upset his pitching and spoil his chances for a major-league bid, forces the boy to cheat.

Produced by Leonard Freeman.
Teleplay by Mel Goldberg.
Story by Robert Stambler and Mel Goldberg.
Directed by Allen Reisner.

Co-Starring Frank Silvera as Andy Towner.
Wayne Grice as Frank Towner.

Also Starring Arch Johnson as Coach Mel Brewer.

With

Juanita Moore ....Ellen Towner.
Leo Durocher..........................Himself.

Reviews:

Athletics meets scholarship head-on in a good Mr. Novak. Wayne Grice is a star baseball pitcher, on the verge of being scouted by the major leagues. But he has fallen behind in English, and if he flunks a midterm exam, he will be ineligible for the big game that the scouts will be watching. Some good points are made here about education, opportunities for Negroes, and ambitious parents. Leo Durocher appears as himself at the climax. — *"TV Tops Tonight,"* Greensboro *(NC)* Record, *November 24, 1964.*

Mel Goldberg has fashioned one of the best scripts yet done on this series. It concerns a brilliant Negro athlete, a baseball pitcher in whom there is a major-league interest, but whose dedication to sports leaves him insufficient time for studies. There are many conflicts in this drama: Should Novak make allowances because of the boy's athletic prowess or declare him ineligible? Is the boy's father right in pushing his son towards sports because of the fate of a college-educated son? To what extent is the boy prepared to sacrifice personal integrity to pass a re-evaluation? Each conflict is well thought out and well handled. The stature of this play is well above the norm for this series and indicates how well drama may be integrated into pedagogy. Even Jim Franciscus as Novak gives a better performance than usual. — *"TV Previews,"* Dover *(OH)* Reporter, *November 24, 1964.*

A performance that particularly touched me was Frank Silvera's feverishly dedicated father of a young negro ballplayer in last week's edition of *Mr. Novak,* "Boy Under Glass." Taking nothing away from the sensitive, effective work of young Wayne Grice as the boy, Silvera's portrait of the eternal father drivingly ambitious for his son, unwilling to block the road he mapped for him, even persuading the boy to cheat, was a picture that sticks in the bosom. His heated exchange with Jim Franciscus on the chance of even an educated black man in a white world was a gem. Allen Reisner expertly directed Mel Goldberg's script. — *Cecil Smith, "The TV Scene,"* The Los Angeles Times, *December 2, 1964.*

One of the best scenes in the play took place between Frank Silvera and Juanita Moore when Silvers (the father), forced the wife (Miss Moore), to help the boy to cheat on the make-up test. The mother had graduated from college as a cum laude as an English major. The moral aspect of the boy's cheating was pointed out in the scene. The good that was in their son came in the climax when he said to his father: "Why didn't you make me study?" Hope the show is repeated. Silvera and Miss Moore were great. — *Hazel Garland, "Video Vignettes,"* The Pittsburgh Courier, *December 5, 1964.*

GRADE B+: This is a superior episode that greatly benefits from the acting skills of Frank Silvera and Juanita Moore as the athlete's parents. There is a beautifully written and played scene between them where they discuss whether to help their son cheat on an important test. The parents are conflicted over the father's pushing his son toward a sports career. Arch Johnson provides fine support as the team's coach who is realistic about academic progress. Wayne Grice is capable as the athlete and has a powerful closing scene where he confronts his father about grandiose expectations. The script brings up interesting points about passing a poor student so that he can become a professional baseball player. It also vividly explores the problem of racism and limited career opportunities for minorities. The inconclusive ending is effective.

ễ ễ ễ ễ ễ

Episode Nine — **Born of Kings and Angels**
Broadcast December 1, 1964

Synopsis:

John Novak accompanies the Jefferson High debating team to a capital city where he becomes involved in one of the strangest experiences of his life. In the city, the captain of the team disappears. All attempts to find the missing student prove futile until Novak, combing the city in a taxicab, finds the youth in a state of shock from a tragic discovery he made during the night.

> Produced by Leonard Freeman.
> Written by George Clayton Johnson.
> Directed by Paul Wendkos.
>
> Guest Star Peter Helm as Vern.
> Lyn Loring as June.
> Ford Rainey as Eason.

With

Mark Slade	Eric.
Jill Hill	Janice.
Jerry Rannow	Lionel.
Mickey Braddock	Ed.
Patrick Moore	Steve.

Faculty

Stephen R., Marjorie C.

Reviews:

Novak (James Franciscus) spends a long night searching for a member of the debate team (guest Peter Helm) who disappears while in a strange city. One of the best series ever to hit television. — *"Previews of Today's TV,"* The Los Angeles Times, *December 1, 1964.*

A boy makes a tragic discovery about himself in a strange city.

"BORN OF KINGS & ANGELS"

starring

- JAMES FRANCISCUS
- DEAN JAGGER
- PETER HELM

The problem children on Mr. Novak are not the ones you might expect in "Born of Kings and Angels." They are the top scholars, members of the debating team which James Franciscus is in charge of during a meet in another town. They run him ragged, especially one lad (Peter Helm), who suddenly thinks he is "Tom Jones" in search of his real father. Viewer's problems are less complicated: the kids, high IQs not with-standing, are a bunch of fast-talking bores. — *"TV Scout,"* Lima *(OH)* News, *December 1, 1964.*

GRADE B: This is an unusual but compelling episode. There is a strange mood to the story that derives from director Paul Wendkos. His use of odd camera angles to highlight the youth's disorientation is effective. Peter Helm is very good as the distracted student who searches for his past while on a field trip. His performance is full of interesting subtleties. Franciscus contributes strongly to the story with his intense effort to find the missing boy. There is a great climatic confrontation between the teacher and the boy which is both powerful and emotional. Lynn Loring is appealing as a coed who tries to understand the youth's confusion. Ford Rainey provides suitable support as a cynical bus driver. Dr. Lois Edinger, the head of the National Education Association, appears in a brief cameo. The majority of the episode is filmed on location which adds a documentary feel to the proceedings. A unique approach to the series.

ῶ ῶ ῶ ῶ ῶ

Episode Ten — **"A" as in Anxiety**
Broadcast Date December 8, 1964

Synopsis:

June Harding guest stars as Karen Parker, an average student driven to strive for excellence by her parents, cracks under the strain of a competitive examination for a college scholarship in "'A' as in Anxiety."

Produced by Leonard Freeman.
Teleplay and Story by Carol O'Brien.
Directed by Allen Reisner.

Guest Star June Harding as Karen Parker.

With

Robert Cornthwaite ....Mr. Gentry.
Norma Connolly.....................Mrs. Parker.
Richard Carlyle ....Mr. Parker.

Faculty

Marian C., Jean Innes as Mrs. Tyman., Warren Kemmerling as Mr. Bloom, Stephen R., Vince H., Marjorie C.

And

Phyllis Avery as Ruth Wilkinson.

June Harding, native of Emporia and a former drama major at the Richmond Professional Institute, will have a guest-star role on the NBC telecast of Mr. Novak at 7:30 Tuesday night. She'll portray an average student who drives herself to attain high marks and finally cracks under the strain, in 'A as in Anxiety.'

Reviews:

" 'A' As in Anxiety" on Mr. Novak almost delivers what it promises: a sharp slap at the American educational system which too often puts too much emphasis on exams. But midway, the heavy blame falls on the parents, the cliché, pushy type who sees their children as geniuses. Story centers on June Harding, a girl with an average IQ but with an abnormal passion to get ahead. When she can't, her thoughts turn to suicide. It's a good episode that fails only when it begins shifting gears. — *"TV Tonight,"* Boston *(MA) Traveler, December 8, 1964.*

Jagger's ability was on display again Tuesday night in a "Novak" story about a girl who drove herself to a breakdown in her studies for a scholarship she thought she needed to live up to the expectations of her parents. June Harding was quite touching as the girl but again it was mainly Jagger's worldly, unaffected handling of unimpressive material that held the viewer. — *Rick Du Brow, "TV in Review — Television Will Sorely Miss Dean Jagger's Huge Talent,"* Oshkosh *(WI)* Daily Northwestern, *December 8, 1964.*

Tuesday's "Mr. Novak" was a rather hysterical one-note plot, that of a student breaking down under parental pressure to achieve scholastic brilliance beyond her capability, but June Harding's expert portrayal of the tragic teen kept it from being too dull. — *Hank Grant, "On the Air — BLOODSHOT SQUARE EYEBALLS DEPT.,"* The Hollywood Reporter, *December 10, 1964.*

GRADE B: A well-written script by young Carol O'Brien and an excellent performance by June Harding highlight this episode. The problem of parents who force a daughter to over achieve beyond her capabilities is presented in a realistic manner. Harding really brings the tragic character to life and is excellent in a scene in which she breaks down during a driving simulation. Director Allen Reisner uses dark lighting to considerable effect. Norma Connolly brings a good support as the dysfunctional mother who is oblivious to her daughter's disintegration. Harding's performance is heartbreaking in a final scene where she goes to pieces after failing an all-important exam. It is very convincing and Franciscus and Jagger contribute powerfully to the intense passage. The ending offers hope but is not conclusive. Well done.

🙶 🙶 🙶 🙶

Episode Eleven — **Johnny Ride the Pony — One, Two, Three**

Broadcast December 15, 1964

Synopsis:

John Novak assumes the duties of adviser for an off-campus boys club headed by Mike Kenyon (Tony Dow). He attends a beach party of the group and gets involved in a near-tragic hazing accident.

Produced by Leonard Freeman.
Written by David Harman.
Directed by Allen H. Miner.

Co-Starring Tony Dow as Mike Kenyon.

With

Robert Logan ....Jerry Hendricks.
Bob Random...........................Denny Bellson.
Stephen Carlson ....Sandy.

And

Denver Pyle as Mr. Brill.

Faculty

Marian C., Peter H., Bill Z., Stephen R., Marjorie C.

Reviews:

This show never seems to run out of problems in America's high schools, and tonight is no exception as they rip into off-campus fraternal clubs. The plot is exactly what you'd expect — hazing, blackballing, power, status, etc. — but it serves its purpose well. Schools in which such clubs tend to get out of hand might find it useful. — *"TV Key Previews,"* Charleston *(WV) Gazette, December 15, 1964.*

GRADE D: This episode is almost completely without merit. The script is full of clichés and the direction is slow-paced to the point of boredom. There is a scene which explores the dangers of hazing but fails to raise much interest. Jagger brings a little life to the story with a scene in which he dresses down the club members for injuring a pledge. Franciscus is good in a classroom passage in which the students interpret *Hamlet* in a modern perspective. However, these short bursts of quality fail to bring any life to the overall limitations of the story. Even the reliable Tony Dow fails to register as an aggressive character. A rare failure for the series.

🙶 🙶 🙶 🙶

Episode Twelve — **Beyond a Reasonable Doubt**

Broadcast December 22, 1964

Synopsis:

A girl who was accused of murdering her parents enrolls at Jefferson High, causing a feeling of uneasiness among students and faculty, in "Beyond a Reasonable Doubt." Mr. Novak tries to help her adjust to her new situation — even after she becomes involved in a mysterious fire at school.

Produced by Leonard Freeman.
Written by Martha Wilkerson.
Directed by Richard Donner.

Introducing Susan Tyrell as Phyliss Freuchen.

With

Bob Random	Eddie.
Melinda Plowman	Mindy.
Jack Chaplain	Bryan.
James Flavin	Fire Chief Hawkins.

Faculty

Marian C., Stephen R., Vince H., Larry T., Marjorie T., André P., Kathaleen E.

Susan Tyrell, acquitted in the slaying of her parents, enrolls at Jefferson High where her presence creates a feeling of uneasiness, in 'Beyond a Reasonable Doubt'. It will be televised on NBC's airing of Mr. Novak at 7:30 Tuesday night.

Reviews:

This program gets an "A" for a good story idea that unfortunately peters out at the climax. Susan Tyrell is an unusual new student, a girl acquitted of the shotgun murders of her parents. Her presence makes people nervous, including teacher Miss Scott (Marion Collier). — *"TV Tonight," Monessen (PA) Valley Independent, December 22, 1964.*

GRADE C: This is an average show that is redeemed by the successful acting of Susan Tyrell as the student who is haunted by her past. She is initially withdrawn and cold but has a powerful scene near the end of the story. The girl breaks down in a darkened theatre and releases her sorrow to Mr. Novak. They have shared a degree of rapport in a few nicely played scenes. Regular Marian Collier has her biggest part in the series and is excellent. She cries when falsely accused of setting a fire at the school. Jagger beautifully supports her in this emotional scene. There are a few amusing vignettes where the teachers are contemplating the girl's guilt or innocence. This is a somewhat sensationalistic script which at times meanders but the positive points succeed. Director Richard Donner does what he can and displays his effective use of great close-ups. This would be his last effort on the series and he would be missed.

ĕ ĕ ĕ ĕ

Episode Thirteen — **Love Among the Grownups**
Broadcast December 29, 1964

Synopsis:

John Novak and teacher Claire Adams (guest star Geraldine Brooks) are targets of poison-pen letters accusing them of having an affair. Principal Vane also receives the letter, and the school board conducts an intensive investigation. Novak is puzzled when Mrs. Andreas suddenly resigns rather than submit to questioning.

Produced by Leonard Freeman.
Written by Harold Gast.
Directed by Abner Biberman.

Guest Star Geraldine Brooks as Claire Andreas.
Co-Starring Lane Bradbury as Ellen Westfall.

With

Stephen Roberts ....Mr. Peeples.
Vince Howard ....Mr. Butler.
Raynes Barron ....Mr. Westfall.
Phillip Terry ....Mr. Burr.

And

Alexander Scourby as George Andreas.

Reviews:

Our teacher becomes the target of poison-pen letters after he and teacher Geraldine Brooks, taking extension courses together at the university, are accused of indecent behavior. This is a realistic look at the results of such an accusation, although the story is slow-moving. Alexander Scourby, in a strangely small role, plays Miss Brook's understanding husband. — *"TV Tonight,"* Monessen *(PA)* Valley Independent, *December 29, 1964.*

There's a bit of romance, or so the students think, between Novak and a pretty French teacher. As a result, both teachers receive poison-pen letters and are deeply troubled. Though the episode doesn't end with the trouble cleared up, it does manage to dig deeper into the motives of the students. — *"Best Bets on TV,"* San Antonio *(TX)* Light, *December 29, 1964.*

GRADE C-: The script veers occasionally into soap opera but not to disastrous consequences. Geraldine Brooks is good as the teacher accused of having an affair with Mr. Novak. She contributes a refined and subtle performance. Alexander Scourby is very good in a brief supporting role as her understanding husband. There are some amusing scenes where each of the teachers mistakenly suspect several students of writing the poison-pen letters. Lane Bradbury is very good as the troubled coed who writes the accusing letters. At first she is flighty and unconcerned but eventually reveals her loneliness and neglect. Franciscus works very well with her in this emotional sequence. Although it is on the melodramatic level, the finale where Brooks confesses her love for Novak is well acted by both. An acceptable episode let down by the script.

ლ ლ ლ ლ

Episode Fourteen — **From the Brow of Zeus**
Broadcast January 5, 1965

Synopsis:

Mr. Novak finds big problems in a small package when Michael Brown, a 10-year-old academic genius, enrolls at Jefferson High in "From the Brow of Zeus." When the boy seems to lose interest in his studies, Mr. Novak learns he is afraid to display his brilliance for fear other students will resent it.

Produced by Leonard Freeman.
Written by Mel Goldberg.
Directed by Ron Winston.

Also Starring Michael Petit as Michael Brown.
Co-Starring Joyce Van Patten as Avis Brown.

With

Rickie Sorensen ....Eddie.
Patricia Morrow ....Sandra.
Harvey Grant ....Dave.
Beverly Washburn ....Edith.

Marian C., Peter Hansen as Mr. Parkson, Marjorie C., Tom Hatten as Mr. Hardin, Vince H., Larry T., André P., Bill Zuckert as Mr. Bradwell.

Reviews:

Problem is what to do with a 10-year-old genius, a boy who in terms of straight, old–fashioned I.Q., is in "orbit." The youngster, deftly played by Michael Petit, comes to Jefferson High and quickly takes over the school — its teachers as well as its students, some of whom, in a fit of jealousy, tear off his trousers and send them flying up a flagpole. The script is an engaging one and only gets heavy-handed when Novak has to deal with the boy's over-protective parents — particularly the father who can't understand why

Dean Jagger counsels Michel Petit, who portrays a child prodigy, in the "Mr. Novak" story on KSD-TV Tuesday at 6:30 p.m.

his super-duper lad isn't like all the other little boys. — *"TV Tonight,"* Monessen *(PA)* Valley Independent, *January 5, 1965.*

Splendid tale about a 10-ten-old genius who goes to high school and hopes to belong with his fellow students. The boy fights his war with his superior brain, so it's touch and go for a while. The script is full of different ways at looking at the problems and should be a special delight to students. A big bow to actor Michael Petit as the genius and Mel Goldberg for the script. — *"NBC Reviews,"* Charleston *(WV)* Gazette, *January 5, 1965.*

Rerun Review:

A generally intriguing study of the problems facing a gifted child in a public-school system. — *"TV Key Previews,"* Waterloo *(IA)* Daily Courier, *July 6, 1965.*

GRADE C-: This show contains an odd storyline that is somewhat believably presented but ultimately becomes unrealistic. At times it is played for whimsy but doesn't always succeed. Michael Petit is very good as the youthful student and only occasionally veers into precociousness. Rickie Sorensen offers fine support as a student who, after initially being adversarial to the boy, becomes a friend. Joyce Van Patten registers as the boy's overprotective mother as does Wally Frank as his dysfunctional father. Beverly Washburn is charming as a fellow student who shares a class with the boy. Jagger is good when he tells the boy not to push his superior intelligence on his classmates. The positive ending is okay but doesn't really resolve the unreality of the script's premise. A weaker episode that is not without interest.

☙ ☙ ☙ ☙ ☙

Episode Fifteen — An Elephant Is Like a Tree
Broadcast January 12, 1965

Synopsis:

Celeste Holm and Tony Bill portray mother and son in "An Elephant Is Like a Tree," a drama about a boy who is accidently blinded and cannot cope with his handicap. His mother, a teacher at Jefferson High, caters to his whims, until Mr. Novak takes the boy to school at night to familiarize him with the surroundings. There the boy faces a crisis which jolts him out of his self-pity.

> Produced by Leonard Freeman.
> Written by John D. F. Black.
> Directed by Abner Biberman.
>
> Guest Star Tony Bill as Chris Herrod.
> Special Guest Star Celeste Holm as Rose Herrod.
> Co-Starring Edward Asner as Mr. Berg.

With

> Zalman King............................Charley.
> Vince Howard.........................Mr. Butler.

Marjorie Corley......................Miss Dorsey.
Ken Lynch............................Walter.

'An Elephant Is Like A Tree'

A blind student is comforted by his mother, who is also a teacher in Jefferson High School which the boy attends, in the drama "An Elephant Is Like a Tree" on NBC-TV's	"Mr. Novak" series Tuesday. Celeste Holm is seen as the mother and the role of the boy trying to make an adjustment to his affliction is played by Tony Bill.

Reviews:

Mr. Novak last night was a touching episode about a blind boy who couldn't adjust to his handicap and required a harsh but steadying hand to guide him back into the hustle and bustle of the world from his self-imposed exile. However, it was not the performance of the cast that held the attention, but the close look into the mental confusion that plagues someone stricken with loss of sight. The understanding of the writer made this hour stand out in dialogue where a less talented man with a pen could have failed so miserably. — *"Television by Sandy Gardiner,"* Ottawa *(ON)* Journal, *January 11, 1965.*

"An Elephant Is Like a Tree" is enough to make the most hard-hearted on Mr. Novak weep. The story centers around a widowed schoolmarm whose only child, a once-promising young man and the key to her future, has been blinded after an accident. She pities the boy (and herself) so much that she wants to pull him out of Jefferson High to teach him Braille at home. The salvation of this tear-jerky script is the acting of Celeste Holm, as the mother, and Tony Bill, as the strong-willed youth. They turn in low-keyed performances that keep the soggy plot from sinking. — *"Highlights Tonight,"* San Antonio *(TX)* Express, *January 12, 1965.*

Tony Bill stars as a blind boy and gives an excellent, emotional performance, and Celeste Holm as his mother trying to do what is best for her son is almost as good. — *"TV Time,"* Decatur *(IL)* Herald, *January 12, 1965.*

GRADE A-: The series returns to form with this first-class episode. The beautifully written script by John D. F. Black contains believable dialogue with great sensitivity to the plights of the sightless. Tony Bill is excellent as the young student who has been blinded and is afraid to return to the school. He is initially cynical but descends into anguish over his condition. Celeste Holm delivers a beautiful performance of vulnerability as the boy's over-protective mother. She is heartbreaking in her frustration in reaching her injured son. Ed Asner contributes a successful cameo as an authoritative teacher at the Braille Institute. Zalman King is good as a rebellious student who trashes the school. Franciscus and Jagger provide superior support in scenes with Bill and

Holm. Director Biberman films the final third at the school with use of much darkness to great dramatic effect. The finale where Bill finds courage is emotionally strong. A winner.

☙ ☙ ☙ ☙ ☙

Episode Sixteen — Enter a Strange Animal
Broadcast January 19, 1965

Synopsis:

The experimental introduction of teaching machines at Jefferson High causes a rift between teachers John Novak and Henry Selkirk in "Enter a Strange Animal." The machine manufacturer's representative is tactless in his claims that the machines can teach faster than faculty members.

Produced by Leonard Freeman.
Written by Alvin Sargent.
Directed by Alvin Ganzer.

Guest Star Martin Landau as Robert Coolidge.
Special Guest Nehemiah Persoff as Henry Selkirk.

NEW TYPE OF TEACHER -- Martin Landau tries to convince David Macklin that the teaching machines he wants to introduce into Jefferson High will improve his grades as James Franciscus observes the clash between them, in "Enter a Strange Animal" on NBC-TV's "Mr. Novak," Tuesday, January 19 (7:30 to 8:30 p.m. on KRON-TV). Nehemiah Persoff is special guest star.

With

David Macklin ....Charles Stoddard.
Adrienne Marden ....Mrs. Selkirk.

Faculty

Marian C., Peter H., Vince H., Bill Z., Larry T.

Reviews:

In "Enter a Strange Animal" Novak (James Franciscus) is out to defeat automation. It seems that his job is threatened by some computer machines that can think "a 1,000 times faster than human instructors." His principal, in a scientific experiment, has set them up in his classroom and the students have gone wild over the "blinking gadgets." But Novak is not nearly so disturbed as his colleague (Nehemiah Persoff), who really believes that the machines will put him out on the street. Neither is helped by the computer's operator (Martin Landau), a tasteless man, with a tasteless wit. It's an obvious script, well-oiled with heavy thoughts on the dignity of man and his machines. — *"TV Tonight,"* Monessen *(PA)* Valley Independent, *January 19, 1965.*

An interesting dramatic essay on automation in education. From the opening scene in which the computers designed to teach at rapid speeds are wheeled in, the entire storyline is telegraphed, but the subject matter is important for an hour of discussion and that's what this is. A bit heavy-handed and overdone at times but worthwhile. — *"TV Key Previews,"* Syracuse *(NY)* Post Standard, *January 19, 1965.*

GRADE A: This is another complete success with a show that predicts the use of computers in the classroom. They are referred to as teaching machines. Martin Landau contributes an excellent performance as the salesman of the new computers. He is initially glib and delivers his lines in a rapid delivery which is very powerful. The salesman later becomes aggressive when challenged. He is matched by Nehemiah Persoff as a veteran teacher who opposes the machine's installation. Adrienne Marden is good in as Persoff 's wife who comforts her distraught husband. David Macklin offers capable support as a sullen student who rejects using the machines. Randy Kirby is also good as an awkward student who learns from the computer. There is a great final scene where Persoff confronts Landau and accuses him of being only interested in profits. This is an excellent, prophetic and thought-provoking episode.

🍎 🍎 🍎 🍎

Episode Seventeen — **Beat the Plowshare,
Edge the Sword**
Broadcast January 26, 1965

Synopsis:

John Novak discovers four Jefferson High senior boys living together with no supervision other than a weekly visit from their so-called "guardian" — ex-hoodlum Joe Garvin. Although he feels sorry for the parentless boys, he is forced to turn them in to the school authorities. Arrangements are made for the boys to remain together on the condition they never see Garvin again — a condition neither the boys nor Garvin finds acceptable.

> Produced by Leonard Freeman.
> Written by Gilbert Ralston.
> Directed by Alvin Ganzer.
>
> Guest Star Harold J. Stone as Joe Garvin.
> Co-Starring Lyle Bettiger as Mr. Brigham.
>
> Mark Slade..............................Lee Manson.
> Stephen Mines ....Stuart Miller.
> Tom Nardini ....Abel King.
>
> And
>
> Jimmy Hawkins as Peter Beatty.
>
> With
>
> Bill Zuckert.............................Mr. Bradwell.
> Carole Shelyne ....Jennifer.
> Caroline Kiddo ....Nancy.

Reviews:

"Beat the Plowshare, Edge the Sword" is one of Mr. Novak's more interesting episodes. Although it's unbelievable, it holds your interest from start to finish. Concerning an ex-hoodlum, who plays father to four orphaned boys, the script is highly reminiscent of the old "Dead End Kids" movies, with sassy, tough dialogues and down-to-earth philosophy right out of the 1930's. Harold J. Stone is fine as the "father," as are his "offspring" — Mark Slade, Stephen Mines, Jimmy Hawkins and Tom Nardini. — *"TV Scout,"* Lima *(OH)* News, *January 26, 1965.*

Good show, if you don't object to corny sentimental tales, you'll enjoy this story of a racketeer who takes it upon himself to supervise and discipline four orphans. The boys happen to be in Novak's class and when our hero discovers they have neither parent nor legal guardian, he must report them to the authorities. Harold J. Stone is excellent as the bad guy with a heart of gold, an over written part which is a throwback to the movies of the 30's. *TV Best Bets* — *San Antonio (TX.) Light, January 26, 1965.*

Rerun Review:

One of the very best episodes. When Novak accidentally learns that four of his good students are living together without parental supervision, he feels compelled to report them. But when he discovers that they are well supervised by a hoodlum to the point where his is a powerful force for education and morality, the situation becomes sticky. — Phoenix *(AZ)* Republic, *July 20, 1965.*

GRADE B: This is a sentimental episode that has a different approach to the series. It is an above-average installment and features a vivid performance by Harold J. Stone as a guardian to four boys. He is a gruff individual with a police record but genuinely cares for his charges. Stone never overplays the role. He is very good in a scene where he discusses his difficult past life with Mr. Novak. Mark Slade delivers a sensitive performance as the leader of the boys. Tom Nardini, Jimmy Hawkins and Stephen Mines are also good as the other members of the household. Franciscus is very effective in scenes with Stone and his integrity is never in question. Lyle Bettiger has a nice supporting role as a counselor who must face the reality of the boy's living conditions. There is an emotionally charged scene near the end where Stone acts tough and leaves the boys for their own good. It has an honest sentiment and is very moving. A showcase for Stone.

🍎 🍎 🍎 🍎

Episode Eighteen — **Faculty Follies: Part 1**
Broadcast February 2, 1965

Synopsis:

Tonight's episode, a two-parter, serves to introduce Burgess Meredith to the faculty — and viewers. He will replace Dean Jagger as principal of Jefferson High, due to Jagger's forced retirement for health purposes. In "Faculty Follies," Meredith portrays Martin Woodridge, who has a lack of enthusiasm for the faculty show being staged to help raise money for exchange students. The show is being directed by teacher Novak and the two clash when the former claims the variety numbers are in poor taste.

Produced by Leonard Freeman.
Written by Meyer Dolinsky.
Directed by Joseph Sargent.

Guest Star Burgess Meredith as Martin Woodridge.
Co-Starring Cloris Leachman as Miss Hummer.
David Sheiner as Al Webb.

Faculty

Marian C., Vince H., Bill Z., Larry T., André P., Peter H., Stephen R., Kathaleen E., Shirley O'Hara as Miss O'Sullivan, Katharine Ross as Mrs. Bellway.

Special Material by Hal Belfer and Meyer Dolinsky.
Musical Numbers Staged by Hal Belfer.

"Droppity Dropouts" sung by James Franciscus, Vince Howard and Bill Zuckert.
"Woodshop Annie" sung by Marian Collier, André Philippe and Larry Thor.
"Oh Friday Day" sung by Vince Howard.

Reviews:

We have a feeling we weren't supposed to feel so strongly inclined toward accepting English teacher Martin Woodridge's point of view that the Novak-directed "Faculty Follies," good cause notwithstanding, is a tasteless show. This may not be the best way to do so, but it's the program on which Burgess Meredith (as Woodridge) enters the cast

THEY STAGE the "Faculty Follies" on NBC's "Mr. Novak" series tonight (KYW, 7:30-8:30), and from the looks of it, folly is the right word. That's Jefferson High's favorite English teacher (James Franciscus) in the Beatle wig being held aloft by Bill Zuckert. It's a two-part show in which Burgess Meredith also makes his bow as a series regular.

to eventually become a regular. For series die-hards and curiosity seekers primarily. — *"TV Tip,"* Phoenix *(AZ)* Republic, *February 2, 1965.*

Burgess Meredith will become Novak's permanent mentor and friend, replacing the retiring Dean Jagger later this season. Tonight he is introduced in the first of a two-parter, "Faculty Follies." Because of a silly script, it's not an audacious debut. As James Franciscus' fellow teacher, Meredith is engaged in a labored variety show, spoofing students in order to raise funds to import foreign youngsters to Jefferson High. — *"TV Tonight,"* Monessen *(PA)* Valley Independent, *February 2, 1965.*

GRADE A-: The high points of this entertaining episode are the regular cast's stage performances and screen times. They are all present throughout to great effect. Franciscus is very good as the Follies' director who has his hands full in handling the production. Burgess Meredith makes a credible debut on the show as an abrasive and cynical teacher. Marian Collier, Larry Thor and André Phillipe are delightful in a musical number. Collier is quite the entertainer. Vince Howard is also impressive with his musical presentation. He displays an excellent singing voice. Cloris Leachman is tragic as a teacher who can't handle the pressures of performing. Semi-regular David Sheiner offers charming support as a wise music teacher. There is a genuinely funny stage routine with the teachers acting as rambunctious students. Director Joe Sargent uses a collage during stage rehearsals that works. This is a very enjoyable and uncommon episode.

🎸 🎸 🎸 🎸

Episode Nineteen — **Faculty Follies: Part 2**
Broadcast February 9, 1965.

Synopsis:

John Novak dons a Beatle wig and plays a guitar while Martin Woodridge (Burgess Meredith, who will later replace Dean Jagger as principal) wears a football uniform to perform in the second episode of the two-parter. Mr. Novak faces a rebellion by cast members, but finally proceeds when Woodridge, leader of the revolt, admits his error and offers to participate.

Produced by Leonard Freeman.
Written by Meyer Dolinsky.
Directed by Joseph Sergeant.

Guest Star Burgess Meredith as Martin Woodridge.
Co-Starring Cloris Leachman as Miss Hummer.
David Sheiner as Paul Webb.
Anna Lee as Mrs. Woodridge.

Michael Hardstark...................Ken Warren.
Gloria Calomeé.......................Betty.
Heather North ....Felicia.

Faculty

Marian C., Vince H., Bill Z., Larry T., André P., Peter H., Stephen R.,
Kathaleen E., Shirley O'H., Katharine Ross as Mrs. Bellway.

NEW PRINCIPAL FOR JEFFERSON HIGH?
Burgess Meredith, who will be seen in "Faculty Frolics" Tuesday on Mr. Novak will be worked into a major part

Special Material by Hal Belfer and Meyer Dolinsky.
Musical Numbers Staged by Hal Belfer.
"Swingin' Composish" sung by Burgess Meredith.

Reviews:

Finally, the curtain falls on "Faculty Follies." In this concluding chapter concerning a very silly variety show put on by the teachers of Jefferson High, Novak (James Franciscus) wears a Beatle wig and plays a guitar, and newcomer to the series, Woodridge (Burgess Meredith) behaves like a juvenile football hero. The crisis is over the object of several instructors, who find it all too banal, and Novak's attempt to keep them in the show. They shouldn't have listened to him. — *"TV Tonight,"* Monessen *(PA)* Valley Independent, *February 9, 1965.*

This should be called "Meet Burgess Meredith," because, unlike part one, he finally gets his teeth into the character of Martin Woodridge (who'll be Principal soon) and comes to life, not as a carbon copy of Dean Jagger's Albert Vane, but with the individuality one expects from Meredith. The producers and the writers deserve credit for making the upcoming principal a different type. — *"TV Best Bits,"* San Antonio *(TX)* Light, *February 9, 1965.*

"Mr. Novak" departed from usual format, one dealing with problems of high schoolers, for a two-parter about the faculty staging a musical. It was not a successful experiment. Aside from fact musicals are not what "Novak" viewers expect, this longie suffered from padding and a generally dull, lightweight script by Meyer Dolinsky, which was lacking any problem of sufficient dimension to hold the viewer's attention. First stanza deals with the faculty going to toss a musical revue, to raise coin for exchange students. A cantankerous, but influential teacher objects on the grounds it's not in good taste, degrades the teaching profession. Chapter two sees the obstructionist mending his ways, and joining in the fun, so they can stage their musical. Big deal. Burgess Meredith was very good as the teacher who is anti, then finds himself and becomes a good human being as everyone in "Novak" should be. (Incidentally, Meredith on the Feb. 23 show becomes principal of the school, replacing Dean Jagger.) Cloris Leachman turns in a good performance; James Franciscus is his customary, clean-cut, noble self; and there is good support from David Sheiner, Marian Collier and Vince Howard. Musical numbers staged by Hal Belfer, with special material by Belfer and Dolinsky are okay. Direction by Joe Sargent is satisfactory. — *Daku, "Telepix Followup,"* Daily Variety, *February 11, 1965.*

GRADE A-: This follow up to the first "Faculty Follies" again finds the whole cast of regulars present throughout. Franciscus is very strong as the director who is conflicted on whether to cancel the production. Meredith grows into his role as Martin Woodridge and after being initially cynical, admits he was wrong and joins in the show. He performs a musical number as a football player and is very charming. Anna Lee makes her debut as Woodridge's wife and works well with Meredith. David Sheiner reappears as the music teacher and is good in reassuring the frazzled Novak. Most of the cast perform a number where they are disruptive students and the scene is very funny. Franciscus, Vince Howard and Bill Zuckert appear in Beatle wigs and bring down the house with their comic song. There is an honestly sentimental ending where the cast and students sing the Jefferson High School song. It is a fine conclusion to the two-part story.

ẽ ẽ ẽ ẽ

Episode Twenty — **The Silent Dissuaders**
Broadcast February 16, 1965

Synopsis:

Claudine Longet (Mrs. Andy Williams) guest stars as an Iranian exchange teacher who tries to steer gifted science student Judy Wheeler away from marriage and into college. But the girl's mother wants her to marry the richest boy in school and forget about college. This is one of the last episodes in which Dean Jagger will appear as Principal Vane.

Produced by Leonard Freeman.
Written by Betty Ulius.
Directed by Allen Reisner.

Guest Star Claudine Longet as Shahri Javid.
Co Starring Kim Darby as Judy Wheeler.
Frances Reid............................Elsie Wheeler.
Edmon Ryan ....Ralph Wheeler.

With

Buck Taylor.............................Scott Lawson.
Peter Hansen...........................Mr. Parkson.
Bill Zuckert.............................Mr. Bradwell.
Kathaleen Ellis ....Mrs. Floyd.
André Phillipe ....Mr. Johns.

FAIR EXCHANGE—Claudine Longet (in private life Mrs. Andy Williams) will be guest star in "The Silent Dissuaders," an episode of NBC-TV's "Mr. Novak" series, on Tuesday, Feb. 16. She portrays an Indonesian exchange student. Here she is seen with Dean Jagger, who plays Principal Albert Vane, in one of the last episodes in which the noted actor will be seen. Burgess Meredith succeeds Jagger in the role he originated.

Reviews:

Viva La Dame! Claudine Longet, a fetchingly trim French actress, contributes a great deal of spunk to "The Silent Dissuaders," an almost nauseating episode that needs all the help it can get. She portrays a foreign-exchange teacher from Iran who can't understand why American High School girls are pushed into marriage before they have time to grow up. Her main interest is a brilliant student (Kim Darby), whose parents can't wait until they get her to the altar. Miss Longet's crusade gets small help from Mr. Novak (James Franciscus), who has wishy-washy thoughts about Cupid, too. — *"TV Tonight,"* Monessen *(PA)* Valley Independent, *February 16, 1965.*

A bugle call to gifted girl students. Handsome French actress Claudine Longet plays an Iranian exchange teacher who tries to dissuade a student from marriage in order to continue her science career. An interesting if not an exciting episode in which a useful point is made. Teenage girls should tune in. — *"Best Bets on TV,"* San Antonio *(TX)* Light, *February 16, 1965.*

Grade B-: The script by Betty Ulius explores the conflict between marriage and a career for graduating coeds. Claudine Longet provides a delicate performance of nuance as a teacher who wants a promising student to pursue a career. She is forthright and charming. Her anguish over the missed potential of the student is palpable. Franciscus is suitably amorous and shares a beautiful scene with Longet in which they discuss romantic poetry. Kim Darby is genuine as the tragic student who is conflicted on which path to take. Buck Taylor is good as the girl's boyfriend who is disdainful of any option than marriage. Frances Reid is also creditable as the girl's dominant mother who clashes with Longet. Jagger is sincere and authoritative in a scene with Longet as he warns her not to get too personally involved with her students. The ending is tragic but Mr. Novak does offer some hope. An intriguing premise marred by lukewarm presentation.

ể ể ể ể ể

Episode Twenty-One — **Mountains to Climb**
Broadcast February 23, 1965
Synopsis:

Burgess Meredith makes his debut as the new principal, Martin Woodridge, and its Dean Jagger's farewell appearance. According to the store, friends persuaded Vane into running for the office of superintendent of Schools against Joe Stillman (Howard Duff), a politically wise gubernatorial aspirant with an experienced team behind him. Election results shock political experts as well as Woodridge, who receives a very unexpected call from Vane. (Dean Jagger is being forced to retire from the series due to health.)

Produced by Leonard Freeman.
Teleplay by Roland Wolpert and John D. F. Black.
Story by Roland Wolpert.
Directed by Paul Wendkos.

Guest Star Howard Duff as Joe Stillman.
Special Guest Star Burgess Meredith as Martin Woodridge.
Co-Starring Milton Selzer as Ted Canford.
Malachi Throne as Tom Norson.
Vaughn Taylor as Ben Rock.

With

Nancy Hadley ....Ann Stillman.
Byron Morrow ....Dr. Haviland.
Ed Prentiss ....Dr. Kellwood.
Johnny Jensen ....Stuart Cranford.
Dort Clark ....Cavanaugh.
Barbara Thye Heimann ....Barbara (Miss American Teenager)

Faculty

Marian C., Stephen R., Vince H., Marjorie C., André P., Kathaleen E.

And

Phyllis Avery as Ruth Wilkinson.

7:30 p. m., 5, **MR. NOVAK:** Mr. Vane runs for the office of state superintendent of schools. Howard Duff is guest star and Burgess Meredith debuts in his rôle as Jefferson High's new principal, Martin Woodridge.

Reviews:

Though Dean Jagger will be missed terribly, this episode is as good a way as could have been conceived to retire him from the series (at his request). The show gets in a few telling points on behalf of education. It also serves to establish Burgess Meredith as the new principal in a logical takeover. It's Jagger's hour in many ways, but Meredith has some strong scenes at the end. — *"TV Time Previews,"* Kansas City *(MO)* Times, *February 23, 1965.*

A show for regular fans. At long last, the baton is finally being passed from Dean Jagger to Burgess Meredith. It's a smooth transition, thanks to a routine election story wherein Vane wins an election for state school superintendent, and guess who's his first appointment as principal. The episode is very well done, and its' too bad that Meredith gets the job just when the school may be cancelled by NBC. — *"TV Best Bets,"* San Antonio *(TX)* Light, *February 23, 1965.*

Dean Jagger takes his leave in a good show that is spoiled only because there is no doubt of the outcome. Jagger is asked to run in opposition to Howard Duff, seeking the job of State Superintendent of Schools (an elective job in California). Naturally, he wins, and Burgess Meredith is named the new principal. Meredith has a fine scene when he realizes a dream has come true. — *"TV Tonight,"* Monessen *(PA)* Valley Independent, *February 23, 1965.*

Rerun Review:

Well done episode that passed the baton from Dean Jagger to Burgess Meredith as Principal of Jefferson High. — Oneonta *(NY)* Star, *July 27, 1965.*

GRADE B+: Dean Jagger makes his final appearance in a well-above-average segment. He displays real presence and integrity in his campaign. Franciscus delivers a powerful speech endorsing his principal during a TV broadcast. Milton Selver is tragic as Vane's campaign manager who is smeared by the opposition. Howard Duff offers effective support as the arrogant opposing candidate and Malachi Throne is suitably smarmy as his devious campaign manager. Burgess Meredith's character of Martin Woodridge is now portrayed as less abrasive and he displays a warmer countenance. John D. F. Black contributed excellent dialogue to the final quarter of the show when Meredith is appointed the new principal. The actor is excellent in this scene and displays humility, astonishment and confidence with complete assurance. His comforting of Selver's character is beautifully played. A fine introduction to the new principal.

ꝭ ꝭ ꝭ ꝭ ꝭ

Episode Twenty-Two — **May Day, May Day**
Broadcast March 2, 1965

Synopsis:

Martin Woodridge (Burgess Meredith) must judge the teaching abilities of some of his former colleagues in his first full day as Jefferson High's new principal. Most of the teachers respect his difficult position, but an English teacher, Bud Walker, resents him. When Woodridge discovers a shocking thing about Walker and fires him, resentment runs high.

Produced by Leonard Freeman.
Teleplay by John D. F. Black.
Story by John D. F. Black and Donald Michael Platt.
Directed by Ida Lupino.

Co-Starring Donald Harrison as George "Bud" Walker.

With

Whit Bissell..............................Karl Bellini.
Irene Tedrow ....Margaret Rina.
Walter Brooke ....Jess Cropper.
Candace Howard.....................Martha Gunn.

Faculty

Marian C., Vince H., Geraldine Lawrence as Miss Randolph, André P., Marjorie C.

Reviews:

This episode is so intent in establishing Burgess Meredith in his new post as Principal Martin Woodridge, complete with duties and responsibilities, you may feel a bit shortchanged in terms of dramatic excitement. However, if you've been an ardent follower of this series, you'll find this an important transitional phase in the series. — *"TV Tips,"* Phoenix *(AZ)* Republic, *March 2, 1965.*

Burgess Meredith, the new principal at Jefferson High on Mr. Novak, starts his first dull day. He is confronted with an assortment of problems, including petty ones like what to do with birds nesting on a window ledge. But his biggest trials are with his former faculty colleagues, who treat him coolly, and what to do about that disrespectful English teacher (Donald Harron), who should be fired. It's Meredith's show all the way, and

Martin Woodridge, the new principal of Jefferson High starts his tenure by firing a former colleague!

"MAY DAY"

starring

**James Franciscus
Burgess Meredith**

on

MR. NOVAK

9 PM

KUTV ₂

James Franciscus has little to do but glumly comment. A slow-moving, but often interesting episode. — *"TV Scout,"* Lima *(OH)* News, *March 2, 1965.*

Absorbing hour. In his first week as principal, Burgess Meredith is blessed with a well-written script and an excellent co-star, Donald Harron. The subject is evaluating new teachers for rehiring purposes. — *"Tonight on TV,"* Lumberton *(NC)* Robesonian, *March 2, 1965.*

GRADE C-: This is a competent episode that is let down by a script that drifts into soap-opera territory. It does bring up the difficulty in firing a teacher with tenure but there are many clichés. Burgess Meredith, in his first full appearance as the new principal, is quite good. He is already developing his character and performs with authority and compassion. The actor works well with Donald Harron, who portrays the concerned teacher fearing termination. Harron is effective as the educator who anticipates being fired and is hiding a secret affair with a student. Geraldine Lawrence is sympathetic as a young teacher who can't handle the pressures of the position. The hour proceeds at a slow pace that ultimately negates the earnest efforts of the actors. A lesser installment.

ༀ ༀ ༀ ༀ ༀ

Episode Twenty-Three — **Where Is There to Go, Billie, but Up?**
Broadcast March 9, 1965

Synopsis:

John Novak falls in love with substitute math teacher Jean Corcoran (Lois Nettleton) and takes up the dangerous sport of skydiving to be near her. As their romance grows, Novak realizes Jean has a driving love of adventure and is not one to settle down. Paul Mantee stars as Jean's boyfriend before Novak.

Produced by Leonard Freeman.
Teleplay by Mel Goldberg.
Story by Herman Graves and Mel Goldberg.
Directed by Abner Biberman.

Guest Star Lois Nettleton as Jean Corcoran.
Co-Starring Paul Mantee as Hal Williams.

With

Alison Mills	Billie.
Jean Iness	Mrs. Tynan.
André Phillipe	Mr. Johns.
Marjorie Corley	Miss Dorsey.
Tony di Milo	Shorty.

Pretty Lois Nettleton stars as a substitute teacher who prefers parachute jumping to classrooms. and who encourages John Novak (James Franciscus) to take up the sport. Mr. Novak finds himself not only falling through the air but falling in love with the teacher in "Where Is There To Go, Billie, But Up", an episode in the Mr. Novak series, which will air on Channel 7, Sunday, March 7.

Reviews:

This show continues its rapid decline by fabricating another story. You see, in real life, James Franciscus has developed quite an interest in sky diving. So tonight we have a tale about how Mr. Novak takes up skydiving to be near Lois Nettleton. — *"Program Highlights,"* Akron *(OH)* Beacon Journal, *March 7, 1965.*

If this weren't such a recurring theme on the series, this would have been a much more affecting episode. It's another in the love finds Mr. Novak skein and it's a good one, involving our earnest English teacher with a substitute math teacher who'd rather sky dive than teach. There are some good scenes between the academic lovers, as well as between the teacher and a student with emotional problems of some sort. — *"TV Previews,"* Rockford *(IL)* Morning Star, *March 9, 1965.*

Rerun Review:

Mr. Novak has a romantic flight into fantasyland in "Where is There to Go, Billie, but Up?" Not only is he smitten by math teacher Lois Nettleton, but takes up sky diving to prove how much he has fallen. Its puppy love all the way and highly recommended for puppies. — *"TV Scout,"* Augusta *(ME)* Kennebec Journal, *August 17, 1965.*

GRADE B: This is a romantic episode that occasionally becomes a soap opera but is redeemed by superior performances. Lois Nettleton is outstanding as the free-spirited substitute teacher who begins an affair with Mr. Novak. She is a thrill-seeking sky diver and has a casual attitude. Franciscus is very good his romantic scenes with Nettleton and there is a genuine chemistry between them. Young Alison Mills provides excellent support as a withdrawn student who is still suffering the loss of her parents. Nettleton mistakenly is rude to the girl but is later informed by Novak as to the cause of her grief. There is a wonderful scene where the substitute teacher apologizes and draws the girl out of her shell. It is beautifully played by the actresses. Nettleton has an emotional scene where she breaks down and reveals the cause of her inability to commit. There is a touching farewell ending among the three principals. Impressive acting.

🍎 🍎 🍎 🍎

Episode Twenty-Four — **The Tender Twigs**
Broadcast March 16, 1965.

Synopsis:

Right-leaning politician Frank Menlow (Robert Culp) accuses teachers John Novak and Walter MacTell (Harry Townes) of spreading Communist doctrine at Jefferson High. The issue becomes city-wide and Novak and MacTell are forced to explain their actions at a school board meeting.

Produced by Leonard Freeman.
Teleplay by Robert Presnell, Jr., and Mel Goldberg.
Story Robert Presnell, Jr.
Directed by Joseph Sargent.

Guest Star Harry Townes as Walter MacTell.
Special Guest Star Robert Culp as Frank Menlow.
Co-Starring Robert Ellenstein as Phillip Goddard.

With

Rita Lynn	Edith MacTell.
Waah Keen	Dr. Manzoni.
Marjorie Corley	Miss Dorsey.

United Nations Assembly

Peter Helm	President.
Allan Hunt	Albania.
Susan White	Ceylon.
Annazette Chase	China.
Robert Crawford	Cuba.
James Henaghan	Ghana.
Charles Briles	Greece.
Cathy Ferraro	Italy.
Keg Johnson	Israel.
Randy Kirby	Lebanon.
Irene Tsu	Mexico.
Tony Dow	United States.
Johnny Crawford	USSR.

Reviews:

Robert Culp, who was in hot water with Kildare a couple of weeks ago as a doctor afraid to take a stand, this week portrays a right-leaning politician. Now there's a switch. He accuses teachers Novak and MacTell (Harry Townes) of spreading Communist doctrine when they act as faculty advisors for a mock U.N. assembly in which students take the roles of member nation representatives. The limelight once again shines on Novak, now that Burgess Meredith is firmly entrenched as the new principal. — Baton Rouge *(LA)* Morning Advocate, *March 16, 1965.*

MR. NOVAK A COMMUNIST?
A mock U.N. assembly triggers investigations into Mr. Novak's political affiliations.

"TENDER TWIGS" on "MR. NOVAK"
TONIGHT - 9:00 PM
KUTV=2

"The Tender Twigs" puts series' star James Franciscus and fellow teacher Harry Townes under considerable pressure. The men, faculty advisors for a mock United Nations assembly, are accused of fostering Communist doctrine. The villain here is Robert Culp, who is more "wrong" than "right." Viewers of the skimpy, hysterical plot will probably feel he is just confused. — *"TV Tonight,"* Monessen *(PA)* Valley Independent, *March 16, 1965.*

Interesting episode on academic freedom. It's framed around a controversy on whether Jefferson High School students can be permitted to take the sides of unfriendly nations while conducting a mock United Nations session in class. It may be very talky, but the speakers are effective, particularly Robert Culp as a "super patriot," Harry Townes as a dedicated teacher and principal Burgess Meredith. — *"Today's TV Tips,"* Phoenix *(AZ)* Republic, *March 16, 1965.*

GRADE A: This is a first-class installment that explores the right to free speech and the harm of political reactionaries. The mock UN set is an impressive one. Robert Culp delivers a vivid performance as the arch conservative. He is self-righteous and becomes more fanatical and vindictive as the story unfolds. Harry Townes is very good as a teacher who becomes fearful after harassment by Culp's followers. Peter Helm, Tony Dow, Johnny Crawford and Randy Kirby are all fine as representatives of the UN panel. Franciscus is riveting in a speech standing up for the right to conduct the mock assembly. The scenes of harassment are realistic. In the final quarter of the hour there is a very impressive scene at a Board of Education hearing. It is well played by all and Burgess Meredith is magnificent confronting Culp for his accusations. There is a realistic and upbeat ending. A winner that is both thought provoking and entertaining.

🍎 🍎 🍎 🍎

Episode Twenty-Five — **Honor and All That**
Broadcast March 23, 1965

Synopsis:

A riot breaks out a Jefferson High's championship basketball game against McClain High despite precautions taken by Mr. Woodridge and John Novak. Beau Bridges guest stars.

Produced by Leonard Freeman.
Written by Jerry McNeely.
Directed by Paul Wendkos.

Guest Star Beau Bridges as Jaytee Bartlett.

With

Michael Pollard ....Gogo Reader.
Stephen Mines ....Bill Graves.
Buck Taylor ....Don.
Charles Briles ....Ken.
Alexander Lockwood...............Collins.

Reviews:

"Honor and All That" concerns students who have too much school spirit. At a basketball game, Jefferson High bursts into a riot when it meets its arch rival, McClain High. How to calm the youngsters is given considerable thought, but not enough action. The charging cast is ably headed by Beau Bridges and Michael Pollard. — *"TV Tonight,"* Monessen *(PA)* Valley Independent, *March 23, 1965.*

The heckling of a rival school gets to be too much for the false pride of Jefferson high students and Novak has his hands full trying to hold them in check. A rumble occurs on the basketball court. Novak and Woodridge have to pick up some pieces when this is over, but it's questionable whether the culprits have really learned much about honor. Beau Bridges and Michael Pollard do nicely as the instigators of the trouble. — *"TV Previews,"* Milwaukee *(WI)* Journal-Sentinel, *March 23, 1965.*

Worth Watching

7:30 p.m.—4—Mr. Novak: Students riot when basketball player is injured in championship game. Beau Bridges (above) stars.

Rerun Review:

Uneven but provocative episode about a trouble-making student who enjoys the power he yields over his classmates by thumbing his nose at authority. Principal Burgess Meredith trods a very hazardous path when he tries to combine understanding with discipline in handling brewing unrest. — *"Today's TV Tips,"* Phoenix *(AZ)* Republic, *August 10, 1965.*

GRADE C-: This is an average episode that is marred by a clichéd script and lackluster direction. Beau Bridges is effective as a hot-headed student who stirs up his fellow students to the point of violence. Michael J. Pollard is appealing as Bridge's dim-witted sidekick who might have more common sense than his leader. Franciscus and Meredith are both competent and give their all despite the clichéd dialogue. The basketball game is filmed well but fails to lift the hour in any considerable way. The riot is also cinematically effective but the dramatic ending is underwhelming due to the slow progress of the hour. An episode that ultimately fails to engage.

ᴇ̃ ᴇ̃ ᴇ̃ ᴇ̃

Episode Twenty-Six — **The Student Who Never Was**
Broadcast March 30, 1965.

Synopsis:

Robert Walker guest stars as Dick Sullivan, a Jefferson High senior who schemes to ridicule the faculty to compensate for loneliness in "The Student Who Never Was." He persuades four other students to enroll in an extra class during their normal free period under the name of Sam Orez.

> Produced by Leonard Freeman.
> Written by Meyer Dolinsky.
> Directed by Paul Wendkos.
> Guest Star Robert Walker as Dick Sullivan.

With

Bonnie Beecher	Valerie.
Bob Random	Phil.
Patricia Morrow	Abigail.
Russell Horton	Ed.
Dennis Whitcomb	Bill.

Faculty

Stephen R., Vince H., Bill Z., André P., Marjorie C.

Reviews:

An intriguing, if somewhat farfetched drama. A brilliant problem student creates a mythical transfer student and gets four friends to join him in a group impersonation. The "gag" flops, but there are some touching moments and young Robert Walker gives

a sensitive performance as the ringleader. — *"The Best on TV Today,"* Des Moines *(IA)* Register, *March 30, 1965.*

Robert Walker on Mr. Novak is a troubled boy. His problem in "The Student Who Never Was" is loneliness. However, from the well-populated and very busy script, it's hard to believe that this is the case. Walker is much too busy plotting schemes to embarrass the faculty at Jefferson High. His most successful and dubious is to invent a mythical student, "Sam Orez," who earns top grades and is

NOVAK GUESTS: Robert Walker, left, reveals some painful truths to Burgess Meredith in "The Student That Never Was," on Mr. Novak tonight over NBC-TV.

expected to graduate with honors. — *"TV Scout — Highlights Tonight,"* San Antonio *(TX)* Express, *March 30, 1965.*

GRADE C: This is another average episode that contains a meandering script and slow direction. Although the high school is heavily featured, the premise is a bit on the absurd side. The saving grace of the episode is a fine performance by Robert Walker as a brilliant student who instigates a prank on the faculty. In the beginning he is both cynical and flippant and appears aloof from feelings. As the story progresses he reveals, to great effect, a lonely and tragic existence. Near the end, in the hour's best scene, Walker reads an essay on loneliness and is very moving in his presentation. Bonnie Beecher is appealing as his girlfriend who struggles to understand the troubled youth. Franciscus and Meredith are good as usual and the finale is underplayed and effective. This is a mediocre show redeemed by Robert Walker.

🐧 🐧 🐧 🐧

Episode Twenty-Seven — **There's a Penguin in My Garden**
Broadcast April 6, 1965

Synopsis:

Vera Miles guest stars as Sister Gervaise, a nun who accuses John Novak of negligence in his duties as a student counselor, in "There's Penguin in My Garden." She blames Novak for her nephew's poor attitude toward his studies, and gets permission from the convent to take a teaching position at Jefferson High.

Produced by Leonard Freeman.
Written by John D. F. Black.
Directed by Alvin Glazer.

Guest Star Vera Miles as Sister Gervaise.
Co-Starring Bob Random as Joey Caldwell.
Pat Harrington, Jr., as Thomas Kelly.

With

Angela Clark ....Mother General.
Maurine Dawson....................Sister Coronada.
Al Freeman, Jr. ....Louis Rider.
Allan Hunt..............................Red.
Rickie Sorensen ....Eddie.

Faculty

Marian C., Walter Brooke as Mr. Capper, Stephen R., André P.,
Kathaleen E., Marjorie C.

GUEST STAR Vera Miles portrays a nun with juvenile delinquency problems—her orphaned nephew—and asks our favorite English teacher to help in tonight's episode of "Mr. Novak" (KYW, 7:30-8:30). It's titled "There's a Penguin In My Garden," which may or may not have anything to do with the plot.

Reviews:

"There's a Penguin in My Garden" on Mr. Novak is a fascinating bit of well-calculated nonsense. Novak (James Franciscus) gets his comeuppance this time by a cool, determined, modern nun, Sister Gervaise (Vera Miles) who scolds him over her nephew's scholastic failings. There's much humor in this one, with a slightly reminiscent ring of the old Ingrid Bergman classic, "Bells of St. Mary," in the humorous scenes. — *"Highlights Tonight,"* San Antonio *(TX)* Express, *April 6, 1965.*

Vera Miles guests as a nun-turned-teacher who blames her nephew's irresponsibility on Novak's failure as a teacher. She decides to take the boy under her wing and try to straighten him out in three months. But, in counseling him, her own problems keep getting in the way. Refreshing dialogue helps keep this one at a high level of interest. — *"Today's Television Tips,"* Phoenix *(AZ)* Republic, *April 6, 1965.*

Grade C-: Yet another average episode that is again let down by a meandering script and lackluster direction. There is a slight whimsical mood to the show that doesn't really engage. Vera Miles is good as the nun turned teacher and her performance is full of nuance. Bob Random is adequate as the irresponsible student that Miles attempts to reform. His lack of presence mars the dramatic conflicts. Pat Harrington, Jr., is also adequate in a supporting role as the boy's former guardian. Young Allan Hunt brings a bit of life to the proceedings as an upbeat student. Franciscus is good in a final scene where he confronts the boy about his future possibilities. The upbeat finale is good but too brief to really register. This was another episode that didn't attract.

🍎🍎🍎🍎🍎

Episode Twenty-Eight — **The Firebrand**
Broadcast April 13, 1965
Synopsis:

Debate-team captain Paul Ryder (Walter Koenig) precipitates an explosive situation at Jefferson High when he leads students in a public demonstration to help passage of a school-bond issue. Mr. Novak permits Ryder to hold the demonstration. However, the boy, carried away by his own oratory, incites student pickets to stop traffic into the school and organizes a mass sit-in on the main stairway, intent on closing the school.

Produced by Leonard Freeman.
Written by Harold Gast.
Directed by Michael O'Herlihy.

Also Starring Walter Koenig as Paul Ryder.
Co-Starring Julie Sommars as Ellen Cable.
Frank Marth as Mr. Gorman.
Ben Yaffee as Mr. Loomis.

With

Tommy Rettig	Frank.
Lauren Gilbert	Mr. Bronson.
George Ives	Mr. Ingram.
Peter Wayne	George.
Keg Johnson	Larry.
Tisha Sterling	Myra.

Faculty

Stephen R., Vince H., Kathaleen E., Lyle Sudrow as Mr. Phillips.

Reviews:

A fascinating study based on the familiar theme that power corrupts. An enigmatic, unusual and bright young man starts agitating for a school bond issue. His oratory inflames his fellow students into uncharacteristic actions, and he becomes more and more obsessed with his influence to the point where he lets it get out of hand. Walter

Koenig makes the most of this difficult role. — *"TV Time Previews,"* Baton Rouge *(LA)* State Times Advocate, *April 13, 1965.*

The usually passive students of Jefferson High show how noisy they can be in "The Firebrand." In this somewhat artificial episode, Walter Koenig, a debate captain, leads his classmates in demonstrations to push passage of a school bond issue. Mostly the young man is caught up in his own oratory, but he does get results: sit-ins, picket lines and some general rioting. Viewers, however, may wonder what all the fuss is about. — *"TV Scout,"* Lima *(OH)* News, *April 13, 1965.*

GRADE B: The series regains some its former quality with this prophetic episode about campus protests. The script makes a good point about the overcrowding of students but drifts at times. Walter Koenig is excellent as a brilliant student reactionary who has a gift for oratory. He has real presence in all his scenes and his protester becomes a vivid character. The actor is very good in a scene where he addresses a committee and calls some of its members on their hypocrisy. Julie Sommars is effective in a supporting role as the boy's girlfriend. Meredith registers in scenes with Koenig and brings complete integrity to the role of the principal. Former child star Tommy Rettig appears as an energetic member of Koenig's class. Near the end, Koenig crumbles when confronted with his real reasons for staging the protests and is a haunting figure. This is a somewhat better than usual episode with a powerful performance by its lead.

🍎 🍎 🍎 🍎

Episode Twenty-Nine — **And Then I Wrote**
Broadcast April 20, 1965.

Synopsis:

Tommy Sands guest stars as a brilliant Jefferson High student who refuses a four-year college scholarship because he does not want to leave his inept father alone in his business. Mike Kellin portrays the father.

Produced by Leonard Freeman.
Teleplay by Mel Goldberg.
Story by Joseph Calvelli and Mel Goldberg.
Directed by Abner Biberman.

Guest Star Mike Kellin as Lewster Lewin.
Norman Fell as Barney Sanders.
Special Guest Star Tommy Sands as Gary Lewin.
Also Starring Louise Latham as Adele.

"Don't Get Around Much Anymore" (Don't Care If You Don't)
By Duke Ellington and Bob Russell.

"How Can I Forget Her"
"Jack, Another Shot of Booze"
By Bob Russell.

Reviews:

Tommy Sands is getting a bit old to be still playing teenage roles, nevertheless turns in a believable performance as a brilliant but troubled Jefferson High student. His problem is that he won't accept a college scholarship because he doesn't want to leave his father, a fumbling tunesmith, alone. Some good scenes, although the finale gets a bit maudlin. Michael Kellin portrays the papa looking for a song. — *"TV Tonight,"* Monessen *(PA)* Valley independent, *April 20, 1965.*

GRADE C+: The script for this episode is a bit on the melodramatic side but the overall excellence of the acting boosts it to better than average. Tommy Sands is very good as a brilliant student who turns down a scholarship to help his inept father run the family music store. Mike Kellin is believable and tragic as the naïve and idealistic songwriter. The actor makes the character come alive and is the main strength of the episode. There is a good supporting performance by Louis Latham as a patient friend of the father who wishes to help him. Norman Fell is also good as a cynical songwriting partner of the father. The episode really comes alive in the last quarter when Novak confronts the father with his lack of musical talent. The scene is beautifully played by Sands, Kellin and Franciscus. The ending is low key, believable and in some ways beautiful. E. Jack Newman has a cameo as a customer at the music store.

ꬲ ꬲ ꬲ ꬲ

Episode Thirty — **Once a Clown**
Broadcast April 27, 1965

Synopsis:

John Novak and Mr. Woodridge receive veiled threats to their jobs when Novak flunks a senior prior to his graduation. The boy is the son of a politically influential attorney (June Lockhart) who refuses to believe her son will never be the brilliant lawyer she is.

Produced by Leonard Freeman.
Teleplay by Mel Goldberg.
Story by John Ryan and Tommy Overton.
Directed by Abner Biberman.

Guest Star Don Grady as Hank Nelby.
Special Guest Star June Lockhart as Mrs. Nelby.

With

Tom Drake............................Mr. Powell.
James Henaghan......................Tommy.
Frank Gerstle..........................Mr. Adams.

Faculty

Marian C., Vince H., André P., Stephen R., Larry T., Kathaleen E., Marjorie C.

Reviews:

Don Grady, who is usually busy as the untroublesome teenager on "My Three Sons," displays the other side of his fine acting talent playing a disturbed senior. A boy who would rather "Top his teachers with a gag than get top grades" he is doomed to flunk, no matter how much his lawyer mom (June Lockhart) tries to pull strings. An interesting script, which unfortunately gets bogged down and never fully graduates to high drama. — "*TV Tonight,*" Monessen *(PA)* Valley Independent, *April 27, 1965.*

GRADE C+: The final episode of *Mr. Novak* proves to be an above-average show with fine performances by Don Grady and June Lockhart. Grady is the campus clown and is genuinely amusing in his efforts to entertain the students. Lockhart plays against type and is very strong as an arrogant and sophisticated lawyer. The script brings up an interesting point of teachers passing students with a gift "D" so that they may graduate with their class. Franciscus is good in arguing against the harm in this practice. There is a powerful scene where Lockhart berates Novak and Woodridge for their perceived inadequacy. Grady and Lockhart also shine in a scene between them where the boy admits his inability with academics. At the end of the episode there is a very moving passage in which Meredith addresses the graduating class. He is most encouraging in this farewell and ends the series with a monologue of superior acting skill.

ꝭ ꝭ ꝭ ꝭ ꝭ

"I flunked English 1 with Mr. Novak."

"If we were in Mr. Novak's class we'd have another crack at this exam during the re-run."

Mr. Novak-Related Programs

Shindig
Broadcast January 6, 1965

Cast:

Hosts: Jimmy O'Neil/Jack Good, Bobby Sherman, Donna Loren, The Blossoms, Adam Faith, Sal Mineo, Jackie & Gayle, The Righteous Brothers, Sandie Shaw.

Producer: Jack Good
Director: Dean Whitmore
Associate Director: Herb Rissman
Art Direction: Lawrence Klein
Unit Manager: Phillip N. Anast
Audio: Dick Wilson
Lighting Director: Truck Krone
Video: Wally Stanard
Costumes: Barbara Murphy
Video Tape Editor: Mike Wenig
Musical Director: Ray Pohlman
Technical Director: Ted Hurley
Choreographer: Andre Tayir.

NOTE: Singing duo Jackie & Gayle performed their Capitol Record "Why Can't My Teacher Look Like Mr. Novak?"

☕ ☕ ☕ ☕ ☕

The Danny Kaye Show
Broadcast January 6, 1965

Cast:

Danny Kaye, Dorothy Collins & Guest Peter Falk.

Review:

Tough guy Peter Falk returns for a "Mr. Novak" takeoff with Danny. Kaye plays a shabby teacher who works in a gas station at night, and Falk plays the father who wonders why his son is failing. — *"TV Key – Best Bets for Today,"* Madison *(WI)* State Journal, *January 6, 1965.*

☕ ☕ ☕ ☕ ☕

The Jack Benny Program
"The Jack Jones Show"
Broadcast January 8, 1965

Cast:

Jack Benny, Don Wilson, Lee Meriwether, Bill Dungan, Victoria Carroll & Guest Jack Jones.

Review:

The Jack Benny Program is kidding the Mr. Novak series, and the teaching profession in general. With guest Jack Jones as an erstwhile young instructor at Benedict Arnold High School, and Benny as the principal who hates his low-paying staff to moonlight, there are some delectable moments of humor — but not many. — *"TV Tonight,"* Appleton *(WI)* Post Crescent, *January 8, 1965.*

꿋 꿋 꿋 꿋

The King Family Show
Broadcast March 6, 1965

Cast: The King Family

Review:

A day in the life of The King Family reveals the singing troupe living in a lush, two-story mansion singing a variety of songs. The set is papier-mâché, but the tunes are solid: There are some novelty outings, including Bill Driggs Jr.'s "Please Don't Take My TV Privileges Away" and Cathy King's "Why Can't My Teacher Look Like Mr. Novak?"

L-R: Jim Franciscus, Barbara Heimann (Miss American Teen-Ager), Marian Collier, and Burgess Meredith on the set of "Mountains to Climb"

April 4
to
April 10
1965

SUNDAY NEWS TV week

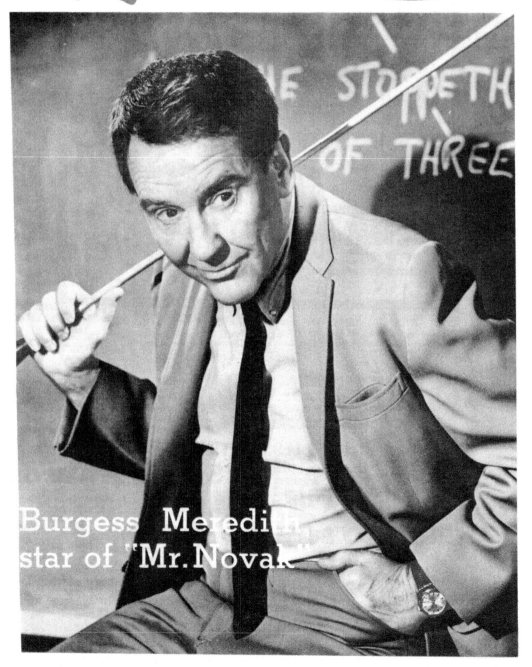

Burgess Meredith,
star of "Mr. Novak"

Appendix #1

Mr. Novak TV Series Awards

1963 — 1964 — 1965

This typewritten list of awards won by the Mr. Novak series was compiled by E. Jack Neuman on August 16, 1965. It is reproduced through the courtesy of Marian Collier Neuman from the Neuman archives.

AWARDS - 1963 - 1964 -1965

(MR. NOVAK TV SERIES)

TO E. JACK NEUMAN

(1) 12-7-63   The JOHN SWETT AWARD (PLAQUE AND CITATION) given
               to California mass media for outstanding interpretation
               of public education programs, achievements, issues and
               needs, - presented during the California Teachers
               Association State Council Meeting in the Ambassador
               Hotel, Los Angeles.

(2) 1-30-64   CITATION - PLAQUE: "Certificate of Commendation
               presented by Los Angeles County School Trustees
               Association to E. Jack Neuman, Executive Producer
               and to the cast of the excellent television series,
               Mr. Novak, for their insight, sympathetic under-
               standing and integrity in depicting intelligently
               the serious problems confronting teachers, ad-
               ministrators and board members in the dynamic field
               of public education."

(3) February
    1964   AWARD (Plaque) "Presented to MGM TV MR. NOVAK for
               exceptional service in the field of education with
               special recognition to Executive Producer E. Jack
               Neuman- ACTORS Jim Franciscus - Dean Jagger - 471
               Dept. of Education California State College, Los
               Angeles, California.

(4) 2-10-64   CITATION(PLAQUE) "In recognition of his distinguished
               service in the creation of the MR. NOVAK series for
               Metro-Goldwyn-Mayer in association with the National
               Broadcasting Company, the National Association of
               Secondary School Principals presents this citation
               to E. Jack Neuman, Executive Producer." (Chicago, Ill.)
               (Honorary membership to Dean Jagger)
               (Special Award Robert E. Kintner, NBC)

(5) 3-19-65   SPECIAL TEACH AWARD - by the St. Louis Suburban
               Teachers Association at the spring conference at
               Kiel Auditorium..."For Television Excellence for
               Advancement of Classroom Humanities".

(6) 3-20-64   ANNUAL COMMUNICATIONS AWARD to a TV producer -
               "who has made an outstanding contribution in
               promoting a better understanding of public education
               and the teaching on the network television program
               Mr. Novak," by California Teachers Association -
               Southern Section presented at a luncheon at the
               Statler-Hilton Hotel, Los Angeles, Calif.
                 (See 1965 Annual Communications Award to MGM-TV
                  for Mr. Novak.)

(7) 4-10-64   AWARD OF MERIT - California Federation of Women's
               Clubs, Los Angeles Metropolitan District 17 - Eighth
               Annual Convention of L.A. at the Ambassador Hotel
               Ballroom, Los Angeles, California. (Messrs. Jagger
               and Franciscus also honored).

(8)   4-17-64   BETTER UNDERSTANDING AWARD "in recognition of an
                 especially outstanding contribution to the cause of
                 education" presented by the Washington Education
                 Association, Seattle, Washington, at the 75th
                 Anniversary Dinner Meeting, Olympia.

(9)   October   HONORARY TEACHER-OF-THE-YEAR by the Iowa State
      15 & 16,   Education Association at their Convention, Des Moines -
      1964   "in recognition of the portrayal of the true image of
                 a teacher". (See James Franciscus also)

(10) 3-6-65   AWARD by Central California Teachers of English
                 held at John Swett High School, Crockett, California.

(11) 3-19-65   Special "TEACH" AWARD - by the St. Louis Suburban
                 Teachers Association at the spring conference at
                 Kiel Auditorium. The award, first ever to be presented
                 by the Association, cited Mr. Neuman for "Television
                 Excellence for Advancement of Classroom Humanities".

(12) 6-30-65   COMMENDATION - by The Citizenship Committee of
                 the National Education Association to E Jack Neuman
                 as Executive Producer of the Mr. Novak TV Series -
                 "for his dramatic and persuasive MOUNTAINS TO CLIMB
                 (episode) interpreting to the public the profession's
                 philosophy about active participation of teachers
                 and teachers' organizations when political decisions
                 affect schools" in the Georgian Ballroom of the
                 Americana Hotel, New York City.

TO DEAN JAGGER

(13) 2-10-64   HONORARY PRINCIPALSHIP - The National Association
                 of Secondary School Principals - presented at the
                 Conrad Hilton Hotel in Chicago.

(14) 3-20-64   ANNUAL COMMUNICATIONS AWARD - California Teachers
                 Association - Southern Section at luncheon at the
                 Statler-Hilton Hotel, Los Angeles, Calif.
                 (See E. Jack Neuman also)

(15) 3-23-64   HONORARY MEMBERSHIP in the CALIFORNIA ASSOCIATION OF
                 SECONDARY SCHOOL ADMINISTRATORS - in the Grand Ball-
                 room of the Jack Tar Hotel, San Francisco, Calif.

(16) 4-10-64   AWARD "Outstanding Portrayal of Principal" by the
                 California Federation of Women's Club (See E. Jack
                 Neuman also)

(17)   1964 EMMY AWARD NOMINATION - National Academy of
                 Television Arts and Sciences - BEST ACTOR

(18)   1965 EMMY AWARD NOMINATION -   BEST ACTOR

TO JAMES FRANCISCUS

(19)   GOLDEN APPLE AWARD - presented by the Los Angeles
         Association of Secondary School Administrators at
         their Annual Spring Dinner Meeting at the New
         Continental Hotel, Hollywood, Calif. on March 11,
         1964.

(20)   AWARD - HONORARY TEACHER-OF-THE-YEAR presented
         at the Iowa State Education Association Convention.
         (See E. Jack Neuman)

(21)   AWARD - The HEDDA HOPPER STAR OF TOMORROW 1964

(22)   AWARD - Sixteen's Magazine (Gee-Gee Award) reader
         poll - as "most popular new male television star on
         a series" - 1964

(23)   CITATION - California State College, Los Angeles,
         1964

(24)   AWARD - TV - Radio Daily Award - selected by a
         nation-wide poll of 443 TV columnists as "most
         promising new talent".

(25)   AWARD - Motion Picture Daily's Fame Award as "most
         promising actor of the year(1964)

(26)   SPECIAL CITATION - Christian College, Columbia,
         Missouri, for his contribution to education through
         his portrayal of a television teacher, Mr. Novak.

TO JEANNE BAL 1964

(27)   AWARD - GOLDEN APPLE presented by the Los Angeles
         Association of Secondary School Administrators.

(28)   AWARD - Women's Vice-Principal Association

(29)   SPECIAL RECOGNITION by California Teachers
         Association, Southern Section.

TO MARIAN COLLIER - 1964

(30)   SILVER TRAY AWARD "for her true professional
         portrayal of a modern American teacher - from
         Niagara Falls Teachers Association.

TO BURGESS MEREDITH - 1965

(31)   ANNUAL COMMUNICATIONS AWARD - Southern California
         School Public Relations Conference held at the
         Statler-Hilton Hotel, Los Angeles, Friday, March 19,
         1965.

TO LEONARD FREEMAN (Producer)

(32   ANNUAL COMMUNICATIONS AWARD - same as Burgess Meredith -

TO "MR. NOVAK"

(33) GEORGE FOSTER PEABODY AWARD (sometimes called Pulitzer
     Prize of broadcasting). This citation given to Mr. Novak
     for distinguished achievement in television entertainment,
     was read by Bennett Cerf, president of Random House, Inc.
     at a luncheon of the Broadcast Pioneers in New Y rk City,
     April 29, 1964.

(34) NOMINATION (1964) FIFTH ANNUAL TV GUIDE POLL for BEST SHOW.

(35) EMMY AWARD (1964) National Academy of TV Arts and Sciences
     for "outstanding dramatic program of the year"

(36) VOTED ONE OF FIVE BEST PROGRAMS in the Look-Listen Poll
     conducted by the American Council for Better Broadcasts.

(37) SCHOOL BELL AWARD 1965 to MGM-TV's MR. NOVAK presented
     specifically for: "distinguished dramatic interpretation
     of education during the year ended April 1, 1965, through a
     single program aired over a national television network -
     MGM-TV for 'The Tender Twigs,' in the Mr. Novak TV series."
     Award was presented at the Thursday evening General
     Assembly of the National Education Association
     Convention in Madison Square Garden, New York City,
     July 1, 1965.

(38) ANNUAL COMMUNICATIONS AWARD for 1965 by California
      Teachers Association, Southern Section - "for out-
      standing interpretation of education and the teaching
      profession", presented at the annual Southern Cali-
      fornia School Public Relations Conference held at
      the Statler-Hilton Hotel, Los Angeles on March 19,
      1965.

(39) THOMAS ALVA EDISON AWARD (1965) as outstanding contri-
      bution to education.

(40) SPECIAL SERVICE TO EDUCATION AWARD -(presented by
      CHRISTIAN COLLEGE, Columbia, Missouri.)

      "For vision; for courage; for setting and maintaining
      the highest possible standards in producing and
      presenting "MR. NOVAK"

                    METRO GOLDWYN MAYER

      is cited for service to education. The creative
      talent which combined to produce this TV show of
      highest merit are acclaimed for their integrity,
      intelligence and the unceasing efforts which have
      culminated in the enhancement of the role of a

teacher, focusing attention on the need and opportunity for dedicated Americans to devote their
lives to this profession.

Awarded by official action of the Board of Trustees
of Christian College this second day of May, nineteen
hundred and sixty-four at Columbia, Missouri."

Presented in 1964

TO THE NATIONAL BROADCASTING ET AL:

(41)   TO ROBERT KINTNER OF NBC - SPECIAL AWARD by Secondary
         School Principals for his efforts in connection with the
         MR. NOVAK program series on NBC Television Network"- in
         Chicago, February 8, 1964.

(42)   CITATION - by The National Association for Better Radio
         and TV - "for outstanding presentation of dramatic enter-
         tainment on network television.....brings to the nation's
         TV screens a consistently high quality of dramatic fare
         marked by good writing and acting on serious themes...."
         presented May 12, 1964 at NBC.

(43)   NATIONAL SCHOOL BELL AWARD - received at the General
         Assembly of the National Education Association Convention
         in the Coliseum, Seattle, Washington on July 1, 1964,
         "For distinguished dramatic interpretation of education
         during the year ended 4-1-64 through a series aired over a
         national television network".

(44)   AWARD to ROBERT KINTNER of NBC - National Education
         Associations Department of Classroom Teachers for "his and
         NBC's contribution to raise the image of education and
         educators by means of the Mr. Novak series"- presentation
         made during "Teaching Career Month" on April 8 at NEA
         headquarters, Washington, D.C. (Vice-president Humphrey
         presented award to Mr. Kintner)

(45)   AWARD:*OHIO STATE UNIVERSITY RADIO-TV DEPT. to ROBERT E.
         KINTNER - "In recognition for his contribution to electronic
         journalism and broadcast communications."....."who has en-
         couraged his news staffs to enlarge the scope and function
         of their operations...." In re "THE EXILE" - Mr. Novak
         episode, 6-4-65.

         "Awards announced at 35th Annual banquet June 3, Columbus,
          Ohio (Institute for Education by Radio-TV of Ohio State U.

         TO NBC, MESSRS. NEUMAN, FRANCISCUS, JAGGER ET AL

         RESOLUTION by Board of Directors, Kansas City
         Education Association - "outstanding contribution
         to the advancement of the teaching profession and
         the understanding and progress of education in
         America...."

To John D. F. Black

(46)   BRAILLE INSTITUTE OF AMERICA CITATION — for
        "An Elephant Is Like a Tree" episode of Mr.
        Novak, 3-1-65.

(47)   WRITER'S GUILD OF AMERICA SCRIPT AWARD — Best
        dramatic episode script, any length, "With a
        Hammer in His Hand, Lord, Lord," 3 23 66.

June Lockhart presents The 1964 National Academy of Television Arts and Sciences
nomination to *Mr. Novak* for Outstanding Program Achievements
in the Field of Drama to E. Jack Neuman

Appendix #2

E. Jack Neuman's Writer's Guide
for *Mr. Novak*

MR. NOVAK

DEAR WRITER:

Welcome to Jefferson High School -

John Novak, your friend and mine, is a young, under
thirty fella who sincerely believes that information and
knowledge and not guns will solve many of the world's
troubles. He figured that out for himself one lonely,
dangerous night during his Air Force duty in the Korean
affair. Novak is like that - he'll do a lot of solitary
thinking about a problem - and then act on it. Although he
was just nineteen at the time,that is where and how and when
John Novak decided to become a teacher. It was two years
later that Novak chose to teach in a high school instead of
a college. He picked high school over college because he
felt that very often a student's mind is already set by the
time he hits college whereas the mind of a teenager is still
malleable in high school - to Novak, high school teaching
offered the most rewards. You may agree with him or you may
not but that's the way Novak feels about his profession
and that's what this series is all about. Mr. Novak is a
practical, hard-working idealist, vital and aggressive, with
his feet on the ground and his head in the clouds. In
"Watch On The Rhine" one character said: "We're all anti-
Fascist." And someone pointed to the hero and remarked:
"Yes, but he works at it."

Well, John Novak is anti-ignorance and he works at it
five days a week and you and I are mainly concerned with <u>him</u>
and what <u>he</u> thinks and <u>feels</u> and <u>does</u>. Don't be misled.
Mr. Novak is <u>not the story of high school kids and their</u>
<u>problems</u>. It <u>is</u> the story of John Novak, a man who happens
to be a high school teacher - and his problems. The story
is always told from Novak's point of view or from the point
of view of Albert Vane, a man who happens to be a high school
principal. Novak and Vane feel very strongly about their
chosen profession - both men are smart, aggressive and active.
Novak is new and Vane is a veteran.

Novak has a Master's degree from State University. He
had experience as a student teacher, as a cadet teacher,
and as a substitute. In this series Novak is wearing his
first long pants, so to speak, with a full schedule and the
full responsibility of a classroom. His inexperience shows
up frequently and then he acts rashly, from anger, outrage,
love and hate. But his good sense and good training invariably
come to his rescue. If they don't, Mr. Vane does. He is
a mountain of information.

A fifty-fifty balance between Novak and Vane would be
desirable in every story; so would a Novak-Vane scene of importance; so would a Novak-somebody and a Vane-somebody scene;
I might add that experience has taught us that a scene that
does not actively include Novak or Vane weakens the image
of the series; we have also discovered that scenes away from
the school are deadly traps that usually can be avoided with
some ingenuity. The deadliest trap of all, however, is a

scene between two kids - these do not work at all. Keep
it in mind as you structure your story. Keep in mind also
that this is an adult series and each story is told from an
adult point of view.

Don't be dismayed when I tell you this series is not
the story of high school kids. Of course we'll tell their
stories; we want their young faces and their active movements
and their beautiful youth in front of the camera as much and
as often as possible; we want to show high school kids for
the attractive, thoughtful human beings they are; we want to
continue to do everything possible to discontinue the
stereotyped image of a wacky teenager. The details of their
portrayals should be included in your writing but your script
and your story must be constructed for Novak or Vane or both.
Two kids who ditch school and discuss the possibility of
getting married is not our story; but the routine administrative notation of their absence - a problem that is introduced across the desk of Mr. Vane -- is very much our story
when the implications of their absence become known.

We have a Teaser and four acts. Since the title of the
series is "Mr. Novak" and the main character is Novak, the
Teaser (one to five minutes) always begins with Mr. Novak,
regardless of whether or not the emphasis shifts to Albert
Vane. The Teaser should be strong and provocative and indicate the upcoming story.

As you may have noticed Albert Vane is a spanking good
principal with a good sense of humor and a good sense of
discipline. Vane is also a married man with a grown and de-

parted family, active and vital and completely engrossed in
his tough job. Wherever and whenever we see Albert Vane he
is the boss with the absolute authority to chastize and advise both students and the Faculty of Jefferson High.

Directly under Vane is the assistant principal, Jean
Pagano. Miss Pagano is an attractive, capable woman in her
mid-thirties. She is terribly efficient as she deals with
kids and Faculty. The artificiality she possesses is a
professional hide-behind for her. She is "Jean" and Vane is
"Al" when they're alone. And her aches and pains as a woman
and an administrator often show through.

Beyond Vane and Pagano are the department heads; i.e.,
the head of the English Department, the head of the Social
Science Department, the head of the History Department, the
head of the Languages Department, the head of the Mathematics
Department, etc. Each department head is invariably a veteran
instructor with a good deal of teaching experience and is the
direct boss of the particular faculty members he or she con-
trols.

Jefferson High is in an unnamed mid-western city; it has
a _four_ year course. They use the track system, accelerated,
average, and modified. Teachers' aides are utilized by some
of the teachers; there is an increasing amount of audio-visual
aids and other technological advances evident in the school;
team teaching, co-ordinated schedules, accelerated innovations
of varying kinds are known, considered, tested and sometimes
argued about at all levels. The students are a representative
cross-section - about ten percent are Negro, about fifteen

percent other minorities, the rest come from rich homes,
poor homes and in-between.

The probation system for teachers is three years; Novak
is in his first year. At the end of three years, John Novak
will be a permanent fixture unless he is discharged for in-
competence, morals, or some such. During his probation
period he can be rated and challenged. You might make use
of that.

Novak has a tough job on his hands. He teaches English
classes at all grade levels from eight o'clock in the morning
until three o'clock in the afternoon. His first class in
the morning might be American Literature to seniors; his
second class of the day might be English Poetry for freshmen;
his third class of the day could be Composition for Juniors,
etc.

During those sessions Novak has on his hands thirty to
forty youngsters with astounding vitality and a natural
restlessness, who must be kept attentive, absorbed, and intrigued. So from eight o'clock in the morning until three
o'clock in the afternoon, Novak is very likely to have taught
and influenced, provoked and excited, angered, disgusted
or exhilarated over two hundred young human beings - at
least that's the chance he takes every day.

Aside from his teaching assignments Novak is expected to
assume extra duties. For instance, he might be asked to
coach the debating team or the elocution team - or both;
Novak is a natural to direct the school play; he is also a
natural to conduct an extracurricular course in the writing

of the short story and the play. He might even elect to coach a minor sport such as fencing or squash or tennis or golf. But Novak would be out of his element if he appeared one week as the high school football coach as much as he would be out of his element if he suddenly took up some amateur detective work or medical work or legal work. The final impression of Novak must be a rigidly authentic picture of what a high school teacher not only does and has to do but what his professional attitude is at all times. The same goes for Albert Vane.

The role of the pretty young Home Economics teacher, Marilyn Scott, is played by Marian Collier. Miss Scott's beaming smile and radiant good looks add immeasurably to the overall picture of a well-rounded Faculty. Miss Scott is pretty - but smart -- breezy - but serious. Neither Mr. Novak nor any of the students gets out of hand with her. Although Miss Scott is often otherwise romantically engaged, she always seems to get back to Mr. Novak. The same thing happens to Mr. Novak where Miss Scott is concerned.

Steve Roberts plays the role of Stanley Peeples, a veteran Mathematics instructor. There is a touch of hardness and cynicism in Mr. Peeples who doesn't get along with everyone and sometimes he doesn't even try. He does try to hide conscientiousness and if you called him an idealist he'd hit you in the mouth - but that's what Peeples is underneath.

Vincent Howard plays the part of Pete Butler, the Negro History Teacher. Mr. Butler is sober and serious and completely competent with ten years' experience under his belt.

He is a big powerful well-conditioned man with that valuable gentleness that often comes with men of size and strength.

Everett Johns, the French teacher, is played by Everett Chambers (né Andre Philippe) who speaks, sings, thinks and acts like a Frenchman. E. Johns can be used for comedy and drama.

Larry Thor plays the part of Jim Hendriks, Science. Mr. Hendriks is a veteran teacher with a quiet, inquiring mind that displays a lot of mischief on occasion. He is also prone to telling bad jokes.

Kathleen Ellis plays the part of Anne Floyd, Business and Typing. Mrs. Floyd is a pretty well-preserved lady of forty or so with a nice capable softness about her. She is prone to laugh heartily and wonderfully on the slightest provocation. Mrs. Floyd is good looking enough to be desirable to most men in her age bracket.

Rosemary Dorsey is the name of the character played by Marjorie Corley, secretary to Mr. Vane and oftentimes in charge of the Administrative Counter. Miss Dorsey is a vital, efficient pretty woman of forty - and also a splendid actress.

All of these people and their characterizations are available to you at your discretion. They are the standard members of the Faculty that we use most frequently, particularly Miss Scott and Mr. Butler who have appeared in four out of every five episodes. The Faculty, however, is quite large, numbering a hundred and two members. Before you create a new character explore the possibility of utilizing one of the established members.

Also in our cast, and by no means least, are the two thousand six hundred and forty-two kids who attend Jefferson High School. You may have noticed that we often show them en masse attending an assembly or moving from class to class - you may also notice that we interrupt them en masse, pluck out one or two or a dozen, and bring them up to Camera so the audience can see what they're like.

They're something, these kids. At their age they still have all of their ideals - somewhere. They certainly have health, looks, and spirit. They have a fierce pride in their school. They have a dread of being condemned by their own kind. Peer pressure is a common administrative device used to control them.

Any of them can stand scrutiny. Ten-eighty-ten is a common phrase among administrators. It means that ten percent of these kids get every last benefit from their high school experience. It means that eighty percent of them get most - but not quite all they can get out of it. It means, sadly enough, that the last ten percent get nothing from their high school careers. This last ten percent are a challenge. The general rule is to try to get to them some way or other. But once you get to them be sure you have something to give them.

There are several stories we don't need. The football star who is flunking Mr. Novak's course is one we don't need the most. We can also do without the Hollywood movie star who visits the Drama Club. Another one is the brilliant, sensitive student who turns in an essay that is going to be

printed by the Atlantic Monthly. We can also do without
the psychological case history that is treated by Dr.
Novak, the delinquent with the switchblade, the pregnant
student who accuses Novak, and the indignant Board of
Education storming for Novak's hide. We don't need the
"big game" or the Nazi who has been hiding all these years
in the History Department, or the old maid school marm.

What we do need are well-researched, contemporary practical stories that are being lived in high schools today.
We want this to look exactly like your neighborhood high
school (unless you live in Beverly Hills). We want you to
acquaint yourself with the high school look and there are some
interesting things to look for. Little things that enhance
the authenticity we want to achieve. For instance, a male
teacher will arrange not to be alone with a female student.
It's simply that he could be accused of improper advances
and public opinion could take it from there. A female teacher
must be just as cautious in relation to a male student. Most
teachers, male and female, make it a point never to touch a
student of either sex for any reason, no pats on the back,
no touching back the hair - nothing. Although such movements
are perfectly natural, sex is predominate in the mind of the
teenager and practically anything can have a sexual connotation.
For that reason teachers are very careful what they say. But
very often they make slips - as in the auditorium scene in
the pilot - I saw that one happen myself.

A conference with a student - for whatever reason - will
often take place in the corridor of the building during a

class change. This is deliberate on the part of the
teacher who wants to make the conference as inconspicuous
as possible. Such an impromptu meeting discourages the
curious and puts the student at ease.

Teachers do their teaching not only by teaching, but by
example. A teacher will not smoke in front of students -
certainly not drink in a kid's presence or, frankly, commit
any action that might be misconstrued as impropriety. In
that sense these modern kids are very often prudish about
their teachers. That's the way things are with teachers
and we have to live with it.

A classroom full of students respects order and authority
as much as a good actor respects the order and authority of
good direction. Many high school teachers have emphasized
to me (and I emphasize to you) that they could not exist a
moment if they ever talked "down" to students. The respect
works both ways.

Don't avoid classroom scenes - this is where Mr. Novak
can show his value - or lack of it. Don't evade your chance
to show faculty and other meetings, testing, calls from
parents, correcting homework, preparing and planning for
classroom. Don't avoid anything a teacher does, the good
and the bad.

High School teachers are quite accustomed to hostility
outside the classroom - not from students but from parents
and non-interested parties in other professions. The teacher
in our society seems to be accepted as only "half" professional
and is often limited to the company of other teachers whether

he likes it or not. Novak does not like it and he resists
it for as many episodes as the traffic will bear. Novak
is the kind of man who,if he does not break some of the
rules,will bend them badly since he is blessed with uncommon
good sense and independence. Albert Vane admires this
quality in Novak -- since it is one of his own qualities.

I could go on with "remember this" and "remember that"
but it would take me a couple of days. The best thing to do
is _research_. Use our technical advisor - ask us - or by far
the best -- go out and find out for yourself. That is
primarily what I mean by research - going to school. Your
story and this series is as good as your research. Make
arrangements to visit the High School in your neighborhood
(or we'll make arrangements for you) and I guarantee that
whether your visit lasts a half hour or a half day you will
see or hear something that can be translated directly onto
the film that you are going to write.

I cannot emphasize too often or too strongly the value
of on-the-spot research. What you and I remember of our own
High School days is almost valueless in light of the quickly
changing scene today. So don't trust your memory - use your
eyes and your ears - at a High School. Think exactly what
you are doing in relation to what Novak and his students are
doing. Novak feels (like all teachers feel) that he knows
and is in contact with everyone of his students; the students,
however, feel that Novak has very little concern for them or
their problems - but they have the same left-out feeling about
their parents - and each other!

If you anticipate a great deal of hard work on this series - you're right. It begins and ends with what you put on paper. It is damned hard work. You might even complain that in a medium where mass entertainment is the objective, that these demands on you are unrealistic. Maybe some details are, but the pursuit of excellence is not only realistic but essential in my opinion. So say something in your story - something dramatic, positive and informative.

For years all of us have wanted a vehicle that would reflect back the contemporary society we live in - the good and the bad of it. This is your chance. Use it.

E. Jack Neuman

Appendix #3

Mr. Novak's Graduation Advice: Think

This was written by James Franciscus in the spring of 1964. It was distributed to various high schools in the United States for the graduating seniors of that year. It was re-distributed for the class of 1965. Courtesy of Marian Collier Neuman from the Neuman archives.

A request I have just received to whip up a commencement address for a high school graduating class leaves me both flattered and frightened. I'm flattered to feel that perhaps I've performed believably enough on NBC-TV every Tuesday night to convince people I'm really "Mr. Novak," or at least an ex-high school teacher. I'm neither. I'm an actor. And I am a little frightened at being invited to step out of my field — like a high school teacher would be, I suppose, if he were asked to turn instant-actor.

Does this mean I won't do the commencement address? No, it doesn't. I am not an educator, but I am human. Even though I didn't teach these kids at "Jefferson High," I did work with them and get to know them. And, twisting an old saying, to know them is to love them. They're great — eager, anxious to please, quick to catch on, amazingly mature for their age. If they're typical of their generation, and I suspect they are, I welcome this chance to share a few thoughts with their real-life "classmates" at this big moment.

I don't have to be there with you to know that you graduating seniors are divided into two groups — those who are going on to college and those who are not. I realize that it is customary these days, with so many going on, to feel sorry for those who are not. With me, frankly, it's the other way around. I'm more concerned, somehow, with those that *are* going on. With so many heading for campus, I feel those who don't will feel they are in a minority — psychologically, if not statistically. They'll realize they're missing something and — hopefully — will try to make up for it in one way or another. This is by no means impossible.

They can read a daily paper — not only the headlines but between the lines. They can take out library cards and use them until they fall apart. They can make sure they never let a year go by without taking in a lecture or two, an occasional travelogue, perhaps even a concert or recital, if the price is right. They can be intelligent shoppers in their television viewing, they can keep an eye out for the decent movies and they can look for friends who do the same.

They can realize, it seems to me, that, even though they do not go to college, they may still become mature citizens in a pushbutton world that needs all the maturity it can get. Toward this, I feel, they can keep trying for the rest of their lives. So can the college group, but there's less likelihood they will. That's why they have the lion's share of my concern.

I'm sure you have all heard the advice, "don't quit after high school, go on to college and get an education." Obviously, there is nothing wrong with either part of this advice, taken separately. Going to college is a fine idea and so is getting an education. I'm no educator, but it seems to me the danger comes in putting the two together.

Joined, these ideas suggest, all too often, that (a) you don't start getting an education until you *reach* college (b) the only time you're being educated is while you're *in* college and (c) — the most dangerous part — you're through getting an education when you *finish* college.

Obviously, you're never through. You can do everything your non-college classmates can do as regards the newspapers, the library cards, the concerts, recitals and all the rest. And you can do it better. You will have four years to get into the habit, four years of additional guide service along the twisting road we all travel.

I hope you make the most of it. Too many before you have not. That's why I'm more worried about you future collegians that you non-collegians I would give anything to see you prove me wrong. Good luck to all of you.

Appendix #4

Principal Vane's
Speech to New Teachers

MR. NOVAK/*NBC-TV*

Credo for New Teachers

From Principal Albert Vane's instructions to Mr. Novak and his associates in the MR. NOVAK episode, "First Year, First Day."

"My secretary, Miss Harvey, has filled you in or will fill you in along those lines least appealing to me — clerical duties, administrative procedures, other handbook highlights. My concern is for you as human beings . . . I'm not going to tell you how to teach or dress or live. You've learned how to do that, or you wouldn't be here. However, there's one thing they can't teach you at Teachers' College — how to teach students. Nor can you be taught how to relate to, understand, tolerate, appreciate or survive students. These things you will learn for yourselves — the quicker the better. And the fact that you were a student yourself not too many autumns ago doesn't help a bit. Today, you are going to meet a new and stunning race. It is going to be a crucial, traumatic meeting and you will wear the scars of it for the rest of your lives. So will your students, I might add.

"However, and this will sound a bit heretical, I am not at all concerned about them right now. High school students have certain magical immunities that are unknown and unavailable to high school teachers. So my real concern is for you. This is your first day — and the students will know it is your first day. To some extent, they will be compassionate. But they are, nevertheless, going to size you up — and they are going to do so sharply and shrewdly and with devastating accuracy. They may not like you, and they may be cruel — but it only hurts a little while and they are only too willing to give it up, once they have cubby-holed you and can turn their minds to more exciting fun-and-games.

"Whether you get their compassion or their cruelty or, God forbid, their indifference, will depend entirely upon you. Show them at once who and what you are. They respect those with a strong self-identity. The young, again unlike their elders, have neither time nor taste for cold wars.

"Cold wars are out. They like friends and enemies to be instantly recognizable. Naturally, you are going to want them to think of you as a friend. But let me offer the advice of experience — don't let this fashionable obsession with Buddyship trip you up. Don't play all your cards at once. Don't wear a sign on your face that reads 'My name is Pal.' They'll think you're a stray dog. And besides, you're simply not going to like every last one of them. It's ten to one that before the day is over you'll privately detest at least one in every class. All right, detest him. But teach him anyway. And teach him well.

"But be aware. The one you don't like can be just as magnetic as the one you favor. Perhaps even more so. Which brings me to my favorite sig-alert. Don't get personally involved. Not for a long while. You don't have your sea-legs, you're inexperienced, you're without the superb defense mechanism called 'seeming indifference,' and you are totally unequipped to deal successfully with personal involvement. If you bump into a problem, send it to the counseling board, or to me. I advise you, no, I order you, to regard your students as a body. When you have learned how to direct and shape and manage a group, you will be ready to cope with individualism. I am adamant about very little, but I am adamant about that!

"You'll go from here directly to the assembly hall. They'll want to look you over, so we oblige by standing you up on stage and saying pleasant, inconsequential things about you. Be confident, act as if you belonged. You do, you know. All of you have worked hard to become teachers and some of you have bypassed more lucrative professions — someday, I'll buy you a drink and ask you why. Right now we can get on with the day. See you in assembly."

Appendix #5

James Franciscus's Columns for 'TEEN Magazine

(1963–1965)

SUBJECTS

Column #1 – October 1963:
A Teacher's View of a Classroom of New Students

Column #2 – November 1963
Classroomances

Column #3 – December 1963
Cheating

Column #4 – January 1964
**Teacher Crushes/Teachers with Chips on their Shoulders/
Physical Education Difficulties**

Column #5 – February 1964
Compatibility between Athletics and Scholarship

Column #6 – March 1964
Fear of New Teachers/Fear of Being a Show-Off

Column #7 – April 1964
Keeping Up Studies if Not Going to College

Column #8 – May 1964
How to Develop Talents while Still in High School

Column #9 – June 1964
See the Movie Version but Read the Book as Well

Column #10 – July 1964
Travel and New Experiences during Summer Vacation

Column #11 – November 1964
Teachers Who Become a Great Influence on Students

Column #12 – December 1964
Creative Imagination

Column #13 – January 1965
Teenagers Can Understand Teenagers Best

Column #14 – February 1965
Teacher's Pets and Pet Teachers

Column #15 – March 1965
Joining Good Deed Groups

Appendix #6

Novelization of the Two-Part *Mr. Novak/Dr. Kildare* Rejected Script "The Rich Who Are Poor" by E. Jack Neuman

Mr. Novak

Part One — Prod. #7517

of

The Rich Who Are Poor

Executive Producer: E. Jack Neuman
Producer: Leonard Freeman
Written by E. Jack Neuman

July 31, 1964

In the corridor of Jefferson High School, John Novak encounters senior Paul Stribling who is standing with fellow student Joyce Kellen. She looks at Paul with a loving expression.

Mr. Novak proceeds to the Counseling Office and meets fellow teacher Pete Butler. They enter the office and join educators Stan Peeples, Anne Floyd and Jim Hendriks. The instructors look over various files and discuss some of the students' problems.

Paul Stribling joins Mr. Novak in a counseling booth. The teacher mentions several unsatisfactory reports and inquires if there is anything wrong. Paul replies that he is going through a slump and there are no problems. He then coughs and Novak tells Paul to go to the Health Office. The student suggests that Novak sounds like his mother who ordered to him see a doctor two days earlier. Mr. Novak looks concerned as Paul leaves.

In a school corridor, Principal Vane encounters Miss Scott, the Home Economics teacher, and tells her to give a ten-minute speech later that afternoon. He wants her to address a PTA meeting and change emerging opinion that Home Ec. is only about cooking and sewing. She agrees and asks Novak if he will help her. He smiles and says that he will.

Novak sees Paul in a phone booth. He is holding the receiver and appears upset. After being encouraged to get to his next class, the angry student departs.

Outside of Jefferson High, Mrs. Stribling, Paul's mother, arrives for the PTA meeting. She is expensively dressed and carries herself with an attitude of affluence. Two other mothers arrive and they all enter the school.

Once inside, Mrs. Stribling inquires about an opportunity to see Principal Vane. In his office, Vane is told by Assistant Principal Dorsey that the three mothers wish to see him. He angrily replies that the PTA meeting is in an hour but agrees to meet Mrs. Stribling. Miss Dorsey says that she will meet with the other two.

Mrs. Stribling enters the principal's office and says that she knows why her son's grades have been slipping. She places the blame on the boy's father who is often away on business. Vane suggests that he should talk with her husband and the mother agrees. The principal asks Miss Dorsey to contact Mr. Stribling for a meeting.

In Novak's classroom, the students discuss a novel by Charles Dickens. Paul coughs slightly and quickly covers his mouth. In the course of the discussion, the class mentions the possible suicide by a character in the novel. Paul suggests that at times suicide can be the only way out. The class soon ends and the students depart. Novak asks Paul if he is all right. He replies that he's okay and leaves the class to meet with his girlfriend.

In the corridor Novak encounters Miss Scott, who relates part of her upcoming speech. She is a bit melodramatic but is confident. Novak, preoccupied with Paul's strange behavior, gives slight approval.

Paul and Joyce are talking by their lockers. She expresses concern about his health. He angrily tells her he's fine. She touches his arm and he recoils. Paul tells Joyce to never touch him again. He leaves as she begins to cry.

Later that evening, while in the administration office, Novak receives a phone call. He is shocked at the news and inquires as to the name of the hospital.

Polly, a hospital employee, tells Novak that the health center is Blair General. Dr. Kildare enters and drops a clipboard on her desk. He proceeds to a corridor and finds Dr. George Siegel examining the unconscious Paul Stribling who is on a gurney. Dr. Siegel wonders why Paul is unconscious. The boy moans and Kildare asks his name. Paul doesn't answer and the physician tells him that he's in a hospital. Dr. Siegel says that the boy has a gastric lavage. Kildare suggests a suicide attempt and tells his colleague to take the boy to a treatment room.

Novak and Vane enter the hospital. Polly calls Kildare and tells him that the boy had a letter sweater from Jefferson High School and a teacher has arrived. Kildare encounters Novak and Vane in a corridor outside of a treatment room. They all go inside and Novak identifies the boy. Kildare says he is very sick and suggests restraints. The doctor and the two educators have a conference with cab driver Ryan. He tells them that he found the boy standing on a corner looking very ill. The cabbie then brought him to the hospital.

Novak says that he knows Paul and had a counseling session with him the previous day. Vane offers to call Paul's mother to let her know what has happened. After he leaves, Novak tells Kildare that the boy had suggested that sometimes suicide *is* the answer in a recent class.

Vane encounters Dr. Gillespie in an office in which he is going to make the call. The principal reaches Paul's mother and suggests she come to the hospital as soon as possible. Gillespie reads Paul's chart and realizes that it *was* a suicide attempt. Vane expresses concern that Paul's situation shouldn't be known around the school. He is assured that this will not happen.

Vane and Gillespie encounter Novak and Kildare in a hallway and they discuss the tense situation.

At dawn the next day an emotionally distraught Mrs. Stribling and Gillespie go outside the hospital for some fresh air. The mother tells the doctor that she can't believe her son's tragic actions. She is informed that Paul almost died from a phenobarbital overdose. Mrs. Stribling assures the doctor that there has been no recent incident that could have caused this situation. She last spoke to her son the previous morning and he was in a positive mood.

Dr. Gillespie is concerned and says he will place Paul in a psychiatric unit. Mrs. Stribling mentions her absent husband and his lack of parental guidance. They enter the admitting area of the hospital. Dr. Siegel shows Kildare the lab report on Paul. He suggests Siegel check it a second time. Gillespie tells Paul's anxious mother to be patient and she can see her son very soon.

In a recovery room, Kildare tells a weak but conscious boy that he is in a hospital. Dr. Siegel takes a second blood sample. Kildare asks Paul if he had seen a doctor about a condition. The youth says he got the bad news the previous day from a Dr. Quayle. Siegel leaves as Kildare refastens the restraints on the boy. Paul says he doesn't want to see his mother.

Kildare tells a nurse that the hospital will have to notify the Public Health Department. Mrs. Stribling overhears this and is informed that her son has syphilis. She is told that it is not a good time to see Paul. The emotional mother says she doesn't want to ever see him again and departs. Gillespie stops her and says the disease is intolerable, not the victim. She then leaves with tears in her eyes.

Kildare tells some nurses and Dr. Siegel that all patients deserve the best possible treatment without moral judgment. He meets with Novak who has brought some of Paul's homework. Kildare suggests that the boy isn't going to get much help from his home situation. Novak says he will talk to his student.

In the hospital room, Novak asks the distraught boy if he can be of any help. Paul tells the teacher that he has syphilis and expects Novak to leave. The instructor assures the boy that the disease can be treated and that he must not try to end his life. He must also quit punishing himself and that he *can* recover. Paul says that he didn't think before and Novak tells him he is thinking now.

Novak leaves the room and Kildare tells a nurse to remove the restraints.

End of Part One.

Dr. Kildare

Part Two — Prod. #6978

of

The Rich Who Are Poor

Executive Producer: Norman Felton
Producer: David Victor
Written by E. Jack Neuman

In the corridor of Blair General Hospital, Dr. Kildare is approaching the room of Paul Stribling. He notices an orderly leaving the room with an untouched tray of food. Kildare enters the room and is told by the boy that he wasn't hungry. The doctor checks his pulse and leaves the room.

Sometime later Kildare meets with Dr. Langley in the residents' office. The older doctor feels that Paul's suicide attempt was caused by the fear that his family and others would reject him because of the infection. It is Langley's view that Paul's guilt has been reduced through conversation with medical professionals. The boy now knows that he can be cured and that normal life can resume with few people knowing of his disease.

Kildare suggests that Paul's mother is one of the few people. Langley tells the young doctor that Paul will have to face his mother very soon. Kildare assures his fellow physician that the youth is physically on the mend. Langley suggests that the mother will be difficult but the youth must deal with her to begin getting back to normality.

Kildare receives a phone call from Mrs. Stribling and informs her that her son will be released in the early afternoon. He asks if someone will arrive to pick up the boy and is assured that it will be done. Dr. Siegel arrives and is told by Kildare that the outcome looks unfavorable.

After a while Kildare, Siegel, Dr. Mikes and Dr. Gillespie all make the rounds of an open ward. They encounter a difficult patient named Bonaparte. Gillespie tells him that Dr. Mikes was an adjuster for an insurance company. He will be able to tell if a patient is faking symptoms to get a hospital stay at the insurance company's expense.

Outside of Paul's room, Gillespie asks Dr. Siegel for the boy's report. He is informed that the patient was admitted for barbiturate poisoning and was found to have secondary syphilis. Gillespie asks why the patient is isolated. Kildare explains that patients with syphilis are routinely isolated until twenty-four hours of penicillin dosage has administered. The Public Health Department has been notified.

Gillespie tells several interns and doctors that syphilis can be cured but that it is rarely mentioned in private practices and medical schools. For the previous seven years, there have been a rising number of cases, especially among teenagers. Young people are experimenting with sex and the result is increasing outbreaks of the disease. There are over 600 reported cases a day and many unreported ones. If smallpox or malaria reached that proportion, medical facilities would mobilize to handle the epidemic. He asks the assembled medical professionals if they've ever seen a case of clinical syphilis. They don't respond and Gillespie takes them to Paul's room.

The group enters the boy's room and Dr. Gillespie questions him about his health for the previous two months. Paul replies that he has been feeling tired and has been coughing. The senior physician explains that lesions disappear in the first stage but a microscopic examination would confirm the presence of the disease.

The doctor asks Paul why he went to see Dr. Quayle. The boy says that his mother made him go because he appeared tired. A few days later Quayle called Paul and told him he had syphilis. The student went to the doctor's office and received a shot of penicillin. He was told he'd have to return for a few more shots to complete the treatment.

Gillespie discovers that Dr. Quayle never submitted a report to the Public Health Department. Paul says his doctor would keep this issue between them and that Quayle is his family's physician.

Dr. Gillespie is very angry at hearing this news. He addresses the group and says that there is often transmission of the disease to others. Many private doctors do not inquire into the source of the disease and the possibility that others have been infected. He says that good medicine must include good epidemiology and departs.

Gillespie is informed that Dr. Quayle is on staff at the hospital. He asks a nurse to contact him for a meeting. On another floor of the hospital Dr. Kildare asks Siegel to get the epidemiology report on Paul Stribling. After Siegel leaves, Mrs. Stribling arrives with some clothes for her son. The mother gives the clothing to Kildare and is told that her son won't be released for a while. She proceeds to the business office.

Kildare and Siegel meet with Paul in a ward office. The boy is told he has a communicable disease and the conversation will be confidential. The doctor tells Paul that if untreated the disease can cause blindness, insanity or heart disease. The boy must have follow-up tests with Dr. Quayle or at the hospital.

Paul is asked how many people he has had sexual intercourse with in the previous year. The boy replies that he thinks it was three. Kildare suggests that some of them may have had the disease and weren't aware of it. Paul mentions a girl named Gloria from another school. She was very promiscuous. The boy also mentions Joan, who he met at a fraternity party. He says that he was only with the two girls.

Kildare mentions that Paul initially said there were three. The boy denies this and insists there were only two. The doctor inquires about Paul's girlfriend. He replies that she is a nice girl, not like the other two. Kildare says if Paul was with her the girl must be told or she could become very ill. The youth insists that she is a nice girl. Kildare suspects Joan could be infected by Paul but the student emphatically denies the possibility. The doctors are told the last names of the other two girls by Paul.

Kildare tells Paul that a man from the Public Health Department will contact them and they'll have to get blood tests and physicals. The boy's name will not be mentioned. The doctor tells Paul one more time that *if* Joan was involved he will personally contact her and cause no embarrassment. The two doctors leave the room.

Siegel suggests that Paul is lying. Kildare tells him to give the boy some time.

At Jefferson High School, Principal Vane meets with two students in his office. He tells the two boys that they are suspended for three days for not obeying a regulation. They are told to get their parents to meet with him.

Donald Stribling, Paul's father, arrives and enters the principal's office. Vane asks Mr. Novak to join them and tells Stribling the teacher is his son's counselor. The father criticizes the school and says that he raised his son to be a moral boy. Paul has syphilis and Mr. Stribling wants to know why his son has it. The father says that he doesn't drink or smoke or run around with women. The boy has been told the facts of life and that he should be careful.

Vane replies that he runs a good school and it is their responsibility to teach the teenagers but not to raise them. The principal says he is sorry that this has happened but the school played no part in this distressing situation. Teachers, priests and printed material cannot substitute for a parent's communication and guidance. Stribling takes offense and says that he is a grown man and leaves. Vane expresses doubt about that statement.

In the Blair Hospital cafeteria, Dr Gillespie tells a nurse that he cannot wait much longer as he is soon to be required elsewhere.

Dr. Quayle enters and Gillespie takes him to a private area. He tells Quayle that he could have done more in the Stribling case and informs him that the boy attempted suicide. Quayle reacts in a shaken manner and is told that the boy will need a serological follow-up.

Dr. Quayle becomes defensive and says he will not discuss his treatment. Gillespie tells the physician that he should have known better than to let Paul leave his office without a complete epidemiologic report. The Public Health Department should have been notified as well. Quayle replies that he had an obligation to the boy's family. Gillespie notes that the infection could cripple or drive insane other people who had never heard of his family obligation.

Principal Vane and Ruth Wilkinson arrive for consultation. Quayle quickly exits while appearing distressed. Gillespie takes to two educators into the cafeteria.

Mrs. Stribling and her son arrive at Jefferson High School. Paul exits the car and is met by teacher Butler who asks him if he is feeling better. The student replies that he is and Butler wishes him well. Joyce, Paul's girlfriend, arrives and asks him if he was in the hospital. He replies that it was nothing and Joyce asks him to come with her. Paul tells her that he will join her in a little while. Mrs. Stribling expresses her disappointment in her son. She says she is not interested in the details and that she'll try and forget it but doubts she ever can. Paul leaves her and heads toward his first class.

Mr. Novak sees Paul running toward the school and approaches Mrs. Stribling who is now in her car. The teacher asks if he can help her and that the boy is only eighteen. She says she doesn't want to discuss the issue and finds it embarrassing. Novak asks her how she thinks her son feels about it. If her boy was injured in a car accident she wouldn't turn her back on him. Paul's been hurt by doing something less dangerous than driving an auto. She ponders this and says she'll think about it.

In the hospital cafeteria Vane tells Gillespie that he wanted to start a course of an hour or two a week on sex education for the students. The Board of Education killed the idea because it was felt that the parents would disapprove. Gillespie says that many parents fail at this type of education.

As they leave Vane tells Gillespie that he had spent an hour with Paul's father who was wondering who or what to blame. Unfortunately, the teachers can't say "sex" or "venereal disease" in the classroom. The principal says that schools should break barriers but have instead become barriers.

In Novak's class the students are discussing the previous lesson. Virginia, a coed, says that Paul had indicated that sometimes suicide is the only way out. The boy announces that you have to be true to yourself. Novak replies that you must be honest with everyone else. Paul agrees with Novak's point of view. The class is dismissed and the students rush into the hall. As Paul leaves he sees that his girlfriend is waiting for him.

Dr. Kildare arrives at Jefferson High School and is mistaken for Mr. Novak by some coeds. He asks the location of the faculty office and is told to go to the location. As he heads toward the office he sees many students clad in band uniforms. Paul and Joyce are walking hand in hand.

They arrive at their lockers and Joyce asks her boyfriend if something is wrong. Paul asks her if she knows what he thinks of her. She replies that he should know what she thinks of him. Paul apologizes for snapping at her the other day. Kildare approaches them and the youth tells his girlfriend that this is his doctor. Joyce asks if her boyfriend will be all right and Kildare assures her that he will. Joyce removes her band uniform from her locker and departs.

Kildare tells Paul that he thinks someone else might be involved. The doctor indicates the departing Joyce and tells Paul he knows what could happen if she was involved. The boy replies that if they had been intimate that he'd have been the only one. Kildare says that she must be told and Paul replies that it would break them up. The doctor tells him it's her whole life that is at stake. Kildare gets her full name and says that he will talk to her. Paul finally admits that she *is* involved and that he will tell her. Novak arrives and takes Kildare down the corridor away from the rushing band members.

The whole band, now in uniform, is rushing toward a dress rehearsal. Joyce emerges carrying her clarinet and sheet music. She hands them to Paul and asks him to help her. They began to talk when the last band member tells Joyce to hurry or she'll be late.

Paul asks Joyce if she remembers a previous Sunday and what they did. The girlfriend replies that they agreed they'd never talk about it. If her parents knew what happened they'd hate her. Joyce hates herself and sometimes she hates Paul. He tells her that she could be sick and must be examined. Joyce replies that she feels fine and prepares to leave and the join the assembled band.

Paul tells her that there was another girl, not like her, that he saw one night. His girlfriend asks what he means by this. Paul tells her that he has syphilis and she might have it too. He offers to take her to a doctor. She tells her boyfriend she doesn't want him to take her anywhere again.

As Paul reaches for her she runs away. He hangs his head in shame. Outside of the school, the band is playing a rousing melody as Kildare and Novak look on. The two men are lost in their individual thoughts.

They both see Paul Stribling walking away from the campus with his head bowed. He is alone, frightened and emotionally shattered. As the boy walks by the band he notices that there is one empty space in the clarinet section.

Fade Out

The End

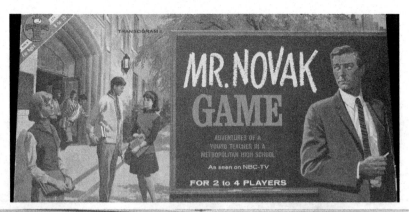

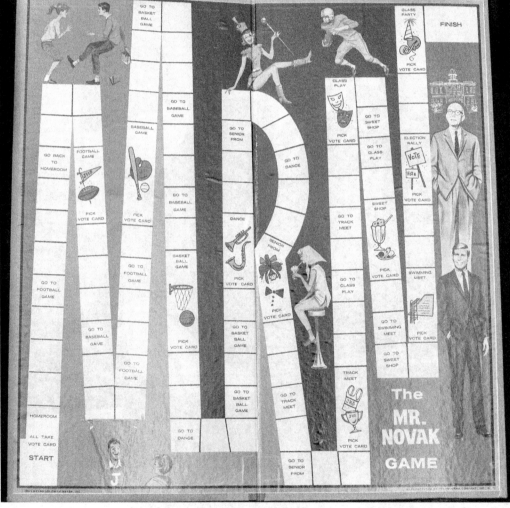

Appendix #6

The Mr. Novak Game

In the late Fall of 1963, the only merchandise associated with the Mr. Novak series was issued in time for the Christmas Season. It was the Mr. Novak Game and was manufactured by the Transogram Company which for many years was a leading producer of board games.

It was designed for 2 to 4 players and was suggested for ages 8 to 15. The game retailed for $1.99 and was very successful due to the popularity of the television series. The box cover of the game featured a colorful painting of James Franciscus and the entrance to Jefferson High School. The game board featured black and white realistic drawings of Teacher John Novak and Principal Albert Vane. The game's instructions carried a copyright of 1963 METRO-GOLDWYN-MAYER, INC.

Accessories included 32 Signal Cards, 50 Vote Cards and 4 Plastic Playing Pieces.

IDEA OF THE GAME

Jefferson High School is holding its annual election for Senior Class President. The students running for President must collect all the votes they can at the various school activities.

Each player is a student candidate in Mr. Novak's Senior Class at Jefferson High. The candidates must go to the school activities to collect votes. In order to attend the activities, each candidate is given a "mental test"; that is, each player must "read his opponents mind." The opponent will ask the question, "Am I for you or against you?" The candidate will answer, "For me," if he thinks the signal cards will match in color. If he thinks the cards will not match, he answers, "Against me." When the candidate "reads his opponent's mind" correctly, he moves ahead the sum of the number on the Signal Cards.

The WINNER and Senior Class President is the player who collects the most votes.

TO START

1. Each player takes a playing piece and places it at Start.
2. One player is the Dealer. He shuffles the Blue and Red Signal Cards, and deals all the cards, one at a time and face down, to all the players.
3. Each player keeps his Signal Cards face down in a pile in front of him for the entire game.
4. The deck of Vote Cards is shuffled and placed down on the board within reach of all the players.
5. Youngest player goes first; play follows to his left.

TO PLAY

When moving your playing piece from Start, take a Bonus Vote Card. Keep your vote cards face down and in front of you until the end of the game. Do not show them to the other players.

You are the first player. The second player, the person to your left, removes the top card from his Signal Card Pile WITHOUT SHOWING IT TO YOU. He concentrates on the color of his card. You look at the top card in your pile. The second player asks you, "Am I for you or Against you?" You must "read his mind" to know the color of his card.

If you think his Signal Card color will match your card, you answer, "For me." You both turn over your cards. If the card colors are the same, you move your playing piece ahead the sum of the numbers on the matching cards. Your turn ends. If the card colors do not match, you do not move and your turn ends.

EXAMPLE: Your card is Blue with the number 2 on it. The other player's card is also Blue with the number 3 on it. You move your playing piece ahead 5 spaces. Your turn ends.

If you think his Signal Card color will not match yours, you answer "Against me." The cards are turned over. If they do not match; that is, a Blue card and a Red card, you move your playing piece ahead the sum of the numbers on the cards.

If the cards do match, you do not move and your turn ends. The used cards are then placed face down at the bottom of their piles.

The third player then removes the top card from his Signal Card pile WITHOUT SHOWING IT TO THE SECOND PLAYER. He asks the second player, "Am I for you or against you?" The second player looks at his card and tries to "read his opponent's mind." The second player answers either "For me or Against me." They show their cards and repeat what was explained before.

The second player moves his playing piece ahead if he answers the question correctly. The game continues in this manner with a player competing with the person on his left.

NOTE: The Signal Cards are never shown until the player doing the "mind reading" answers the question asked of him. Whenever a player correctly answers the question, he moves ahead the sum of the numbers on the Signal Cards.

ACTIVITY SPACES

The Activity Spaces tell you to pick a Vote Card. Each time you land on an Activity Space by an exact count, you draw the top card from the Vote Card Pile.

EXAMPLE: The sum of the cards is 5. You move ahead and land on the Activity Space which reads: "Football game Pick Vote card." You draw the top card from the Vote Card Pile and place it face down in front of you. Your playing piece remains in that Activity Space, and your turn ends.

DIRECTION SPACES

When you land on a Direction Space by an exact count, you must follow the instructions immediately. The Direction Spaces may move you ahead or back. With one exception, all of these spaces will direct you to an Activity Space where you pick a vote card. EXCEPTION: *When a player is sent back to Homeroom, he does not draw a vote card.*

EXAMPLE: Your playing piece is in the Class Play Activity Space. The sum of the cards is 4 and you move ahead. Your count takes you to the Direction Space which reads: "Go to the Class Play." You immediately move back to the Class Play space and draw a vote card. Your turn ends.

TO WIN

Play continues until all the players pass "Finish." If a player finishes before the others, he no longer moves his playing piece or collects vote cards. However, he continues to play his Signal Cards so the remaining players may finish the game. That is, he will ask the player to his left, "Am I for you or against you?"

When all players pass "Finish," they will add the votes on their vote cards.

EXAMPLE: A player finishes the game with four vote cards which have these votes printed on them:

10	50	40	20
Votes	Votes	Votes	Votes

This player's total number of votes is 120.

The WINNER is the player with the highest total number of votes.

The *Mr. Novak* Game can be found on Ebay.

Index

Photo by Ani Berberian of Ani Berberian Photography

About the Author

Chuck Harter is an author, musician and popular culture consultant. He is the author of four previously published books which include... *Superboy & Superpup: The Lost Videos* (Cult Movies Press — AMAZON); *Superman on Broadway*, co-authored with Bob Holiday (Holiday Press); *Johnnie Ray: 1952 The Year of the Atomic Ray* (self-published); and *Little Elf: A Celebration of Harry Langdon*, co-authored with Michael J. Hayde (Bear Manor Media — AMAZON).

Chuck wrote the acclaimed television documentary *Hey! Hey! We're the Monkees* (Rhino/Disney Channel) and... among others... *Gossip: Tabloid Tales* for A&E. He has appeared as a commentator on many TV programs, including *North Mission Road; Cops: America's Most Wanted; Places of Infamy; A&E Biography; Mysteries and Scandals;* and *Unsolved Mysteries.*

Under his musical performing name of Chuck Winston, he has produced five CDs of musical recordings and has two music videos on Youtube: *Another Rock and Roll Christmas* and *Time Is Passing By.* The musician has performed in concert many times in the Los Angeles area. Chuck lives in Culver City near Los Angeles and the former MGM studio. He can be reached by writing in care of the publisher at srgrabman@cableone.net. The author can also be contacted through the website mrnovakbook.com.

CPSIA information can be obtained
at www.ICGtesting.com
Printed in the USA
LVOW04*2009100817
543974LV00003BA/5/P